Advancing in Romans
From Faith to Faith

By Bob Warren

Published by The Hill Publishing, LLC
PO Box 13
Hardin, KY 42048
www.lifeonthehill.org

ISBN: 978-1-62727-130-1

Table Of Contents

Acknowledgments

I'll never forget Bob Warren saying how much he enjoyed studying and teaching Romans 1-4 in depth, after years of having summarized it in order to quickly arrive at the meat of the book, chapters 5-8. Shortening the teaching time spent in those four chapters was the best way to make it fit into a semester. Bob never considered Romans 1-4 unimportant. Those four chapters are the foundation needed to understand the truths of the entire book. Wonderful treasures lay hidden there. Bob found many of them when he began teaching this greatly expanded version, *Advancing in Romans*. Eliminating the previous time constraints allowed him to pursue every rabbit found lurking in the scriptural underbrush.

Bob's passing in August of 2014 came on the heels of his finishing a teaching series in Romans 9 and one session of Romans 10. To say his departure left a void in the ministry is like calling the Grand Canyon a roadside ditch. Its founder, leader, visionary, teacher, and mentor had gone to be with Jesus. My thoughts inescapably focused on how we would finish the works he had started. In addition to everything that was unpublished, Bob was in the middle of updating all of his previous works.

However, Bob didn't show up in heaven without invitation and catch the Father by surprise, nor was a contingent of angels hurriedly dispatched to prepare a room for him. He was fully expected and his absence from earth and this ministry had already been carefully considered. The Father's desire to have Bob at home with Him, and His plan for the rest of us, outweighed our loss and perceived need.

The Father's solution for one of our dilemmas was already in place— Bob's editor, Jhonda Johnston, who had been editing his work at least three years by this time. She was initially hired to take the "Western Kentucky" out of his writing style, but quickly became much more to all of us at The Hill: a writing coach and editor, a source of encouragement and humor, a tireless warrior for truth, a friend, and ray of sunshine when she comes to visit.

The truth is, none of the publications done since Bob's homegoing would have been accomplished without Jhonda. She followed the Lord and became what we lacked. The Holy Spirit used her skillful pen and creativity to reduce years of work into months and to turn what may have never happened into a possibility. Her faithfulness to this ministry will continue to impact the lives of others for years to come. Her contribution to this and many other books will be greatly rewarded.

We are extremely grateful for Bob and his faithful pursuit of all those spiritual rabbit trails, for Jhonda, and others who have been instrumental in bringing *Advancing in Romans* to publication. It has been a wonderful collaboration of talents, led by the Holy Spirit, to craft what you now hold in your hand. I hope you agree the results are outstanding.

Brent Armstrong

Introduction

Paul studied Scripture in context, making certain that nothing he believed contradicted a single word (or phrase, or verse, or chapter, or book) recorded in God's letter to man. Thus, he could say to the elders from Ephesus:

> *For I have not shunned to declare unto you all the*
> *counsel of God.* (Acts 20:27 KJV)

This *Advancing in Romans 1-8* study contains much deeper theology than its predecessor, the foundational *Romans 1-8* study, which I thought necessary due to a theological shift within Christendom that classifies contradiction as "mystery" in an attempt to justify its error. Since writing the original foundational *Romans 1-8* study, I have written several books and Bible studies. While generating and teaching these materials and, at the same time, observing major theological changes engulfing Christendom, I sensed a need to produce this present work. I trust that your passion for the God of truth, Who never contradicts Himself, will be stimulated by its content.

To take the full counsel of God's Word and expand the foundational *Romans 1-8* course will be adventuresome indeed. To observe how flawlessly this new input meshes with previously studied truths will validate, to an even greater degree, the consistency and non-contradictory nature of the Scriptures.

If you are a passionate student of God's letter to man, this journey should be extremely intriguing—regardless of your theological background. Even if you should disagree with our findings, they will serve as a profitable use of your time—for passionate students of the Word welcome all arguments against what they believe. Otherwise, they become isolated and unteachable, injuring themselves and those who follow in their footsteps.

Recently, while teaching on the topic of faith, I asked if the faith required prior to salvation originates with man or with God. Much to my surprise, many of the students answered, "with God." Some who said, "with God," had even completed the foundational *Romans 1-8* study (written over twenty years ago), which made me realize the need to expand the subject matter.

I wrote in that original work: "Several years ago I saw my need for a Savior. When this occurred, I just basically made a choice to look up and God did all the rest. He (at that moment) granted me *"repentance"* (2Timothy 2:25; Acts 11:18), gave me *"faith"* (Romans 12:3), and then justified me." I have been intrigued by the number of students who, as a result of these words, have misunderstood my beliefs regarding faith. If you are one of those students, I apologize for not writing more clearly concerning the subject. I assumed that the statements, "Several years ago I saw my need for a Savior" and "When this occurred, I just basically made a choice to look up and God did all the rest," communicated that the repentance and faith I exercised prior to spiritual regeneration (and while depraved) originated with me. Of course, once I exercised personal repentance and faith while depraved, God granted me *"a measure of faith"* (Romans 12:3) to function within my particular spiritual gifting—for every New Testament believer receives a spiritual gift (1Peter 4:10) in conjunction with being placed in Christ and made new (2Corinthians 5:17). The gift of faith of Romans 12:3, therefore, is not equivalent to the personal faith we exercised in our depravity prior to being made new (a subject covered in depth later).

"Depravity" points to our spiritual state before we were spiritually regenerated/saved. In other words, to be depraved means to be lost. Yet, the depraved are capable of exercising personal repentance and faith. Remember this fact as we continue, for the terms "depravity" and "depraved" are used throughout the study. The *God's Heart* series addresses this subject in great detail.

When teaching God's Word, I no longer assume that the student's definition of a theological term is equivalent to mine. This mindset has served me well in the present postmodern era, which denies absolutes and disregards contradictions. I have discovered, in fact, that when a system, regardless of its label, redefines words for the sake of preserving a preconceived notion, truth is viewed as inferior to the system. Hence, pragmatism takes precedence over truth, and truth takes a backseat to man's ideology. In such cases, pragmatism rules, and the system billed as producing life produces agonizing death. Compromise of this sort has inundated our society, even the church. Therefore, our only hope is to know truth based on its context, allowing definitions to remain as they were when God penned His infallible letter to man. As a friend of mine states: "Proper Biblical interpretation is dependent on one thing only—context, context, context." We will attempt to abide by this guideline.

In order to link the truths from the foundational *Romans 1-8* study to this advanced study of the same Scriptures, I have simply added additional input to the original study. Three goals will be accomplished: (1) We will address new subject matter and blend it with previously studied materials; (2) We will review the foundational *Romans 1-8* series, which is normally needed after a student's first trek through. In fact, more than half of the participants in our annual *Romans 1-8* Retreat have taken the foundational course multiple times. (3) Should a person choose to forego the foundational study and engage himself in this study alone, he will have access to the entire body of truth.

No one can scuba dive without first learning to swim on the water's surface. We learned to swim in the original *Romans 1-8* study; time has arrived to observe the wonders of the deep. In the Gulf of Aqabah, off the coast of Elat in southern Israel, I discovered the fascinating world of the depths of the sea. I was forever changed by that experience! In fact, that one glimpse of an unfamiliar portion of God's creation made Him, in my mind at least, even more sovereign and omnipotent. My prayer is that your awareness of God's awesomeness will be enhanced through our diving into the depths of *Romans 1-8!*

Take time to read all Scripture references. You will be glad you did. Scripture text is taken from the New American Standard Bible (NASB) unless otherwise noted. If you do not own a copy of the NASB, it might be wise to obtain one. I have used this version for years and found it to be a wonderful resource for Biblical study. Of course, you can use the version you have, but pay special attention to the NASB rendering of the passages provided in this work.

Much of the new material in this commentary has been added due to a resurgence in the popularity of Reformed Theology. You will find a discussion of its various tenets woven throughout our study; although for brevity's sake we keep it on a basic level. If you desire to dig deeper into this topic, our *God's Heart* series is available. This series contains four volumes: *God's Heart As It Relates To Foreknowledge – Predestination, God's Heart As It Relates To Sovereignty – Free Will, God's Heart As It Relates To Depravity, and God's Heart As It Relates To Election–Atonement–Grace–Perseverance.*

Note: For emphasis, specific words or phrases are sometimes underlined in selected verses.   Comments are also inserted within brackets [ ] for the sake of clarity.

Romans 1

We know that Paul wrote this epistle in Corinth while on his third missionary journey (Romans 16:23; 1Corinthians 1:14), for he delivered the contribution, mentioned in Romans 15:25-26, to Jerusalem at the end of that third journey. Then, he was arrested and eventually sent to Rome (Acts 20-28). Phoebe, who was in Cenchrea (near Corinth), delivered the letter to the Roman believers (Romans 16:1-2). Since Paul had not yet visited his readers, he addresses the fundamentals of the gospel in more detail than in his other epistles. He not only defines the gospel, but also explains its energizing effect as we enjoy the adventure of faith.

Romans chapters 1-8 may very well be the most important section of the entire Word of God. No portion of Scripture has marked my life like these eight chapters. Your in-depth study of this book should: (1) Result in a deeper understanding of Christ's sacrifice on the cross; (2) Give you a greater desire to love Him with all of your heart. After all, *"faith"* can only work effectively *"through love"* (Galatians 5:6).

Profound theological truths pack this first chapter. Paul, a *"bond-servant"* (Romans 1:1) of Christ, after having been set free by his Master, chose to remain with and serve Him for life. This mindset greatly impacted Paul's perception of his relationship with the Lord (read Exodus 21:5-6 and Deuteronomy 15:12-17 for additional input). Jesus had set him free, but Paul chose to submit to Christ the remainder of his days. As we learn more about our freedom in Christ, we too, if we aren't already, will desire to become His bond-servants.

Paul was *"called as an apostle"* (Romans 1:1), *"apostle"* meaning "one sent forth."

> *Paul, a bond-servant of Christ Jesus, <u>called as an apostle,</u>*
> *<u>set apart</u> for the gospel of God,* (Romans 1:1)

To be an *"apostle"* one had to have seen the resurrected Lord (1Corinthians 9:1), a prerequisite Paul fulfilled according to Acts 9:3-5 and Acts 22:6-8. Paul compared his apostleship *"to the uncircumcised"* (the Gentiles) with Peter's *"apostleship to the circumcised"* (the Jews) in Galatians 2:7-9 and urged the Corinthians to acknowledge his office in 1Corinthians 9:2 and 2Corinthians 12:12. Paul was an *"apostle"*

(Romans 1:1) who had been *"set apart"* to share the *"gospel"* with the Gentiles.

According to Galatians 1:15-16, Paul was *"set...apart"* to his apostleship *"from"* his *"mother's womb"*:

> But when He who had <u>set</u> me <u>apart</u>, even from my
> mother's womb, and <u>called</u> me through His grace, was
> pleased to reveal His Son in me, that I might preach Him
> among the Gentiles,... (Galatians 1:15-16)

God desired *"to reveal His Son in"* Paul as he preached the gospel *"among the Gentiles."* This truth ties in perfectly with Romans 1:1, which confirms that Paul was *"set apart"* as an *"apostle"* to take the good news of the gospel to non-Jews. Thus, Paul was not only *"called"* as an *"apostle"* (Romans 1:1; Galatians 1:15), but was *"set apart"* as *"an apostle"* (Romans 1:1). This fact is also substantiated by Acts 13:2:

> And while they were ministering to the Lord and fasting,
> the Holy Spirit said, <u>"Set apart</u> for Me Barnabas and Saul
> for the <u>work</u> to which I have <u>called</u> them." (Acts 13:2)

Paul was *"set apart...for the work to which"* he had been *"called."* Combining Romans 1:1, Galatians 1:15, and Acts 13:2, Paul was *"set apart"* for a specific *"work"* that God would perform through him as he yielded to Christ's indwelling presence. He was <u>not</u> *"set apart"* for salvation, as some theologians wrongfully suppose.

The boldness to *"persuade"* men came with Paul's apostleship:

> And he was reasoning in the synagogue every Sabbath
> and trying to <u>persuade</u> Jews and Greeks. (Acts 18:4)

> And Agrippa replied to Paul, "In a short time you will
> <u>persuade</u> me to become a Christian." (Acts 26:28)

> And when they had set a day for him, they came to him at
> his lodging in large numbers; and he was explaining to
> them by solemnly testifying about the kingdom of God,
> and trying to <u>persuade</u> them concerning Jesus, from both

> *the Law of Moses and from the Prophets, from morning*
> *until evening.* (Acts 28:23)

> *Therefore knowing the fear of the Lord, we persuade*
> *men, ...* (2Corinthians 5:11)

If the depraved are incapable of understanding truth, as some have incorrectly concluded, why would Paul have attempted to *"persuade"* the depraved (the lost)? Persuading an individual who is incapable of believing is impossible! Also, should God have chosen (elected) certain persons to salvation from eternity past (a popular, yet incorrect teaching of our day), Paul would have been disobedient in offering salvation to those who rejected his gospel. Yet, he offered salvation to all his listeners throughout his missionary journeys, many choosing to remain in their sin. Because the depraved <u>are</u> capable of understanding truth, Paul attempted to persuade them with the truth. He understood well the power of God's Word, for the depraved (when convicted by the truth) can choose to exercise personal repentance and faith. This fact is verified by Acts 26:16-18, where Paul quotes Jesus' words while presenting his testimony before King Agrippa:

> *'But arise, and stand on your feet; <u>for this purpose I have</u>*
> *<u>appeared to you, to appoint you a minister and a witness</u>*
> *not only to the things which you have seen, but also to the*
> *things in which I will appear to you; delivering you from*
> *the Jewish people and from the Gentiles, to whom I am*
> *sending you, <u>to open their eyes so that they may turn from</u>*
> *<u>darkness to light</u> and from the dominion of Satan to God,*
> *in order that they may receive forgiveness of sins and an*
> *inheritance among those who have been sanctified by*
> *faith in Me.'* (Acts 26:16-18)

Jesus *"appeared"* to Paul for the purpose of appointing him as a *"minister and...witness."* Jesus did <u>not</u> appear to Paul for the purpose of appointing him to salvation. Even those to whom he would speak were required to *"turn from darkness to light,"* proving that the depraved can make a choice to repent and believe—note the word *"turn."* Although the depraved (lost) live in *"darkness,"* they must *"turn from darkness to light"* before they can receive God's salvation, as also confirmed by 2Corinthians 3:16:

> *but whenever a man turns to the Lord, the veil is taken away.* (2Corinthians 3:16)

Once man *"turns to the Lord"* in the midst of his depravity, the *"veil is taken away."* Reversing this sequence, or order, simply will not work! God is not required to spiritually regenerate the depraved (lost) and give them the gifts of repentance and faith before they can *"turn"* (repent), believe, and be saved (Reformed Theology's view). They can *"turn"* to Christ in the midst of their *"darkness"* (Acts 26:18) and receive God's salvation.

Some theologians use John 6:70 in an attempt to prove that God's choice, not man's, determines man's destiny:

> *Jesus answered them, "Did I Myself not choose you, the twelve, and yet one of you is a devil?"* (John 6:70)

Jesus chose *"the twelve."* *"Chosen"* and *"election"* are synonymous, as verified by 1Peter 1:1-2 in the NASB and KJV:

> *Peter, an apostle of Jesus Christ, to those who reside as aliens, scattered throughout Pontus, Galatia, Cappadocia, Asia, and Bithynia, who are chosen according to the foreknowledge of God the Father, by the sanctifying work of the Spirit, that you may obey Jesus Christ and be sprinkled with His blood: May grace and peace be yours in fullest measure.* (1Peter 1:1-2 NASB)

> *Peter, an apostle of Jesus Christ, to the strangers scattered throughout Pontus, Galatia, Cappadocia, Asia, and Bithynia, Elect according to the foreknowledge of God the Father, through sanctification of the Spirit, unto obedience and sprinkling of the blood of Jesus Christ: Grace unto you, and peace, be multiplied.* (1Peter 1:1-2 KJV)

Therefore, to be chosen is to be elected, allowing the NASB to use *"chosen"* while the KJV inserts *"elect."* Let's again read John 6:70:

> *Jesus answered them, "Did I Myself not <u>choose</u> you, the twelve, and yet one of you is a devil?"* (John 6:70)

All the disciples were chosen (elected)—note the words, *"the twelve."* However, one of *"the twelve"* was *"a devil,"* confirming the impossibility of the disciples being chosen (elected) to salvation. We also know of Judas' betrayal, Jesus calling him *"the son of perdition"* in John 17:12. Thus, to be chosen (elected) doesn't point to being chosen (elected) to salvation from eternity past. It can point to being chosen (elected) to a particular office within the body of Christ, as was the case with the twelve, including Judas, who alone declined the offer and betrayed the Savior. Paul replaced Judas as the twelfth apostle, allowing him to write:

> *Paul, a bond-servant of Christ Jesus, <u>called</u> as an <u>apostle</u>, <u>set apart</u> for the gospel of God,* (Romans 1:1)

> *and last of all, as it were to one untimely born, He appeared to me also. For I am the least of the apostles, who am not fit to be <u>called an apostle</u>, because I persecuted the church of God.* (1Corinthians 15:8-9)

Paul was *"called"* and *"set apart"* to be an *"apostle,"* not *"called"* and *"set apart"* to be saved. In fact, nowhere do the Scriptures teach that God selects some of mankind to be saved. Man determines where he will spend eternity by the exercise of his will while depraved.

Jesus was *"chosen" ("elected")* to an office, which is confirmed by Isaiah 42:1:

> *"Behold, My Servant, whom I uphold; My <u>chosen</u> one in whom My soul delights. I have put My Spirit upon Him; He will bring forth justice to the nations.* (Isaiah 42:1 NASB)

> *"Behold my servant, whom I uphold; mine <u>elect</u>, in whom*
> *my soul delighteth; I have put my spirit upon him: he*
> *shall bring forth judgment to the Gentiles.* (Isaiah 42:1
> KJV)

Jesus was *"chosen"* to office, the office of Messiah. He was not chosen for salvation, for He has always been the perfect second Person of the Trinity. Neither we, nor any other person, were chosen to be saved.

This truth explains Jeremiah's calling as a prophet as described by God's words in Jeremiah 1:5:

> *"Before I formed you in the womb I <u>knew</u> you, and before*
> *you were born I consecrated you; I have <u>appointed you a</u>*
> *<u>prophet</u> to the nations."* (Jeremiah 1:5 NASB)

The word *"knew"* (Jeremiah 1:5) points to God's infinite knowledge of Jeremiah as a person. Jeremiah became a person at conception, *"<u>Before</u>"* he was *"formed...in the womb"* (Jeremiah 1:5)—conception precedes the formation of a child in the womb. God, in His infinite foreknowledge, knew (from eternity past) that Jeremiah would be born and serve as a prophet; He did not know Jeremiah as a person until conception. Even God can't have a relationship with an idea; He has relationships with people. Thus, *"knew"* (Jeremiah 1:5) does not point to his chosenness as a prophet, although he most definitely was chosen to be one *("I have appointed you a prophet to the nation"*—Jeremiah 1:5)—a position (office) he could have rejected had he desired. Rather, *"knew"* (Jeremiah 1:5) points to God's infinite knowledge of Jeremiah as a person once he was conceived in the womb.

Yes, *"before"* Jeremiah was *"born,"* and while he was in his mother's womb, he was *"appointed* [as] *a prophet"* to the southern kingdom of Judah, an office he could accept or reject—as verified by Judas' response to his calling as an apostle. He was <u>not</u> appointed to salvation, as some have incorrectly assumed.

Even Jesus was *"called...from the womb"* (Isaiah 49:1) to function as Messiah, confirming that His calling was to office rather than salvation:

> *...The* LORD *called Me from the womb; from the body of*
> *My mother He named Me.* (Isaiah 49:1)

Isaiah 49:2-7 verifies that verse 1 is speaking of Jesus, who was *"called"* to offer redemption to the Jews and Gentiles alike. He was not called to salvation, for He was never lost.

Conclusion: New Testament believers are *"called"* to a special office once they are placed in Christ and made new—after having exercised personal repentance and faith while depraved. This fact will be verified to a greater degree when we study Romans 1:6.

Understanding Paul's definition of *"the gospel"* (Romans 1:1) is imperative. In 1Corinthians 15:1-8, the gospel refers to Jesus' death, burial, and resurrection. However, these truths do not reveal the entire story. The gospel also includes the fact that Jesus is seated *"at the right hand of the Majesty on high"* (Acts 1:11; Hebrews 1:3) and now lives in every New Testament believer (Colossians 1:27; Galatians 2:20). New Testament believers also live in Him (2Corinthians 5:17; Ephesians 2:6). What exciting news!

This reality applies to our everyday experiences in that our Father desires that Christ live His life through us, since He lives in us—instead of us working for Him. This concept is supported by the fact that Christ is the only Person (He is also *"God"*—Hebrews 1:8) Who has lived void of sin.

The gospel was *"promised beforehand through* [the] *prophets"* (Romans 1:2). Isaiah 53 and Psalm 22 speak of a suffering Savior. In fact, much of the Old Testament points to Christ. Genesis 3:15 tells of the *"seed,"* Who is *"Christ"* (Galatians 3:16), Who would usurp Satan's authority through submitting to the unfairness of the cross. Satan bruised *"him on the heel"* (Genesis 3:15), pointing to Jesus' crucifixion; His resurrection allowed the *"gospel"* to become a living reality—an event that transpired in space and time. These facts explain Paul's words in Romans 1:2:

> *which was promised beforehand through His prophets in*
> *the holy Scriptures,* (Romans 1:2)

Paul uses the term *"holy"* when referring to the Scriptures. Paul's words express a complete, and unwavering belief in the reliability and validity of what God had spoken. Do you view the Scriptures from this same vantage point?

Paul realized that Jesus was required to be a descendant of David, mentioned in Romans 1:3, if He was to hold the office of Messiah. In 1Chronicles 17:11-14, God promised David an eternal *"son,"* Who would reign on an eternal *"throne,"* and rule over an eternal *"kingdom."* This unconditional covenant is known as the Davidic Covenant, the "son" being the eternal Son, Jesus Christ. The genealogy of Matthew 1:1-16 reveals an amazing truth about Jesus' earthly lineage.

Matthew, a Jew, wrote his gospel to the Jews with the goal of proving that Jesus is the Son of God, not the son of Joseph. He recorded Joseph's lineage in Matthew 1:1-16, which includes *"Jeconiah"* found in verse 11. According to Jeremiah 22:24-30, no descendant of *"Jeconiah"* *("Coniah")* would be a successful King, sitting on the throne of David. Matthew recorded Joseph's lineage to prove the impossibility of Jesus being Joseph's offspring. Stated plainly, had Joseph been Jesus' father, Jesus could not be Messiah. Furthermore, *"by whom"* in verse 16 is feminine, pointing to Mary rather than Joseph, confirming once again the *"virgin"* birth of Isaiah 7:14.

Luke records Jesus lineage through Mary in Luke 3:23-38. In verse 23 the definite article *"the"* (preceding *"son of Joseph"*) is in italics, meaning that it was not in the original manuscripts. Intriguingly, *"Joseph"* is the only name in this genealogy that does not have the definite article *"the"* preceding it. The reason is because Mary's lineage is recorded here, not Joseph's. *"Jeconiah"* of Matthew 1:11 is nowhere to be found in these verses. Mary was a descendant of David through *"Nathan"* (Luke 3:31), not Solomon; Joseph was Solomon's descendant according to Matthew 1:6. Thus, Jesus, Who was born of a virgin, His Father being our heavenly Father, will rule successfully on the throne of David during the Millennium—His literal one thousand year reign on earth. However, these events cannot transpire without God fulfilling the three unconditional covenants (Abrahamic, Palestinian, and New) He established with physical Israel:

(1) The Abrahamic Covenant (Genesis 12:1-3; 13:14-17; 15:1-21; 17:1-14; 22:15-18; 26:2-5; 28:13-15)

Abraham would become the father of a multitude of nations (be a blessing to many nations), with the physical Jewish nation (Abraham's physical descendants through Isaac and Jacob) controlling (and inhabiting) the land from *"the river Euphrates"* to the *"river of Egypt"* (Genesis 15:18)—the holy land (something the Jews have yet to accomplish). This covenant also promised that *"those who bless"* physical Israel will be blessed, and *"the one who curses"* physical Israel will be cursed.

Some people cite Joshua 2:24 and Joshua 21:43 in an attempt to prove that the Jews have already possessed (and inhabited) the land promised in Genesis 15:18, thus fulfilling the promise (in their minds at least):

> *And they said to Joshua, "Surely the LORD has given all the land into our hands, and all the inhabitants of the land, moreover, have melted away before us."* (Joshua 2:24)

> *So the LORD gave Israel all the land which He had sworn to give to their fathers, and they possessed it and lived in it.* (Joshua 21:43)

The full counsel of God's Word verifies that these statements are general, because after Joshua's death, and during the time of the Judges, pockets of the land remained unconquered:

> *Now it came about after the death of Joshua that the sons of Israel inquired of the LORD, saying, "Who shall go up first for us against the Canaanites, to fight against them?" And the LORD said, "Judah shall go up; behold, I have given the land into his hand."* (Judges 1:1-2)

Joshua 23:1-13 authenticates our findings as well.

> *For if you ever go back and cling to the rest of these nations, these which remain among you, and intermarry with them, so that you associate with them and they with you, know with certainty that the LORD your God will not <u>continue to drive these nations out</u> from before you; but*

> *they shall be a snare and a trap to you, and a whip on*
> *your sides and thorns in your eyes, until you perish from*
> *off this good land which the LORD your God has given*
> *you.* (Joshua 23:12-13)

The phrase, *"continue to drive these nations out,"* validates that Israel did not inhabit all the land at this time—again confirming that Joshua 2:24 and Joshua 21:43 are general statements.

The remainder of the Old Testament proves that Israel failed to inhabit the land promised in Genesis 15:18, and the same situation continues today. Israel will control and inhabit the land in its entirety during the Millennium, the one thousand year reign of Christ on the earth.

(2) The Palestinian Covenant (Deuteronomy 30:1-10)

Since 1948, many Jews have lived in a portion of this real estate—but in a state of unbelief. The nation will eventually be driven out and return a second time (in a state of belief) shortly after Christ's Second Coming (Isaiah 11:11-16). At this time, and for the first time, they will control and inhabit all of the land originally promised in Genesis 15:18.

(3) The New Covenant (Jeremiah 31:31-33):

Every Jew on the earth at the end of the Tribulation will choose to repent and exercise faith in the Messiah, while depraved. Then, God will write the Law on their hearts through the power of the Holy Spirit and save them.

Through Jesus, the Abrahamic, Palestinian, Davidic, and New Covenants will be fulfilled. Yet, some individuals attempt to allegorize these unconditional covenants, perceiving the church as fulfilling the conditions of the four covenants instead of the physical Jewish nation. They view physical Israel's return to the land in 1948 as irrelevant and, in some cases, desire that America cease supporting the Jews. America needs to remember Genesis 12:3 when confronted with such unscriptural dogma. Our *God's Heart* series addresses this subject in much greater depth.

According to Romans 1:4, Jesus' resurrection was the final proof of His Sonship and right to reign. 1Corinthians 15:12-19 also speaks of the power of Jesus' resurrection. Yes, Jesus *"was declared the Son of God with power by the resurrection from the dead"* (Romans 1:4). The Father confirmed that Jesus was His *"beloved Son"* both at His baptism (Matthew 3:17) and His transfiguration (Matthew 17:5), but He *"was declared the Son of God with power"* through His *"resurrection"* (Romans 1:4). The resurrection has attracted so much attention for the past two thousand years, for no other "religious leader" has come out of the grave. Jesus not only arose from the dead, but *"appeared"* to many in His resurrected body before ascending to the Father (1Corinthians 15:1-8). The event was real and in no way fabricated by the mind of man.

Through Christ, Paul *"received grace and apostleship"* (Romans 1:5). Thus, God's *"grace"* did more than save Paul after he exercised repentance and faith while depraved. God's *"grace"* also empowered Paul as he served as an apostle, as verified by 1Corinthians 15:10:

> *But by the grace of God I am what I am, and His grace*
> *toward me did not prove vain; but I labored even more*
> *than all of them, yet not I, but the grace of God with me.*
> (1Corinthians 15:10)

By receiving God's *"grace"* on a consistent basis, we are empowered to function in the area of our calling (gifting) as well. According to Romans 1:6 every New Testament believer is *"called"* to an office, which is received in conjunction with being made new subsequent to exercising repentance and faith while depraved:

> *among whom you also are the called of Jesus Christ;*
> (Romans 1:6)

Choosing to reject God's *"grace"* causes one to withdraw from the battle. Paul realized that God's daily provision of *"grace"* in his own life would be sufficient *"to bring about the obedience of faith among all the Gentiles"* (Romans 1:5). The book of Acts verifies that God's grace empowered and sustained Paul throughout his three missionary journeys and his trip to Rome.

According to verse 7, New Testament believers *"are beloved of God"* and *"called as saints":*

> *to all who are <u>beloved of God</u> in Rome, <u>called as saints:</u>...* (Romans 1:7)

Because *"God is love"* (1John 4:8, 16), He is capable of loving His own. Hence, Paul viewed his readers as *"beloved of God,"* for God's boundless love is showered on everyone who repents and believes. *"God"* also loves the *"world,"* every human being (John 3:16)—even those who reject the salvation offered through the gospel. He can display such compassion on the unbeliever and believer alike because He loves with *agape* love, unconditional love, desiring that *"all"* be *"saved"* (1Timothy 2:4; 2Peter 3:9) even though all will not.

New Testament believers are also *"called as saints"* (Romans 1:7). We learned earlier that we were *"called"* to a specific office just as Paul was *"called as an apostle"* (Romans 1:1). This calling occurred once we were placed in Christ subsequent to repenting and believing while depraved. To properly function in this office, we must understand what God made us into the moment He made us *"new"* (2Corinthians 5:17). Are we lowly sinners saved by grace, or are we *"saints"* who sometimes sin? We are *"saints"* who sometimes sin according to Romans 1:7 and 1Corinthians 1:2, a topic that will be covered in greater depth when we study Romans 5:1.

"Grace to you and peace" (Romans 1:7) is a phrase used by Paul in a majority of his epistles. He does not say, peace and grace because grace must be received before peace can be experienced, as verified by Paul's words to the church at Corinth:

> *And because of the surpassing greatness of the revelations, for this reason, to keep me from exalting myself, there was given me a thorn in the flesh, a messenger of Satan to buffet me — to keep me from exalting myself! Concerning this I entreated the Lord three times that it might depart from me. And He has said to me, "My grace is sufficient for you, for power is perfected in weakness." Most gladly, therefore, I will*

> *rather boast about my weaknesses, that the power of*
> *Christ may dwell in me.* (2Corinthians 12:7-9)

That *"power is perfected in weakness"* is demonstrated when Jesus submitted to the cross. His enemies said, *"we win";* yet the resurrection forever confirmed that they lost.   Paul realized that God's grace sustained him in his ministry as an apostle. We must come to the same realization as we function in our unique calling (gifting—1Peter 4:10).

No verse in the New Testament is more convicting than Romans 1:8. Paul states that the *"faith"* of the Roman believers was *"being proclaimed throughout the whole world."* As I read this verse, I wondered if my faith is being proclaimed in my city, county, or state. However, I'm certain it won't happen if my faith is not maturing and being enlarged—a wonderful benefit of studying and praying through the Scriptures. Through knowing and applying God's Word, our faith is broadened.

Romans 1:9-10 explains Paul's burden for these saints. He prayed for them *"unceasingly,"* asking that God allow him to visit Rome. He was genuinely concerned about their welfare, longing to see them firmly *"established"* in the faith (Romans 1:11). I don't view the *"spiritual gift"* mentioned in Romans 1:11 as one of the spiritual gifts of Romans 12:6-8, 1Corinthians 12 and 14, and Ephesians 4. I expect, rather, that Paul is referring to the spiritual growth that would occur in their lives as a result of his visit. On the heels of this thought, he makes an astounding statement. Paul, the mature man of God, declares that his time with the believers in Rome would serve to encourage him (Romans 1:12). Yes, a less mature believer can minister to the giants of the faith. We must never forget this reality!

Paul desired to bear *"fruit"* among the believers in Rome (Romans 1:13)—allow Jesus to bear *"fruit"* through him. Even though he had experienced difficulty in arranging a visit, he refused to give up the idea. In fact, in Romans 1:14-15 Paul mentions that he was *"under obligation"* when it came to preaching *"the gospel"*—which should explain his desire to visit his readers.   *"Under obligation"* actually means "in debt." Thus, Paul viewed himself as a debtor while serving the church at Rome. Can you believe Paul's heart? Can you believe the calling the Lord had placed upon him to preach to the Gentiles? Read 1Corinthians 9:16 for additional insight.

Romans 1:16-17 addresses Paul's view of *"the gospel":*

> *For I am not ashamed of the gospel, for it is the power of*
> *God for salvation to everyone who believes, to the Jew*
> *first and also to the Greek. For in it the righteousness of*
> *God is revealed from faith to faith; as it is written, "BUT*
> *THE RIGHTEOUS man SHALL LIVE BY FAITH."* (Romans 1:16-
> 17)

Paul was *"not ashamed"* of what Jesus had accomplished through His death, burial, resurrection, and ascension (Romans 1:16). Why should he be ashamed of such good news? Today, many men who claim to proclaim truth water down *"the gospel"* in the presence of those who might take offense—or, worse yet, teach without openly disclosing what they believe regarding the more divisive theological matters of our day. What one believes <u>always</u> affects what one speaks. Thus, the listener has every right to know the teacher's theological bent <u>before</u> deciding to listen to that teacher. Paul was not *"ashamed"* of what he believed, nor did he attempt to conceal it with illogical assumptions adorned with excessive vocabulary designed to covertly sway his listener's beliefs—a common practice of our day. *"The gospel...is the power of God for salvation to everyone who believes"* and no other legitimate *"gospel"* exists (Galatians 1:8-10). The gospel of Christ was and is the only gospel with the power to transform lives. Being an eloquent speaker is not a requirement for communicating the gospel's profundity:

> *And when I came to you, brethren, I did not come with*
> *superiority of speech or of wisdom, proclaiming to you*
> *the testimony of God. For I determined to know nothing*
> *among you except Jesus Christ, and Him crucified. And I*
> *was with you in weakness and in fear and in much*
> *trembling. And my message and my preaching were not*
> *in persuasive words of wisdom, but in demonstration of*
> *the Spirit and of power, that your faith should not rest on*
> *the wisdom of men, but on the power of God.*
> (1Corinthians 2:1-5)

Paul was not impressed with man's natural abilities but with God's ability to communicate through mortal servants.

The reason the world is ashamed of the gospel is given in 1Corinthians 1:18:

> *For the word of the cross is to those who are perishing foolishness, but to us who are being saved it is the power of God.* (1Corinthians 1:18)

The fact that God would die for the sin of the world is *"foolishness,"* or folly, to the lost—as long as they reject Christ's perfect work. However, when they realize (in their depravity) that they are sinners the gospel becomes magnificent news to them. We must never forget this reality, especially while enduring scorn or ridicule from the lost. In fact, our greatest enemy today may become our most treasured comrade tomorrow. I am grateful for those who exemplified godly lives before me while I lived as an unbeliever. They were extremely offensive to me before I submitted to the Lord, but their willingness to risk the friendship for the sake of the truth spoke volumes concerning their courage and faith. I have since thanked them for loving me enough to demonstrate the more excellent way.

Paul uses the phrase, *"to the Jew first and also to the Greek"* in Romans 1:16. When Paul entered a city he had not previously visited, he preferred preaching in the Jewish synagogue first (as is evidenced by the book of Acts). He believed that the gospel should be presented *"to the Jew first"* and then *"to the Greek"* (Gentiles). What had affected his thinking? The Law was given *"to the Jew first"* in Exodus 20. Also, our Lord instructed His disciples to preach *"to all the nations,"* but to begin in *"Jerusalem,"* the city of the Jews (Luke 24:46-47; Acts 1:8).

Paul realized, too, that *"the righteousness of God"* is *"revealed"* in the gospel (Romans 1:17) through the cross of Christ. God is holy; He will have nothing to do with sin, and must always judge sin. Man is unholy in his spiritually unregenerated state, inundated with sin—but capable of exercising personal repentance and faith. A just act took place on the cross, for sin was judged through the perfect God-man, Jesus Christ. Because *"righteousness"* means to be right, the Father's rightness was *"revealed"* when He judged sin through His sinless Son.

Consequently, the gospel demonstrates *"the righteousness* [the rightness] *of God."*

The last phrase of Romans 1:17, which is taken from Habakkuk 2:4, could easily be the theme of this epistle:

> … *"But the righteous man shall live by faith."* (Romans 1:17)

You would do well to memorize this phrase, for its rock-solid truth sums up the book of Romans and is dealt with quite often—especially the terms *"righteous," "live,"* and *"faith."* Paul repeatedly emphasizes that God gives *"righteousness"* to only one group of people—to those who exercise personal repentance and faith while depraved. God not only makes the depraved, repentant sinner *"new"* (2Corinthians 5:17 KJV), but also allows him to *"live"* spiritually due to having accepted Jesus through *"faith."*

Romans 1:18-32 explains the progression of sin in man, for the heathen is condemned in these passages. This section of Romans proves that a Godless society will self-destruct, so we will examine these verses in great depth.

Paul first states *"the wrath of God is revealed...against all ...who suppress the truth in unrighteousness"* (Romans 1:18).

> *For the wrath of God is revealed from heaven against all ungodliness and unrighteousness of men, who* <u>*suppress the truth in unrighteousness,*</u> (Romans 1:18)

The depraved who reject Christ receive *"the wrath of God,"* not the depraved who choose to repent and believe and experience God's salvation. Because *"suppress"* can also be interpreted "hold" or "possess," those who reject Christ have access to the truth. After all, you can never *"suppress"* what is unavailable to you. Romans 1:19 confirms our findings:

> *because that which is known about God is evident within them; for God made it evident to them.* (Romans 1:19 NASB)

> *Because that which may be known of God is manifest in*
> *them; for God hath shewed it unto them.* (Romans 1:19*
> KJV)

Even the English Standard Version renders the passage:

> *For what can be known about God is plain to them,*
> *because God has shown it to them.* (Romans 1:19 ESV)

The lost have opportunity to know *"about God"* in the midst of their depravity, for the individuals addressed here choose to disregard the obvious. God's *"eternal power and divine nature...have been clearly seen, being understood through what has been made"* in the physical realm. As a result, *"they are without excuse":*

> *For since the creation of the world His invisible*
> *attributes, His eternal power and divine nature, have been*
> *clearly seen, being understood through what has been*
> *made, so that they are without excuse.* (Romans 1:20)

Paul's point is that the depraved who reject God's truth will have no *"excuse"* for not believing, for He has revealed Himself *"through what has been made."* Some reject His offer of salvation choosing instead to *"suppress the truth"* through living *"in unrighteousness"* (Romans 1:18). You can't *"suppress"* what is not accessible, confirming that the depraved have every opportunity to know and believe the truth.

Be careful with verse 21. The phrase, *"For even though they knew God,"* does not mean that they *"knew"* Him as a result of exercising repentance and faith while depraved and receiving God's salvation. It means only that they knew <u>about</u> Him through His disclosure of the truth in visible creation and what was *"evident within them"* (verses 19-20).

We also find that the hearts of the depraved who *"did not honor Him as God"* were *"darkened"* more extensively as they progressed in sin (Romans 1:21).

> *For even though they knew God, they did not honor Him*
> *as God, or give thanks; but they became futile in their*

speculations, and their foolish heart was darkened.
(Romans 1:21)

This verse is another encumbrance for those who perceive the depraved as incapable of recognizing their need for a Savior and exercising repentance and faith. How could *"their foolish heart"* be *"darkened"* more extensively if they are, as some people incorrectly assume, born a spiritual corpse? A corpse is as dead as dead can be—it cannot experience additional deadness. Yet the word *"darkened"* is in the passive voice in the Greek, meaning that the subject is being acted upon by an outside source—the source being the powers of darkness. Consequently, this verse proves that man is not as spiritually *"darkened"* at physical birth as some might believe. We were not born spiritual corpses.

The fruit of a *"darkened...heart"* is mentioned in verses 22-23:

Professing to be wise, they became fools, and exchanged
the glory of the incorruptible God for an image in the
form of corruptible man and of birds and four-footed
animals and crawling creatures. (Romans 1:22-23)

Those who profess *"to be wise"* become *"fools."* God honors humility—never pride. He, in fact, opposes *"the proud, but gives grace to the humble"* (James 4:6). *"Every knee"* will *"bow"* and *"every tongue"* will *"confess that Jesus Christ is Lord,"* including those who reject Him and experience His condemnation (Philippians 2:10-11). The fool won't win, no matter how wise he professes to be in the realm of the natural. Paul verifies this fact in the following passages:

For it is written, "I WILL DESTROY THE WISDOM OF THE
WISE, AND THE CLEVERNESS OF THE CLEVER I WILL SET
ASIDE." Where is the wise man? Where is the scribe?
Where is the debater of this age? Has not God made
foolish the wisdom of the world? (1Corinthians 1:19-20)

Those who become *"fools,"* due to *"Professing to be wise"* (Romans 1:22), are irrational enough to exchange *"the glory of the incorruptible God for an image in the form of corruptible man and of birds and four-*

footed animals and crawling creatures" (Romans 1:23). God classifies such behavior as *"idolatry":*

> *Therefore consider the members of your earthly body as*
> *dead to immorality, impurity, passion, evil desire, and*
> *greed, which amounts to idolatry.* (Colossians 3:5)

The *"glory"* (Romans 1:23) they exchange is the physical manifestation of God's presence, which in the Scriptures is displayed in the form of fire, smoke, clouds, thunder, lightning, and the second Person of the Trinity, Jesus Christ.

God's glory appeared to Moses in a burning bush in Exodus 3:2, to Israel in Exodus 19:16-18 and 20:18-19, and entered the tabernacle in Exodus 40:34-35. It led Israel throughout the forty years of wilderness wanderings (Exodus 40:36-38), entered King Solomon's temple (2Chronicles 5:13-14; 7:1-3), returned to heaven in Ezekiel's day (Ezekiel 9-11), and remained there for approximately six hundred years. It returned to earth at Jesus' First Coming, appearing to the shepherds in Luke 2:8-9; for Jesus, the Son of God, is the *"...glory as of the only begotten from the Father..."* (John 1:14). "*Glory,*" in the form of a *"cloud," "received Him"* back into heaven subsequent to His resurrection (Acts 1:9; 1Timothy 3:16). God's glory was also manifested on the day of Pentecost when *"tongues as of fire...rested"* on the Jewish believers in Jerusalem (Acts 2:3). This same *"glory"* dwells inside all New Testament believers (Colossians 1:27); for Jesus, the *"glory"* of God (John 1:14), *"lives"* inside them (Galatians 2:20). Therefore, this glory is manifested as we yield to His indwelling presence, making life the most fulfilling journey imaginable. Paul verifies these truths while writing to the church at Corinth:

> *For God, who said, "Light shall shine out of darkness," is*
> *the One who has shone in our hearts to give the light of*
> *the knowledge of the <u>glory</u> of God in the face of Christ.*
> *But <u>we have this treasure in earthen vessels</u>, that the*
> *surpassing greatness of the power may be of God and not*
> *from ourselves;* (2Corinthians 4:6-7)

> *For we who live are constantly being delivered over to*
> *death for Jesus' sake, <u>that the life of Jesus also may be</u>*
> <u>*manifested in our mortal flesh.*</u> (2Corinthians 4:11)

When the Rapture occurs, all church saints (those who are on the earth as well as those who have experienced physical death and dwell in heaven) will receive their resurrected bodies and *"be caught up…in the clouds"* (1Thessalonians 4:16-17)—meaning they will be *"caught up"* in glory. The church will also return with Christ in *"glory"* at His Second Coming (Colossians 3:4).

This same *"glory"* appeared on Moses' *"face"* as he returned from the Mount on which he received the Law:

> *But if the ministry of death, in letters engraved on stones,*
> *came with glory, so that the sons of Israel could not look*
> *intently at the face of Moses because of the glory of his*
> *face, fading as it was,* (2Corinthians 3:7)

"…the sons of Israel could not look intently at the face of Moses…," confirms that the Law cannot bring a person into a place of intimacy with God. The *"glory of his face"* was *"fading,"* verifies that the new covenant of grace would replace the old covenant of Law. This subject is addressed in the book of Hebrews, with the pronoun *"He"* pointing to Jesus:

> *But now He has obtained a more excellent ministry, by as*
> *much as He is also the mediator of a better covenant,*
> *which has been enacted on better promises. For if that*
> *first covenant had been faultless, there would have been*
> *no occasion sought for a second.* (Hebrews 8:6-7)

New Testament believers are not under Law, as validated by Paul's words in Romans 6:14:

> *…for you are not under law, but under grace.* (Romans
> 6:14)

Without question, the *"glory"* is a fascinating subject! The fact that it lives in us through the Person of Christ (Colossians 1:27) should forever encourage us! Is it not amazing that anyone would exchange this glory for the shallowness of worshipping the creature?

As we continue, realize that God loves the lost as well as the saved:

> *"For God so loved the world, that He gave His only begotten Son, that whoever believes in Him should not perish, but have eternal life.* (John 3:16)

God loves the liar, the thief, the fornicator, the adulterer, the homosexual, the lesbian, and even the reprobate. In fact, He loves them so much that He will give them over to their desires; He would never force individuals to submit to His will by removing their freedom of choice. As we address the progression of sin in man, know that the Father loves those who participate in the deeds of darkness. In fact, He would welcome them with open arms should they choose to repent and accept His Son as Savior.

God gives man over to man's own desires when man rejects truth, as is validated by Old and New Testament Scripture:

> *"But My people did not listen to My voice; and Israel did not obey Me. "So I gave them over to the stubbornness of their heart, to walk in their own devices.* (Psalm 81:11-12)

> *"And at that time they made a calf and brought a sacrifice to the idol, and were rejoicing in the works of their hands. "But God turned away and delivered them up to serve the host of heaven;...* (Acts 7:41-42)

God is saying: "If you long to discard truth and live in sin, I will give you over to as much sin as you desire." A high price is paid for such rebellion, as indicated by verses from Romans 1:

> *Therefore God gave them over in the lusts of their hearts to impurity, that their bodies might be dishonored among them. For they exchanged the truth of God for a lie, and*

> *worshiped and served the creature rather than the*
> *Creator, who is blessed forever. Amen.* (Romans 1:24-
> 25)

These verses portray the downward spiral of mankind throughout history. First, truth is rejected. Then comes sexual immorality (sex outside of marriage), and man actually begins worshipping *"the creature rather than the Creator."* In other words, *"idolatry"* runs rampant (Colossians 3:5). This scenario is unfolding at an accelerated pace in our day, as evidenced by the rapid spread of pornography, adultery, premarital sex, etc. When the *"creature"* is worshipped the *"bodies"* of those who participate are *"dishonored"* to their shame. Should you doubt the validity of this statement, examine the lives of those who have trodden this Godforsaken path. Nothing but devastation is left in their wake, leaving the participants and their offspring perplexed, confused, and in most cases void of the stability to live a meaningful life. Infidelity rips a society to shreds, as evidenced by the present state of our surroundings.

Many people (even believers) view premarital sex as socially permissible. As a result, an alarming percentage of Christian youth are sexually active prior to marriage. They argue that the Scriptures have nothing to say regarding the subject, when in essence God's Word has much to say about remaining pure until the wedding day. Let's begin with the issue of virginity, for Paul speaks of a man giving his *"virgin daughter"* in marriage:

> *But if any man thinks that he is acting unbecomingly*
> *toward his virgin daughter, if she should be of full age,*
> *and if it must be so, let him do what he wishes, he does*
> *not sin; let her marry.* (1Corinthians 7:36)

In Paul's day, the bride was expected to be a virgin, as confirmed by 1Corinthians 7:28 as well:

> *But if you should marry, you have not sinned; and if a*
> *virgin should marry, she has not sinned. Yet such will*
> *have trouble in this life, and I am trying to spare you.*
> (1Corinthians 7:28)

This truth ties in perfectly with 2Corinthians 11:2; for the church, who will one day marry Christ (Ephesians 5:22-27; Revelation 19:7-9), will be presented to Christ *"as a pure virgin":*

> *For I am jealous for you with a godly jealousy; for I*
> *betrothed you to one husband, that to Christ I might*
> *present you as a pure virgin.* (2Corinthians 11:2)

This same truth is expressed in different terminology in Ephesians 5:27:

> *...that He might present to Himself the church in all her*
> *glory, having no spot or wrinkle or any such thing; but*
> *that she should be holy and blameless.* (Ephesians 5:27)

Tying Ephesians 5:27 in with Ephesians 5:25-27, we find that the church will be presented to Christ as a pure virgin when their marriage is consummated in heaven:

> *Husbands, love your wives, just as Christ also loved the*
> *church and gave Himself up for her; that He might*
> *sanctify her, having cleansed her by the washing of water*
> *with the word, that He might present to Himself the*
> *church in all her glory, having no spot or wrinkle or any*
> *such thing; but that she should be holy and blameless.*
> (Ephesians 5:25-27)

The marriage between a man and a woman is a picture of Christ's relationship with the church. The church will be presented as a pure virgin to Christ on the wedding day. Consequently, premarital sex is not endorsed by the Creator.

The account of Tamar and Amnon verifies the sinfulness of premarital sexual activity:

> *Then David sent to the house for Tamar, saying, "Go now*
> *to your brother Amnon's house, and prepare food for*
> *him." So Tamar went to her brother Amnon's house, and*
> *he was lying down. And she took dough, kneaded it, made*

cakes in his sight, and baked the cakes. And she took the pan and dished them out before him, but he refused to eat. And Amnon said, "Have everyone go out from me." So everyone went out from him. Then Amnon said to Tamar, "Bring the food into the bedroom, that I may eat from your hand." So Tamar took the cakes which she had made and brought them into the bedroom to her brother Amnon. When she brought them to him to eat, he took hold of her and said to her, "Come, lie with me, my sister." But she answered him, "No, my brother, do not violate me, for such a thing is not done in Israel; do not do this disgraceful thing! "As for me, where could I get rid of my reproach? And as for you, you will be like one of the fools in Israel. Now therefore, please speak to the king, for he will not withhold me from you." However, he would not listen to her; since he was stronger than she, he violated her and lay with her.

Then Amnon hated her with a very great hatred; for the hatred with which he hated her was greater than the love with which he had loved her. And Amnon said to her, "Get up, go away!" But she said to him, "No, because this wrong in sending me away is greater than the other that you have done to me!" Yet he would not listen to her.
(2Samuel 13:7-16)

Sexual activity of this sort is grossly unacceptable, for Absalom killed Amnon as a result of his misdeed (read 2Samuel 13:23-29).
Exodus 22:16 also explains the severity of the issue:

"And if a man seduces a virgin who is not engaged, and lies with her, he must pay a dowry for her to be his wife.
(Exodus 22:16)

The priests under the Law were allowed to marry only virgins:

'*A widow, or a divorced woman, or one who is profaned by harlotry, these he may not take; but rather he is to marry a virgin of his own people;* (Leviticus 21:14)

The magnitude of the issue of virginity is described in Deuteronomy 22:13-21 as well:

> *"If any man takes a wife and goes in to her and then turns against her, and charges her with shameful deeds and publicly defames her, and says, 'I took this woman, but when I came near her, I did not find her a virgin,' then the girl's father and her mother shall take and bring out the evidence of the girl's virginity to the elders of the city at the gate. And the girl's father shall say to the elders, 'I gave my daughter to this man for a wife, but he turned against her; and behold, he has charged her with shameful deeds, saying, "I did not find your daughter a virgin." But this is the evidence of my daughter's virginity.' And they shall spread the garment before the elders of the city. So the elders of that city shall take the man and chastise him, and they shall fine him a hundred shekels of silver and give it to the girl's father, because he publicly defamed a virgin of Israel. And she shall remain his wife; he cannot divorce her all his days. But if this charge is true, that the girl was not found a virgin, then they shall bring out the girl to the doorway of her father's house, and the men of her city shall stone her to death because she has committed an act of folly in Israel, by playing the harlot in her father's house; thus you shall purge the evil from among you.* (Deuteronomy 22:13-21)

Virginity was expected by the man taking a wife in marriage, for the blood shed by the virgin bride (on the wedding night) is a visible picture of the sealed covenant of marriage. The Father sealed the covenant of marriage with Israel by the shedding of blood (read Exodus 24:1-8).

For a man to lie with a woman prior to marriage meant that he had *"violated her"*:

> *"If a man finds a girl who is a virgin, who is not engaged, and seizes her and lies with her and they are discovered, then the man who lay with her shall give to the girl's father fifty shekels of silver, and she shall become his wife*

> *because he has violated her; he cannot divorce her all his*
> *days.* (Deuteronomy 22:28-29)

God's will is purity prior to marriage in every case, as verified by both Old and New Testament Scripture. However, sexual sin can be forgiven. Any sin can be forgiven, but the consequence of sexual sin in this life is staggering even among believers (Colossians 3:25), for the memories it creates are impossible to erase. Paul said:

> *Do you not know that your bodies are members of Christ?*
> *Shall I then take away the members of Christ and make*
> *them members of a harlot? May it never be! Or do you*
> *not know that the one who joins himself to a harlot is one*
> *body with her? For He says, "THE TWO WILL BECOME ONE*
> *FLESH."* (1Corinthians 6:15-16)

Paul isn't teaching that a sexual relationship between a man and a woman consummates a true marriage. His point is that the two participants in the sin are *"one body"* due to the physical intimacy associated with the sin, a counterfeit of what occurs in a God-sanctioned marriage when *"two...become one flesh."* Paul follows later with:

> *Flee immorality. Every other sin that a man commits is*
> *outside the body, but the immoral man sins against his*
> *own body. Or do you not know that your body is a temple*
> *of the Holy Spirit who is in you, whom you have from*
> *God, and that you are not your own? For you have been*
> *bought with a price: therefore glorify God in your body.*
> (1Corinthians 6:18-20)

Paul also teaches:

> *Now the deeds of the flesh are evident, which are:*
> *immorality, impurity, sensuality,* (Galatians 5:19)

> *But do not let immorality or any impurity or greed even*
> *be named among you, as is proper among saints;*
> (Ephesians 5:3)

> *Therefore consider the members of your earthly body as*
> *dead to immorality, impurity, passion, evil desire, and*
> *greed, which amounts to idolatry.* (Colossians 3:5)

Scripture confirms that God forbids immoral sexual relationships. Jesus describes the seriousness of the issue as well as it can be stated in Matthew 5:27-28:

> *"You have heard that it was said, 'You shall not commit*
> *adultery'; but I say to you, that everyone who looks on a*
> *woman to lust for her has committed adultery with her*
> *already in his heart.* (Matthew 5:27-28)

Before exiting this subject matter, we need to emphasize that believers who have compromised their virginity prior to marriage will be presented to Christ as pure virgins at the marriage ceremony in heaven:

> *For I am jealous for you with a godly jealousy; for I*
> *betrothed you to one husband, that to Christ I might*
> *present you as a pure virgin.* (2Corinthians 11:2)

> *...that He might present to Himself the church in all her*
> *glory, having no spot or wrinkle or any such thing; but*
> *that she should be holy and blameless.* (Ephesians 5:27-28)

Even the nation of Israel, after centuries of disobedience, will return to the Father at the end of the Tribulation. This remnant, after accepting Jesus as Messiah, will return as a pure virgin:

> *"At that time," declares the* LORD, *"I will be the God of*
> *all the families of Israel, and they shall be My people."*
> *Thus says the* LORD, *"The people who survived the sword*
> *found grace in the wilderness-Israel, when it went to find*
> *its rest." The* LORD *appeared to him from afar, saying, "I*
> *have loved you with an everlasting love; therefore I have*
> *drawn you with lovingkindness. "Again I will build you,*
> *and you shall be rebuilt, o virgin of Israel! Again you*

> *shall take up your tambourines, and go forth to the*
> *dances of the merrymakers. "Again you shall plant*
> *vineyards on the hills of Samaria; the planters shall plant*
> *and shall enjoy them. "For there shall be a day when*
> *watchmen on the hills of Ephraim shall call out, 'Arise,*
> *and let us go up to Zion, to the* LORD *our God.'"*
> (Jeremiah 31:1-6)

Can there be any doubt that God is a God of grace, love, and forgiveness?

When a society ignores the warnings regarding sexual sin between a man and a woman, greater repercussions occur as described in Romans 1:26-27:

> *For this reason God gave them over to degrading*
> *passions; for their women exchanged the natural function*
> *for that which is unnatural, and in the same way also the*
> *men abandoned the natural function of the woman and*
> *burned in their desire toward one another, men with men*
> *committing indecent acts and receiving in their own*
> *persons the due penalty of their error.* (Romans 1:26-27)

Because their previous unwise choices resulted in a passion to enter into greater rebellion, men desired sexual relationships with men and women with women. As a result, *"God gave them over to"* their desires even though their desires were *"unnatural."* This stage is next to last and precedes the destruction of a society, for time is normally short when behavior of this type appears. Genesis 18-19, Jude 7, and 2Peter 2:6-8 confirm this fact by addressing the sin and destruction of Sodom.

Three men appeared to Abraham, one of Whom was the Lord (Genesis 18:1-2). The other two men were angels (Genesis 19:1). Angels appear as men, and for this reason *"some* [people] *have entertained angels without knowing it"* (Hebrews 13:2). As the Lord was departing, He revealed to Abraham that He would visit Sodom to evaluate its sin (Genesis 18:16-21). Abraham, aware that Lot resided there, asked if it was right for Him to *"sweep away the righteous with the wicked"* (Genesis 18:22-23). The Lord promised Abraham that if as many as *"ten"* righteous lived in the city it would not be destroyed (Genesis 18:24-32).

Genesis 19 deals with the events surrounding Lot's deliverance from wicked Sodom. Lot was sitting in the gate of the city when the two angels arrived (Genesis 19:1). This positioning tells us that Lot held a place of leadership in the city or was close friends with those who did (city officials met at the city gate). Lot asked that the two angels (who appeared as men) stay in his house rather than in the court square (Genesis 19:1-2), for homosexuality ran rampant in the city. Once the angels entered Lot's home, the men of Sodom asked that they might have sexual relations with Lot's visitors (Genesis 19:3-5). Lot refused and even offered his two daughters instead (Genesis 19:6-8), but the men of the city objected and turned against him (Genesis 19:9). Lot's two visitors (the two angels) rescued him and struck the mob with blindness (Genesis 19:10-11). Lot was then delivered from the city (Genesis 19:12-29).

This account places Jude 7 in proper context:

> *Just as Sodom and Gomorrah and the cities around them,*
> *since they in the same way as these indulged in gross*
> *immorality and went after* <u>*strange flesh*</u>*, are exhibited as*
> *an example, in undergoing the punishment of eternal fire.*
> (Jude 7)

Genesis 18-19 verifies the type of sin that Jude is addressing while stating: *"indulged in gross immorality and went after strange flesh."* According to Jamieson, Fausset and Brown, *"Strange flesh"* refers to "departing from the course of nature."[1] Consequently, *"strange flesh"* points to men with men and women with women, homosexuality and lesbianism in other words, *"unnatural"* acts according to Romans 1:26-27.

Merriam Webster's definition of "natural" is:

"…in conformity with the ordinary course of nature…"[2]

Thus, the *"unnatural"* of Romans 1:26-27 points to that which is not "in conformity with the ordinary course of nature"—something out of the ordinary. Homosexuality and lesbianism are *"unnatural"* lifestyles contrary to God's original design. Thus, Lot was *"oppressed by the sensual conduct"* of the inhabitants of Sodom:

> *and if He condemned the cities of Sodom and Gomorrah*
> *to destruction by reducing them to ashes, having made*
> *them an example to those who would live ungodly*
> *thereafter; and if He rescued righteous Lot, oppressed by*
> *the sensual conduct of unprincipled men (for by what he*
> *saw and heard that righteous man, while living among*
> *them, felt his righteous soul tormented day after day with*
> *their lawless deeds),* (2Peter 2:6-8)

Even during the days of the judges the same behavioral flaws were manifested. They were manifested because *"every man did what was right in his own eyes"* (Judges 17:6) rather than what was right in God's eyes. Homosexuality prevailed, for in Judges 19 men from the tribe of Benjamin desired to perform homosexual acts with a Levite, again confirming the type of sin that prevails when God's truth is replaced with man's fleshly desires:

> *While they were making merry, behold, the men of the*
> *city, certain worthless fellows, surrounded the house,*
> *pounding the door; and they spoke to the owner of the*
> *house, the old man, saying, "Bring out the man who came*
> *into your house that we may have relations with him."*
> (Judges 19:22)

We should be grieved as we observe the downward spiral of morality within our land, for our souls are *"tormented day after day with their lawless deeds"* (2Peter 2:8). However, God's grace will sustain and *"rescue"* us for Peter writes:

> *then the Lord knows how to rescue the godly from*
> *temptation,...* (2Peter 2:9)

What a mighty, faithful, and loving God we serve! Yet, our land is accepting this corrupt lifestyle on an ever-increasing basis—confirming God's ability to predict sin's toll on a wayward people. The fact that

Paul penned these words some two thousand years ago verifies that truth is not only unchanging and fixed, but also applicable to any society in any season of time. Yes, truth is eternal and impossible to alter, regardless of how man perceives it in this present age. Note: God loves the adulterer and homosexual, for He accepts them with open arms when they repent and exercise faith while depraved. However, their sinful actions break His heart. After all, marriage communicates that God alone is enough; adultery communicates that God alone is not enough; homosexuality communicates that God is not needed at all.

Before leaving this topic, I would like to describe a personal experience that gave me tremendous compassion for those involved in a homosexual lifestyle.

One evening, I was counseling a man who desired to be freed from his homosexual past. He was a believer in Christ, but his previous experiences had generated habits and memories that persistently unsettled his soul. On top of this, he had developed a friendship with a man with homosexual tendencies. When his friend walked by the room where we were talking, I noticed a dramatic change in the man I was counseling. He had broken into a sweat and was bolting for the door when I stood in his way to prevent his leaving. The expression on his face of reckless abandonment, rage and evil intent, yet tempered with an unnerving look of despair, remains etched in my mind to this day. I could visibly observe (and feel) the powers of darkness waging war with the power of light. Never have I witnessed an environment more intense than that moment. When I said, "Over my dead body will you leave this room," the Spirit of God extinguished the darkness and he wept. He then thanked me for blocking his path and a few months later married a wonderful lady whose passion is Christ. He has remained faithful to the Lord and is a wonderful testimony of God's grace. After all, he, as a believer, was not a homosexual. He was a saint who struggled with the sin of homosexuality. A great difference exists between these two perspectives, as will be validated throughout the remainder of this study.

I believe that Jesus Christ can deliver an individual from any spiritual stronghold. This fact is confirmed time and time again in the Scriptures, and my experience that evening is a living testimony to the validity of God's transforming power.

As was addressed earlier, Ephesians 5:25-27 states that Christ, Who is referenced as *"He,"* will be married to the *"church,"* which is referenced as *"she"*:

> *Husbands, love your wives, just as Christ also loved the*
> *church and gave Himself up for her; that He might*
> *sanctify her, having cleansed her by the washing of water*
> *with the word, that He might present to Himself the*
> *church in all her glory, having no spot or wrinkle or any*
> *such thing; but that she should be holy and blameless.*
> (Ephesians 5:25-27)

Marriage, therefore, is between a man and woman, as indicated by Ephesians 5:31-33:

> *For this cause a man shall leave his father and mother,*
> *and shall cleave to his wife; and the two shall become one*
> *flesh. This mystery is great; but I am speaking with*
> *reference to Christ and the church. Nevertheless let each*
> *individual among you also love his own wife even as*
> *himself; and let the wife see to it that she respect her*
> *husband.* (Ephesians 5:31-33)

The words *"his"* and *"himself,"* along with *"she"* and *"her husband,"* verify that Christ, Who is male in gender, will marry the church, which is female in gender. Scripture, therefore, defines the proper and natural definition of marriage. A man is to marry a woman, not a man. A woman is to marry a man, not a woman. Man with man or woman with woman is *"unnatural,"* as shown by Romans 1:26-27. After all, Adam and Eve were commanded to *"Be fruitful and multiply,"* something that a same-sex marriage cannot fulfill due to the *"unnatural"* nature of the union:

> *And God created man in His own image, in the image of*
> *God He created him; male and female He created them.*
> *And God blessed them; and God said to them, "Be fruitful*
> *and multiply, and fill the earth, and subdue it; and rule*
> *over the fish of the sea and over the birds of the sky, and*

over every living thing that moves on the earth. "
(Genesis 1:27-28)

God will in no way accept unrepentant sinners who reject the gospel. In fact, He will give them over to their sin (Acts 7:42; Romans 1:24, 28), never forcing them to obey. For this reason Paul writes:

> *But we know that the Law is good, if one uses it lawfully, realizing the fact that law is not made for a righteous man, but for those who are lawless and rebellious, for the ungodly and sinners, for the unholy and profane, for those who kill their fathers or mothers, for murderers and immoral men and homosexuals and kidnappers and liars and perjurers, and whatever else is contrary to sound teaching, according to the glorious gospel of the blessed God, with which I have been entrusted. (1Timothy 1:8-11)*

> *Or do you not know that the unrighteous shall not inherit the kingdom of God? Do not be deceived; neither fornicators, nor idolaters, nor adulterers, nor effeminate, nor homosexuals, nor thieves, nor the covetous, nor drunkards, nor revilers, nor swindlers, shall inherit the kingdom of God. And such were some of you; but you were washed, but you were sanctified, but you were justified in the name of the Lord Jesus Christ, and in the Spirit of our God. (1Corinthians 6:9-11)*

Homosexuality is a sinful deed in the eyes of the Father. Yet, once homosexuals exercise repentance and faith while depraved, they are made into holy and blameless saints by the God Who loves and saves them. They will be tempted to return to their previous lifestyle, just as all believers are tempted to return to the sins of their past. God's grace, however, when accepted by the passionate pursuer of truth, will bring deliverance.

The final stage of a rebellious populace is described by Romans 1:28-32, verses that explain the fruit of a *"reprobate mind"* (KJV):

> *And even as they did not like to retain God in their*
> *knowledge, God gave them over to a <u>reprobate mind</u>, to*
> *do those things which are not convenient;* (Romans 1:28
> KJV)

> *And just as they did not see fit to acknowledge God any*
> *longer, God gave them over to a <u>depraved mind</u>, to do*
> *those things which are not proper,* (Romans 1:28 NASB)

The NASB uses *"depraved mind,"* yet the context is better suited for *"reprobate mind"* found in the KJV. Every person is born depraved, for all people are Adam's descendants. Not everyone, however, follows the rebellious path described in these passages. A *"reprobate mind"* (KJV) not only rejects truth but also basks in *"things which are not proper"*— the final stage before a society is completely destroyed. Paul describes the behavior exhibited by such individuals in verses 29-32:

> *being filled with all unrighteousness, wickedness, greed,*
> *evil; full of envy, murder, strife, deceit, malice; they are*
> *gossips, slanderers, haters of God, insolent, arrogant,*
> *boastful, inventors of evil, disobedient to parents, without*
> *understanding, untrustworthy, unloving, unmerciful; and,*
> although *they <u>know the ordinance of God</u>, that <u>those who</u>*
> *<u>practice such things are worthy of death</u>, they not only do*
> *the same, but also give hearty approval to those who*
> *practice them.* (Romans 1:29-32 NASB)

Paul's description of a *"reprobate"* society could very easily describe America today. Yet, with all of the rebellion and decadence addressed in these passages, Paul solidifies the fact that the depraved, even those who have become *"reprobate,"* know *"the ordinance of God."* In fact, they know enough truth to realize that *"those who practice such things are worthy of death."* Therefore, Romans 1:29-32 describes something other than a spiritual corpse, for these individuals can comprehend the consequence of sin. Comprehension can be obtained only through understanding, to some degree at least, unadulterated truth! If the *"reprobate"* can draw such conclusions, the depraved who have been less rebellious can comprehend even more. After all, Adam, subsequent to sinning in the garden and becoming depraved, understood his nakedness:

> *Then the eyes of both of them were opened, and <u>they knew</u>*
> *<u>that they were naked</u>; and they sewed fig leaves together*
> *and made themselves loin coverings.* (Genesis 3:7)

Even though we were born with the same nature that Adam possessed <u>after</u> he sinned (the Adamic nature, sinful nature, old self, old man, dead spirit—all synonymous terms), we could realize that we were naked (sinful) in our depravity, repent of our sins, exercise personal faith, and receive God's salvation. No one is born a spiritual corpse incapable of comprehending truth—as some have wrongfully supposed. The third book in our God's Heart series, *God's Heart as it Relates to Depravity,* covers this subject in great depth.

As a nation, we are presently headed toward the last stage at an alarming rate. Can you see the need to equip ourselves with truth? A great battle awaits us, and we must be ready.

Romans 2

Romans 2 can be divided into two sections. The first section condemns the moral man who does not know Christ (vv.1-16), while the second section condemns the Jew who does not know Christ (vv.17-29). Romans 2:1-16 is one of the most difficult sections of Romans 1-8. Therefore, digest what you can and leave the remainder for later.

The Unbelieving Moral Man will be Condemned

Had we lived in Paul's day, we would have heard the moral man say, "Preach on, Paul! You are exactly right! The man who sins to the degree that you have discussed in Romans 1:18-32 is deserving of judgment! Tell it like it is, Paul!"

Paul had a response for the good, upstanding, self-righteous, moral man, who trusted in his good works as his ticket to heaven: *"You are without excuse."*

> *Therefore you are without excuse, every man of you who passes judgment, for in that you judge another, you condemn yourself; for you who judge practice the same things.* (Romans 2:1)

This man was without excuse because he was practicing *"the same things"* as those who receive God's condemnation! He may not have been practicing them outwardly, but he was practicing them within his heart. The man in Romans 2:1-16 didn't know the Lord any more intimately than the man in Romans 1:18-32, for neither had repented and exercised faith in Christ. After all, repentance means to call sin by name and turn from it.

Have you attempted to share Jesus with a good upstanding citizen, a dedicated church worker, a faithful father who provides for his family, or any such outwardly pure individual who has failed to accept Christ as Savior? Of all the people Paul mentions, this type may be the most deceived. In fact, the man described in Romans 1:18-32 is, normally, much easier to address than the one in Romans 2:1-16. However, no difference exists, for both types will receive God's *"judgment"* unless

they choose to repent and exercise faith while depraved. Romans 2:2-3
states this fact very plainly:

> *And we know that the judgment of God rightly falls upon*
> *those who practice such things. And do you suppose this,*
> *O man, when you pass judgment upon those who practice*
> *such things and do the same yourself, that you will escape*
> *the judgment of God?* (Romans 2:2-3)

These verses are not teaching that displaying righteous judgment is
improper; if this were the case, the Old Testament writing prophets, John
the Baptist, and Paul would stand condemned. Even Jesus would stand
condemned, for He frequently spoke against the sins of the Jewish
people. These passages are teaching the incorrectness in passing
judgment if you are practicing the same things. In other words, the man
who steals, lies, or cheats is incapable of passing judgment on those who
commit similar sins. The scribes and Pharisees walked away from the
woman caught in adultery (John 8:1-11) since they were guilty of
adultery themselves.

The politically correct position today (although scripturally incorrect)
is tolerance at all costs, even at the expense of truth. As a result, most
people sidestep conflict, refusing to involve themselves regardless of the
severity of the injustice. I heard a man recently state that he knew of
only two people who would address wrong, and that he never involved
himself in such matters. Hence, he perceived it improper to discipline or
rebuke anyone for anything, citing that no man is perfect.

He is right on one count. No person living on the earth walks in
sinless perfection (1John 1:8). Only Jesus did that, and He was God-
man. However, Paul instructed the church at Corinth to dis-fellowship
the man who was committing sexual sin with his stepmother
(1Corinthians 5:1-8) and also wrote to Timothy about rebuking sinners:

> *Those who continue in sin, <u>rebuke</u> in the presence of all,*
> *so that the rest also may be fearful of sinning.* (1Timothy
> 5:20)

Did Paul believe in passivity? Never! Was he fearful of conflict? Not in a million years! He consistently pointed out error in the lives of others, even with the apostle Peter (Cephas) while in Antioch:

> *But when Cephas came to Antioch, I opposed him to his face, because he stood condemned. For prior to the coming of certain men from James, he used to eat with the Gentiles; but when they came, he began to withdraw and hold himself aloof, fearing the party of the circumcision. And the rest of the Jews joined him in hypocrisy, with the result that even Barnabas was carried away by their hypocrisy. But when I saw that they were not straightforward about the truth of the gospel, I said to Cephas in the presence of all, "If you, being a Jew, live like the Gentiles and not like the Jews, how is it that you compel the Gentiles to live like Jews?* (Galatians 2:11-14)

Nevertheless, Peter wrote subsequent to this encounter, and shortly before his physical death, that Paul was his *"beloved brother"* in Christ (2Peter 3:15). Yes, blatant honesty, even negative input, can serve to deepen our friendships with others.

Jesus regularly condemned the Jewish leaders for their unrighteousness (Matthew 23:13-36), cleansing the temple on at least two occasions. Yet, He taught:

> *"Do not judge lest you be judged.* (Matthew 7:1)

In Matthew 7:1, Jesus was addressing situations similar to Romans 2, where men were condemning others for sins they were committing themselves (read Matthew 7:2-5). However, people who passionately pursue God's heart need to point out wrong when situations arise that can benefit from their input. Much wisdom is required to know when to speak and when to remain silent. Only God's Word, anointed by the Holy Spirit, can provide discernment for one to know how to appropriately respond in all situations (Hebrews 5:14).

Paul was free to correct others because he understood his identity—who he was in Christ. (We will study this subject in depth while addressing Romans 5:1.) Paul realized that what he did was not who he was, but that who he was had a tremendous impact on what he did. He was a perfect, blameless, and holy saint, who sometimes sinned, who was not on a performance-based acceptance with God. He was a new creation who hated sin—but at the same time, was free to fail while attempting to stand for truth. In fact, should he fail while trusting God to rectify the error within the hearts of those to whom he was called to instruct, he could live with the consequence, knowing that God would honor his willingness to get involved. Indeed, Paul was not passive in his relationships with others, and paid the ultimate price that accompanies this noble undertaking (read 2Corinthians 11 and 12).

Correcting others reaps consequence, even when the correction is done in love; we open ourselves to criticism from those whom we have corrected. This "fallout" keeps many people from addressing sinful behavior, even in the confines of their own home. Thus, husbands and dads are refusing to lead, which creates the perfect environment for abundant discord. Conflict, disharmony, and resentment are impossible to rectify without compassionate and honest dialogue that points out error for the good of all parties involved.

My prayer is that we exit our study of Romans 1-8 with a compassionate boldness explained only in terms of our Savior—freeing us to be ourselves, and at the same time, speak truth to anyone who could benefit from its transforming power. After all, God corrects us for our good through His Word; yet we love and respect Him all the more:

> *All Scripture is inspired by God and profitable for*
> *teaching, for reproof, for correction, for training in*
> *righteousness; that the man of God may be adequate,*
> *equipped for every good work.* (2Timothy 3:16-17)

Romans 2:4 is one of the most powerful verses in the entire New Testament:

> *Or do you think lightly of the riches of His kindness and*
> *forbearance and patience, not knowing that the kindness*
> *of God leads you to repentance?* (Romans 2:4)

For years, I believed that a knowledge of God's wrath is the main player in bringing the lost to repentance. I then read this passage, and something clicked. Paul taught that God's *"kindness,"* not His wrath, motivates the depraved to turn from sin! Do you comprehend the significance of this truth? Christ's death on the cross, along with the Father's *"kindness"* displayed through that gruesome injustice inflicted by unrighteous man, reveals to unregenerate man that *"God is love"* (1John 4:8, 16). This truth serves as a tremendous catalyst for the depraved to repent and exercise faith. Truly, the greatest motivator is God's love—never His wrath! Note: The Law convicts the lost (depraved) of their need to repent as well.

The "source" of repentance is highly debated. One school of thought holds to the following beliefs:

> The depraved (lost) are so spiritually dead that they cannot exercise personal repentance and faith.
>
> Therefore, God makes the choice for them by predestining and electing them to salvation from eternity past—by means of an eternal decree.
>
> At God's specified time, He spiritually regenerates those who have been predestined and elected to salvation from eternity past. He follows by giving them the gift of repentance, along with the gift of faith, so they can repent, believe, and be saved.

In the above arrangement, spiritual regeneration precedes repentance and faith. Also according to this view, repentance and faith are God's gifts to those whom He has previously spiritually regenerated.

Another school, which is diametrically opposed to the view just described, subscribes to the following:

> The depraved are capable of exercising their own repentance and faith prior to experiencing God's spiritual regeneration (salvation).
>
> All people are drawn by God (John 6:44; 12:32), for God desires that all might repent, believe, and be saved (1Timothy 2:4; 2Peter 3:9). However, only the depraved who exercise personal repentance and faith will be saved (spiritually regenerated).

Which school is in agreement with the full counsel of God's Word? We will allow the Scriptures to decide.

"Peter and the apostles" (Acts 5:29) stated that both *"repentance"* and *"forgiveness"* have been granted to *"Israel"* (Acts 5:31):

> *"He is the one whom God exalted to His right hand as a Prince and a Savior, to grant repentance to Israel, and forgiveness of sins.* (Acts 5:31)

The word *"Israel"* is extremely important in this context and must be properly defined, for theologians perceive the term from two polarized vantage points:

> *"Israel"* points to believers only. God has washed His hands with the physical nation of Israel (the Jews) and is dealing with the church alone.

> *"Israel"* points to the physical nation of Israel, the Jews, and God remains committed to the unconditional covenants He sealed with the nation.

The word *"Israel"* in Acts 5:31 points to everyone of Jewish descent, not just Jewish believers; the apostles were speaking to unsaved Jewish leaders who would have viewed *"Israel"* as pointing to the entire Jewish nation. Had *"Israel"* referenced Jewish believers only, the apostles would have stated it in the text. Yet, nothing is mentioned that could justify such a mindset. Consequently, Acts 5:31 proves that God has granted *"repentance to Israel"* in the sense that He grants every Jew the right and freedom to repent. Acts 5:31 most definitely does not teach that God is the source of repentance for any Jew who believes.

Acts 5:31 also validates unlimited atonement, for just as all Jews have been granted the right to repent, they have also been granted the right to receive *"forgiveness of sins."* This right could not have been granted had *"forgiveness"* not been accessible to all. *"Forgiveness of sins"* is not received from God until repentance and faith are exercised. This same principle applies to the Gentiles, as is validated by Acts 11:18 and 2Timothy 2:25.

God requires repentance from those who desire to be saved. Thus, God grants the depraved the right and freedom to repent (Acts 11:18; 2Timothy 2:25); for *"repentance...leads to life"* as well as *"to the knowledge of the truth"*:

> … *"Well then, God has granted to the Gentiles also the repentance that leads to life."* (Acts 11:18)

> ...*if perhaps God may grant them repentance leading to the knowledge of the truth,* (2Timothy 2:25)

Until the lost come to Christ through personal repentance and faith, the deeper truths of God are unattainable. The depraved (lost) possess ample truth to repent and believe; nature reveals the Godhead and His invisible attributes, so that all *"are without excuse"* who reject the Savior (Romans 1:20).

Repentance also applies to the believer's experience subsequent to justification (salvation). Knowing the loving nature of God, we should be compelled to confess and repent soon after sins are committed. Paul writes to the church at Corinth:

> *For though I caused you sorrow by my letter, I do not regret it; though I did regret it—for I see that that letter caused you sorrow, though only for a while—I now rejoice, not that you were made sorrowful, but that you were made sorrowful to the point of repentance; for you were made sorrowful according to the will of God, in order that you might not suffer loss in anything through us. For the sorrow that is according to the will of God produces a repentance without regret, leading to salvation; but the sorrow of the world produces death.* (2Corinthians 7:8-10)

The *"repentance"* mentioned here is exercised by the believer who is walking in disobedience. This *"repentance"* leads to *"salvation"* from the power of sin. Therefore, Paul is not alluding to the *"salvation"* associated with justification (salvation from the penalty of sin), but to *"salvation"* from the power of sin in our daily experience (three types of *"salvation"* are taught in the Scriptures—a subject addressed later). Unconfessed sin prevents us from walking in a place of close communion with the Lord which can only be restored through repentance—calling sin what it is and moving on.

We now have the context of Paul's words in Romans 2:4:

> *Or do you think lightly of the riches of His kindness and*
> *forbearance and patience, not knowing that the kindness*
> *of God leads you to repentance?* (Romans 2:4)

The depraved do the repenting and believing. God does the saving.
Romans 2:5 states that even the moral man will receive God's
"wrath" due to his *"stubbornness and unrepentant heart":*

> *But because of your stubbornness and unrepentant heart*
> *you are storing up wrath for yourself in the day of wrath*
> *and revelation of the righteous judgment of God,*
> (Romans 2:5)

Man's decision to remain in his depravity causes God to condemn
man. Thus, God's *"wrath"* is directed toward the lost due to a decision
they make, not a decision He makes; the lost (depraved) are free to
choose to repent and believe. This *"judgment"* of *"wrath"* is a
"righteous judgment," since man has a choice. He never makes a
contradictory decision, speaks a contradictory word, or performs a
contradictory deed. Hence, He can *"rightly"* judge the lost:

> *And we know that the judgment of God rightly falls upon*
> *those who practice such things.* (Romans 2:2)

Taking this truth into account, let's pause for a moment and consider
the ramifications of some of the popular theology of our day.
Some people incorrectly assume that God elected and predestined
certain persons to salvation from eternity past by means of an eternal
decree. They also assume that He withholds the freedom to believe from
those who were not selected. Under these circumstances, God's *"wrath"*
would be placed upon persons incapable of believing. Yet, Romans 2:5
states that God's *"judgment"* is *"righteous." "Righteous"* means "to be
right." Thus, God's *"judgment"* is always "right," meaning that the
punishment in every case is equal to the wrongdoing. However, if the
lost were punished for not believing, when it was God's choice that
prevented them from believing, God would be totally unjust. Yet, this

contradiction is being promoted in our day. <u>Mystery</u> is often cited as the solution, which is no solution at all; it fails to answer the ultimate question:

> If God is capable of saving all, yet chose to save only
> some (through predetermining their destiny from eternity
> past—as come advocate), how can He remain a God of
> love?

The dilemma generated by this question is insurmountable for those who classify contradiction as mystery. If God, by means of an eternal decree, chose some to be saved (as they advocate) when He could have chosen all (as they also advocate), how could He remain a God of *"love"* (1John 4:8, 16)?   I have never heard or read a satisfactory, non-contradictory answer from those who cite mystery as the solution.   In fact, they often present the following argument:

> "God is so sovereign that He must cause all things.
> Therefore, He chose the elect to salvation from eternity
> past. Should man possess the freedom to determine his
> destiny through the exercise of his will (especially while
> depraved), man would be more sovereign than God.
> Consequently, God, Who is capable of saving all, chose
> from eternity past to save only some so that He might
> have someone upon which to display His wrath. This
> violent display of His wrath causes those who were
> chosen to salvation to appreciate His grace."

Does this mindset properly portray the God that you know, the God of *"love"* that John addresses so passionately in 1John 4:8 and 16? Impossible! Individuals who adhere to such unbiblical thinking elevate God's sovereignty at the expense of His love. God is sovereign, but He never allows His sovereignty to override, supersede, or violate His love. Had God chosen some to salvation from eternity past, thus preventing others from being saved, yet judged those "others" for failing to exercise repentance and faith, He would be cruel and totally unjust. (This subject is covered in much detail in our *God's Heart* series.)

God's *"judgment"* is *"righteous"* (Romans 2:5), for He condemns only one class of people—those individuals who choose to reject His offer of salvation through the exercise of their will.

Paul also states that the lost are *"storing up wrath for...the day of wrath"* (Romans 2:5). God's *"wrath"* will be poured out on unbelievers in proportion to the quantity of *"wrath"* they have stored up—in proportion to the degree of their sin. They will face the *"great white throne"* judgment (Revelation 20:11-15), a judgment of condemnation for all who discard His free offer of grace—a judgment from the *"books"* that list the sins of all the unredeemed.

The *"great white throne"* judgment (Revelation 20:11) differs from *"the judgment seat of Christ"* (2Corinthians 5:10). No believer will be judged at the *"great white throne,"* for it is a judgment of <u>wrath</u>. A New Testament believer faces *"the judgment seat of Christ,"* a judgment bestowing <u>rewards</u>. Each of our works will be tested *"with fire"* (1Corinthians 3:10-15), and our rewards will be contingent upon the deeds done in faith. Thus, we will be rewarded for those times when we have trusted Christ to perform a particular deed through us, regardless of the outcome. The deeds performed in our own strength will burn, even if good has resulted from our efforts.

God *"will render to every man according to his deeds"* (Romans 2:6). Those who do *"good"* will receive *"glory...honor...peace...and immortality, eternal life"* (Romans 2:7, 10). Those who *"do not obey the truth"* receive *"wrath...indignation...tribulation and distress"* (Romans 2:8-9). Verses 7-10 teach, therefore, that all who habitually do *"evil"* and enjoy it, proving that repentance and faith are non-existent in their lives, will receive God's *"wrath."* These passages also teach that all who do *"good,"* if their good deeds result from yielding to Christ's indwelling presence, will receive *"glory...honor and peace."* After studying this comparison, do you wonder how anyone could choose to reject Christ?

These verses do <u>not</u> teach that good deeds yield a right standing with God. Paul will confirm this fact to a greater degree later.

The statements, *"of the Jew first and also of the Greek"* (Romans 2:9), and, *"to the Jew first and also to the Greek"* (Romans 2:10), are interesting in that the Jews were the first to receive the Law—not the Gentiles. Paul preached first in the synagogue, and later to the Gentiles, upon his arrival in a new city. The Jews are also God's *"first-born"*

(Exodus 4:22), meaning that they are doubly cursed for their sin (Isaiah 40:1-2; Jeremiah 16:18; Jeremiah 17:18) and doubly blessed for their obedience (as will be evidenced most vividly during the Millennium, when Israel is elevated above all the nations)—for the first-born received a double portion of the inheritance (Deuteronomy 21:17). Israel's sin has caused her to reap more persecution and hardship than any other nation. This situation will change when she repents at the end of the Tribulation and calls Christ back, for she, more than any other nation, will be blessed while basking in the awesomeness of the Millennium. In fact, the Gentiles will serve the Jews throughout the Millennium, as is confirmed by Isaiah 14:2. Hence, Paul's words of Romans 2:9-10 are totally compatible with the full counsel of God's Word.

Paul teaches that, *"...there is no partiality with God"* (Romans 2:11). Any person who is unsaved, due to refusing to repent and believe while depraved, will be condemned and *"thrown into the lake of fire"* (Revelation 20:15). Yes, God loves man enough to allow man to live eternally separated from His presence should he (man) so desire.

Paul makes an extremely interesting statement in Romans 2:12, teaching that *"all who have sinned without the Law will also perish without the Law."* The word *"sinned"* in this instance points to a lifestyle of habitual sin without choosing to receive Christ as Savior. Is it fair for God to respond to the unsaved in this manner? Can individuals who have never been exposed to the Law given to Moses, know about God? They certainly can, for Romans 1:20 teaches that God's creation reveals *"...His invisible attributes, His eternal power and divine nature...."* Many people were declared righteous by God (after exercising repentance and faith while depraved) before Moses received the Law. Therefore, Paul's statement in verse 12 is contextually sound.

In addition, we know that *"all who have sinned under the Law will be judged by the Law"* (Romans 2:12); *"sinned"* again points to a lifestyle of habitual sin without submitting to Christ as Savior. Thus, everyone who has been exposed to the Law, and refused to accept Christ while depraved, *"will be judged by the Law"* at the *"great white throne"* judgment of Revelation 20:11-15.

Those who have heard the Law, but refused to believe in the *"seed"* of Genesis 3:15, Who *"is Christ"* (Galatians 3:16), have not received a *"just"* standing *"before God"* (Romans 2:13).

Paul's last statement in verse 13, when studied in context, brings much truth into focus:

> ...*but the doers of the Law will be justified.* (Romans 2:13)

How can individuals be *"doers of the Law"* (v.13) when through breaking the Law on one count they are guilty of breaking it on all counts (James 2:10)? We can be *"doers of the Law"* only under the condition that we repent and exercise faith in Christ, Who lived the Law perfectly (Galatians 4:4; Hebrews 4:15) and takes up residence in us after we repent and believe while depraved (Galatians 2:20). Only through Jesus living in us (Galatians 2:20), and us living in Jesus (2Corinthians 5:17; Ephesians 2:6), can God justify us by taking away our guilt—and perceive us as having lived the Law perfectly. Thus, Jesus' life in us, the God-man Who carried out the Law perfectly, allows the Father to view us as *"doers of the Law."* We will deal with this wonderful truth in more detail in Romans 5.

The statements, *"do instinctively the things of the Law"* (Romans 2:14) and *"they show the work of the Law written in their hearts"* (Romans 2:15), are challenging to interpret. If they point to the work of the Holy Spirit in a New Testament believer, these Gentiles are believers. If they address the moral law written on the conscience of every man, these Gentiles are unbelievers. Several scholars agree with the second interpretation due to Romans 2:16, which speaks of the judgment of the ungodly at the *"great white throne"* (Revelation 20:11). No believer will face this judgment, yet the individuals of Romans 2:14-15 seem to be present when this judgment occurs, in which case, they are lost and without eternal life. *"The secrets of"* the lost will be judged (Romans 2:16, Revelation 20:11-15); no sin or motive will be veiled, not even among the "morally pure" who have (due to a choice of their own) rejected Christ. All sin will be exposed.

The Unbelieving Jew will be Condemned

The second half of this chapter, consisting of verses 17-29, explains why the unbelieving Jew will be condemned. Up to now the Jews could say,

58

"Preach on, Paul. We are in total agreement." But Paul had not yet addressed, in depth at least, why the unbelieving Jew will receive God's wrath. The Hebrew male normally viewed himself as right with God based on three counts: (1) He was a Jew (2) He had been circumcised (3) The Jewish nation had received the Law—and he was part of that nation. All or any of these avenues provided passage to heaven as far as the average Jew was concerned. Paul disagrees and spends the remainder of the chapter, along with part of the next, explaining why.

In verses 17-24, Paul mentions the disparity between possessing the Law and living by its requirements. In fact, he writes that those *"who boast"* about possessing *"the Law...dishonor God" "through...breaking"* the Law's commands (v.23)!

Since the unbelieving Hebrews assumed that their Jewishness made them part of God's family, Paul writes:

> *But if you bear the name "Jew," and rely upon the Law,*
> *and boast in God,* (Romans 2:17)

The unbelieving Jew also viewed himself as knowing God's *"will"* and approving *"the things that are excellent"* due to possessing *"the Law"* (Romans 2:18). As a result, he considered himself *"a guide to the blind, a light to those who are in darkness"* (Romans 2:19), as well as *"a corrector of the foolish, a teacher of the immature"* (Romans 2:20). A problem existed, however, for he was guilty of the same sin that he condemned in others (Romans 2:21-22)—which brought gross *"dishonor"* to God's name (Romans 2:23). Thus, Paul wrote:

> *For "THE NAME OF GOD IS BLASPHEMED AMONG THE*
> *GENTILES BECAUSE OF YOU," just as it is written.* (Romans 2:24)

Next, Paul addresses the subject of circumcision in Romans 2:25. Due to misguided thinking, the unbelieving Jew viewed *"circumcision"* as a guarantee of salvation. This arrangement could not be the case, for Abraham was circumcised <u>after</u> he was declared righteous (read Genesis 15:6 and Genesis 17:24). Actually, circumcision was given to the Jewish nation as *"a seal of the righteousness of the faith which he [Abraham] had while uncircumcised"* (Romans 4:11). In other words, circumcision was a reminder to the Jewish nation that repentance and faith, exercised in one's depraved (lost) state, result in God granting salvation. Paul wrote:

> *For indeed circumcision is of value, if you practice the*
> *Law; but if you are a transgressor of the Law, your*
> *circumcision has become uncircumcision.* (Romans 2:25)

Paul was quick to mention that *"circumcision"* could result in salvation only if the one circumcised kept the Law perfectly. However, Romans 3:20 and 28 verify that salvation is impossible to obtain through the *"works of the Law"*:

> *because by the works of the Law no flesh will be justified*
> *in His sight; for through the Law comes the knowledge of*
> *sin.* (Romans 3:20)
>
> *For we maintain that a man is justified by faith apart*
> *from works of the Law.* (Romans 3:28)

The Law, which the unbelieving Jew relied upon to grant passageway to heaven (Romans 2:17), was incapable of providing salvation even for a Jew. Its purpose was to convict the lost, Jew and Gentile alike, of their need for a Savior so they might be *"justified"* by God subsequent to exercising repentance and *"faith"* while depraved:

> *Therefore the Law has become our tutor to lead us to*
> *Christ, that we may be justified by faith.* (Galatians 3:24)

Therefore, Paul confirms that to break the Law in one point makes physical *"circumcision"* *"uncircumcision"* for those who trust in *"circumcision"* for salvation:

> *For indeed circumcision is of value, if you practice the*
> *Law; but if you are a transgressor of the Law, your*
> *circumcision has become uncircumcision.* (Romans 2:25)

Every person breaks that Law in some fashion (Romans 3:20; 1John 1:8); yet Jesus, the sinless God-man, kept it perfectly (2Corinthians 5:21;

Hebrews 4:15). Do not overlook this critical fact, for it will serve us well as we continue.

Romans 2:26-27 proves that New Testament Gentile believers, even though physically *"uncircumcised,"* are perceived by God as having kept *"the requirements of the Law."* As a result, He views their *"uncircumcision"* as *"circumcision."*

> *If therefore the uncircumcised man keeps the*
> *requirements of the Law, will not his uncircumcision be*
> *regarded as circumcision? And will not he who is*
> *physically uncircumcised, if he keeps the Law, will he not*
> *judge you who though having the letter of the Law and*
> *circumcision are a transgressor of the Law?* (Romans
> 2:26-27)

God can perceive physically *"uncircumcised"* New Testament Gentile believers as having kept *"the requirements of the Law"* because Jesus, who kept the Law perfectly, lives inside them (Galatians 2:20). Additional benefits accompany this wonderful reality. Because Jesus' presence is within them, along with the presence of the Holy Spirit, their behavior begins to line up with the righteous *"requirement of the Law"* (Romans 8:4)—a subject covered in considerable detail later.

In Romans 2:28-29, Paul explains that a *"Jew"* is not a true *"Jew"* until the *"Spirit"* has circumcised his *"heart."*

> *For he is not a Jew who is one outwardly; neither is*
> *circumcision that which is outward in the flesh. But he is*
> *a Jew who is one inwardly; and circumcision is that*
> *which is of the heart, by the Spirit, not by the letter; and*
> *his praise is not from men, but from God.* (Romans 2:28-
> 29)

Paul's point is that the *"heart"* of a church saint is circumcised by *"the Spirit"* (Romans 2:29), a circumcision that occurs in conjunction with the New Testament believer being placed *"in Christ"* (2Corinthians 5:17) through the power of the Holy Spirit (1Corinthians 12:13) subsequent to exercising repentance and faith while depraved (Acts 16:31; Acts 26:18; Romans 10:9-10). Colossians 2:11 verifies this truth:

> *and in Him you were also circumcised with a*
> *circumcision made without hands, in the removal of the*
> *body of the flesh by the circumcision of Christ;*
> (Colossians 2:11)

We must be extremely careful with Romans 2:28-29, for these passages have been misinterpreted by those who view the church as having replaced physical Israel as God's covenant people. Understanding verses 28-29 in their context is absolutely essential. When Jews or Gentiles exercise repentance and faith during the church age, God makes them members of the body of Christ, the universal church. However, this transformation does not mean that the church is fulfilling God's unconditional covenants granted to the physical Jewish nation, covenants that we addressed in Romans 1. For example, God promised Abram that he and his physical descendants, the physical Jewish nation, would possess the territory *"From the river of Egypt as far as the great river, the river Euphrates"* (Genesis 13:15; 15:18; 17:8). Genesis 26:2-5 and 28:13-15 also verify that the land was given to physical Israel. The Jews will not possess and inhabit this land in its entirety until the Millennium, the one thousand year reign of Christ on the earth (Revelation 20:4, 6). This fulfillment must occur if God is to remain faithful to His Word. However, many people have misunderstood Romans 2:28-29 and accepted the following error:

> Because a true Jew is one who is circumcised inwardly,
> and since every member of the body of Christ fits this
> category, God is not obligated to fulfill the unconditional
> covenants granted to the <u>physical</u> Jewish nation. In fact,
> God is done with physical Israel and is concerned with the
> church alone.

How can this conclusion be valid if God is uncompromisingly faithful to His Word? He guaranteed a literal nation a literal land, along with other unconditional promises. He must fulfill these promises if He is the God of truth and faithfulness portrayed in the Scriptures. We will address this subject matter in more detail later.

Make sure to desire the *"praise…from God"* rather than the *"praise…from men"* (Romans 2:29) as you serve this glorious Creator! The dividends reaped from such a mindset are limitless.

Romans 3:1-8

Romans 3:1-8 reveals some of the arguments presented by the Jews who rejected Paul's gospel. These eight verses should be linked to Romans 2:17-29, for Romans 2:17 through 3:8 comprise a complete section, dealing entirely with the Jews. A Jew who rejected Jesus as Messiah considered himself right with Jehovah on three counts: (1) He was a descendent of Abraham, and thereby a Jew (2) He was part of the nation that had received the Law (3) He had been circumcised. As far as the unbelieving Jew in Paul's day was concerned, any or all of the three would suffice. But Paul's gospel stated that man, any man, be he Jew or Gentile, was right with God only if he had, while depraved, repented and received Christ as Savior. One can only imagine the degree to which Paul's Jewish opponents resented his teaching.

The Theology of the Jew who Rejected Paul's Gospel

I, a Jew, believe that Jehovah has chosen/elected every member of the Jewish nation to enter into covenant with Him and be His covenant people.

I am right with Jehovah because I am part of Jehovah's covenant people.

All Jews are descendants of Abraham.

Jehovah commanded that Abraham and his male offspring be circumcised.

This circumcision is an outward sign of a Jew's participation in Jehovah's covenant with Israel. It seals my position in Jehovah's family.

Being a Jew, I am a member of the nation that received the Law, the nation that God chose/elected as a covenant people to belong to Him forever. Jehovah married Israel at the base of Mount Sinai.

Through keeping the commandments of the Law I maintain the covenant that God made with me as a member of the Jewish nation.

Should I fail to obey the Law to the degree that Jehovah desires, and die physically, Jehovah will reincarnate (*gilgul*) me so I (being a soul) can be perfected in another lifetime as I seek more diligently to keep the Law's commands.

Reincarnation has been a factor in Jewish thinking for many centuries. The following quote is from Rabbi Simmons:

> There are many Jewish sources dealing with what is popularly called "reincarnation." In Hebrew, it is called "gilgul ha'ne'shamot," literally the recycling or transmigration of souls. This concept can be compared to a flame of one candle lighting another candle. While the essence of the second flame comes from the first one, the second flame is an independent entity. Still, the new flame contains imperfections inherited from the initial flame, and it is these imperfections that are to be corrected....
>
> Many sources say that a soul has a maximum of three chances in this world. One example given is that the great Talmudic sage Hillel was a reincarnation of the Biblical figure Aaron. The soul only comes into this world in the first place in order to make a spiritual repair. If that is not fulfilled by the end of one's lifetime, then the soul will be sent down once again. The return trip may only be needed for a short time or in a limited way. This in part explains why people are born with handicaps or may live a brief life.[3]

Additional quotes from a variety of resources could be cited, but the previous quote is sufficient to understand the influence of the false doctrine of *gilgul* on the minds of Paul's audience. The Jew had much to overcome before accepting Jesus as Messiah. Paul, being a Jew, could understand; he was required to do the same. He remained steadfast while presenting Jesus to his Jewish brethren, although the majority rejected his message.

According to Paul's theology, the Jews could no longer view their Jewishness, the Law, or circumcision as providing a righteous standing before God. Paul had annihilated all of these arguments in Romans 2:17-29. Consequently, their only alternative was to attack Paul's theology. Paul, therefore, addresses the questions he must have faced time after time as he spoke with Jews who resisted the gospel.

Romans 3:1 records two of these questions:

> *"Then what advantage has the Jew?" "Or what is the benefit of circumcision?"* (Romans 3:1)

Paul's Jewish opponents were bewildered to the point of asking: "If what you are teaching is true, does being a Jew carry any advantage at all?" Paul is quick to answer, stating:

> *Great in every respect. First of all, that they were entrusted with the oracles of God.* (Romans 3:2)

Paul taught that *"Great"* advantage is attached to being Jewish and much benefit is associated with circumcision. After all, the Jews *"were entrusted with the oracles of God"!*

The *"oracles of God,"* also mentioned in Acts 7:37-38, were received by Moses on Mount Sinai. *"Oracles"* in this case are synonymous with the Law. Romans 1:20 tells that God initially revealed Himself to mankind through creation. That revelation was minor compared to the degree to which He revealed Himself through the Law; an oracle is a divine communication or revelation. Through these *"oracles,"* the Jewish nation had opportunity to know God in a way that had not been provided for the Gentiles. No other nation had received such a revelation. Thus, giving the Jewish nation a distinct advantage.

Most Jews, however, misinterpreted the Law's purpose. Instead of allowing it to reveal their sin and confirm their need for the Savior, they perceived it as an end in itself. In fact, the Law (Genesis through Deuteronomy) and the Prophets (Isaiah through Malachi) were passionately memorized—but had little impact on their daily living due to sin. This fact is vividly portrayed in Matthew 2:3-6, for the Jewish leaders revealed to Herod the exact location of the Messiah's birth and, at the same time, were directly responsible for Jesus' death (Matthew 27:20). They knew the letter of the Law but did not know the God Who provided the letter.

The Father requires repentance and faith from the depraved (the spiritually unregenerated) prior to delivering them from the Law and awarding them new *"life"* in Christ (read 2Corinthians 3:1-18). Note what 2Corinthians 3:16 states concerning the individual who *"turns to the Lord"* while depraved:

> *but whenever a man turns to the Lord, the veil is taken*
> *away.* (2Corinthians 3:16)

Once a Jew or Gentile *"turns to the Lord,"* the veil that has hindered (yet not totally blinded) his spiritual vision is removed. While depraved, one has ample vision to understand his need for a Savior (Romans 1:20; 2Corinthians 3:16; Galatians 3:24), but the veil prevents one from understanding the deeper things of God—truths which can be easily understood subsequent to salvation/justification.

Comparing Exodus 34:27-35 with 2Corinthians 3:1-18 reveals that the old covenant (Law) is temporary in the life of a believer while the *"new covenant"* is eternal (although the Law itself, being part of *"the word of the Lord," "abides forever"*—1Peter 1:25). Paul uses some intriguing terminology in 2Corinthians 3:6-11 while comparing the old covenant with the new:

> *who also made us adequate as servants of a new*
> *covenant, not of the letter, but of the Spirit; for the letter*
> *kills, but the Spirit gives life. But if the ministry of death,*
> *in letters engraved on stones, came with glory, so that the*
> *sons of Israel could not look intently at the face of Moses*
> *because of the glory of his face, fading as it was, how*
> *shall the ministry of the Spirit fail to be even more with*
> *glory? For if the ministry of condemnation has glory,*
> *much more does the ministry of righteousness abound in*
> *glory. For indeed what had glory, in this case has no*
> *glory on account of the glory that surpasses it. For if that*

> *which fades away was with glory, much more that which*
> *remains is in glory.* (2Corinthians 3:6-11)

Paul states that *"the letter* [the old covenant] *kills, but the Spirit* [the new covenant] *gives life"* (v.6). He also speaks of *"the ministry of death"* (v.7) and *"condemnation"* (v.9) brought on by the Law (Exodus 20:18-21 and Hebrews 12:18-24 relate very well to this topic). A right standing with God is unattainable through the deeds of the Law, for it was given as a *"tutor to lead us to Christ"* (Galatians 3:24; 1Timothy 1:8-11).

The followers of a discredited theology often misrepresent the views of those who have proven them incorrect, which is exactly how Paul's Jewish opponents responded once he dismantled their contradictory beliefs. Their arguments, however, did nothing to sway Paul or refute the truth of his gospel.

Romans 3:3 contains another question directed toward Paul by his Jewish opponents:

> *What then? If some did not believe, their unbelief will not*
> *nullify the faithfulness of God, will it?"* (Romans 3:3)

These Jews were asking: "Suppose that Christ is the Messiah spoken of in the Law and the Prophets, and yet some of us do not believe. Will not God be obligated to save the whole Jewish nation?" Their goal was to prove that should God condemn a portion of the nation, He would be required to condemn the whole nation. They believed the converse as well, that should God save a portion of the Jewish nation, He would be obligated to save the entire nation. They perceived God in this manner due to an improper view of their chosenness/election. We will dig deeper to discover where and why they went awry.

As has already been verified, Paul's Jewish opponents perceived Jehovah as having chosen the Jewish nation to salvation due to having chosen them as His covenant people. In other words, they viewed themselves as part of God's family due to a choice God had made prior to their arrival on the earth. After all, several passages speak of God as having chosen the nation, some of which are listed below:

> *"For you are a holy people to the LORD your God; the*
> *LORD your <u>God has chosen you to be a people for His</u>*
> *<u>own possession</u> out of all the peoples who are on the face*
> *of the earth.* (Deuteronomy 7:6)

> *For you are a holy people to the LORD your God; and <u>the</u>*
> *<u>LORD has chosen you to be a people for His own</u>*
> *<u>possession</u> out of all the peoples who are on the face of*
> *the earth.* (Deuteronomy 14:2)

> *"The beasts of the field will glorify Me; The jackals and*
> *the ostriches; Because I have given waters in the*
> *wilderness, and rivers in the desert, to give drink to <u>My</u>*
> *<u>chosen people.</u>* (Isaiah 43:20)

> *And Thy servant is in the midst of <u>Thy people which Thou</u>*
> *<u>hast chosen,</u> a great people who cannot be numbered or*
> *counted for multitude.* (1Kings 3:8)

> *O seed of Israel His servant, sons of Jacob, <u>His chosen</u>*
> *<u>ones!</u>* (1Chronicles 16:13)

> *And He brought forth His people with joy, <u>His chosen</u>*
> *<u>ones</u> with a joyful shout.* (Psalm 105:43)

> *For <u>the LORD has chosen Jacob for Himself, Israel for His</u>*
> *<u>own possession</u>.* (Psalm 135:4)

All Jews have been chosen/elected by God, for God chose to marry the nation of Israel at the base of Mount Sinai (Exodus 24). Were they chosen/elected so all Jews could be saved, or were they chosen/elected to office? Their office would be taking the good news of the Messiah, Who would be born a Jew, to the Gentiles.

Exodus 19:6 confirms that Israel was declared to be *"a kingdom of priests,"* the priests being the teachers of God's truth:

> *and you shall be to Me a kingdom of priests and a holy*
> *nation.'…* (Exodus 19:6)

The Jews failed to accept this responsibility and kept the truth to themselves, for they viewed the Gentiles as unworthy of hearing the great news of the coming Messiah. Therefore, they sat on the truth instead of taking it to the Gentile nations. In fact, they worshipped the truth rather than the Source Who spoke it. Due to the disobedience exemplified by the Jews in their storied past, the seven years of Tribulation will be in progress before they will fulfill, in fullest measure, that to which they were originally chosen (elected). The 144,000 Jewish evangelists, empowered by God, will assist in bringing about this fulfillment by taking the good news of the gospel to the Gentiles. At that time, God's original covenant with Abraham will be fulfilled to an even greater degree. This covenant guaranteed the patriarch the privilege of not only being the father of the Jewish nation, but the father of a multitude of nations:

> *Now the LORD said to Abram, "Go forth from your*
> *country, and from your relatives and from your father's*
> *house, to the land which I will show you; and I will make*
> *you a great nation, and I will bless you, and make your*
> *name great; and so you shall be a blessing; and I will*
> *bless those who bless you, and the one who curses you I*
> *will curse. And in you all the families of the earth shall*
> *be blessed."* (Genesis 12:1-3)

Israel's chosenness/election has nothing to do with the eternal destiny of the individual Jews who make up the nation, for the whole nation is chosen/elected—yet many Jews have failed to repent and believe. These realities explain why Romans 9:27 and 30-33 teach that only a remnant of the Jews will be saved:

> *And Isaiah cries out concerning Israel, "Though the*
> *number of the sons of Israel be as the sand of the sea, it is*
> *the remnant that will be saved;* (Romans 9:27)

> *What shall we say then? That Gentiles, who did not*
> *pursue righteousness, attained righteousness, even the*
> *righteousness which is by faith; but Israel, pursuing a law*
> *of righteousness, did not arrive at that law. Why?*

> *Because they did not pursue it by faith, but as though it*
> *were by works. They stumbled over the stumbling stone,*
> *just as it is written, "Behold, I lay in Zion a stone of*
> *stumbling and a rock of offense, and he who believes in*
> *Him will not be disappointed."* (Romans 9:30-33)

A Jew is chosen/elected (to office) only because he is born into the nation that Jehovah chose/elected to office. Yet, it was commonly taught in Paul's day that a Jew was righteous before Jehovah due to his/her Jewish heritage. Even Gentiles, such as Ruth, were perceived as right before the Father solely due to their having become a proselyte to Judaism. This assumption could not be further from the truth, for Ruth received God's salvation through believing in the *"seed"* of Genesis 3:15. This *"seed"* is Christ (Galatians 3:16). Abraham, Moses, Joshua, David, Isaiah, John the Baptist (all Old Testament believers), and, yes, all who repent and believe during the church age (which began in Acts 2) have been saved in the same manner—through believing in the *"seed,"* Jesus Christ.

This truth is critical, for the Jews who rejected Jesus perceived themselves as right with Jehovah on the basis of ancestry. Yet, they viewed Jehovah as requiring unwavering obedience to the Law if they were to maintain their covenant position and chosenness (election). The hollow deeds of the Law, no matter how righteous and sincere, cannot verify that the performer of the deeds is right with God (Romans 3:20; James 2:10). After all, how many deeds would Jehovah require under such an arrangement? He does not specify because the theology behind such a mindset is totally unscriptural. How could a man who had previously sinned ever hope to live by the righteous standard of the Law when the Law is broken in all points at the first hint of disobedience (James 2:10)?

Also, as a result of Jehovah having chosen (elected) Israel (the nation) to office, He, according to Numbers 6:27, put His *"name upon the"* nation:

> *And they shall put my <u>name</u> upon the children of Israel;*
> *and I will bless them.* (Numbers 6:27 KJV)

Paul, in speaking of the disobedience of Israel, wrote:

> *For "the <u>name</u> of God is blasphemed among the Gentiles*
> *because of you," just as it is written.* (Romans 2:24)

God's name has been *"blasphemed among the Gentiles"* due to Jewish disobedience, for the Jews have misunderstood the purpose of God's election. They have viewed God's choice/election of the nation as being to salvation rather than to office. This fact brings us to a fork in the road, a fork impossible for the New Testament believer to bypass. In fact, the branch of the fork which one pursues is dependent on how one answers the following question: "Can God's name be blasphemed by church saints through misunderstanding and, therefore, misrepresenting what the Scriptures teach regarding the believer's chosenness/election during the church age?" As you ponder this question, realize that the Jews *"blasphemed"* God's name (made Him out to be something that He is not) by misunderstanding and, therefore, misrepresenting His view of the election of Israel. We, as church saints, must make certain to avoid this same error. Consequently, how we view the following passages is critically important:

> *"For the sake of Jacob My servant, And Israel My <u>chosen</u>*
> *one, I have also called you by your name; I have given*
> *you a title of honor though you have not known Me.*
> (Isaiah 45:4)

> *The LORD did not set His love on you nor <u>choose</u> you*
> *because you were more in number than any of the*
> *peoples, for you were the fewest of all peoples,*
> (Deuteronomy 7:7)

> *"The God of this people Israel <u>chose</u> our fathers, and*
> *made the people great during their stay in the land of*
> *Egypt, and with an uplifted arm He led them out from it.*
> (Acts 13:17)

> *From the standpoint of the gospel they are enemies for*
> *your sake, but from the standpoint of God's <u>choice</u> they*
> *are beloved for the sake of the fathers;* (Romans 11:28)

73

Israel was <u>not</u> *"chosen"* (elected) to salvation, for many Jews have died unsaved. Thus, the word *"chosen"* (or election) can point to something other than God choosing/electing certain persons (or nations) to salvation from eternity past. In fact, the Scriptures have confirmed that Israel's chosenness/election granted her an office, a special office indeed—that of bearing the Messiah and taking the news of His coming to the Gentiles.

Paul strongly taught that the chosenness/election of the nation (Israel) to the office of a kingdom of priests was not enough. The Jews of his day were in need of entering into the *"election of grace"* (Romans 11:5 KJV)—that which God bestows upon <u>all</u> individuals who accept His grace (by exercising personal repentance and faith while depraved) during the church age.

> *Even so then at this present time also there is a remnant according to the election of grace.* (Romans 11:5 KJV)

All individuals during the church age who choose to repent and believe while depraved are placed into Christ (1Corinthians 12:13)—the *"chosen one"* of Isaiah 42:1 (NASB), the *"Elect one"* of Isaiah 42:1 (NKJV). Through this means they enter into His chosenness/election. They also become *"new"* creations in Christ (2Corinthians 5:17). Jesus was not chosen/elected to salvation. He was chosen/elected to the office of Messiah, a very special position (office) indeed. Thus, once New Testament believers have been placed into Christ and have become part of His body (1Corinthians 12:18-20), they enter into His chosenness/election and receive a special position (office) as well. This position (office) is used by God to accomplish His purposes, just as Jesus was elected/chosen as Messiah to accomplish, through the Father's strength, the most important purpose of all.

The Jews who rejected Paul's message failed to realize that God is faithful to His promises regarding salvation no matter how few Jews accept Christ, the *"seed"* of Genesis 3:15, as Savior. Isaiah spoke of this fact some 700 years before Christ's First Coming:

> *And Isaiah cries out concerning Israel, "THOUGH THE NUMBER OF THE SONS OF ISRAEL BE AS THE SAND OF THE SEA, IT IS THE remnant THAT WILL BE SAVED;* (Romans 9:27)

God is faithful and will remain faithful throughout eternity. He is faithful to every Jew or Gentile who has placed faith in the *"seed"* of Genesis 3:15, the *"seed"* being *"Christ"* (Galatians 3:16). Consequently, if all of your friends reject the gospel, deny Christ, curse Him, walk away and never look back, His faithfulness to you will remain steadfast. God reminded Elijah of this truth in Romans 11:2-4:

> *Or do you not know what the Scripture says in the passage about Elijah, how he pleads with God against Israel? "Lord, THEY HAVE KILLED THY PROPHETS, THEY HAVE TORN DOWN THINE ALTARS, AND I ALONE AM LEFT, AND THEY ARE SEEKING MY LIFE." But what is the divine response to him? "I HAVE KEPT for Myself SEVEN THOUSAND MEN WHO HAVE NOT BOWED THE KNEE TO BAAL."*
> (Romans 11:2-4)

Paul's gospel was rejected by Jews on numerous occasions. No better example is found than in Acts 28:23-26:

> *And when they had set a day for him, they came to him at his lodging in large numbers; and he was explaining to them by solemnly testifying about the kingdom of God, and trying to persuade them concerning Jesus, from both the Law of Moses and from the Prophets, from morning until evening. And some were being persuaded by the things spoken, but others would not believe. And when they did not agree with one another, they began leaving after Paul had spoken one parting word, "The Holy Spirit rightly spoke through Isaiah the prophet to your fathers, saying, 'GO TO THIS PEOPLE AND SAY, "YOU WILL KEEP ON HEARING, BUT WILL NOT UNDERSTAND; AND YOU WILL KEEP ON SEEING, BUT WILL NOT PERCEIVE;* (Acts 28:23-26)

Only a portion of the Jews have accepted the gospel, meaning that many have died unredeemed. The unredeemed will not be given a second or third opportunity to "get it right" through *gilgul* (reincarnation), for this falsehood is taught nowhere in the Scriptures. Is it not amazing the hoops through which an incorrect system of thought must jump in an attempt to justify their contradictory reasoning? Now back to Romans 3:3:

> What then? *If some did not believe, their unbelief will not nullify the faithfulness of God, will it?* (Romans 3:3)

Paul's Jewish opponents asked this question because they believed they were right with Jehovah due to their belonging to the chosen/elect nation of Israel. In their minds, God's *"faithfulness"* would be nullified should He save some of Israel and not all. Yet, according to 2Kings 22-23, a time existed when a majority of the Kingdom of Judah had submitted to sin. In fact, the Law of God was no longer perceived as the standard for righteous living. Then Josiah, a godly king, reinstated the Law. God, however, needed no reinstating. He had remained faithful to the believing remnant even while the majority of the nation floundered in disobedience. Time and time again God has displayed His relentless faithfulness; the magnificent news is that faithfulness continues today! In fact, when *"we are faithless, He remains faithful"* (2Timothy 2:13). Read about His faithfulness in 2Timothy 1:12, 1Corinthians 10:13, 1Corinthians 1:9, 1Thessalonians 5:24, 2Thessalonians 3:3, Hebrews 2:17, Hebrews 3:6, and other similar passages.

In Romans 3:4, Paul responds to the unbelieving Jews' question of Romans 3:3:

> *May it never be! Rather, let God be found true, though every man be found a liar, as it is written, "THAT THOU MIGHTEST BE JUSTIFIED IN THY WORDS, AND MIGHTEST PREVAIL WHEN THOU ART JUDGED."* (Romans 3:4)

The apostle uses the strongest language possible, saying, *"May it never be."* *"May it never be"* that the overall unbelief within the Jewish nation should nullify God's faithfulness to the Jews who believe. Paul understood well that God will *"be found true, though every man be found a liar."* He does not stop here. He goes on to say, *"That Thou mightest be justified in Thy words, and mightest prevail when Thou art judged."* The words, *"art judged,"* can be interpreted, *"dost enter into judgment."* Therefore, the last phrase of the passage can be rendered: *"and mightest prevail when Thou dost enter into judgment."* Yes, when

God passes judgment, no one, not even an unbelieving Jew, can accuse Him of responding unjustly.   Keep this fact in mind as we continue.

Worthy of our time is King David's quote in Romans 3:4:

> *"THAT THOU MIGHTEST BE JUSTIFIED IN THY WORDS, AND MIGHTEST PREVAIL WHEN THOU ART JUDGED."* (Romans 3:4)

David made these statements in Psalm 51:4, a Psalm of repentance written subsequent to his sin with Bathsheba.   In mentioning these words, Paul reminded his Hebrew opponents of David's view of sin in the life of a Jew.   David also penned in Psalm 51:16:

> *For Thou dost not delight in sacrifice, otherwise I would give it; Thou are not pleased with burnt offering.* (Psalm 51:16)

David realized that *"sacrifice"* and *"burnt offering"* were not what ultimately restored fellowship with Jehovah once sin was committed. What restored fellowship was *"a broken spirit; A broken and a contrite heart"*:

> *The sacrifices of God are a broken spirit; A broken and a contrite heart, O God, Thou wilt not despise.* (Psalm 51:17)

In quoting David in Romans 3:4, Paul demonstrated his desire that his Jewish opponents realize that even a Jew is in need of repentance, and that personal repentance and faith, exercised in Christ while depraved, is required by Jehovah before ushering anyone, Jew or Gentile, into His kingdom.

In verse 5, Paul records even more questions offered by his Jewish opponents.

> *But if our unrighteousness demonstrates the righteousness of God, what shall we say? The God who inflicts wrath is not unrighteous, is He? (I am speaking in human terms.)* (Romans 3:5

The Jews who disagreed with Paul's teaching presented the following argument. They realized that Paul considered them lost so long as they rejected Jesus' Messiahship:

> "If what you are teaching is true, then our unrighteousness demonstrates the righteousness of God. However, if our acts of disobedience present opportunity for God's righteousness to be manifested to an ever-increasing degree, which in turn enhances His reputation, how can He condemn our sin and remain just? In fact, if you are correct Paul, we need to sin to an even greater degree so His righteousness can be manifested all the more. If His judgment against the non-elect, whom He gave no opportunity to believe, enhances the elect's appreciation of His grace, He is grossly unjust and unworthy of anyone's praise."

Intriguingly, these Jews, who were lost and without Christ, properly understood that God would be unjust by judging those who do not believe should He withhold from them the freedom to believe. However, their argument did not stop there. They correctly understood that should God's righteousness be magnified through judging the sin of those who had no opportunity to exercise faith, the non-elect Jews (if there were such a thing) would be free to sin excessively—all to God's glory. This argument presented by Paul's Jewish opponents adds much flavor to what follows.

The Jews in opposition to Paul's message viewed God as having chosen/elected them to be part of His family prior to physical birth. Should Paul be correct, the Jews questioning his theology had no alternative, in their minds at least, but to view God as having chosen/elected some Jews as His covenant people, and by default, rejecting the remainder. They concluded, therefore, that should God judge the sins of the Jews He failed to choose/elect, He would be totally *"unrighteousness"* (v.5)—for those judged would have had no opportunity to repent and believe.

This input makes Romans 3:6 extremely intriguing:

> *May it never be! For otherwise how will God judge the*
> *world?* (Romans 3:6)

To understand Paul's words in Romans 3:6, one must realize that the unsaved Jew perceived God's judgment as directed toward Gentiles only. Thus, they would have interpreted the word *"world"* as Gentiles. This conclusion is totally out of context, for Paul is emphasizing the impossibility of God judging the *"world"* (Jews and Gentiles alike) should He fail to judge the unsaved Jews. The judgment addressed here is the *"great white throne"* judgment of Revelation 20:11-15, a judgment directed toward all persons who reject the Father's provision through Christ.

In Romans 3:7-8, Paul's enemies make their final assault:

> *But if through my lie the truth of God abounded to His*
> *glory, why am I also still being judged as a sinner? And*
> *why not say (as we are slanderously reported and as some*
> *affirm that we say), "Let us do evil that good may come"?*
> *Their condemnation is just.* (Romans 3:7-8)

By accusing Paul of teaching, *"Let us do evil that good may come"* (v.8), Paul's Jewish opponents verified that their only alternative was to distort the theology of the man who had proven them incorrect. Paul had never taught such an outlandish notion—that of granting man a license to sin so man's disobedience could enhance God's *"glory."* This falsehood explains Paul's response:

> *And why not say (as we are slanderously reported and as*
> *some affirm that we say), "Let us do evil that good may*
> *come"? Their condemnation is just.* (Romans 3:8)

God would be unjust in judging the lost should they be incapable of believing, especially if their sin magnified His righteousness, which is why Paul records, *"as we are slanderously reported and as some affirm that we say."* Bondage to the Law many times produces such erroneous thinking, yet a similar mindset is being promoted within Christendom today.

The interpretation of these verses allows us to draw some interesting conclusions regarding the theological shift of our day that promotes the falsehood that God determines man's destiny from eternity past by means of an eternal decree. According to this view, He chooses and predestines the elect to salvation and, either condemns the non-elect to damnation (one branch of this system of thought) or leaves them to the consequences of their sin (another branch of this same system). This view portrays God, in His sovereignty, as electing only some to salvation so He will have persons on which to display His wrath. Those receiving His wrath serve as a catalyst for the elect to appreciate His grace. Yet, according to this view, the non-elect lack the ability to believe. If this scenario were true, the non-elect would be judged for failing to believe when it was God who created them with an inability to believe—making Him totally unjust.

Paul's Jewish opponents detected the flaw in this arrangement, for God would be entirely unjust should the sin of those incapable of believing enhance His glory. This flaw, as obvious as it seems to be, has not been reconciled by those who presently accept the flaw as proper theology. Their response to why God would create people who have no ability to believe and then punish them for their unbelief, is "mystery," which is no answer at all. Yet, according to this popular contradictory view, God is capable of saving all (due to His sovereignty), yet chooses to save only some, so His wrath against the non-elect will enhance the elect's appreciation of His grace. Is this your perception of the God of the Scriptures? The unbelieving Jews of Paul's day could see through this inconsistency. They could not bear to believe that God chose/elected only a portion of the Jews so His wrath displayed toward the non-elect of the nation could enhance His glory. Neither did Paul believe this irrational notion, for Paul taught something totally different regarding the believer's chosenness/election!

...Their condemnation is just. (Romans 3:8)

"Their condemnation is just" because their reasoning confirmed that they were lost and without Christ. After all, they considered themselves as belonging to Jehovah due to a choice that Jehovah had made, having chosen/elected them as His covenant people (as part of His family) prior to birth. Therefore, Paul's gospel, which required personal repentance

and faith in Christ (while depraved) prior to God bestowing salvation, was viewed as ludicrous. Thus, they resisted Paul's teaching and labeled him a blasphemer of the truth. Although these arguments presented by the unredeemed Jews could not refute Paul's theology, they gave rise to a popular, although contradictory teaching of our day. This teaching is addressed below in a numbered format.

A Popular, yet Contradictory Teaching of our Day

1. God is capable of saving all, but chooses to save only some.
2. God, in His sovereignty, and by means of an eternal decree, chose/elected from eternity past each person who will be saved.
3. Those who were not chosen/elected were either damned (according to one branch of this system) or given over to the consequence of their sin (according to another branch of this same system).
4. Only the chosen/elect can believe, and all of the chosen/elect will believe. God will ensure that all of the chosen/elect will be saved.
5. The non-elect can never believe.
6. The depraved (those who are spiritually unregenerated) cannot exercise personal repentance and personal faith due to their spiritual deadness. They are spiritual corpses.
7. Even those who have been chosen/elected to salvation from eternity past cannot believe in their depraved state.
8. When the time arrives for the chosen/elect to believe, God draws them to Himself, spiritually regenerates them, gives them repentance and faith, and they repent, believe, and are saved.
9. God did not choose/elect everyone to salvation because He desired to have someone on which to display His wrath.
10. God's wrath will be displayed on those who have had no opportunity to believe, causing the chosen/elect to have a greater appreciation of His grace.
11. The chosen/elect must persevere for the purpose of proving that they are part of the chosen/elect.

12. If a person sins excessively, it verifies that he was never chosen/elected to salvation. Excessive sin proves, in fact, that he is part of the non-elect.

Can you see how Paul's Jewish opponents, should they live today, could detect the error in several aspects of this popular teaching? Our *God's Heart* series provides an in-depth study of this topic.

The Rebuttal to this Popular yet Contradictory Teaching

1. If God were to judge the sin of the non-elect, who according to this popular teaching have no opportunity to believe, He would be totally unjust.
2. Should God receive glory through judging the sin of the non-elect, who according to this same teaching have no opportunity to believe, the non-elect would be free to sin all the more.
3. Should the chosen/elect be required to persevere for the purpose of proving their chosen/elected status, as this contradictory teaching promotes, Scripture does not mention the standard of perseverance required.
4. Because no such standard is addressed in the Scriptures, the chosen/elect, who, according to this popular teaching are chosen/elected to salvation from eternity past, can never be assured of their chosenness/election, and in turn, their salvation.

Unsurprisingly, many individuals who agree with this widespread yet contradictory teaching perceive God as the cause of all things, even sin. If God were the cause of all things, He would cause the elect to believe and the non-elect to fail to believe, yet judge the non-elect for failing to believe—making Him totally unjust. God would have also caused Satan to rebel against His authority and to continue in that rebellion. Yet, according to Revelation 20:10, God will cast him *"into the lake of fire"* where he *"will be tormented day and night forever and ever."* He will be sent there for his disobedience, which can be traced to the heart of

God should God be the cause of all things. Contradiction abounds in such thinking, making a mockery of God in the process.

This contradictory thinking confused one of the greatest minds to grace the earth. Hugh Ross, on pages 73-74 of his work, *The Creator and the Cosmos*, tells of Albert Einstein as he (Einstein) was confronted with the fact that his theory of relativity had proven that the universe had a "Beginner":

> Einstein's "superior reasoning power," however, was not the God of the Bible. Though he confessed to the rabbis and priests who came to congratulate him on his discovery of God that he was convinced God brought the universe into existence and was intelligent and creative, he denied that God was personal.
>
> Of course, those clergy had a stock response to Einstein's denial: How can a Being who is intelligent and creative not also be personal? Einstein brushed past their objection, a valid one, by raising the paradox of God's omnipotence [His unlimited power] and man's responsibility for his choices: If this Being is omnipotent, then every occurrence, including every human action, every human thought, and every human feeling and aspiration is also His work; how is it possible to think of holding men responsible for their deeds and thoughts before such an almighty Being? In giving out punishment and rewards He would to a certain extent be passing judgment on Himself. How can this be combined with the goodness and righteousness ascribed to Him?
>
> None of the clergy Einstein encountered ever gave him a satisfactory answer to his objection. Typically, they responded by saying that God has not yet revealed the answer. They encouraged him to endure patiently and blindly trust the All-Knowing One.
>
> Regrettably, Einstein lacked the perseverance to pursue an answer further. He took for granted the biblical knowledge of those religious professionals and assumed

that the Bible failed to adequately address the crucially important issue. Of what value, then, could such a "revelation" be?

Lacking a solution to the paradox of God's predestination and human beings' free choice, Einstein, like many other powerful intellects through the centuries, ruled out the existence of a personal God. Nevertheless, and to his credit, Einstein held unswervingly, against enormous peer pressure, to belief in a Creator.

I am grieved that no one ever offered Einstein the clear, biblical resolution to the paradox he posed. I am also sad that Einstein did not live long enough to see the accumulation of scientific evidence for a personal, caring Creator. These might have sparked in him a willingness to reconsider his conclusions.[4]

Had Einstein searched the Scriptures, instead of accepting the contradictory theology of the "clergy" of his day, he would have discovered that God can remain sovereign without causing all things. In fact, he would have understood that God is a righteous judge, judging only one class of individuals—those who fail to exercise their freedom to repent and believe while depraved.

Man dislikes admitting error, which can be evidenced by the arguments of the unsaved Jews of Paul's day. However, to grow in the knowledge of the Lord we must remain teachable, never hardened by sin's deceitfulness, always maintaining a willingness to admit our mishandling of the truth. Paul's Jewish opponents failed to realize this fact and reaped the consequence of their error, as do many individuals who follow the contradictory teachings inundating Christendom today.

Our study of Romans 3:1-8 may be summed up in one statement:

"The strictest legalism leads to the greatest license" (author unknown).

May we forever be delivered from the bondage of the Law through the grace we have been granted in Christ!

Our foundation is getting stronger. In fact, it will be completed by the time we reach Romans 4:25. We will then be equipped to build amazing truths on an uncompromised footing!

Romans 3:9-31

Paul has proven that the heathen (Romans 1:18-32), the moral man (Romans 2:1-16), and the Jew (Romans 2:17-3:8) can be lost and in need of a Savior. Man's only hope is to have God save him once he (while depraved) exercises personal repentance and faith in Christ. Paul next condemns the whole world in Romans 3:9-18, that is, all people who refuse to repent and believe.

Both Jews and Greeks Under Sin

Paul begins by writing:

What then? Are we better than they?... (Romans 3:9)

Paul, a Jew, asks his Gentile readers who have accepted Christ if they (along with him) are better than the Jews who have rejected Christ. These questions must be interpreted in context or they generate confusion. Romans 3:9 provides the proper context:

...Not at all; for we have already charged that both Jews and Greeks are all under sin; (Romans 3:9)

The apostle emphasizes that everyone, regardless of nationality, is born *"under sin."* All Jews and Gentiles *("Greeks")* are born with a need for a Savior. Consequently, Paul and his Gentile readers, prior to receiving Christ, were no *"better"* than the unbelieving Jews—nor anyone else as far as salvation was concerned. Thus, Jews cannot claim that they are part of God's family when they exit their mother's womb. They are born with a nature that loves sin, a nature that makes them *"children of wrath"* (Ephesians 2:3). God eradicates this nature when the depraved during the church age repent and believe, for He makes them *"new"* creations (2Corinthians 5:17)—a subject addressed in depth in Romans 5.

Verses 10-18 of Romans 3, some of the most controversial verses of our day, describe the condition of a society that does not know Christ. Paul's words are chilling, for his description of lost mankind parallels the world of today. When man refuses to fear God, destruction is inevitable, no matter what stage of history he experiences.

Some individuals use Romans 3:10-18 in an attempt to prove that the depraved are incapable of exercising personal repentance and faith. These passages teach no such thing, for they are general statements regarding the depraved rather than a precise description of every moment of their existence. Romans 3:10-12:

> *as it is written, "THERE IS NONE RIGHTEOUS, NOT EVEN ONE; THERE IS NONE WHO UNDERSTANDS, THERE IS NONE WHO SEEKS FOR GOD; ALL HAVE TURNED ASIDE, TOGETHER THEY HAVE BECOME USELESS; THERE IS NONE WHO DOES GOOD, THERE IS NOT EVEN ONE. "* (Romans 3:10-12)

When taken through the full counsel of God's Word, Romans 3:10 teaches that everyone is born unrighteous due to Adam's sin. Romans 5:18 verifies this fact:

> *So then as through one transgression there resulted condemnation to all men,* (Romans 5:18)

Some people perceive Romans 3:11-12 as teaching that the depraved are incapable of repenting and believing—that God (prior to salvation) must spiritually regenerate the depraved (those who make up the elect, in their opinion), and give them repentance and faith, before they can repent, believe, and be saved. They also, due to their view of man's depravity and God's sovereignty, perceive God as choosing/electing from eternity past who will be saved, yet condemning the non-elect to damnation (or giving them over to the consequence of their sin). Romans 3:11-12 is then perceived as communicating that the depraved are totally *"useless"*— spiritual corpses, incapable of choosing Christ.

Paul's words to his Jewish opponents in Romans 3:1-8 prove that he did not perceive the depraved as incapable of repenting and believing. Should God elect some individuals to salvation, giving them no choice as to where they would spend eternity, He would, by default, later judge the non-elect who had no opportunity to believe. This scenario would make Him totally unjust. The answer to what Paul is communicating is extremely simple when all of the verses in God's Word are considered rather than a select few.

Paul, in Romans 3:11-12, is stressing that the depraved will never seek God without the Father's drawing (John 6:44) and the Spirit's convicting (John 16:8). Yet, he also viewed man as capable of repenting and exercising personal faith while depraved (read Acts 16:31, Acts 26:18, and Romans 10:9-10).

No verse is to be isolated and interpreted as an island. Neither are a few verses to be insulated from what the Scriptures teach overall. All of the verses in God's Word are required for proper, contextual understanding—that is, if you adopt Paul's method of interpretation:

> *For I have not shunned to declare unto you all the*
> *counsel of God.* (Acts 20:27 KJV)

Without the aid of *"all the counsel of God,"* we could conclude that Paul taught error in stating:

> *if somehow I might move to jealousy my fellow*
> *countrymen and save some of them.* (Romans 11:14)

Paul did not view himself as possessing the power to *"save"*—which would have been heretical and, thus, totally void of truth. He believed that God alone saves the depraved, repentant sinner, as confirmed by a hoard of passages in the apostle's epistles! Therefore, the proper meaning of Romans 11:14 is determined by taking Paul's thought through all of what he writes rather than isolating it. He viewed his teaching of the truth as a vehicle through which the depraved could be persuaded to exercise personal faith in Christ, faith that God requires before granting salvation.

The following passages confirm that the depraved can pursue the Lord, with the assistance of the Father's drawing (John 6:44) and the Spirit's conviction (John 16:8), prior to being spiritually regenerated. Additional verses could be cited, but for the sake of time and space, a limited number are included. Just these few passages, however, are more than sufficient to validate that the depraved can exercise repentance and faith prior to spiritual regeneration. Our *God's Heart* series examines the subject in much greater depth.

Genesis 3:6-7

When the woman saw that the tree was good for food, and that it was a delight to the eyes, and that the tree was desirable to make one wise, she took from its fruit and ate; and she gave also to her husband with her, and he ate. <u>*Then the eyes of both of them were opened, and they knew*</u> <u>*that they were naked;*</u> *and they sewed fig leaves together and made themselves loin coverings.*

The fact that the term "death" in Scripture can mean separation is critical. Cain's birth in Genesis 4:1, after Adam and Eve's sin in Genesis 3:6, confirms this truth. Adam's sin, therefore, caused him to experience spiritual death (Genesis 2:17), a spiritual separation from God, leaving him depraved. As a result, all of Adam's offspring are born depraved (Romans 5:12-19), separated from God. That Adam realized his nakedness subsequent to sinning confirms that he recognized his lost condition while depraved. He also desired to please God while depraved, for he *"sewed fig leaves together"* for a covering due to his shame. He, likewise, feared God and heard God's voice while depraved (Genesis 3:10). After Adam responded in this manner, God provided covering for Adam and Eve through shedding the first blood from the animal kingdom (read Genesis 3:21).

Conclusion: Adam recognized his lost condition and need for forgiveness <u>after</u> becoming depraved. He was not a spiritual corpse.

Psalm 10:4

The wicked, through the pride of his countenance, will not seek after God: God is not in all his thoughts. (KJV)

Inability to believe in the midst of their depravity is <u>not</u> what prevents the *"wicked"* from seeking the Lord. Their *"pride"* leads to an unwillingness to pursue God's heart. The Scriptures teach clearly that the depraved are to humble themselves (Matthew 23:12). The Scriptures also stress that God opposes *"the proud, but gives grace to the humble"* (James 4:6). For this reason the Law was given to the depraved

(1Timothy 1:9) so they might repent of their pride and come to Christ (Romans 3:19).

1Chronicles 28:9

"As for you, my son Solomon, know the God of your father, and serve Him with a whole heart and a willing mind; for the LORD searches all hearts, and understands every intent of the thoughts. If you seek Him, He will let you find Him; but if you forsake Him, He will reject you forever.

David, the man after God's own heart, told Solomon (his son) that the Lord would allow him (Solomon) to find Him should Solomon *"seek Him."* Therefore, God must be sought before He can be found. In other words, the Lord is found by the depraved who *"seek Him."*

2Chronicles 15:1-4

Now the Spirit of God came on Azariah the son of Oded, and he went out to meet Asa and said to him, "Listen to me, Asa, and all Judah and Benjamin: the LORD is with you when you are with Him. And if you seek Him, He will let you find Him; but if you forsake Him, He will forsake you. And for many days Israel was without the true God and without a teaching priest and without law. But in their distress they turned to the LORD God of Israel, and they sought Him, and He let them find Him.

These words were not directed toward Asa alone, but toward *"all Judah and Benjamin,"* many of whom were not (at this juncture at least) followers of Jehovah—one of many examples where the Lord urges the unregenerate (the depraved) to *"seek"* Him. When *"they turned to the Lord"* in their depravity, *"and...sought Him"* in their depravity, God allowed them to *"find Him."*

Isaiah 55:6-7

Seek the LORD while He may be found; Call upon Him while He is near. Let the wicked forsake his way, And the unrighteous man his thoughts; And let him return to the LORD, And He will have compassion on him; And to our God, For He will abundantly pardon.

The *"wicked"* man is to *"forsake his way,"* meaning that the depraved are to make a choice to submit to the Lord before they can be pardoned (saved). They are to *"Seek"* and *"Call upon"* God <u>prior</u> to being spiritually regenerated.

Jeremiah 29:13

'And you will seek Me and find Me, when you search for Me with all your heart.

One must *"seek"* the Lord <u>before</u> finding the Lord, Who alone, can save (spiritually regenerate). Thus, seeking, <u>prior</u> to spiritual regeneration, precedes finding.

Acts 26:16-18

'But arise, and stand on your feet; for this purpose I have appeared to you, to appoint you a minister and a witness not only to the things which you have seen, but also to the things in which I will appear to you; delivering you from the Jewish people and from the Gentiles, to whom I am sending you, to open their eyes so that they may turn from darkness to light and from the dominion of Satan to God, in order that they may receive forgiveness of sins and an inheritance among those who have been sanctified by faith in Me.'

Having realized that God appointed him to preach the gospel (not to be saved), Paul attempted to persuade the depraved, the spiritually unregenerated, to believe (Acts 18:4; 26:28; 28:23; 2Corinthians 5:11).

Therefore, he understood that the depraved can *"turn from darkness to light"* (Acts 26:18) prior to spiritual regeneration.

2Corinthians 5:11

Therefore knowing the fear of the Lord, we <u>persuade</u> men, but we are made manifest to God; and I hope that we are made manifest also in your consciences.

Paul spoke of his attempt to *"persuade men"* to come to Christ, realizing that a choice was required on their part (in the midst of their depravity) <u>before</u> God would bestow salvation (spiritual regeneration).

Philippians 2:8-11

And being found in appearance as a man, He humbled Himself by becoming obedient to the point of death, even death on a cross. Therefore also God highly exalted Him, and bestowed on Him the name which is above every name, that at the name of Jesus EVERY KNEE SHOULD BOW, of those who are in heaven, and on earth, and under the earth, and that every tongue should confess that Jesus Christ is Lord, to the glory of God the Father.

These verses refute the contradictory teaching that portrays the depraved (the spiritually unregenerated) as incapable of believing (incapable of confessing *"that Jesus Christ is Lord"*). This erroneous mindset views the depraved as spiritually dead corpses, incapable of responding to any spiritual stimulus. However, the lost (depraved) present in Philippians 2:8-11 (all the lost, of all the ages) will <u>not</u> be spiritually regenerated, yet confess Jesus as Lord. This confession will not result in salvation, for they will receive God's wrath for failing to repent and believe while depraved while on earth (Revelation 20:11-15). (Our *God's Heart* series, distributed by this ministry, has much more to say regarding this topic.)

As we address Romans 3:13-14, keep in mind that Romans 3:10-18 contains general statements regarding the depraved rather than a precise description of every moment of their existence.

> *"THEIR THROAT IS AN OPEN GRAVE, WITH THEIR TONGUES THEY KEEP DECEIVING," "THE POISON OF ASPS IS UNDER THEIR LIPS"; "WHOSE MOUTH IS FULL OF CURSING AND BITTERNESS";* (Romans 3:13-14)

The spiritually unregenerated (depraved) find it extremely difficult to control what proceeds from their mouths; that is, until they turn to Christ and are made new.

The *"feet"* of the spiritually unregenerated (depraved) are *"swift to shed blood"* due to their possessing a nature that enjoys sin:

> *"THEIR FEET ARE SWIFT TO SHED BLOOD,* (Romans 3:15)

As a result of their sin:

> *Destruction and misery are in their paths, AND THE PATH OF PEACE HAVE THEY NOT KNOWN."* (Romans 3:16-17)

The depraved live a miserable existence, never finding *"peace"*—that is, unless they choose to repent and believe and receive God's salvation.

Romans 3:18 is another highly debated verse due to the theological shift that has occurred within Christendom.

> *"THERE IS NO FEAR OF GOD BEFORE THEIR EYES."* (Romans 3:18)

Individuals who view the depraved as incapable of exercising repentance and faith cite this passage in an attempt to prove that the depraved can never *"fear...God"*—that the depraved are unable to repent and believe. Their theology stems from their improper view of God's sovereignty, which they perceive as compromised should the depraved be capable of choosing their own destiny. After all, should the depraved possess the capacity to choose Christ, no need would exist for God to determine man's destiny from eternity past. Paul, however, as was stated earlier, is making a general statement regarding the depraved rather than a precise description of every moment of their existence. Remember, he has already proven that should God's choice from eternity past determine who will or will not be saved, He would be a God who condemns those who have no opportunity to believe—making Him totally unjust (review notes on Romans 3:1-8). Consequently, Romans 3:18 does not teach that the depraved are incapable of fearing God and exercising personal repentance and faith.

The Law's Function

Even more good news is forthcoming in Romans 3:19, regarding the freedom granted to the depraved to repent and believe!

> *Now we know that whatever the Law says, it speaks to*
> *those who are under the Law, that every mouth may be*
> *closed, and all the world may become accountable to*
> *God;* (Romans 3:19)

The Law *"speaks"* to those *"who are under the Law."* Purposefully, Paul uses the present active indicative verb *"speaks"*—which points to action that is occurring (indicative mood) at the present time (the present tense). Would an all-wise God generate a Law which *"speaks"* to those *"under the Law"* (the depraved) should *"those under the Law"* (the depraved) be incapable of comprehending what the Law is speaking? Never! Consequently, the depraved can understand what the Law is saying—confirming that the depraved can comprehend spiritual truth, for the Law *"is spiritual"* (Romans 7:14):

> *For we know that the Law is spiritual;* (Romans 7:14)

We also know that only the spiritually unregenerated (depraved) are under the Law:

> *But we know that the Law is good, if one uses it lawfully,*
> *realizing the fact that law is not made for a righteous*
> *man, but for those who are lawless and rebellious, for the*

> *ungodly and sinners, for the unholy and profane, for those*
> *who kill their fathers or mothers, for murderers and*
> *immoral men and homosexuals and kidnappers and liars*
> *and perjurers, and whatever else is contrary to sound*
> *teaching, according to the glorious gospel of the blessed*
> *God, with which I have been entrusted.* (1Timothy 1:8-
> 11)

These verses from 1Timothy 1:8-11 confirm what is taught in Romans 3:19, that the Law *"speaks to those who are under the Law"*—the spiritually unregenerated (the depraved):

> *...it* [the Law] *speaks to those who are under the Law...*
> (Romans 3:19)

Romans 3:19 does <u>not</u> say that the Law speaks to those under the Law who have previously been spiritually regenerated. Because the depraved are capable of understanding the Law while yet unregenerated, the Law is given as a *"tutor to lead"* them *"to Christ"* so they might *"be justified by faith"*:

> *Therefore the Law has become our tutor to lead us to*
> *Christ, that we may be justified by faith.* (Galatians 3:24)

A *"tutor"* is hired only for the purpose of a student understanding the subject matter. God would never generate a Law for the purpose of leading the depraved to Christ should the depraved be incapable of comprehending what the Law is speaking. Such an endeavor would be a waste of God's time.

Paul taught that the New Testament believer is *"not under Law, but under grace"*:

> *For sin shall not be master over you, for you are not*
> *under law, but under grace.* (Romans 6:14)

Only the depraved who reject Christ's provision live under the Law. Once they exercise personal repentance and faith while depraved, they are made new and live *"under grace."* For this reason Paul wrote to the

Galatians, who erroneously believed that they were saved by grace but kept by Law:

> *You foolish Galatians, who has bewitched you, before*
> *whose eyes Jesus Christ was publicly portrayed as*
> *crucified? This is the only thing I want to find out from*
> *you: did you receive the Spirit by the works of the Law, or*
> *by hearing with faith? Are you so foolish? Having begun*
> *by the Spirit, are you now being perfected by the flesh?*
> (Galatians 3:1-3)

Conclusion:

> The Lord used the Law to allow us to see our need for a Savior while we were spiritually unregenerated (depraved).

> We were under Law only so long as we were spiritually unregenerated (depraved).

> Once we were saved (spiritually regenerated), through exercising personal repentance and faith while depraved, we were forever freed from the Law to live under grace.

The depraved can comprehend ample truth to realize their need for a Savior. God, therefore, spoke *"the Law"* into existence to shut man's *"mouth"* and make him *"accountable to God"* (Romans 3:19).

> *Now we know that whatever the Law says, it speaks to*
> *those who are under the Law, that every mouth may be*
> *closed, and all the world may become accountable to*
> *God;* (Romans 3:19)

To put it simply, the Law was given to reveal to all of the depraved (not just the depraved who will be saved) their need for a Savior, *"for through the Law comes the knowledge of sin"*:

> *because by the works of the Law no flesh will be justified*
> *in His sight; for through the Law comes the knowledge of*
> *sin.* (Romans 3:20)

Of course, the depraved must exercise personal repentance and faith before receiving God's salvation from the penalty of sin.

The Law's function remains the same today. It was given so man would cease trying to please God by his own efforts *("works")* and submit to His saving grace, grace granted to all who exercise personal repentance and faith while depraved:

> *because by the works of the Law no flesh will be justified*
> *in His sight;* (Romans 3:20a)

We have proven from a Scriptural basis that the depraved can recognize their need for a Savior, repent and believe, and receive God's salvation. The depraved, most definitely, do not need to be spiritually regenerated by God before they can turn to Christ.

The Righteousness of God Revealed

According to verse 21, more wonderful news awaits us!

> *"But now apart from the Law the righteousness of God*
> *has been manifested, being witnessed by the Law and the*
> *Prophets."* (Romans 3:21)

Purposefully, the phrase, *"the righteousness of God,"* is inserted twice in Romans 3:21-22. Neither is it accidental that *"His righteousness"* is recorded twice in Romans 3:25-26. Paul's goal is to prove that God is righteous and, in the process, disprove his critic's argument in verse 5— that his (Paul's) teaching led one to believe that God is unrighteous.

To be righteous means "to be right." God has always been righteous (right), a righteousness (rightness) that will continue throughout eternity future. He is correct, accurate, just, exact, precise, and more in all matters, regardless of what accusation man directs His way. In fact, His righteousness and holiness result in glory being manifested when He appears—as demonstrated in Exodus 24:16-18, Exodus 40:34-35, 1Kings 8:11, Ezekiel 1:28, 3:23, 8:4, 9:3, 10:4, 10:18-19, 11:22-23, and additional Old Testament passages. God's glory was manifested often during Old Testament times, each appearance validating His *"righteousness"* (Romans 3:21).

God's *"righteousness...has been manifested"* (Romans 3:21) even more magnificently through the death, burial, and resurrection of Christ. According to New Testament Scripture, Jesus is *"God"*:

> *But of the Son He* [the Father] *says, "THY THRONE, O GOD, IS FOREVER AND EVER, AND THE RIGHTEOUS SCEPTER IS THE SCEPTER OF HIS KINGDOM.* (Hebrews 1:8)

Jesus is, therefore, *"righteous"*:

> *My little children, I am writing these things to you that you may not sin. And if anyone sins, we have an Advocate with the Father, Jesus Christ the righteous;* (1John 2:1)

Accordingly, Jesus possesses the same *"glory"* as that of *"the Father"*:

> *And the Word became flesh, and dwelt among us, and we beheld His glory, glory as of the only begotten from the Father, full of grace and truth.* (John 1:14)

Paul wrote that Jesus is the visible manifestation *"of the invisible God"*:

> *And He is the image of the invisible God,...* (Colossians 1:15)

Thus, Jesus could state with much boldness:

> *... He who has seen Me has seen the Father;...* (John 14:9)

Jesus is, hence, *"one"* with *"the Father"*:

"I and the Father are one." (John 10:30)

Not only was the Father's righteousness *"revealed"* through Jesus' life, but His righteousness was also revealed through Jesus' death—which explains Paul's words of Romans 1:17:

"For in it [the gospel] *the righteousness of God is revealed from faith to faith…"* (Romans 1:17)

The necessity of the cross is progressively revealed to those who passionately pursue truth. So, God's *"righteousness…is revealed from faith to faith"* as we mature in the faith.

Because the God of the gospel is righteous, Paul describes the Scriptures (God's letter to man) as *"holy":*

which He promised beforehand through His prophets in the holy Scriptures, (Romans 1:2)

Peter describes the Scriptures as *"pure":*

long for the pure milk of the word, (1Peter 2:2)

Jesus describes the Scriptures as *"truth":*

…Thy word is truth. (John 17:17)

Therefore the gospel is unadulterated truth, free of contradiction. Otherwise, it is error—a fact disregarded by an increasing number of "so called" believers. Should the gospel contain contradiction, God would be a contradiction—and thus unrighteous. Praise God that the gospel, when studied in context and according to all the Scriptures rather than a select few interpreted out of context, is free of even the slightest inconsistency. Otherwise, God is not the righteous, holy, just, and sovereign Ruler of the universe He claims to be.

God must be righteous, for His *"righteousness"* (Romans 3:21) is what allows Him to make the repentant, believing sinner righteous. In other words, remove God's righteousness and He can make no man righteous.

God's righteousness was vividly displayed through both the giving of the Law and the cross of Christ. However, a great disparity exists between what either could accomplish.

God's righteousness was powerfully manifested on Mount Sinai as He spoke the Ten Commandments to Israel (Exodus 20:1-19). However, their response exposed the weakness of the Law:

> *And all the people perceived the thunder and the lightning flashes and the sound of the trumpet and the mountain smoking; and when the people saw it, they trembled and stood at a distance. Then they said to Moses, "Speak to us yourself and we will listen; but let not God speak to us, lest we die."* (Exodus 20:18-19)

Instead of the conditional covenant of Law drawing the Israelites to Jehovah, it hampered their fellowship with their Creator: *"but let not God speak to us, lest we die"* (Exodus 20:19). This fact proves that even though God's righteousness has been revealed through the Law, the Law is incapable of establishing an intimate relationship between God and man. Thus, the deeds of the Law can never result in salvation:

> *because by the works of the Law no flesh will be justified in His sight; for through the Law comes the knowledge of sin.* (Romans 3:20)

Although the sacrifices offered under the Law covered sin (when offered in faith), they could never remove sin:

> *For it is impossible for the blood of bulls and goats to take away sins.* (Hebrews 10:4)

If the Law is broken in one point, it is broken in all points:

> *For whoever keeps the whole law and yet stumbles in one point, he has become guilty of all.* (James 2:10)

Actually, the Law was given not so we might earn our salvation through keeping its requirements, but as a means through which God could break us—show us our need for a Savior:

> *Therefore the Law has become our tutor to lead us to*
> *Christ, that we may be justified by faith.* (Galatians 3:24)

In fact, the Law was given so we might sin more, and in turn, recognize our sinful state:

> *And the Law came in that the transgression might*
> *increase;...* (Romans 5:20)

Therefore, the old covenant of Law is inadequate to save:

> *who also made us adequate as servants of a new*
> *covenant, not of the letter, but of the Spirit; for the letter*
> [Law] *kills, but the Spirit gives life.* (2Corinthians 3:6)

Yet, *"the Law is holy"*:

> *So then, the Law is holy, and the commandment is holy*
> *and righteous and good.* (Romans 7:12)

"The Law is holy" because it functions in the manner that God prescribes: It convicts the depraved of their need for a Savior. This truth makes Paul's words of 2Corinthians 3:7-11 extremely intriguing:

> *But if the ministry of death, in letters engraved on stones,*
> *came with glory, so that the sons of Israel could not look*
> *intently at the face of Moses because of the glory of his*
> *face, fading as it was, how shall the ministry of the Spirit*
> *fail to be even more with glory? For if the ministry of*
> *condemnation has glory, much more does the ministry of*
> *righteousness abound in glory. For indeed what had*
> *glory, in this case has no glory on account of the glory*
> *that surpasses it. For if that which fades away was with*

glory, much more that which remains is in glory.
(2Corinthians 3:7-11)

The old covenant (Law) *"kills"* and is, thus, totally incapable of making a person righteous. Therefore, it came with *"fading...glory."* The new covenant of grace, however, empowered by God's *"Spirit,"* came with *"even more...glory," "glory...which remains"*— which explains John's words in John 1:17:

> *For the Law was given through Moses; grace and truth*
> *were realized through Jesus Christ.* (John 1:17)

These passages also explain the transformation that occurred in the apostles on the day of Pentecost (Acts 2). Having chosen to repent and believe prior to Acts 2, they (on Pentecost) were empowered by the Holy Spirit so they might understand the accomplishments of Christ in light of the Old Testament Scriptures. This fact is confirmed by Peter's words in Acts 2:14-26, where he used Old Testament passages to validate Jesus' Messiahship. Even Jesus, prior to His ascension and, thus, prior to Pentecost, showed two traveling companions every instance where He is mentioned in the Old Testament:

> *And beginning with Moses and with all the prophets, He*
> *explained to them the things concerning Himself in all the*
> *Scriptures.* (Luke 24:27)

The only *"Scriptures"* available at that time were those of the Old Testament, for none of the New Testament books were yet written. Even Stephen's sermon in Acts 7 was inundated with Old Testament truth. Stephen's closing words included this statement:

> *"Which one of the prophets did your fathers not*
> *persecute? And they killed those who had previously*
> *announced the coming of the Righteous One, whose*
> *betrayers and murderers you have now become;* (Acts
> 7:52)

Yes, the Old Testament *"prophets...announced the coming of the Righteous One."*

Conclusion: The Old Testament *"Law"* and *"Prophets"* are filled with truth regarding the suffering Messiah and the new covenant that would follow. As a result of the new covenant, our righteous God makes us righteous subsequent to our exercising repentance and faith while depraved. Thus Paul writes:

> *"But now apart from the Law the righteousness of God*
> *has been manifested, being witnessed by the Law and the*
> *Prophets."* (Romans 3:21)

Paul's point in Romans 3:21 is that God's righteousness is bestowed to man *"apart from the Law,"* a truth *"witnessed by"* the portion of the Bible known as *"the Law and the Prophets."* For example, Abraham came on the scene in the book of Genesis, a section of the Bible known as *"the Law,"* consisting of Genesis through Deuteronomy. Abraham is first mentioned in Genesis 11:26-32. God declared him righteous on the basis of his (Abraham's) faith (Genesis 15:6) prior to issuing the Law in Exodus 20—proving that God declared Abraham righteous *"apart from the Law"* even though it is mentioned in one of the five books of the Bible titled *"the Law."* Romans 3:21 makes an extremely valid statement.

This *"righteousness of God" "apart from the Law"* is also *"witnessed by...the Prophets"* (Romans 3:21). For instance, Isaiah the prophet *"witnessed"* (prophesied) that a suffering Savior would die for the sin of man, Jesus being the avenue through which *"righteousness"* would be bestowed (apart from the Law) to those who repent and believe while depraved:

> *All of us like sheep have gone astray, each of us has*
> *turned to his own way; but the LORD has caused the*
> *iniquity of us all to fall on Him.* (Isaiah 53:6)

> *By oppression and judgment He was taken away; and as*
> *for His generation, who considered that He was cut off*

> *out of the land of the living, for the transgression of my*
> *people to whom the stroke was due?* (Isaiah 53:8)

> *As a result of the anguish of His soul, He will see it and*
> *be satisfied; by His knowledge the Righteous One, My*
> *Servant, will justify the many, as He will bear their*
> *iniquities.* (Isaiah 53:11)

Jesus' sacrifice, not the sacrifices offered under the Law, allowed Him to *"justify"* (Isaiah 53:11) us—make us as righteous as Himself. Thus, Isaiah spoke of the bestowal of God's righteousness upon those who repent and believe in the portion of the Old Testament known as the Prophets.

Romans 4:6-8 also teaches that David, a prophet, spoke *"of the blessings upon the man to whom God reckons righteousness apart from works,"* that is, *"apart from"* the *"works"* of the Law.

God communicated through the prophet Jeremiah that a day would come when He would establish a *"new covenant"* that would replace the old covenant of Law:

> *"Behold, days are coming,"* declares the LORD, *"when I*
> *will make a new covenant with the house of Israel and*
> *with the house of Judah, not like the covenant which I*
> *made with their fathers in the day I took them by the hand*
> *to bring them out of the land of Egypt, My covenant which*
> *they broke, although I was a husband to them,"* declares
> *the LORD. "But this is the covenant which I will make*
> *with the house of Israel after those days,"* declares the
> *LORD, "I will put My law within them, and on their heart I*
> *will write it; and I will be their God, and they shall be My*
> *people. "And they shall not teach again, each man his*
> *neighbor and each man his brother, saying, 'Know the*
> *LORD,' for they shall all know Me, from the least of them*
> *to the greatest of them,"* declares the LORD, *"for I will*
> *forgive their iniquity, and their sin I will remember no*
> *more."* (Jeremiah 31:31-34)

This new covenant came about as a result of Jesus' death, which is recorded in New Testament Scripture:

> *And when He had taken some bread and given thanks, He broke it, and gave it to them, saying, "This is My body which is given for you; do this in remembrance of Me." And in the same way He took the cup after they had eaten, saying, "This cup which is poured out for you is the new covenant in My blood.* (Luke 22:19-20)

The *"new covenant"* is also addressed in the book of Hebrews, the writer quoting Jeremiah 31:31-33:

> *But now He has obtained a more excellent ministry, by as much as He is also the mediator of a better covenant, which has been enacted on better promises. For if that first covenant had been faultless, there would have been no occasion sought for a second. For finding fault with them, He says, "BEHOLD, DAYS ARE COMING, SAYS THE LORD, WHEN I WILL EFFECT A NEW COVENANT WITH THE HOUSE OF ISRAEL AND WITH THE HOUSE OF JUDAH; NOT LIKE THE COVENANT WHICH I MADE WITH THEIR FATHERS ON THE DAY WHEN I TOOK THEM BY THE HAND TO LEAD THEM OUT OF THE LAND OF EGYPT; FOR THEY DID NOT CONTINUE IN MY COVENANT, AND I DID NOT CARE FOR THEM, SAYS THE LORD. "FOR THIS IS THE COVENANT THAT I WILL MAKE WITH THE HOUSE OF ISRAEL AFTER THOSE DAYS, SAYS THE LORD: I WILL PUT MY LAWS INTO THEIR MINDS, AND I WILL WRITE THEM UPON THEIR HEARTS. AND I WILL BE THEIR GOD, AND THEY SHALL BE MY PEOPLE. "AND THEY SHALL NOT TEACH EVERYONE HIS FELLOW CITIZEN, AND EVERYONE HIS BROTHER, SAYING, 'KNOW THE LORD,' FOR ALL SHALL KNOW ME, FROM THE LEAST TO THE GREATEST OF THEM. "FOR I WILL BE MERCIFUL TO THEIR INIQUITIES, AND I WILL REMEMBER THEIR SINS NO MORE." When He said, "A new covenant," He has made the first obsolete. But whatever is becoming obsolete and growing old is ready to disappear.* (Hebrews 8:6-13)

This *"new covenant"* ushered in the age of *"grace,"* which allowed Paul to state that the New Testament believer is *"not under Law, but under grace"*:

> *For sin shall not be master over you, for you are not*
> *under law, but under grace.* (Romans 6:14)

We live in the age of *"grace"* because Jesus, our high priest, serves under a different priesthood than is required by the Law. The priesthood associated with the Law is the Aaronic priesthood. Jesus, on the other hand, is a *"priest...according to the order of Melchizedek"*:

> *For it is witnessed of Him, "THOU ART A PRIEST FOREVER*
> *ACCORDING TO THE ORDER OF MELCHIZEDEK."* (Hebrews
> 7:17)

Based on the book of Hebrews, *"when the priesthood is changed,"* the *"law"* changes as well:

> *for when the priesthood is changed, of necessity there*
> *takes place a change of law also.* (Hebrews 7:12)

Through becoming *"partakers"* of the new covenant of *"grace"* (Philippians 1:7), we live under the *"law* [or principle] *of the Spirit"*— which brings *"life."* We no longer live under *"the letter"* of the old covenant of Law—which results in *"death"* (Romans 8:2; 2Corinthians 3:6):

> *For it is only right for me to feel this way about you all,*
> *because I have you in my heart, since both in my*
> *imprisonment and in the defense and confirmation of the*
> *gospel, you all are partakers of grace with me.*
> (Philippians 1:7)
>
> *For the law* [principle] *of the Spirit of life in Christ Jesus*
> *has set you free from the law of sin and of death.*
> (Romans 8:2)

> *who also made us adequate as servants of a new*
> *covenant, not of the letter, but of the Spirit; for the letter*
> *kills, but the Spirit gives life.* (2Corinthians 3:6)

By means of the new covenant, therefore, God imparts His righteousness to all who repent and believe while depraved:

> *He made Him who knew no sin to be sin on our behalf,*
> *that we might become the righteousness of God in Him.*
> (2Corinthians 5:21)

The fact that God would impart His righteousness to the repentant sinner apart from the Law is taught not only in the portion of the Old Testament known as the Law but also in the portion of the Old Testament known as the Prophets (Romans 3:21).

Isn't it wonderful to know that once you were placed in Christ, subsequent to repenting and believing while depraved, you were made as righteous in the Father's eyes as Jesus is righteous in the Father's eyes? Wow! This subject is covered in great depth as we continue, so magnificent news awaits us. Furthermore, Romans 3:21 lines up perfectly with the full counsel of God's Word.

In verse 22, Paul confirms that God, Who is righteous, imparts *"righteousness"* on the basis of *"faith in Jesus Christ."*

> *even the righteousness of God through faith in Jesus*
> *Christ for all those who believe; for there is no*
> *distinction;* (Romans 3:22)

This truth verifies that God withholds righteousness under only one condition: When the depraved refuse to exercise repentance and faith in Christ. Those individuals who view the depraved as incapable of exercising repentance and faith would disagree. They would argue that God must spiritually regenerate the depraved, and follow by giving them the gifts of repentance and faith, underline before they can repent, believe, and be saved. I disagree for the following reasons.

The Contextual View of Repentance and Faith

The Scriptures teach that God does the saving and man does the repenting and believing, for God saves those who exercise repentance and faith while depraved. However, a debate exists regarding the source of this repentance and faith. In fact, at least two schools of thought exist within Christendom: (1) Repentance and faith are God's gifts to those who will subsequently believe and be saved (2) Repentance and faith originate with the depraved (the spiritually unregenerated) and are exercised prior to God bestowing salvation.

The first school (1) views the depraved (the spiritually unregenerated) as totally incapable of exercising personal repentance and faith. In fact, they view the depraved as spiritual corpses—unable to respond to any spiritual stimulus. Therefore, they view the depravity of man as being a Total Depravity—thus the "T" of the TULIP.

The remaining letters of the acrostic (ULIP) rest on the foundation of this extreme view of depravity. Under this arrangement, God must, by means of Unconditional Election (the "U" of the TULIP), elect (choose) each family member (to salvation) from eternity past by means of an eternal decree. Based on this view, the depraved are incapable of repenting and believing due to their spiritual deadness. Hence, God must make that choice for them.

Limited Atonement (the "L" of the TULIP), a mindset that views Jesus as dying for the elect alone, naturally follows. Any of His blood shed for the non-elect would be wasted according to this view.

The next letter of the TULIP (the "I") must logically (not scripturally) follow. If the depraved are incapable of exercising personal repentance and faith, as is incorrectly assumed, God must, through Irresistible Grace (the "I"), draw the elect to Himself when it is their time to repent and believe. Thus, the following sequence is incorrectly assumed: (1) God must spiritually regenerate the depraved prior to salvation (2) God follows by awarding the spiritually regenerated the gifts of repentance and faith (3) The spiritually regenerated who have received God's gifts of repentance and faith then repent, believe, and are saved. This arrangement is unacceptable, for to be spiritually regenerated is equivalent to being saved. So, according to this sequence, the believer is saved twice—a direct violation of the Scriptures.

This system also necessitates that the elect persevere for the purpose of validating their election—thus the "P" of the TULIP, Perseverance of the Saints.   Consequently, the TULIP leaves its followers lacking assurance of their salvation. After all, to what degree must one persevere to validate his election?   The answer is unattainable due to the unscriptural nature of this system's dogma.

Because the TULIP rests upon the foundation of the "T," Total Depravity, it rests upon shaky ground.   Numerous Scriptures confirm that the depraved can recognize their lost state and, in turn, understand their need for a Savior.   Adam and Eve (as mentioned earlier) are prime examples, for after sinning and becoming depraved *"...they knew that they were naked..."* (Genesis 3:7).   Thus, *"...they sewed fig leaves together..."* to cover themselves due to their sin:

> *Then the eyes of both of them were opened, and they knew*
> *that they were naked; and they sewed fig leaves together*
> *and made themselves loin coverings.* (Genesis 3:7)

Also Philippians 2:11, a passage addressed previously, states:

> *that at the name of Jesus EVERY KNEE SHOULD BOW, of*
> *those who are in heaven, and on earth, and under the*
> *earth, and that every tongue should confess that Jesus*
> *Christ is Lord, to the glory of God the Father.*
> (Philippians 2:10-11)

Many people who *"bow"* in this instance and *"confess that Jesus is Lord"* will be depraved (spiritually unregenerated), for *"every knee"* of mankind will *"bow"* instead of just some. The depraved will respond in this manner without being spiritually regenerated—negating the "T" of the TULIP, along with the other letters of the acrostic (ULIP), altogether.

The subjects of repentance and faith must be perceived properly if God is to be perceived properly.

> *For by grace you have been saved through faith; and that*
> *not of yourselves, it is the gift of God; not as a result of*
> *works, that no one should boast.* (Ephesians 2:8-9)

110

Paul emphasizes that salvation is most definitely by God's *"grace"* (also reference Romans 3:24 and Titus 3:7). Paul also affirms that *"...the righteous man shall live by faith"* (Romans 1:17), a quote from Habakkuk 2:4.

The word *"that"* in the phrase, *"and that not of yourselves"* (Ephesians 2:8), is a major source of contention between (1) People who view faith as God's gift and (2) People who perceive faith as originating with the depraved (the spiritually unregenerated—the lost). Individuals in the first camp view *"that"* as pointing to *"faith."* The second camp views *"that"* as pointing to *"saved."*

The grammar of the Greek language offers the answer. The word *"that"* (in Ephesians 2:8) refers to *"saved"* because *"faith"* is a feminine noun and the demonstrative pronoun *"that"* is neuter—making it impossible for *"that"* to refer to *"faith."* Alford, F. F. Bruce, A. T. Robertson, W. E. Vine, Scofield, and additional Greek authorities agree according to Dave Hunt, in *What Love Is This?*, page 452.[5] In addition, the following notation is written in the margin of the New American Standard Bible relating to *"that"* in Ephesians 2:8:

> I.e., that salvation

Even John Calvin believed that salvation rather than faith is the gift in Ephesians 2:8. On page 453 of *What Love Is This?*, Dave Hunt writes:

> Calvin himself acknowledged, "But they commonly misinterpret this text, and restrict the word 'gift' to faith alone. But Paul...does not mean that faith is the gift of God, but that salvation is given to us by God...."[6]

Yet, many individuals who view themselves as Calvinists would disagree with Calvin's interpretation of this passage! I find that amazing!

Ephesians 2:9, when coupled with Ephesians 2:8, also confirms that salvation, not *"faith,"* is the *"gift."* Ephesians 2:9 applies:

> *not as a result of works, that no one should boast.*
> (Ephesians 2:9)

Paul is teaching that salvation *("saved"*—Ephesians 2:8) is *"not...a result of works..."* (Ephesians 2:9). Salvation is a *"gift"* (Ephesians 2:8) received by those who exercise *"faith"* (Ephesians 2:8) while depraved. Thus, one cannot work himself into a right standing with God. This truth is exactly what Paul teaches elsewhere. Read Romans 3:27-28, for example, realizing that *"justified"* points to salvation:

> *Where then is boasting? It is excluded. By what kind of*
> *law? Of works? No, but by a law of faith. For we*
> *maintain that a man is <u>justified by faith apart from works</u>*
> *<u>of the Law</u>.* (Romans 3:27-28)

Paul proves once again that we are *"justified"* (saved) *"apart from works"* (Romans 3:28). This truth is identical to what Paul conveys in Ephesians 2:8-9. Paul also confirms that *"boasting"* is *"excluded"* in such cases (Romans 3:27). Thus, to exercise *"faith"* while depraved is <u>not</u> a work. In fact, Paul contrasts *"faith"* and *"works"* on many occasions in the Scriptures. Consequently, choosing to exercise personal *"faith"* in the midst of one's depravity is <u>not</u> a meritorious deed. Paul teaches the same principle in Romans 4:5, contrasting *"work"* with believing:

> *But to the one who <u>does not work, but believes</u> in Him*
> *who justifies the ungodly, his faith is reckoned as*
> *righteousness,* (Romans 4:5)

Romans 9:30-32 confirms the same truth:

> *What shall we say then? That Gentiles, who did not*
> *pursue righteousness, attained righteousness, even the*
> *righteousness which is by faith; but Israel, pursuing a law*
> *of righteousness, did not arrive at that law. Why?*
> *<u>Because they did not pursue it by faith, but as though it</u>*
> *<u>were by works</u>...* (Romans 9:30-32)

Scripture has a great deal more to say about *"faith."* We have already determined that *"faith"* (Ephesians 2:8-9) originates within the heart of the depraved (also read Acts 16:31, Acts 26:18, and Romans 10:8-10). The faith required prior to salvation is not God's gift, for *"faith"* springs forth from the lost (the depraved—the spiritually unregenerated) who desire to be saved. I exercised faith in my depravity when I said, "God help, I need a Savior." In that statement, I exhibited not only faith, but repentance as well (we will address repentance shortly). Thus, faith was not the Father's gift prior to His saving me. On the other hand, we must not overlook the Father's drawing (John 6:44) and the Spirit's conviction (John 16:8) that have been ever-present in our lives. But the faith we exercised prior to salvation was our own faith, initiated in our depravity. It was not the Father's gift!

The faith addressed in Ephesians 2:8-9 cannot be classified as God's gift. Salvation is His gift (Ephesians 2:8-9)—given to those who exercise personal repentance and faith while depraved. Some people would suggest that Romans 12:3 refutes this fact:

> *For through the grace given to me I say to every man*
> *among you not to think more highly of himself than he*
> *ought to think; but to think so as to have sound judgment,*
> *as God has allotted to each a measure of faith.* (Romans
> 12:3)

The *"faith"* addressed in Romans 12:3 cannot be the faith that God requires prior to effecting salvation. God only saves under only one condition: When the depraved repent and choose to believe (Acts 16:31; Acts 26:18; and Romans 10:9-19). We will confirm that God's gift of *"faith"* (Romans 12:3) is the faith needed to function within the area of the New Testament believer's spiritual gifting, a gift received <u>after</u> repenting and believing while depraved. After all, Romans 12:3-8 addresses the subject of spiritual gifts.

According to 1Peter 4:10, Romans 12, 1Corinthians 12 and 14, and Ephesians 4, every church saint receives a spiritual gift. This spiritual gift is received in conjunction with being placed into Christ through the avenue of the Holy Spirit (1Corinthians 12:13; Ephesians 1:3) subsequent to exercising repentance and faith while depraved. The *"faith"* addressed in Romans 12:3 is of utmost importance if we are to function efficiently within the area of our spiritual gifting. This gift of *"faith"* is <u>not</u> the same *"faith"* as is mentioned in Ephesians 2:8-9. Considering the above, we can conclude the following.

Once we exercised repentance and faith while depraved, we were baptized into Christ's body through the avenue of the Holy Spirit (1Corinthians 12:13) and were *"saved"* (Acts 16:31). In other words, we were *"born again"* (John 3:3-6), became new creations (2Corinthians 5:17), and were made part of the *"body"* of Christ (Ephesians 5:30). In conjunction with being saved, subsequent to exercising personal repentance and faith while depraved, we received the *"measure"* of *"faith"* mentioned in Romans 12:3, the *"faith"* given to every member of Christ's body, the church, so each gift within His body might function as efficiently and powerfully as possible. This *"faith"* is God's gift (Romans 12:3), unlike the *"faith"* of (Ephesians 2:8-9), which is exercised by the depraved prior to spiritual regeneration.

The *Wycliffe Bible Commentary* adds concerning Romans 12:3:

> Paul is not here speaking of "saving faith"... "Saving faith" would be no standard for correct self-judgment. Only pride would say: "See how much saving faith I have." But it is a humbling experience to say: "Here is the faith I have for carrying out this or that particular task for God." This can only lead to the prayer, "Lord, increase our faith" (see Luke 17:5). In the account of the heroes of faith in Heb 11, we see that the measure of faith given corresponds to the task to be accomplished.[7]

The *"faith"* of Ephesians 2:8-9, exercised by the depraved in conjunction with their recognizing their need for a Savior, must not be confused with God's gift of *"faith"* (Romans 12:3) granted to those who have previously chosen to repent and believe. Yes, God gives believers faith (Romans 12:3), but it is the faith needed to function within the area of their spiritual gifting—not the faith required prior to God's redemptive work of spiritual regeneration. We can draw this conclusion because Paul is addressing spiritual gifts in Romans 12. Thus, the *"measure of faith"* of Romans 12:3, given to New Testament believers once they are in Christ, cannot be equated with the *"faith"* of Ephesians 2:8-9—the *"faith"* exercised by the depraved prior to salvation. Those who fail to make this distinction entangle themselves in numerous

114

theological inconsistencies. After all, why would God plead for the lost (depraved) to exercise faith, all of whom will not be saved, if He were the source of such faith, determining from eternity past who will or will not receive it? Such a scenario would make Jesus appear foolish in passages such as Matthew 23:37:

> *"O Jerusalem, Jerusalem, who kills the prophets and*
> *stones those who are sent to her! How often I wanted to*
> *gather your children together, the way a hen gathers her*
> *chicks under her wings, and you were unwilling.*
> (Matthew 23:37)

The unbelieving Jews rejected Jesus' offer of salvation due to being *"unwilling."* Their unbelief, therefore, did not result from God failing to provide repentance and faith, as some have incorrectly assumed. (Matthew 23:37 is discussed in much greater depth in our *God's Heart* series.)

God's *"purpose,"* desire, and will for man can be rejected:

> *But the Pharisees and the lawyers rejected God's <u>purpose</u>*
> *for themselves, not having been baptized by John.* (Luke
> 7:30)

> *who <u>desires</u> all men to be saved and to come to the*
> *knowledge of the truth.* (1Timothy 2:4)

> *The Lord is not slack concerning his promise, as some*
> *men count slackness; but is longsuffering to us-ward, not*
> *<u>willing</u> that any should perish, but that all should come to*
> *repentance.* (2Peter 3:9 KJV)

Before moving forward, we must correctly answer the following question: "Is the repentance needed for salvation God's gift, or does it originate with man?"

> *He is the one whom God exalted to His right hand as a*
> *Prince and a Savior, to grant repentance to Israel, and*
> *forgiveness of sins.* (Acts 5:31)

Must God give us faith and repentance <u>before</u> we can repent and believe? Some people would answer with a resounding, "Yes!" Does this idea line up with the full counsel of God's Word? *"Peter and the apostles"* (Acts 5:29) stated that both *"repentance"* and *"forgiveness"* have been granted to *"Israel"* (Acts 5:31).

For proper interpretation, we must first understand that the word *"Israel"* in this context points to everyone of Jewish descent, not just Jewish believers. The apostles were speaking to the leaders of the Jews, most of whom had rejected Jesus' Messiahship. Had the apostles been speaking of Jewish believers only, and not the entire Jewish nation, they would have stated this fact in the text. Hence, for *"Israel"* in this context to mean anything other than the entire Jewish nation would have been misleading to their unbelieving Jewish audience. Consequently, those who view the word *"Israel"* as pointing to believers alone are in error.

Here is where our study becomes extremely interesting. First, note that *"repentance"* (Acts 5:31) is <u>granted</u> in the same sense that *"forgiveness"* is <u>granted</u>. Second, if repentance should be God's <u>gift</u>, then the entire Jewish nation has been given *"repentance"* and *"forgiveness."* In that case, every Jew would be saved, which the Scriptures vehemently deny. How then is Acts 5:31 to be viewed? God <u>grants</u> *"repentance"* and *"forgiveness"* to Israel in the sense that He offers all of Jewish descent the <u>opportunity</u> to repent as well as the <u>opportunity</u> to receive forgiveness. The choice is theirs as to whether they, in their depravity, will or will not repent and exercise faith. The same opportunity is made available to both Jews and Gentiles according to Acts 11:18 and 2Timothy 2:25:

> *...then, God has granted to the Gentiles also the*
> *repentance that leads to life."* (Acts 11:18)

> *with gentleness correcting those who are in opposition, if*
> *perhaps God may grant them repentance leading to the*
> *knowledge of the truth,* (2Timothy 2:25)

Conclusion: God grants all Jews and Gentiles the right to exercise personal repentance and faith while depraved. This fact refutes the false teaching that He must give the gifts of repentance and faith to the spiritually regenerated before they can repent and believe.   More information regarding faith and repentance is available in our series titled, *"God's Heart."*

This correct view of repentance and faith is necessary if we are to properly view God and His gospel. What we have gleaned will enhance our understanding of Romans 3:22:

> *even the righteousness of God through faith in Jesus*
> *Christ for all those who believe; for there is no*
> *distinction;* (Romans 3:22)

Subsequent to our repenting and believing while depraved, God made us as righteous as He is righteous through placing us *"in Christ"* (1Corinthians 12:13; 2Corinthians 5:17, 21):

> *For by one Spirit we were all baptized into one body*
> [Christ's body],... (1Corinthians 12:13)

> *Therefore if any man is in Christ, he is a new creature;*
> *the old things passed away; behold, new things have*
> *come.* (2Corinthians 5:17)

> *He made Him who knew no sin to be sin on our behalf,*
> *that we might become the righteousness of God in Him.*
> (2Corinthians 5:21)

This gift of *"righteousness"* is why we are saints instead of lowly sinners saved by grace—a topic addressed in much depth when we arrive at Romans 5:1. (Remember for future reference that the word *"all"* in Romans 3:22 points to believers only.)

Romans 3:23 is deeper than initially meets the eye. It declares:

> *"for all have sinned and fall short of the glory of God."*
> (Romans 3:23)

We should have no problem understanding that *"all have sinned."* Paul has made this remarkably clear. Yet, we need to pay special attention to the word *"all"* (Romans 3:23). In this case, *"all"* points to every person, not just some. However, in Romans 3:22 *"all"* points to believers alone. If *"all"* is misinterpreted in Romans 3:23, then an argument could be made that only believers *"fall short of"* God's *"glory"*—which we know to be incorrect.

Some theologians who have failed to interpret words such as *"all, they, us, we, our, my,* and *world"* in their proper context view the word *"world"* in John 3:16 (for instance) as pointing to the *"world"* of believers only. As a result, they teach that God loves the elect and hates the non-elect— a false assumption indeed:

> *"For God so loved the world, that He gave His only*
> *begotten Son, that whoever believes in Him should not*
> *perish, but have eternal life.* (John 3:16)

The above-mentioned false assumption is easily refuted, for the word *"world"* is from the Greek word *kosmos*, meaning the inhabited earth. Also, the word *"whoever"* validates that all (all persons) are free to partake of the life offered through the Son—although, a majority of people refuse to do so.

The word *"world"* is limited in scope in some cases, however, such as in Luke 2:1:

> *And it came to pass in those days, that there went out a*
> *decree from Caesar Augustus, that all the world should be*
> *taxed.* (Luke 2:1 KJV)

"World" in this instance points to the Roman world (not the entire inhabited earth), just as Romans 11:12 makes reference to the Gentile world:

> *Now if their transgression be riches for the world and*
> *their failure be riches for the Gentiles, how much more*
> *will their fulfillment be!* (Romans 11:12)

The fact that *"world"* can be interpreted in this manner in no way means that it, in every case, is used in a limited sense. Nor does it always point to the entire inhabited earth, as has already been confirmed.

How then does one determine the proper meaning? As always, it is context based on the full counsel. Let's observe some additional passages that verify the value of context.

> *For if while <u>we</u> were enemies, we were reconciled to God through the death of His Son, much more, having been reconciled, <u>we</u> shall be saved by His life.* (Romans 5:10)

Was Paul teaching that only he and the church at Rome were *"reconciled to God through the death of His* [the Father's] *Son"?* Of course not! Such a conclusion could be drawn should context be disregarded.

> *to all who are beloved of God in Rome...* (Romans 1:7)

God loved the believers at Rome. However, this passage cannot be used in an attempt to confirm that God loves the elect only. If that were the case, it could also be argued that He loved the believers at Rome only.

> *But God demonstrates His own love toward <u>us</u>, in that while we were yet sinners, Christ died for us.* (Romans 5:8)

Does Romans 5:8 teach that God loves only Paul and the believers at Rome (note the word *"us"*)? Of course not! Therefore, it cannot be used by the adherents of limited atonement to attempt to prove that God's love is particular.

> *Just as it is written, "JACOB I LOVED, BUT ESAU I HATED."* (Romans 9:13)

The word *"hated"* in this instance means "to love less." Paul was also, based on Genesis 25:23, speaking of nations rather than individuals:

> *And the LORD said to her, "Two nations are in your womb; And two peoples shall be separated from your*

body; And one people shall be stronger than the other;
And the older shall serve the younger. " (Genesis 25:23)

Based on these findings, the apostle (in Romans 9:13) is communicating that God loved Jacob (the nation of Israel) more than He loved Esau (the nation of Edom). God married Israel. He did not marry the Edomites. This verse, therefore, cannot be used in an attempt to verify limited atonement—an unsuitable system of thought that rests on the assumption that God's love is particular. Consider 1Thessalonians 1:4 for instance:

knowing, brethren beloved by God... (1Thessalonians 1:4)

If God's love is limited, as Reformed Theology (extreme and hyper-Calvinism) suggests, is it limited in the sense that He loves only the believers at Thessalonica? (Observe Diagrams 11, 13-15 in the Reference Section for additional information regarding Reformed Theology.) This supposition is not what Reformed theologians conclude, for they advocate that God's love is limited in the sense that He loves the elect alone. However, by disregarding context and full counsel (which is what Calvinism does while attempting to prove that God loves only the elect), one could conclude that God loves only the believers at Thessalonica. Proper context and full counsel resolve the issue by confirming that God loves all—all being everyone, in fact, all *"the world"* of John 3:16.

Let's take this input and again consider Romans 3:23:

"for all have sinned and fall short of the glory of God." (Romans 3:23)

"All [all descendants of Adam]...*fall short of the glory of God"* (Romans 3:23) prior to salvation due to being born with a sin nature that enjoys sin. Even so, the depraved (the spiritually unregenerated) are free to repent and exercise faith in Christ.

To comprehend the depth of the second phrase, *"and fall short of the glory of God,"* we must review what was discussed in Romans 1:23 regarding God's *"glory."*

The phrase, *"the glory of God,"* points to the physical manifestation of God's presence—which appeared in the Old Testament in the form of a cloud and (or) fire. This glory appeared to Moses in Exodus 3:2 and to Israel in Exodus 13:21-22 and Exodus 19:16-18. It reappeared and remained on the earth after the completion of the tabernacle in Exodus 40:34-38, even filling King Solomon's temple in 2Chronicles 5:13-14. This same glory departed from Jerusalem and ascended into heaven in Ezekiel 11:22-25, remaining there until Luke 2:8-9. Because Jesus is the *"glory"* of God (John 1:14), the glory returned to earth in the Person of Christ. After Jesus' resurrection, the glory ascended into heaven (Acts 1:9), only to reappear on the day of Pentecost (Acts 2:3) to live in every New Testament believer. God placed His *"glory"* inside us (Colossians 1:27) subsequent to our exercising repentance and faith while depraved (Acts 16:31; Romans 10:9-10). What wonderful news, for we are not second-class citizens of the kingdom! We are glorified saints who sometimes sin!

Note the word *"justified"* in Romans 3:24.

> *being justified as a gift by His grace through the*
> *redemption which is in Christ Jesus;* (Romans 3:24)

"Justified" means "to be made righteous (right) in the eyes of God." It also means, "just as if I never sinned or ever will sin again." Consider too that we were *"justified as a gift by His grace,"* "grace" being defined as "unmerited favor." God's justification of the New Testament believer is, therefore, a *"gift;"* it is not earned. *"Faith,"* exercised while depraved, and prior to spiritual regeneration (salvation), is not a *"work"* (Romans 3:27; 4:5; 9:32).

Even more good news is forthcoming. *"Redemption"* (v.24) means "to be set free, to liberate by paying a price." Therefore, our sins were redeemed (paid for) on the cross by God's grace. In addition, our sinful nature was eradicated through Christ's death, which will be addressed in Romans 6. Thus, we were *"justified"* (made righteous) by God's *"grace"* (God's unmerited favor) *"through the redemption which is in Christ Jesus,"* a *"redemption"* that was applied once we exercised repentance and faith while depraved and were placed in Christ (1Corinthians 12:13; 2Corinthians 5:17). Jesus paid for our sins in 30 AD, but the payment was not credited to our account until we repented and believed while depraved and were placed in God's holy Son. The payment was not credited to our account while Jesus was on the cross, as some theologians have incorrectly assumed.

As we examine the cross in greater depth, we will become increasingly aware of the Father's unfathomable love for us. He placed our sins, along with the sins of all mankind, upon His selfless Son! He also established a friendship with us subsequent to our exercising repentance and faith while depraved.

God's mercy demonstrated toward the repentant sinner is what *"propitiation"* is all about (Romans 3:25), for the same Greek word rendered *"propitiation"* in Romans 3:25 is rendered *"mercy seat"* in Hebrews 9:5.

> *whom God displayed publicly as a __propitiation__ in His blood through faith. This was to demonstrate His righteousness, because in the forbearance of God He passed over the sins previously committed;* (Romans 3:25)

> *And above it were the cherubim of glory overshadowing the __mercy seat__; but of these things we cannot now speak in detail.* (Hebrews 9:5)

The mercy seat, positioned on top of the Ark of the Covenant in the tabernacle, and later in the temple, was where sins were atoned, or covered. The high priest would enter the holy of holies *"...once a year... taking blood...for himself and for the sins of the people..."* (Hebrews 9:7). This blood was sprinkled on the mercy seat, after which the sins of Israel were covered. Jesus' death removed the need for this blood to be offered, a topic addressed in more depth in Hebrews 9:1-28. Thus, the *International Standard Bible Encyclopedia* defines *"propitiation"* as, "the removal of wrath by the offering of a gift."

How did the cross of Christ *"demonstrate"* God's *"righteousness"* (Romans 3:25)? In other words, was God right in judging sin? Of course He was, for He had to judge sin to remain just! He has never sinned, never will sin, and cannot condone sin. Since man is born lost and incapable of saving himself, the only remedy was crucifying a sinless God-man on the cross. Because Jesus was without sin (and remains without sin), He was the only being capable of dying for man's misdeeds. He was the perfect offering. Indeed, God's *"righteousness,"* the fact that He was right in judging sin, was demonstrated on the cross. Consequently, God's *"righteousness"* is revealed to an ever-increasing degree *("from faith to faith")* as we mature in our understanding of His heart:

> *For in it* [the gospel] *the righteousness of God is revealed from faith to faith; as it is written, "BUT THE RIGHTEOUS man SHALL LIVE BY FAITH."* (Romans 1:17)

Sins were only atoned, or covered, through the sacrifices offered under the Mosaic Law and were not forgiven until the cross. Consequently, no Old Testament believer's sins were forgiven until Jesus died. Thus, Paul states:

> *"God...passed over the sins previously committed"* (Romans 3:25).

Also, Hebrews 10:4 and 10:11 verify that *"the blood"* of animals could never *"take away sins."* Only the blood of Christ could accomplish such a feat.

The cross demonstrated God's *"righteousness"* to an even greater degree than it was demonstrated in Old Testament times.

> *for the demonstration, I say, of His righteousness at the present time, that He might be just and the justifier of the one who has faith in Jesus.* (Romans 3:26)

Old Testament believers understood that God is righteous, but not like church saints understand His *"righteousness at the present time."* We received God's righteousness the moment we repented and believed while depraved. Old Testament believers, who were saved on credit, were not made righteous until the cross. Indisputably, the cross was the most vivid demonstration of God's righteousness imaginable.

Because God is righteous, He is *"just."* Only the righteous can rule justly. Because He is *"just,"* He possesses the ability to justify those who choose to repent and believe while depraved. In other words, unless

God is just, He cannot justify those who desire to become part of His family.

Due to God's impeccable justness, He, one hundred percent of the time, attaches the proper punishment to all wrongdoing.   He is omniscient and, therefore, knows every detail surrounding each misdeed. No need for additional witnesses, as in our courts of Law, for nothing transpires that escapes His omniscience.   In fact, His foreknowledge allows Him to know every detail of all events before they occur—without being required to cause them!   God truly is the all-knowing One—Who never violates His love while exercising His justice.

This knowledge of God allows us to recognize that He would never condemn anyone unjustly.   Thus, all who receive His wrath must have opportunity to believe.   Yet, a popular teaching of our day portrays God as judging those who never have opportunity to exercise personal repentance and faith.   The adherents of this view depict God as electing certain individuals to salvation from eternity past, yet leaving the remainder to the consequence of their sin.   The "remainder" never have opportunity to believe, however, yet receive God's wrath for failing to believe!   Such a view makes God totally unjust—a fact that the proponents of this system vehemently deny.   In fact, a popular supporter of this view proclaims that one must perceive God as judging those who have no opportunity to believe (for failing to believe) before he can understand the value of this assessment of the Scriptures.   Wow!

Because God is *"...just and the justifier of the one who has faith in Jesus"* (v.26), we can take no credit for our salvation.   All *"boasting...is excluded"* when we realize that we are *"justified by faith"* rather than by the *"works of the Law":*

> *Where then is boasting? It is excluded. By what kind of*
> *law? Of works? No, but by a law of faith. For we*
> *maintain that a man is justified by faith apart from works*
> *of the Law.* (Romans 3:27-28)

Don't misunderstand.   Paul is not saying that the faith we exercised while depraved saved (justified) us, but rather that God saved (justified) us once we exercised faith while depraved.   Therefore the faith we exercised while depraved is not a work—the point that Paul is stressing in verses 27-28.

Be sure to notice the phrase, *"law of faith"* (v.27). The word *"law"* in this case, when viewed in context, can be translated "principle" and should not be confused with Law (rules and regulations). We are *"free"* from the Law of rules and regulations (Galatians 5:1) once we accept the *"law"* (principle) *"of faith"* (Romans 3:27). We will discuss this subject in more detail later.

According to Romans 3:29-30 and Ephesians 2, *"God"* is not only *"the God of Jews," "the circumcised,"* but He is also *"the God of Gentiles," "the uncircumcised."* In fact, Ephesians 2:14 states that Jesus *"made both groups into one."* Thus, during the church age, both Jews and Gentiles become *"one body"* through being placed in Christ subsequent to repenting and believing while depraved.

> *Or is God the God of Jews only? Is He not the God of Gentiles also? Yes, of Gentiles also, since indeed God who will justify the circumcised by faith and the uncircumcised through faith is one.* (Romans 3:29-30)

> *For He Himself is our peace, who made both groups into one, and broke down the barrier of the dividing wall, by abolishing in His flesh the enmity, which is the Law of commandments contained in ordinances, that in Himself He might make the two into one new man, thus establishing peace, and might reconcile them both in one body to God through the cross, by it having put to death the enmity.* (Ephesians 2:14-16)

Repentance and faith must be exercised by the depraved before God will award salvation. Therefore, Paul is not teaching that the repentance and faith exercised by the depraved saves (justifies) them. Rather, he is teaching that God saves (justifies) the depraved once they exercise repentance and faith. In this case, does our *"faith"* in any way *"nullify the Law"*? Paul says it does not:

> *Do we then nullify the Law through faith? May it never be! On the contrary, we establish the Law.* (Romans 3:31)

The initial purpose of *"the Law,"* to follow Paul's line of thinking, was to expose sin (Romans 3:19-20) and to show man his need for a Savior (Galatians 3:24). Thus, we do not *"nullify the Law through faith"* but *"establish"* it (Romans 3:31). Isn't this fun!

Romans 4:1-12

Abraham's Faith Apart from Works

In this section, Paul brings up Abraham, a man of faith as well as one of the great names in history. Abraham obeyed God and moved from Haran to Canaan (Genesis 12:1-5). He also believed God's promises (Genesis 15:6), after which, through obedience, he and his entire household were circumcised (Genesis 17:9-27). When asked by God, he offered up Isaac, his son of promise, on the altar (Genesis 22:1-19). Abraham could respond in this manner for only one reason: God had promised that Isaac would have descendants (Genesis 17:19, 21:12). Therefore, he knew that God would resurrect Isaac (back to natural life) should he (Abraham) take Isaac's physical life (Hebrews 11:17-19). Can you see the importance of knowing God's promises? Doesn't this encourage you to know God's Word!

Abraham possessed tremendous faith. But he also, like us, was beset with weakness. For instance, he twice asked Sarah to lie about their relationship as husband and wife and pose as his sister, Genesis 12:10-20 and Genesis 20. She was, in actuality, his half-sister (Genesis 20:12), but God hates the sin of half-truths. However, Sarah was supernaturally protected in Genesis 20:6 when Abimelech, king of Gerar, took her:

> *Then God said to him in the dream, "Yes, I know that in the integrity of your heart you have done this, and I also kept you from sinning against Me; therefore I did not let you touch her.* (Genesis 20:6)

Some theologians use this passage in an attempt to prove that man does not possess a free will. They argue that God, in His sovereignty, prevented Abimelech from sinning—that Abimelech had no choice in the matter. They then contend that God does the same with all mankind not only in the area of preventing sin but also in the area of causing it. In fact, they conclude that God is the cause of all things: every sin, heartache, trial, difficulty—everything that occurs from eternity past through eternity future. God, in their minds, must rule in this manner if He is to retain His rightful position as the Sovereign of the Universe.

Thus, they believe that should anything transpire that God has not caused, He would lose His sovereignty.

Genesis 20:6 proves nothing in regard to God causing man to refrain from sin. It simply shows that Abimelech's prudent choice to honor Sarah was based on information supplied through the avenue of a dream whose source was God. If you read the entire account (Genesis 20:1-18), you discover that Abimelech was totally blameless in the matter. Yes, God warned him through a *"dream"* (verse 3) that Sarah was Abraham's wife, but that warning did not control Abimelech's actions. In fact, once Abimelech understood the severity of the matter, he immediately returned her to her husband.

Even though Abraham possessed great faith, he possessed character flaws that only God could mend. His sinful impatience carried a huge consequence. Yet, God mentions none of his sins in Hebrews 11:8-12 and 17-19. Instead of waiting for Sarah to conceive and bear the son of promise, his impatience resulted in Ishmael's birth through Hagar (Genesis 16). The enormity of Abraham's sin is proven by the instability of Ishmael and his descendants (Genesis 16:12):

> *"And he will be a wild donkey of a man, his hand will be*
> *against everyone, and everyone's hand will be against*
> *him; and he will live to the east of all his brothers."*
> (Genesis 16:12)

The scope and correctness of this prophecy, regarding Abraham's son through Hagar is staggering. Ishmael's descendants are the Arab nations who have brought persistent grief to the Jews—the Jews being Abraham's descendants through Sarah. In fact, the ever-present problems in the Middle East can be traced back to Ishmael's birth. Even September 11, 2001, that horrendous day when many innocent people died, can be linked to Abraham's error. Ishmael's descendants were responsible for the calamity. The Arab nations view America as pro-Israel, and a thorn in their side. In their minds, anyone who is a friend of Israel is the enemy of Ishmael's descendants, the Arab nations.

The tiny nation of Israel is incapable of defending herself without the support of her allies; her most prominent ally is America. In fact, should the United States cease backing Israel, Israel would lack the military means (planes, tanks, and weapons) to remain in the land. She has the most highly trained military personnel in the world, but these personnel are powerless without the state of the art equipment needed for present-day warfare (that is, so long as she refuses to trust God for victory in battle). Israel has every right to defend herself. The land for which she is fighting was promised to Abraham (Genesis 13:17; 17:8) and his descendants (Genesis 15:18; 17:8), the Jews, many generations before Mohammad and Islam existed. Furthermore, Isaac was the son of *"promise,"* not Ishmael:

> *For it is written that Abraham had two sons, one by the bondwoman and one by the free woman. But the son by the bondwoman* [Ishmael] *was born according to the flesh, and the son by the free woman* [Isaac] *through the promise.* (Galatians 4:22-23)

According to the Scriptures, the Jews own (as a gift from God) from *"the river of Egypt"* to *"the river Euphrates"* (Genesis 15:18), a territory she has never fully inhabited. She will inhabit it in its entirety during the one thousand year reign of Christ (the Millennium), as confirmed by Ezekiel 47:13—48:29. In the meantime, however, she will struggle significantly to remain in part of the land due to personal sin.

A major political debate rages in the United States over what to do with Israel. One line of reasoning parallels a movement within modern Christendom teaching that God is done with Israel, and that the Arabs possess as much right to the holy land as do the Jews. Such a position is rooted in Replacement Theology where the writing prophets are allegorized and the church takes Israel's place in the unconditional covenants promised to the Jewish people. Should the church fully embrace that ideology and decide that Israel is no longer a viable component in God's strategy and support the election of men who are not pro-Israel, an adventure awaits us, for God has promised to *"bless"* the nations who support Israel but *"curse"* the nations who do not:

> *And I will bless those who bless you, and the one who curses you I will curse. And in you all the families of the earth shall be blessed."* (Genesis 12:3)

History verifies that the nations who have cursed Israel have been cursed, and the nations who have blessed Israel have been blessed. The United States of America has been blessed for several reasons, the main one being her commitment to the Jewish people—God's chosen people.

The Netherlands is another nation who found blessing through her favorable attitude toward Israel. The Dutch welcomed Jews who had been expelled from Spain and Portugal in the fifteenth century. As a direct result, the tiny nation became a great colonizing influence in the new world building a commercial empire that stretched from Brazil to the West Indies. Likewise, the Ottoman Empire enjoyed the fruit of God's blessing by welcoming Jewish immigration during that same era. That blessing enriched them for centuries.[8]

The list of nations who have mistreated God's chosen people and reaped the negative consequences begins with Egypt and Pharaoh's refusal to let the children of Israel go and includes: the people of Amalek who fought against Israel soon after they left Egypt and were defeated (Exodus 17:8-16) [Moses reminded the Jews that once they were given rest from their enemies they were to *blot out the memory of Amalek from under heaven* (Deuteronomy 25:17-19)], Spain, Portugal, England, Germany, Poland, and most Arab nations.

> *What then shall we say that Abraham, our forefather according to the flesh, has found? For if Abraham was justified by works, he has something to boast about; but not before God. For what does the Scripture say? "AND ABRAHAM BELIEVED GOD, AND IT WAS RECKONED TO HIM AS RIGHTEOUSNESS."* (Romans 4:1-3)

To the Jews, none is greater than Abraham; he is their father (Romans 4:1; John 8:37-39). The answer to how Jews, being descendants of Abraham, obtain a righteous standing before God is embedded in Romans 4.

Had Abraham been *"...justified by works, he has something to boast about..."* (Romans 4:2). However, no one can work his way into a right standing with God. Abraham's faith, exercised while depraved, caused God to reckon (count) him as righteous (Romans 4:3).

> *Now to the one who works, his wage is not reckoned as a*
> *favor, but as what is due.* (Romans 4:4)

So long as we perceive our good works as gaining points with God, we may wrongly view God as owing us something. Unless this attitude is replaced with repentance and *"faith"* (Romans 4:5), the holder will face God's judgment of Revelation 20:11-15.

God is in the business of justifying *"the ungodly"* (Romans 4:5):

> *But to the one who does not work, but believes in Him*
> *who justifies the ungodly, his faith is reckoned as*
> *righteousness,* (Romans 4:5)

Before God made us righteous, we were required to acknowledge (while depraved) that we were *"ungodly"*—totally and completely shipwrecked in regard to righteousness and holiness. This *"repentance,"* a change of attitude concerning sin, *"leads to life"* (Acts 11:18), the eternal *"life"* that God gives to the depraved who choose to repent and believe. These facts negate the argument that God must spiritually regenerate the depraved and grant them *"the hidden wisdom"* of 1Corinthians 2:6-8 before they can repent and believe. Paul wrote to the church at Corinth concerning the subject:

> *Yet we do speak wisdom among those who are mature; a*
> *wisdom, however, not of this age, nor of the rulers of this*
> *age, who are passing away; but we speak God's wisdom*
> *in a mystery, the hidden wisdom, which God predestined*
> *before the ages to our glory; the wisdom which none of*
> *the rulers of this age has understood; for if they had*
> *understood it, they would not have crucified the Lord of*
> *glory;* (1Corinthians 2:6-8)

The depraved who repent and believe are *"ungodly"* (Romans 4:5), not spiritually regenerated beings who have been given God's *"hidden wisdom"* of 1Corinthians 2:7. This *"hidden wisdom"* is the *"wisdom"* possessed by the *"mature"* believer—a truth discovered when 1Corinthians 2:6-8 is studied in context and according to the full counsel of God's Word. How could a man who is spiritually regenerated, but unsaved, possess the wisdom of a mature believer? He cannot!

In Romans 4:6, Paul speaks of David, the man after God's own heart, the man beloved of God:

> *just as David also speaks of the blessing upon the man to whom God reckons righteousness apart from works:* (Romans 4:6)

Paul's point, when taken through all of the Scriptures, is that David believed that God's *"righteousness"* is bestowed (apart from the works of the Law) upon those who exercise repentance and faith while depraved. In fact, these passages prove that the Lord does not *"take"* a New Testament believer's *"sin...into account"* (vv.7-8). Thus, God has no record of any sin we have committed in the past. Neither does He record any sin we commit in the present or future. We will discuss this truth in greater depth later.

Abraham's Faith Apart from Circumcision

In Romans 4:9-10, Paul again discusses circumcision to prove that God declared Abraham righteous <u>before</u> Abraham was circumcised. By making his case from the Scriptures alone, he removes the Jews' ability to say that Abraham was declared righteous because of circumcision. Observe as Paul develops his argument.

First, in Romans 4:9 he asks the Jews if the *"blessing"* mentioned by David in Romans 4:7-8 is *"...upon the circumcised, or upon the uncircumcised also...."* Then he again references Abraham, because through Abraham the covenant of circumcision was instituted (Genesis 17:9-27). Next, in Romans 4:10, Paul asks if Abraham was declared righteous by God before or after he was *"circumcised."* To answer this question, the Jews would have consulted the book of Genesis and discovered that Abraham was declared righteous in Genesis 15:6, at least thirteen years before he was circumcised (read Genesis 15:6; 16:16; 17:24). Therefore, the uncircumcised can be declared righteous, proving that circumcision guarantees no one a right standing before God. As usual, Paul proves his point while refuting his challengers' allegation!

Romans 4:11 explains that the purpose of *"circumcision"* is both a *"sign"* and *"a seal"*:

> *and he received the sign of circumcision, a seal of the*
> *righteousness of the faith which he had while*
> *uncircumcised, that he might be the father of all who*
> *believe without being circumcised, that righteousness*
> *might be reckoned to them,* (Romans 4:11)

Circumcision is a *"sign"* because every time a Jew sees someone circumcised, or is reminded of his own circumcision, he is to remember that God bestows righteousness on the basis of *"faith."* Circumcision is *"a seal"* because it cannot be undone. It proves-that once God makes us righteous, subsequent to our exercising repentance and faith while depraved, we cannot lose our righteousness and become unrighteous (John 10:29, Ephesians 1:13, Hebrews 7:25, and Jude 1 verify the same truth). The identical principle applied in Paul's day. In fact, it applied to believers who lived before the cross, although they were only <u>declared</u> righteous prior to Jesus' perfect sacrifice. The compelling news is that they were <u>made</u> righteous through Jesus' death, burial, and resurrection. If you are somewhat confused do not worry because this subject is addressed in great depth in subsequent verses.

Abraham is *"the father of all who believe"* (vv.11-12), whether they are physically circumcised or not. This truth verifies that Jews and Gentiles alike become descendants of Abraham through faith. In other words, they become true Jews (Romans 2:28-29). Paul addresses this subject in Ephesians 2:11-16, where he states that *"both groups,"* believing Jews and Gentiles during the church age, are *"made...into one"* (Ephesians 2:14). Consequently, through repentance and faith, and God's resulting salvation, Jews and Gentiles partake of the "spiritual" blessings promised to Abraham.

Don't misunderstand. God continues to deal with the physical Jewish nation as a separate nation, as He has done since Genesis 12—when He began making promises to Abraham. He, therefore, will fulfill the physical and spiritual promises made to physical Israel.

Man can misinterpret God's purpose. God's purpose in circumcision was pure and wholesome, yet man misunderstood it and suffered the consequence of improper theology. Are we not guilty of the same mistake when we mishandle the truth of the gospel? Oh, if we could but perceive truth from God's perspective! This clarity should be our goal as we continue.

Romans 4:13-25

Abraham's Faith Apart from Law

In Romans 4:9-12, Paul uses Abraham to prove that physical circumcision has nothing to do with making man right with God. In Romans 4:13-25, he again refers to Abraham, this time to illustrate that righteousness, a right standing with God, is unattainable through the works of the Law.

According to Romans 4:13, God promised Abraham *"...that he would be heir of the world...":*

> *For the promise to Abraham or to his descendants that he would be heir of the world was not through the Law, but through the righteousness of faith.* (Romans 4:13)

God made this promise in Genesis 17:4-6 and again in Genesis 22:17.

> *"As for Me, behold, My covenant is with you, and you shall be the father of a multitude of nations. "No longer shall your name be called Abram, but your name shall be Abraham; for I will make you the father of a multitude of nations. "And I will make you exceedingly fruitful, and I will make nations of you, and kings shall come forth from you.* (Genesis 17:4-6)

> *...indeed I will greatly bless you, and I will greatly multiply your seed as the stars of the heavens, and as the sand which is on the seashore; and your seed shall possess the gate of their enemies.* (Genesis 22:17)

Shortly, we will study the details of this promise. But for now, note that it was made prior to the issuing of the Law: The promise given in the book of Genesis, the Law issued later in the book of Exodus.

Do you see Paul's point? Many Jews had believed the lie that the Law was their ticket to heaven. Paul exposes the error in their thinking, for God's *"promise"* to Abraham came some *"four hundred and thirty years"* <u>before</u> the Law:

> *What I am saying is this: the Law, which came four*
> *hundred and thirty years later, does not invalidate a*
> *covenant previously ratified by God, so as to nullify the*
> *promise.* (Galatians 3:17).

Thus, the apostle writes:

> *"...if those who are of the Law are heirs, faith is made*
> *void and the promise* [given to Abraham] *is nullified"*
> (Romans 4:14).

Paul again proves that the Law cannot save.

The Law cannot save because *"...the Law brings about wrath..."* (Romans 4:15):

> *for the Law brings about wrath, but where there is no*
> *law, neither is there violation.* (Romans 4:15)

The Law was given to shut our mouths (Romans 3:19) and show us our need for a Savior (Galatians 3:24). No one will ever be saved by keeping the Law (Romans 3:20), for its purpose is to reveal man's need for Christ. Anyone who declines to acknowledge this need and refuses to exercise repentance and faith while depraved will be condemned at the *"great white throne"* judgment of Revelation 20:11-15. No doubt, *"...the Law brings about wrath..."* (Romans 4:15).

The latter part of Romans 4:15 is extremely interesting: *"...but where there is no law, neither is there violation."* Is Paul teaching that sin was not judged prior to the Law (the Law given to Moses)? No way! The Law was given in Exodus 20, yet sin was consistently judged between Genesis 1:1 and Exodus 20. This judgment resulted because man lived under moral law prior to the issuing of the Mosaic Law. Paul is saying that the Law was given to increase the lost man's awareness that he is in violation of God's standard for holiness. Paul emphasizes this point in Galatians 3:24, where he states that *"the Law"* was given as a *"tutor to lead us to Christ."* The Law's main purpose is to show the lost (depraved) that they need a Savior and are living a life of *"violation"* (Romans 4:15). These truths confirm why Paul wrote that the Law is only *"for the ungodly and sinners"*:

> *But we know that the Law is good, if one uses it lawfully,*
> *realizing the fact that law is not made for a righteous*
> *man, but for those who are lawless and rebellious, for the*
> *ungodly and sinners, for the unholy and profane, for those*
> *who kill their fathers or mothers, for murderers and*
> *immoral men and homosexuals and kidnappers and liars*
> *and perjurers, and whatever else is contrary to sound*
> *teaching,* (1Timothy 1:8-10)

These truths also verify why Paul taught that the New Testament believer is *"not under law, but under grace"*:

> *For sin shall not be master over you, for you are not*
> *under law, but under grace.* (Romans 6:14)

Abraham's Faith in the "Seed" (Christ)

The story doesn't end here, for Paul writes:

> *For this reason it is by faith, that it might be in*
> *accordance with grace, in order that the promise may be*
> *certain to all the descendants, not only to those who are*
> *of the Law, but also to those who are of the faith of*
> *Abraham, who is the father of us all, (as it is written, "A*
> *FATHER OF MANY NATIONS HAVE I MADE YOU") in the sight*
> *of Him whom he believed, even God, who gives life to the*
> *dead and calls into being that which does not exist.*
> (Romans 4:16-17)

God saves the lost (depraved), once they exercise *"faith"* (and repentance), in order that salvation might be presented to man on the basis of His *"grace"* (Romans 4:16). By doing so, He offers salvation to everyone—not just the recipients of the Law (the Jews). In fact, God makes all New Testament believers spiritual descendants of Abraham regardless of their nationality (Romans 4:16-17).

"Christ" is Abraham's *"seed"* (Galatians 3:16):

> *Now the promises were spoken to Abraham and to his*
> *seed. He does not say, "And to seeds," as referring to*
> *many, but rather to one, "And to your seed," that is,*
> *Christ.* (Galatians 3:16)

When a person during the church age exercises faith in Christ (while depraved), he is placed *"in Christ"* and made *"new"* (2 Corinthians 5:17):

> *Therefore if any man is in Christ, he is a new creature;*
> *the old things passed away; behold, new things have*
> *come.* (2Corinthians 5:17)

Once *"in Christ,"* that individual, regardless of nationality, is Abraham's spiritual descendant (Galatians 3:7 and 29). The book of Galatians was written to Gentiles:

> *Therefore, be sure that it is those who are of faith who are*
> *sons of Abraham.* (Galatians 3:7)

> *And if you belong to Christ, then you are Abraham's*
> *offspring, heirs according to promise.* (Galatians 3:29)

Abraham is the father of many nations because all believers from Acts 2 (the beginning of the church age) through the Rapture become a member of the body of Christ, the church, through being placed in Christ (Abraham's descendant) the moment they exercise repentance and faith while depraved. We will discuss how the New Testament believer is placed in Christ later in the commentary.

Abraham understood that through his lineage the *"seed"* of Genesis 3:15 would be born. The degree to which he understood this truth is debatable, but Paul's words in Galatians 3:6-9 verify that Abraham possessed at least some knowledge of the gospel prior to Jesus' birth:

> *Even so Abraham BELIEVED GOD, AND IT WAS RECKONED TO*
> *HIM AS RIGHTEOUSNESS. Therefore, be sure that it is those*
> *who are of faith who are sons of Abraham. And the*
> *Scripture, foreseeing that God would justify the Gentiles*

*by faith, preached the gospel beforehand to Abraham,
saying, "ALL THE NATIONS SHALL BE BLESSED IN YOU." So
then those who are of faith are blessed with Abraham, the
believer.* (Galatians 3:6-9)

"The gospel" was *"preached"* to Abraham by God when He stated: *"All the nations shall be blessed in you."* These words are taken from Genesis 12:3:

*...And in you all the families of the earth shall be
blessed."* (Genesis 12:3)

Following Genesis 12:3 (the passage confirming that Abraham heard *"the gospel"*), several significant events transpired. First, he moved from Haran to Canaan (Genesis 12:4-5). After building altars to the Lord in Shechem and Bethel (Genesis 12:6-8), he traveled toward the Negev (Genesis 12:9). As a result of a famine, he moved to Egypt (Genesis 12:10-20)—afterwards returning to the Negev in Canaan with Sarah and Lot (his nephew), along with an abundance of livestock, silver, and gold (Genesis 13:1-2). After proceeding to Bethel, and to the altar he had previously constructed (Genesis 13:3-4), Abraham and Lot eventually separated due to strife between their herdsmen (Genesis 13:5-8). Abraham told Lot to choose the land best suited for his needs. Lot chose the valley of the Jordan (an extremely fertile land), which included Sodom (Genesis 13:9-13). Abraham, meanwhile, elected to live in Canaan (Genesis 13:12).

Upon Lot's departure, God promised Abraham that he would eventually possess all the land (which included Lot's portion—*"the valley of the Jordan"*) as well as have an abundance of descendants (Genesis 13:14-17). Subsequently, Abraham moved to Hebron and *"built an altar to the Lord"* (Genesis 13:18). After saving Lot from a band of evil kings (Genesis 14:1-16), Abraham was blessed by Melchizedek, who was *"king of Salem"* and *"priest of God Most High"* (Genesis 14:17-20). Interestingly, after Abraham gave a tenth of the spoils of battle to Melchizedek (Genesis 14:20), the king of Sodom insisted that Abraham take the remainder (Genesis 14:21). Abraham declined because he had *"sworn to the Lord God Most High"* that he would take nothing from the king. In fact, Abraham responded in this manner to prevent the king from claiming that he had made him rich (Genesis 14:22-23). Thus, Abraham desired that the blessings upon his life be explained in terms of God alone—never man. As a result, Abraham took only what his men had eaten while engaged in battle. He did suggest, however, that Aner, Eshcol, and Mamre (his assistants) take their share of the spoils (Genesis 14:24). How they reacted is not stated in the text.

At this juncture in Abraham's life an amazing event transpired. *"The word of the Lord came to Abram in a vision"* in Genesis 15:1 and communicated that: (1) He was his *"shield"* (2) Abraham's *"reward"* would *"be very great."* In other words, God richly honored Abraham's commitment to having his life explained in terms of Him alone. After God's promise to supply Abraham an abundance of descendants (Genesis 15:4-5), we arrive at that famous verse from Genesis 15:

> *Then he believed in the LORD; and He reckoned it to him*
> *as righteousness.* (Genesis 15:6)

This statement is intriguing considering that the gospel had been preached to Abraham earlier in Genesis 12:3 (reference Galatians 3:6-9). Thus, Abraham did not believe the gospel initially offered in Genesis 12:3 to the degree that he later believed it in Genesis 15:6! How encouraging to be reminded that as we grow *"from faith to faith"* (Romans 1:17) in our understanding of God's righteousness displayed through the gospel we are increasingly willing to believe His promises! (Remember for future reference that Abraham's offspring would have been exposed to his knowledge of the subject.)

Do you realize that *"...God...gives life to the dead and calls into being that which does not exist"* (Romans 4:17)? According to Romans 4:18-21, God met Abraham's need through responding in this miraculous manner. After all, God spoke the world into existence, *"...so that what is seen was not made out of things which are visible"* (Hebrews 11:3). But someone might ask, "Does God function in the same fashion in the present?" Absolutely, for many believers today walk in the realm of the supernatural through yielding to Christ's life within (Galatians 2:20; Colossians 3:4). In such cases, God is perceived as the God in charge, the God capable of performing the impossible regardless of the circumstance—and God miraculously provides. God accomplishes these feats by merely speaking a word. Truly, nothing is more exhilarating than the life of faith.

Much of what we will experience as a believer is described in the first phrase of Romans 4:18:

> *In hope against hope he believed, in order that he might become a father of many nations, according to that which had been spoken, "SO SHALL YOUR DESCENDANTS BE."*
> (Romans 4:18)

Abraham knew how to *"hope against hope,"* and so must we. To *"hope against hope"* means to *"hope"* when no logical reason exists to remain hopeful. Only through perceiving God as capable of speaking into existence that which we lack can we continue to *"hope."* Abraham continued to *"hope"* because of God's promise. As a result, God did the "impossible," giving him a son in the midst of adverse circumstances (Romans 4:19-20). He will allow the "impossible" to occur in our lives as well if we will but rest in His promises. Where are His promises found? They are found in His letter to man! Need I say more!

The last extremely powerful phrase of Romans 4:20 states that Abraham *"...grew strong in faith, giving glory to God."* Hence, Abraham's faith was enlarged as a result of praise, for praise is the fuel for faith. We can't read Psalms 145-150, Psalms of praise, without witnessing the value of worship. Praise energizes faith by restoring the worshippers' perception of Who God is—the One and Only Sovereign of the universe. Once God is perceived in this light, His promises are easily appropriated. Praise isn't always easy, for Hebrews 13:15 states that we are to *"...continually offer up a sacrifice of praise to God...."* Yes, praise can be *"a sacrifice,"* but praise always empowers faith to the glory of God.

In Romans 4:22, Paul again emphasizes that God *"reckoned"* (counted) Abraham as righteous due to Abraham's faith. Thus, Abraham was *"reckoned"* (counted) as righteous before he was made righteous through Jesus' death in 30 AD. According to Romans 4:23-24, every person during the church age who exercises faith in Christ receives this same righteousness (is made righteous). No Jew could say, therefore, that anything but faith (coupled with repentance) could result in God making man righteous. Paul has proven his point and proven it well.

141

(Have you noticed the degree to which Paul repeats himself? Every good teacher realizes the importance of hammering home his point.)

The last verse in this chapter speaks of the death and resurrection of Christ along with the purpose of each:

> *He who was delivered up because of our transgressions,*
> *and was raised because of our justification.* (Romans
> 4:25)

Jesus died for *"our transgressions."* Consequently, the penalty associated with our past, present, and future sins has been eternally pardoned—a subject covered in greater depth later. Isn't it wonderful to know that everything needed for *"our justification,"* *"justification"* being God's gift to those who repent and believe while depraved, was also provided through the cross? Had this not been the case, Jesus would have remained in the grave—*"He...was raised because of our justification."* In other words, had the cross been an insufficient means through which God could *"justify the ungodly"* (Romans 4:5), Christ's resurrection would have never occurred.

Let's take this truth and dig deeper into the issue of justification. Should the following input bring confusion, don't be concerned. This subject will be covered in great depth in our study of Romans 5-8.

Indeed, forgiveness of sin was accomplished through Jesus' blood:

> *....To Him who loves us, and released us from our sins*
> *by His blood,* (Revelation 1:5)

For God to justify us, however, the Adamic nature (old man, old self, sinful nature, dead spirit—all synonymous) that we inherited from Adam had to be eradicated because this *"nature"* made us *"children of wrath"*:

> *Among them we too all formerly lived in the lusts of our*
> *flesh, indulging the desires of the flesh and of the mind,*
> *and <u>were by nature children of wrath</u>, even as the rest.*
> (Ephesians 2:3 emphasis added)

Therefore, our acts of sin did not condemn us before God. Our nature condemned us—who we were in our person. Consequently, for God to justify our person, our person had to change. In fact, it had to be made new:

> *Therefore if any man is in Christ, he is a new creature;*
> *the old things passed away; behold, new things have*
> *come.* (2Corinthians 5:17)

How were we made *"new"?* The Adamic nature was eradicated through the avenue of Jesus' body:

> *Therefore, my brethren, you also were made to die to the*
> *Law through <u>the body</u> of Christ, ...* (Romans 7:4 emphasis
> added)

> *knowing this, that our old self was crucified with Him, ...*
> (Romans 6:6)

> *"I have been crucified with Christ; and it is no longer I*
> *who live, but Christ lives in me; and the life which I now*
> *live in the flesh I live by faith in the Son of God, who*
> *loved me, and delivered Himself up for me.* (Galatians
> 2:20)

Only after the Adamic nature was eliminated was the new man (new self, new creation—all synonymous) born. Thus, when we exercised personal repentance and faith while depraved, God killed who we used to be and made us new. Hence, should any portion of the Adamic nature remain alive in us, we would remain unjustified. We cannot be the Adamic nature (old man) plus new man, with the Adamic nature (old man) wounded. We are the "new man" only! Otherwise, the cross was an insufficient work—a subject addressed in much depth in Romans 5:1.

Romans 4:25 will become more meaningful as we progress through Romans 5-8. In fact, as we transition into Romans 5 and examine justification in greater depth, be prepared to enjoy some of the most exciting Scripture in the entire Word of God.

Unfortunately, some theologians use the phrase, *"He who was delivered up because of our transgressions"* (Romans 4:25), in an attempt to validate the "L" of the TULIP, Limited Atonement—that

Jesus died for believers only. We must be careful to interpret terms such as *"all, they, us, we, our, my*, and *world"* in their proper context. Just because this passage states that Jesus *"was delivered up because of our transgressions"* does not rectify all the verses that plainly teach that Jesus died for believers and unbelievers alike—John 3:14-15, John 3:16, John 7:37, Romans 5:6, Romans 5:18-19, 2Corinthians 5:14-15, 2Corinthians 5:19, 1Timothy 2:3-4, 1Timothy 2:6, 1Timothy 4:10, Hebrews 2:9, 2Peter 2:1, 1John 2:2, 1John 4:14, and many more. Again, context is critical, especially when coupled with the full counsel of God's Word. Truly, what an amazing sixty-six books the Creator penned for our enjoyment!

Romans 5:1 (Part 1)

Justification by Faith

Are you ready to consider a most fascinating dimension of the Christian life? This section tells us that Jesus did more than get us out of hell and into heaven. His obedience, coupled with the faith and repentance God requires from the depraved, is why the Father justified us! He made us not guilty by saving us through His Son. He did it in the instant of time that we, while lost and depraved, realized our need for a Savior, repented of our sins, and asked Jesus Christ into our hearts through faith. This news is not merely exceptional! It is life!

Justification was defined earlier as "just as if I never sinned or ever will sin again." God, in a moment's time, ushered us out of a state of condemnation (Ephesians 2:1-3) and made us righteous (right) on the basis of our own personal repentance and faith exercised while depraved! Paul speaks of this astounding transformation in Romans 5:1:

> *Therefore having been justified by faith, we have peace*
> *with God through our Lord Jesus Christ,* (Romans 5:1)

The phrase, *"having been justified by faith,"* is not Paul teaching that *"faith"* saves. *"Faith"* has never saved anyone. God does the saving. Man does the believing. Thus, *"faith,"* exercised by the depraved, cannot be classified as a work—as verified by Romans 3:28 and Romans 4:4-5.

> *For we maintain that a man is justified by faith apart*
> *from works of the Law.* (Romans 3:28)

> *Now to the one who works, his wage is not reckoned as a*
> *favor, but as what is due. But to the one who does not*
> *work, but believes in Him who justifies the ungodly, his*
> *faith is reckoned as righteousness,* (Romans 4:4-5)

"Faith" and *"works"* are contrasted. Thus, to exercise *"faith"* while depraved cannot be classified as a work (although some theologians

believe otherwise). This truth will be confirmed to a greater degree as we continue.

Paul uses *"Therefore"* as the first word in Romans 5 because the first four chapters of this epistle prove that God bestows righteousness upon those who repent and believe while depraved. We were *"justified"* by God as a result of exercising faith <u>prior</u> to being born again! Yes, God saves; man believes. However, man in his lost (depraved) state must believe before God will bestow salvation. Furthermore, *"...it* [the salvation that comes through God alone] *is by faith, that it might be in accordance with grace..."* (Romans 4:16). Thus, justification is available to man solely as a result of God's grace.

I view justification in this manner: Several years ago, in the midst of my depravity, I saw my need for a Savior (repented, in other words) and exercised personal faith. I did this by looking to heaven and saying, "God help, I need a Savior." God then did all the rest. Much more occurred than initially meets the eye, so let me attempt to explain by offering the following illustration.

When I gave my life to Christ (when I exercised personal repentance and faith while depraved), God, seated in heaven behind His huge gold desk, took His huge gold gavel (no desk or gavel are mentioned in Scripture—again, this is an illustration), stood up behind His desk, raised up on His tip-toes, and with all the force that He could muster through that right arm of power, struck that huge, gold, glistening desk. As a result of this powerful act, all heaven shook—even the angels took notice—and every eye in the heavenly places gazed at the Creator. As He prepared to speak, they could not help but notice the love and compassion that characterized His stature. As they gazed more intently, they could see tears of joy rushing down those cheeks from which the glory of His Majesty was manifested. Then, when everything in heaven settled, the Creator pointed at me. (Here is where our illustration ends and Scriptural reality kicks in, although some of what is stated previously may very well have occurred.) With great boldness and authority, and yet with great joy, my God said the following: "You are holy, perfect, redeemed, complete, blameless, accepted, glorified, a brother of Christ, not condemned, a saint, a son, forgiven, and I take you as my very own!"

Wow! Can you believe that the Father did all of that (and more) in an instant of time? This entire transformation occurred at the point of justification, subsequent to our exercising repentance and faith while depraved. God did it all through His grace!

Let's observe a few New Testament verses that confirm what has been stated regarding justification. The verse reference is listed on the left. What God says about us in each verse is recorded on the right. Keep in mind that everything addressed here happened in an instant, at the point of justification. Bask in the greatness of what you find. These verses describe who you are at this moment in time if you are a believer. You most definitely are not required to experience physical death before the truths recorded in these passages apply.

What Happened at the Point of Justification:
A Description of the New Testament Believer
The New Man (New Self)

2 Corinthians 5:17 ....New Creation

Galatians 2:20 ....Crucified With Christ - Christ Lives In Me!

2 Corinthians 5:21...............Righteousness Of God

Romans 8:1 ....Not Condemned

Ephesians 1:13 ....Sealed In Him (Secure)

Ephesians 1:4 ....Holy And Blameless Before Him

Ephesians 2:6 ....Seated In The Heavenly Places

Colossians 3:1 ....Raised Up With Christ

Colossians 3:3 ....Have Died — My Life Is Hidden With Christ In God!

Colossians 3:13 ....Forgiven

Ephesians 4:32 ....Forgiven

Colossians 2:13 ....Forgiven

Romans 8:30 ....Justified, Glorified

Romans 6:6 ....Old Self (Adamic Nature) Was Crucified

Colossians 3:9,10 ....Laid Aside Old Self, Put On New Self

Ephesians 4:22-24...............Laid Aside Old Self, Put On New Self

Hebrews 10:10 ....Sanctified

Hebrews 10:14 ....Perfected

Hebrews 9:28 ....Forgiven

Ephesians 5:30 ....Member Of His Body

Colossians 1:22 ....Holy, Blameless, And Beyond
                                     Reproach

Colossians 2:10 ....Complete

1 Corinthians 1:30...............In Christ, Righteous, Sanctified,
                                     Redeemed

1 Corinthians 1:2.................A Saint

1 Corinthians 1:8.................Confirmed To The End, Blameless

1 Corinthians 6:11...............Washed, Sanctified, Justified

Ephesians 2:19 ....Member Of God's Household

Philippians 3:20 ....Citizenship In Heaven

Colossians 3:12 ....Holy And Beloved

Colossians 2:12 ....Buried With Him

1 John 5:20..........................In Christ

Jude 1 ....Kept For Jesus Christ

Everything listed in the previous thirty-two verses pertains to the New Testament believer who, while depraved, repented and exercised personal faith. Can you see why the gospel is called *The Good News?* This truth is not "positional" truth, as some theologians have incorrectly assumed. It is much more. It is reality! "Positional Truth," which is taught in many Christian circles, is misleading. It carries with it the idea that God somehow <u>sees</u> us in the manner that these verses describe us— but in actuality we are just lowly sinners saved by grace, who will someday (in heaven) become all of these things.

Scripture presents a totally different view, for we are <u>now</u> (present tense) everything these thirty-two verses say about us—and more. The evidence is in the tenses of the verbs used in these passages. The action is past tense action that occurred when we met Jesus. Therefore, we are <u>now</u> holy, perfect, righteous, complete, and all of the rest—not lowly sinners saved by grace. In fact, we are saints who sometimes sin! Can you see the difference in these two perspectives? Pray that God will enlighten your spiritual eyes so you might perceive yourself as He sees you.

The Father's view of the New Testament believer means that He isn't required to look at us through Jesus to "stomach" what He sees. The Father loves us because of who we are—because of what He has made us into. Jesus alone is the reason the Father could make us new, subsequent to our repenting and believing while depraved. But our identity (who we are as the Father's children—new creations) allows Him to view us as the apples of His eye. He isn't required, therefore, as I supposed as a new believer, to view us through His peripheral vision due to a lowliness we possess as His sons. He can look at us straight on because of what He made us into at the point of justification, for He totally accepts us as His holy and eternal possession. As a result, He is accessible, ready to listen to our every concern—and ready to defend us to the very end.

The writer of Hebrews tells us *"There remains...a Sabbath rest for the people of God"* (Hebrews 4:9). New Testament believers can *"rest"* because God, in an instant of time, made us into the most holy and righteous beings imaginable. The work is a finished work. We are blameless before Him. We are also set free to enjoy, for all eternity, all that Christ has done for the redeemed.

Because we are blameless and free, our focus should center on knowing—really *KNOWING*—Christ and yielding to His indwelling presence (Philippians 3:10; Galatians 2:20). When we do, we are *"filled"* with God's Spirit (Ephesians 5:18), and those around us cannot help but see Jesus. Thus, we *"rest"* as God lives His holy and omnipotent life through us. What a deal!

Examining Ephesians 1:4 in greater depth would be wise as it is the most debated of the thirty-two verses listed earlier:

> *...just as He chose us in Him before the foundation of the*
> *world, that we should be holy and blameless before Him.*
> *In love* (Ephesians 1:4)

Paul teaches that the New Testament believer is made *"holy and blameless"* at the point of justification. This truth, although rejected by some (maybe many), is not a major source of tension within Christ's body. The phrase, *"just as He chose us in Him before the foundation of the world,"* is the cause of disharmony. Some people use these words in an attempt to prove that God chooses (elects) some persons to salvation before they are born—in fact, from eternity past by means of an eternal decree. Are they correct? Let's allow the full counsel of God's Word to provide the proper answer.

When we made the choice to accept Christ as Savior (while depraved), we were placed into Christ through the avenue of the Holy Spirit (1Corinthians 12:13), into the Father's *"chosen one"* (Luke 9:35; Isaiah 42:1), and made *"new"* (2Corinthians 5:17). This action by God on our behalf, subsequent to our exercising personal repentance and faith while depraved, is the only means through which we could enter into Christ's chosenness! Once in Christ, the Father's *"chosen one"* (Isaiah 42:1), we also received His kind of *"life"* (Colossians 3:4), eternal life, having no beginning and no end. Consequently, once we were placed into Christ and received eternal life, the Father saw us as having always been in Christ, even though our entry point into Christ was <u>after</u> we repented and believed while depraved. This sequence makes it possible for us to have been chosen *"...in Him before the foundation of the world...,"* even though we did not accept Him until almost two thousand years after the cross.

Thus, the phrase, *"chose us in Him <u>before</u> the foundation of the* *world"* (Ephesians 1:4a), does not communicate that God selected us to salvation before we were born—selected us to be placed into Christ from eternity past. It means, rather, that we were chosen once we were placed into Christ, into the Father's *"chosen one"* (Isaiah 42:1), subsequent to our exercising personal repentance and faith while depraved. Because Christ possesses eternal life, life with no beginning or end, we received eternal life the moment we were placed in Him. Consequently, the Father sees us as having always been in Christ—even *"...before the foundation of the world..."* (Ephesians 1:4a)—although our entry point into Christ occurred when we repented and believed while depraved.

Jesus was chosen to office—the office of Messiah. He was not chosen to salvation. Accordingly, all New Testament believers, as a result of being placed into Christ (after repenting and believing while depraved), receive a special office, or *"gift"* (1Peter 4:10), so Christ's body might function efficiently and effectively to the Father's glory. To this office or *"gift,"* we were chosen once placed in Him—subsequent to repenting and believing while depraved. Note: Our *God's Heart as it Relates to Foreknowledge - Predestination* and *God's Heart as it Relates to Sovereignty - Free Will* address this subject in much greater depth.

Romans 5:1-5

Peace with God

Paul used the phrase, *"peace with God"* (Romans 5:1) because not only does He wipe away all sin, but He also builds a peaceful relationship between Himself and those whom He justifies. God is not angry with us. He is at peace with us! In other words, His idea of a good time is <u>not</u> pouncing on us to see how much damage He can inflict. Peace has been established. We are His children. Yes, He will chasten us when we sin, but He does so in love (read Hebrews 12:4-11). Therefore, when we repent as a believer, we are not restoring our relationship, but our fellowship with the Father. The relationship established through justification is eternal, incapable of being severed by sin.

Possessing *"peace with God"* (Romans 5:1) is quite different from possessing the peace of God. *"Peace with God"* was established for all eternity when He *"justified"* us subsequent to our exercising *"faith"* while depraved. The *"peace"* of God, on the other hand, is a *"fruit of the Spirit"* (Galatians 5:22) and must be received on a moment-by-moment basis. Isaiah was right when he wrote, *"The steadfast of mind Thou wilt keep in perfect peace, because he trusts in Thee"* (Isaiah 26:3). God's *"peace"* is ever present among those who spend more time being a friend to God than a friend to others.

"Peace with God" was made available *"through"* a Person, *"the Lord Jesus Christ"* (Romans 5:1). Yes, Jesus gives every individual the opportunity to live in *"peace with"* the Godhead. However, for this *"peace"* to become a reality repentance and faith must first be exercised by the depraved.

Ample Grace for Trials

We need to know as much as possible about *"grace,"* for through Jesus Christ *"...we have obtained our introduction by faith into this grace in which we stand..."* (v.2). This *"introduction... into...grace"* results in justification and everything this wonderful act encompasses. We must not think for a moment, however, that this initial measure of grace will perpetually sustain us. We need new grace, daily grace, as we trust Christ to keep the trials of life in check.

The great news is that grace is available for any situation. However, believers do have the option of either accepting or rejecting this grace. Those who reject it experience defeat, while those who accept it soar like *"eagles"* (Isaiah 40:31). Yes, it is God's grace that causes Him to justify (save) the depraved who repent and believe. It is also His grace that empowers the believer for service. Paul understood this truth as well as anyone according to 2Corinthians 12:9-10, 2Corinthians 4:7-12, 1Corinthians 15:10, and 2Timothy 2:1. For the purpose of understanding the context of these powerful passages, let's consider for a moment the trials that Paul encountered as he carried the gospel to the Gentiles by examining 2Corinthians 11-12 and 2Corinthians 4. This input should be particularly encouraging since the believability of a statement is determined by the integrity and character of the person issuing the statement. Paul's lifestyle backed up everything he taught regarding the value of grace in the midst of adversity. Note that the Scripture references are posted to the left with commentary to their right:

2Corinthians 11:1-6   Although having been inundated with the *"simplicity"* of the gospel through Paul's message, the believers at Corinth were being led astray by false teachers. Apparently, Paul was *"unskilled in speech,"* but he was not unskilled *"in knowledge."* In fact, he considered himself *"not in the least inferior to the most eminent apostles."* The words, *"the most eminent apostles,"* may very well point to the *"false apostles"* addressed in verse 13. If not, they point to the disciples who traveled with Jesus for the duration of His public ministry (Acts 1:21-22)—of which Paul was not a part. Paul's attitude confirms that he was secure in his apostleship, even when perceived as inadequately trained. Unlike the eleven, he was basically taught (after his conversion) one-on-one with the Savior, an honor about which he *"boasted"* in Galatians 1:15-24. Thus, seminary training does not equal preparation. Some of the deepest thinkers I have known gained their insights from sitting alone with Jesus. The most educated men of Jesus' day failed to recognize His Messiahship. Don't misunderstand. If I were younger I would probably attend seminary and major in Hebrew and Greek. However, seminary is not a prerequisite for proper Biblical understanding—although many people might disagree. Having to validate himself to those whom he freely served must have been excruciatingly painful to this man of God.

2Corinthians 11:7-13 Paul refused financial support from the Corinthian church, in fact, all the churches *"in the regions of Achaia."* He allowed gifts from churches elsewhere to provide for his physical needs while in Corinth. His response was partially due to the false teachers' financial demands on the Corinthian believers. Paul demonstrated much wisdom here, realizing that he could not be accused of improper motives while offering *"the gospel...without charge."* His heart was pure, unlike those distorting the teachings of Christ. Can you imagine the depths of Paul's concern for these believers?

2Corinthians 11:14-15 The false teachers in Corinth greatly disturbed Paul, for they were disguising *"themselves as servants of righteousness."* Yet the people received their lies and deception as absolute truth. Nothing concerns a teacher more than watching those he has instructed follow individuals deficient in understanding. Paul endured considerable heartache in this area as he carried the gospel to the Gentiles. We will experience the same.

2Corinthians 11:16-33 Paul discusses his qualifications as a teacher of the gospel. One cannot study these verses without concluding that God's grace in Paul's life was amazingly adequate. Most of us, when comparing our trials with his, must blush with embarrassment. Paul's heart was deeply grieved over the abuse the church was encountering through false teachers (v.20). However, his heart had to leap with joy as he reviewed God's grace in his life through his many sufferings (verses 21-33). We, like Paul, will pay a price as we carry truth to an ill-informed world. The price, however, never supersedes His grace.

2Corinthians 12:1-10 Paul continues listing his qualifications as an apostle by mentioning the *"visions and revelations"* received *"of the Lord"* (v.1). Paul was blessed in that he had received a vision of *"the third heaven"* (v.2). He *"was caught up into Paradise, and heard inexpressible words, which a man is not permitted to speak"* (v.4). Could this extraordinary event have occurred when Paul was stoned and left for dead at Lystra (Acts 14:19)? To prevent Paul *"from exalting"* himself, he *"was given...a thorn in the flesh, a messenger of Satan to buffet"* him (2Corinthians 12:7). After entreating *"the Lord three times"* for deliverance (v.8), the Lord *"said"* to him, *"My grace is sufficient for you, for power is perfected in weakness"* (v.9). Paul accepted this *"grace,"* realizing that when he was *"weak"* he was *"strong"* (vv.9-10).

2Corinthians 12:11-13   Paul mentions *"the signs and wonders and miracles"* performed through him to further validate his ministry. Can we even begin to imagine Paul's pain as he addressed those who were once deeply committed to his teaching but had been led astray by false teachers? This scenario is the absolute worst for any defender of the truth.

2Corinthians 12:14-18   That Paul sought the people rather than their material possessions is again emphasized. Considering all he had done for these believers, astonishingly he was required to mention this subject? Truly, ministry is not for the faint hearted.

2Corinthians 12:19-21   The apostle's burden for the church is again expressed.

Using this input as our backdrop, let's now consider Paul's words in 2Corinthians 4. You will be encouraged by his response to the trying circumstances recorded in 2Corinthians 11 and 12, for 2Corinthians 4 was written after his experiences described in those two chapters.

2Corinthians 4:1   With all that Paul had suffered, he did not *"lose heart."* He *"received"* God's *"mercy."* God's *"mercy"* will sustain the believer, regardless of the degree of pain and heartache.

2Corinthians 4:2   That Paul had stood for *"truth"* explains why victory superseded his pain. After all, life is a matter of perspective. Viewing agonizing circumstances through the prism of God's heart is the only hope for the troubled soul.

2Corinthians 4:3-4   Paul knew that Satan, *"the god of this world,...blinded the minds of the unbelieving, that they might not see the light of the gospel of the glory of Christ...."* The apostle understood that

Satan blinds *"the minds of the"* unredeemed. Consequently, those who perceive God as the cause of all things must be incorrect. Under such an arrangement God would cause Satan to blind *"the minds"* of the unredeemed, making Satan God's ally. Should this be the case, God would be totally unjust in judging Satan for his evil deeds. These verses also dispel the falsehood that the depraved are incapable of comprehending absolute truth, and in turn, exercising personal repentance and faith. Why would Satan need to blind the depraved (the lost) if the depraved are incapable of understanding truth? Paul preached the gospel to many individuals who rejected his message, for He perceived all mankind as capable of choosing Christ prior to spiritual regeneration. Yes, Paul believed that Satan is real, even possessing the power to blind the depraved in an attempt to prevent them from believing. The apostle did not view our enemy as a wimpy being with horns, carrying a pitchfork. He was the source of Paul's difficulties, trials, and sufferings; and the apostle despised him. Yet, the reality of Satan was frequently a hard sell to those who opposed Paul's message. Amazing!

2Corinthians 4:5 When Paul preached, he preached *"Christ Jesus as Lord"*—not himself. Paul was not only a bond-servant of Christ, but a bond-servant of the believers at Corinth. No pride here, for Paul served those whom he taught rather than requiring himself to be served. What humility! Thus, he could speak with such remarkable authority.

2Corinthians 4:6 Once the depraved see their need for a Savior, God's *"light"* shines in their *"hearts to give the light of the knowledge of the glory of God in the face of Jesus Christ."* This truth is verified by 2Corinthians 3:16: *"but whenever a man turns to the Lord, the veil is taken away."* Man *"turns"* (in his depravity), at which time *"the veil is taken away"* through God's *"light"* penetrating his heart—never the other way around! However, a popular yet incorrect teaching of our day suggests that God's light shines in the heart prior to man turning from sin. Certainly, God *"draws"* man to himself (John 6:44; 12:32), but this *"drawing"* by no means forces man to believe. What Paul expresses here is that God's *"glory,"* God's *"light,"* Who is *"Jesus Christ,"* enters into man once man chooses to repent and believe while depraved. This truth carried Paul through every trial, as verified by 2Corinthians 4:7.

2Corinthians 4:7 The *"treasure"* that Paul mentions is God's *"glory,"* Jesus being that *"glory"* according to John 1:14. This *"treasure"* lived inside Paul's *"earthen"* vessel, his body. Therefore, Jesus' indwelling presence empowered him rather than Paul empowering himself. He wrote: *"...that the surpassing greatness of the power may be of God and not from ourselves."* Because Jesus' presence and power sustained him through an abundance of excruciating circumstances, he could view them as positive experiences used to God's glory.

2Corinthians 4:8-9 As a result of Jesus' indwelling presence, Paul was *"...afflicted...but not crushed; perplexed, but not despairing; persecuted, but not forsaken; struck down, but not destroyed.* The *"perseverance"* (Romans 5:3-4) he displayed was a remarkable testimony to God's grace!

2Corinthians 4:10-15 Paul perceived his pain, not as a detriment, but as an opportunity to have Jesus' *"life...manifested in"* his *"body."* Can we even begin to imagine the degree to which Satan feared this man of God?

2Corinthians 4:16-17 Paul viewed his *"inner man"* as *"being renewed day by day"* through the power of Christ's indwelling presence. His adversity, therefore, as severe as it was in the flesh, was perceived as *"momentary, light affliction"* through the eyes of the Spirit. After all, it was *"...producing...an eternal weight of glory far beyond all comparison."* His pain also allowed him to see the unseen. Yes, an amazing adventure awaits those who make pain their friend!

Paul exulted (rejoiced) *"in hope of the glory of God"* (Romans 5:2). He also exulted (rejoiced) *"in...tribulations"* (Romans 5:3). Paul viewed all suffering as his ally; pain had become his friend. How else could he have survived the many hardships described in 2Corinthians 11 and 12? He regarded God as sovereign and working everything *"for good"* (Romans 8:28). That is how he made it. That is how he finished the race!

Most of us do not possess the maturity to view life from Paul's perspective, for we have not yet learned to *"...look...at the things which...are not seen..."* (2Corinthians 4:18). Without Paul's perspective, we normally draw our conclusions from that which is visible. In fact, most of us attempt to rectify negative circumstances through our own strength. However, the Lord allows the same negative circumstances to arise until we have learned to trust Him in the midst of our various trials. Only then do we pass the class—be it in the area of finance, a sinful habit, loneliness, a difficult relationship, or whatever. Through an increased understanding of God's capabilities, we learn to rest in His provision, sovereignty, and grace—the by-product of which is a perseverance explained only in terms of Christ.

What, then, is perseverance? Perseverance is the ability to remain encouraged when things look thoroughly hopeless, trusting our heavenly Father when most people are dropping out of the race. Yes, we persevere through accepting His grace for every challenge of life. Perseverance, characterized in this manner is a necessity to possess.

If we hold fast in *"tribulation,"* allowing God to produce *"perseverance," "proven character"* will result. Isn't it wonderful to hang out with people who have had their character tried and proven? I believe that everyone seeks to know at least one person of that sort—and that God is looking for that individual as well (2Chronicles 16:9). As I think of those who possess *"proven character,"* I realize that none of them arrived at that place void of hardship. We all suffer in some form or other, and it certainly is not enjoyable. When we allow our trials to choke and stifle us, they seem virtually unbearable. However, no matter how difficult they become knowing that God is using them for good encourages us to yield to His grace to see us through. And yes, He will see us through!

We need to take a moment to address God's character, for if we fail to understand Who He is we may hinder the work He desires to accomplish in and through us. In fact, when adversity comes our way, we may attempt to fix the problems ourselves, or worse yet, perceive Him as the cause of it all. The statement: "When we don't understand His hand, we can trust His heart" is so very accurate. Viewing our trials through the lens of His character is essential for abundant living. The deeper we know Him, therefore, the more we will trust Him in the heat of the battle.

After *"proven character"* comes *"hope"* (v.4). *"Hope"* is the ability to look positively at the future regardless of the present circumstance. Those who possess hope in Christ will never, ever be disappointed (v.5). The Object of their hope will ensure that.

"...Hope does not disappoint, because the love of God has been poured out within our hearts through the Holy Spirit who was given to us" (v.5). *"The Holy Spirit...was given to us"* at the point of justification, subsequent to our exercising repentance and faith while depraved—a one-time shot that never needs repeating. Furthermore, this *"love"* is continually accessible.

To *"...be filled with the Spirit"* (Ephesians 5:18; Galatians 5:22) is different, occurring repetitively as we walk in fellowship with God. When we are *"filled with the Spirit,"* the love of God—along with His peace, joy, patience, and all the rest—is manifested to those around us regardless of what comes our way.

God always uses tribulation for our good. However, only through knowing His heart do we comprehend the value of this truth. Romans 5:6-11 will supply additional insight into Who God is and what He has done for man.

Romans 5:6-11

Helpless to Save Ourselves

Romans 5:6 tells that man is *"helpless"* to save himself:

> *For while we were still helpless, at the right time Christ died for the ungodly.* (Romans 5:6)

Ephesians 2:8-9, Titus 3:5, and Romans 3:20 confirm that no matter how hard man labors, he can never perform sufficient deeds to merit God's favor. Many people, however, attempt to gain salvation through their own effort. If man will but realize his ungodliness (which he is capable of doing while depraved), repent (turn from sin), and exercise faith, God will save him.

Some theologians emphasize the word *"helpless"* (Romans 5:6) and teach a spiritual deadness that prevents the depraved from exercising personal repentance and faith. They argue that God must spiritually regenerate the depraved, give them repentance and faith, before they can repent, believe, and be saved. In their opinion, the depraved (spiritually unregenerated) are nothing more than corpses, totally incapable of understanding truth prior to God's spiritual enlightenment. Adam disproves this error, for immediately after sinning and becoming depraved he realized his spiritual nakedness (Genesis 3:7, 10). Also consider that God gave the Law to convict the depraved of sin (Galatians 3:24; 1Timothy 1:9-10) so they might repent and believe. Such a Law would be useless should the depraved (spiritually unregenerated) lack the capability of recognizing their need for a Savior.

Have you wondered why so few people choose to repent and come to Christ? John communicates it best in John 3:19-21, where he states that *"...men loved the darkness rather than the light...,"* as evidenced by the fact that *"...their deeds were evil."* He then states that *"...everyone who does evil hates the light, and does not come to the light, lest his deeds should be exposed."* In other words, many people refuse to turn from sin due to fearing the Lord will expose their error. If man refuses to perceive himself as sinful (ungodly) and, therefore, fails to repent while depraved, he simply cannot become God's child. Paul spent much time proving this truth in Romans 1-3.

Jesus Died at the Right Time

Read Romans 5:6, paying special attention to the phrase *"...at the right time Christ died for the ungodly."* What a powerful statement for Paul to make at this point in his epistle! Could it be that God appointed a specific time in history, even to the very day and hour, for Jesus to die— all along granting man a free will to choose as he pleases? The answer is "yes!" After all, Jesus was crucified at 9:00 a.m. on Passover morning (30 AD), at the exact time the Passover Chagigah sacrifice was being offered in the temple.

The Jews deal with the days of the week differently than the days of the month. They consider the day of the week as beginning at sundown and ending the following sundown. However, they regard the day of the month as beginning at midnight and continuing until the following midnight. This fact is confirmed in Leviticus 23:26-32, where verse 27 points out that the Day of Atonement was to be observed on *"the tenth day of"* the *"seventh month."* However, verse 32 indicates that it <u>began</u> on the *"evening"* before, the *"evening"* of *"the ninth of the month."* Thus, even though the Jewish day of the week changed when three stars appeared in the evening, the day of the month did not change until midnight.

This same principle applies to the Passover addressed in Leviticus 23:5-6. The lamb was killed and eaten at *"twilight"* (when three stars appeared) on the evening of the *"fourteenth"* (v.5), but the Feast of Unleavened Bread did not begin until the next calendar day, the *"fifteenth"* of the month (v.6). This fact allows us to better understand the events surrounding the Passover in Jesus' day. The lamb for Jesus' last Passover with His disciples was killed on Thursday afternoon, the fourteenth of Nisan, and eaten at evening (when three stars appeared), the beginning of Jewish Friday but the same calendar day, the fourteenth. However, the special Passover sacrifice offered at 9:00 a.m. the next morning, the Chagigah sacrifice, was offered on Friday, the same day of the week, but a different calendar day, the fifteenth.

The Jews who delivered Jesus to Pilate *"...did not enter into the Praetorium in order that they might not be defiled, but might eat the Passover"* (John 18:28). This statement has caused some individuals to misinterpret the context, for they view the word *"Passover"* as pointing to the Pascal Supper eaten on Thursday evening, the beginning of Jewish

Friday. The truth of the matter is that the word *"Passover"* in Scripture can point to the Pascal Supper (eaten on Thursday evening) as well as the Chagigah sacrifice offered on Friday morning—in fact, all the Passover sacrifices. Jesus ate the Pascal Supper with His disciples on Thursday evening, the beginning of Jewish Friday. However, substantial proof exists confirming that the word *"Passover"* (John 18:28) points to the special Chagigah Passover sacrifice offered at 9:00 a.m. on Friday morning. The Chagigah is addressed in the Old Testament, for instance, in Deuteronomy 16:2-3. The following (somewhat technical) quote comes from *A Commentary on the New Testament from the Talmud and Hebraica*, (John Lightfoot):

> That therefore which John saith, that "the Jews would not go into the judgment hall lest they should be polluted, but that they might eat the Passover," is to be understood of that Chagigah of the fifteenth day, not of the paschal lamb: for that also is called the Passover, Deuteronomy 16:2; "Thou shalt sacrifice the Passover to the Lord of thy flocks and of thy herds." *"Of thy flocks*; this indeed, by virtue of that precept, Exodus 12:3: but what have we to do with *herds?"* "'Of thy herds,' saith R. Solomon, for the Chagigah."

> …So that John said nothing strange to the ears of the Jews, when he said, "They went not into the judgment hall lest they might be polluted, but that they might eat the Passover"; pointing with his finger to the Chagigah, and not to the lamb, eaten indeed the day before.[9]

The defilement mentioned in John 18:28 was produced through contact with a Gentile (read Acts 10:28 as well as the following quote from the Mishnah).

> If a man went through the country of the gentiles in hilly or rocky country, he becomes unclean….The dwelling places of gentiles are unclean. *(Mishnah— Oholoth, 18:7—p. 675):*

Any person who had contracted Levitical defilement could not offer the Chagigah, to which the following quote refers as "festal offering":

> But when it is offered on a Sabbath, or is sufficient, or [is offered] in uncleanness, none may bring a [freewill] festal offering. *(Mishnah—Pesahim, 6: 3—p. 144)*

This defilement continued until sundown (Leviticus 22:4-7). Therefore, had the Jews entered the Praetorium early Friday morning, to observe the Chagigah sacrifice later that same morning would have been impossible (the Chagigah could not be offered on behalf of a defiled person). Entering the Praetorium would have been of no concern had the Pascal Supper been the issue, for that defilement would have ceased at sundown (Leviticus 22:4-7), freeing them to partake of the meal. The only way John 18:28 can be reconciled with Matthew, Mark, and Luke is for the word *"Passover"* to point to the Chagigah sacrifice of Friday morning rather than the Pascal Supper of Thursday evening, the beginning of Jewish Friday.

Pilot's dilemma was that had he released a man claiming to be king of the Jews, he would have been viewed as having released a rival to Caesar. Such a scenario could have cost Pilate more than his governorship. It might very well have cost him his life. This political pressure caused Pilate to bring Jesus out, place himself on the judgment seat (John 19:13) and say to the Jews, *"...Behold, your King"* (John 19:14). This event occurred at *"about the sixth hour"* on *"the day of preparation for the Passover"* (v.14), *"the...preparation for the Passover"* (v.14) pointing to the Chagigah Passover sacrifice offered later that Friday morning. The following quote is from *A Commentary on the New Testament from the Talmud and Hebraica*, (John Lightfoot):

> "It was the preparation of the Passover, and about the sixth hour." It was the preparation to the Chagigah, and not to the lamb.[10]

It seems proper, therefore, for the word *"Passover"* (John 19:14) to point to the Chagigah sacrifice offered on Friday morning—not to the paschal lamb eaten on Thursday evening. *"About the sixth hour"* (John 19:14) is based on the Roman perception of time, which was 6:00 a.m. in the morning. The time of the crucifixion is placed at *"the third hour"* (Mark 15:25), which according to the Jewish frame of reference, was 9:00 a.m. Thus, Jesus was crucified at the same time the official Passover sacrifice (the Chagigah sacrifice) was being offered in the temple on Friday morning.

Jesus died *"...at the right time..."* (Romans 5:6). In fact, it was the only *"time"* that would fulfill the Father's purpose. Note: Our commentary, *The Gospels from a Jewish Perspective,* addresses this subject in greater detail.

Atonement Unlimited

The last portion of Romans 5:6 speaks volumes regarding the scope of Jesus' atonement:

> *"...Christ died for the ungodly."*

The term *"ungodly"* points to every descendant of Adam, for all persons are born *"...a child of wrath..."* according to Ephesians 2:3. Thus, all people are born *"ungodly."* Hence, Jesus *"died"* for all mankind.

Romans 5:6 alone, without assistance from the wealth of additional passages that could be cited, negates limited atonement—the "L" of the TULIP. Because Jesus *"died for the ungodly"* (Romans 5:6), should atonement be limited, only the elect (those who believe) would be born *"ungodly."* Such a scenario would mean that those who reject Christ are godly—a total impossibility according to passages such as Romans 3:9 and Ephesians 2:3. Most proponents of limited atonement avoid Romans 5:6. In the few cases where they offer commentary, contradiction abounds. (Our *God's Heart* series covers this subject in greater detail.)

Unlimited atonement is validated by an abundance of passages, some of which are listed and discussed below:

> *"For God so loved the <u>world</u>, that He gave His only*
> *begotten Son, that <u>whoever</u> believes in Him should not*
> *perish, but have eternal life.* (John 3:16)

> *...and He Himself is the propitiation for our sins; and not*
> *for ours only, but also for those of <u>the whole world</u>.*
> (1John 2:2)

> *And we have beheld and bear witness that the Father has*
> *sent the Son to be the <u>Savior of the world</u>.* (1John 4:14)

Those who perceive Jesus' atonement as limited view the word *"world"* in John 3:16, 1John 2:2, and 1John 4:14 as pointing to the "world" of the elect. The context of these verses never suggests such a notion.

> *...who gave Himself as a ransom for <u>all</u>,...* (1Timothy
> 2:6)

The supporters of limited atonement teach that the term *"all"* points to "all" of the elect—the elect alone. This conclusion is ill founded, for Paul taught two verses earlier in First Timothy that Jesus died for *"all"* mankind, desiring that *"all men...be saved and...come to the knowledge of the truth"* (1Timothy 2:4).

Among the proponents of limited atonement, the phrase, *"He might taste death for everyone"* (Hebrews 2:9), is perceived as pointing to "everyone" who believes—the elect alone.

> *But we do see Him who has been made for a little while*
> *lower than the angels, namely, Jesus, because of the*
> *suffering of death crowned with glory and honor, that by*
> *the grace of God He might <u>taste death for everyone</u>.*
> (Hebrews 2:9)

Jesus' goal was to die, *"...that by the grace of God He might taste death for everyone"* (Hebrews 2:9). Also, the fact that Jesus tasted *"death"* means that He literally died. He tasted *"death for everyone,"* confirming that all sin for all time was placed on the innocent Messiah. Therefore, He didn't just die for those who would receive Him as Savior. He took on all the pain and agony of believers and unbelievers alike.

> *For it is for this we labor and strive, because we have*
> *fixed our hope on the living God, who is <u>the Savior of all</u>*
> <u>*men, especially of believers.*</u> (1Timothy 4:10)

The words, *"the Savior of all men, especially of believers"* (1Timothy 4:10), which clearly communicate that Jesus died for all mankind, are viewed by some theologians as validating limited atonement—that Jesus died only for the elect. Yet, to avoid the devastating impact of this passage on their contradictory ideology, they teach that Jesus' death provided temporal benefits for the non-elect while securing eternal benefits for the elect. No way!

Adherents of universal salvation also cite 1Timothy 4:10 in an attempt to prove that not one person will be lost, yet 1Corinthians 6:9-10 and 2Thessalonians 1:1-10 clearly teach otherwise.

> *But false prophets also arose among the people, just as*
> *there will also be false teachers among you, who will*
> *secretly introduce destructive heresies, even denying <u>the</u>*
> <u>*Master who bought them,*</u> *bringing swift destruction upon*
> *themselves.* (2Peter 2:1—emphasis added)

Proponents of limited atonement view Peter's words as follows: (1) The false teachers viewed themselves as believers (2) Peter mocks them by verifying their certain destruction.

This interpretation is flawed, for Peter communicates that Jesus died for the *"false teachers"* who were lost, verifying unlimited atonement.

> *"And as Moses lifted up the serpent in the wilderness,*
> *even so must the Son of Man be lifted up; that whoever*
> *believes may in Him have eternal life.* (John 3:14-15)

Because the context of Jesus' words to Nicodemus is crucial, let's first examine Numbers 21:4-9 to determine the backdrop of this account:

> *Then they set out from Mount Hor by the way of the Red*
> *Sea, to go around the land of Edom; and the people*
> *became impatient because of the journey. And the people*
> *spoke against God and Moses, "Why have you brought us*

> *up out of Egypt to die in the wilderness? For there is no*
> *food and no water, and we loathe this miserable food."*
> *And the LORD sent fiery serpents among the people and*
> *they bit the people, so that many people of Israel died. So*
> *the people came to Moses and said, "We have sinned,*
> *because we have spoken against the LORD and you;*
> *intercede with the LORD, that He may remove the*
> *serpents from us." And Moses interceded for the people.*
> *Then the LORD said to Moses, "Make a fiery serpent, and*
> *set it on a standard; and it shall come about, that*
> *everyone who is bitten, when he looks at it, he shall live."*
> *And Moses made a bronze serpent and set it on the*
> *standard; and it came about, that if a serpent bit any man,*
> *when he looked to the bronze serpent, he lived.* (Numbers
> 21:4-9)

Israel rebelled by speaking *"...against God and Moses..."* (vv.4-5).
As a result, *"...the Lord sent fiery serpents among the people...,"* they
were bitten, and *"...many people of Israel died"* (v.6). Once the people
repented, *"Moses interceded"* (v.7), and God presented the remedy.
Moses was to *"...Make a fiery serpent, and set it on a standard..."* (v.8)
so everyone who was *"bitten"* might *"live"* (v.8). They could *"live"*
through only one means—gazing at the *"serpent."* So *"...Moses made a*
bronze serpent and set it on the standard; and it came about, that if a
serpent bit any man, when he looked to the bronze serpent, he lived"
(v.9).

The context reveals the meaning of Jesus' words to Nicodemus in
John 3:14-15. When Israel sinned in Numbers 21, anyone *"bitten"* was
automatically healed *"when he looked to the bronze serpent."* The
choice was left to the *"bitten"* ones—not God. Therefore, the
correlation is simple. All mankind has been *"bitten"* by sin, being
descendants of Adam. The *"bronze serpent,"* (Numbers 21:9; John
3:14) points to Jesus, who was *"lifted up"* (John 3:14) on a cross so
"that whoever believes may in Him have eternal life" (John 3:15). Just
as a *"bronze serpent"* was raised by Moses as the remedy to the poison
injected by the *"serpents,"* Jesus became *"sin"* (2Corinthians 5:21)
while on the cross, taking on the misdeeds of all mankind to eradicate the
poison of sin in all who choose (while depraved) to repent and believe.

The Jews in Numbers 21, through choosing to believe God's Word by gazing upon His provision, made the choice to obey. The fact that the choice was made <u>before</u> they were healed illustrates that the depraved can choose Christ <u>before</u> being born again. After all, not all who made that choice were believers in Jehovah when the rebellion of Numbers 21:4-5 broke out.

Why must those who support limited atonement go to such lengths while attempting to validate their position? In their opinion, should Jesus' atonement be unlimited, a portion of His blood would be wasted since all are not saved. What they fail to consider is this: <u>All</u> of His blood was required to save just me—or you—or whomever.

Take a moment to consider Romans 5:7-8:

> *For one will hardly die for a righteous man; though*
> *perhaps for the good man someone would dare even to*
> *die. But God demonstrates His own love toward us, in*
> *that while we were yet sinners, Christ died for us.*
> (Romans 5:7-8)

As I ponder these passages, I can't help but ask myself if I would be willing to die for my brothers and sisters in Christ. Until we are placed in a situation requiring such a decision, I doubt if any of us can know how we would respond. Christ not only *"...died for us,"* but He did so *"...while we were yet sinners...."* What love! He actually demonstrated His love through the cross by dying *"...for the ungodly"* (Romans 5:6), an act sanctioned by His Father. We can demonstrate this same love as we walk by God's Spirit and lose our lives for others (Matthew 10:39; John 15:12-13; 2Corinthians 4:11-12).

Romans 5:8 is used by the adherents of limited atonement in an attempt to validate their position. They argue that the *"us"* in the passage proves that Jesus died for believers only:

> *But God demonstrates His own love toward <u>us</u>, in that*
> *while we were yet sinners, Christ died for <u>us</u>.* (Romans
> 5:8)

Jesus died for *"us"*—for believers. However, passages of this sort do not negate the fact that He died for all—for believers and unbelievers alike (reference notes on Romans 5:6). Nowhere in the verse, nor anywhere else in God's Word, do we find that Jesus died for the elect alone. To isolate verses for the purpose of establishing a faulty doctrine is an affront against the authority of God's Word. Context is everything in all areas of Biblical interpretation. Avoiding the context of *"us"* in Romans 5:8 would also allow for an argument that Jesus died only for Paul and the believers at Rome. Similarly, by sidestepping context, one could contend that Paul alone was *"crucified with Christ"* (read Galatians 2:20). It could be said as well that Paul was capable of saving the lost (read Romans 11:14)—heresy indeed.

Many advocates of limited atonement also use Romans 5:8 in an effort to prove that God loves only believers. The phrase, *"But God demonstrates His own love toward us...,"* is cited as proof for their position. They then suppose that the phrase, *"For God so loved the world..."* (John 3:16), points to the world of the elect alone. They then conclude that God loves the saved and hates the lost, a direct violation of Ezekiel 18:32 and Ezekiel 33:11. (Our *God's Heart* series covers this subject in much greater depth.)

Saved from God's Wrath through Christ's Death

Paul continues by saying:

> *Much more then, having now been justified by His blood,*
> *we shall be saved from the wrath of God through Him.*
> (Romans 5:9)

Jesus' *"blood,"* once applied to our lives, allows the Father to justify us (make us not guilty before Him)—since the shedding of *"blood"* is a symbol of the fact that a death has occurred, *"the life of the flesh"* being *"in the blood"* (Leviticus 17:11). At that point, everything we have studied concerning justification applies to us. As a result of being righteous, holy, blameless, complete, and all the rest, we will escape God's *"wrath."* We will not stand before the *"great white throne"* judgment of Revelation 20:11-15. Only unbelievers will experience that horrible ordeal. We will face *"the judgment seat of Christ"*

(2Corinthians 5:10)—a judgment for rewards, not condemnation (Romans 8:1).

Paul repeats himself quite often, for he realizes the necessity of a deep and abiding understanding of the cross. After all, *"...the cross is to those who are perishing foolishness, but to us who are being saved it is the power of God"* (1Corinthians 1:18).

Saved Daily from Sin's Power by Christ's Life

I don't know of any verse that better communicates the essence of the Christian experience than Romans 5:10:

> *For if while we were enemies, we were reconciled to God through the death of His Son, much more, having been reconciled, we shall be saved by His life.* (Romans 5:10)

This passage first states that we, in our lost state, *"were enemies"* to God (although He loved us in our unredeemed state—John 3:16). This truth lines up perfectly with John 8:44, which verifies that we were sons of Satan so long as we walked in rebelliousness:

> *"You are of your father the devil, and you want to do the desires of your father. He was a murderer from the beginning, and does not stand in the truth, because there is no truth in him. Whenever he speaks a lie, he speaks from his own nature; for he is a liar, and the father of lies.* (John 8:44)

Thus, we were *"children of wrath"*:

> *Among them we too all formerly lived in the lusts of our flesh, indulging the desires of the flesh and of the mind, and were by nature children of wrath, even as the rest.* (Ephesians 2:3)

However, once we repented and believed while depraved *"we were reconciled to God through the death of His Son"* (Romans 5:10),

171

"reconciled" meaning to be granted favor with the Father. Christ's *"death"* serves as the means through which God reconciles those who repent and believe while depraved. This fascinating reality will be studied in depth when we arrive at Romans 6:6, but for now realize that the death and eradication of who we used to be (who we were in our lost state) allowed God to welcome us into His family. In other words, the Father, by placing us in His Son on the cross (1Corinthians 12:13; Romans 6:6; 7:4; Galatians 2:20) subsequent to our repenting and believing while depraved, eradicated the "person" previously living in our bodies and made us new (2Corinthians 5:17). Therefore, we did the repenting and believing, but God did the saving—our choice to repent and believe while depraved in no way being a work (Romans 3:27-28; 4:5).

God smiled on us at the point of justification, and for the first time we could call Him *"Father"* (Galatians 4:6). We were finally at peace with our Creator. Is this reconciliation all that we received? Did He restore us to a place of favor so we could flounder around until He calls us home? Based on the remainder of Romans 5:10, absolutely not!

Most believers understand at least something regarding the first half of Romans 5:10, but only a minority of the body of Christ comprehends the awesomeness of the remainder of the verse. In fact, the phrase, *"...we shall be saved by His life,"* holds the key to abundant living.

We understand well by now that at the point of salvation (justification) we, as church saints, were freed from the penalty of sin. But salvation includes more than forgiveness of sins. It includes, among other things, being saved on a day-to-day basis from the temptations we face as believers. This salvation (deliverance) is accomplished by Jesus' life that moved into our spirit the moment we repented and believed while depraved (Galatians 2:20; Colossians 3:4)! Read it: *"...we shall be saved by His life"* (Romans 5:10). This continual, moment-by-moment salvation is not addressing the issue of getting out of hell and into heaven. The first part of the verse dealt with that topic—salvation from the penalty of sin. Paul is saying that the life of Christ residing inside us is the only means through which we experience salvation from Satan's ever-present schemes. Therefore, by yielding to Christ's life within, victorious living becomes a reality rather than remaining an obscure idea understood by God alone.

Thus, Paul stated *"...neither circumcision nor uncircumcision means anything, but faith working through love"* (Galatians 5:6). Did you catch that? Love, not duty, causes us to yearn to live by faith, to live a life characterized by trust in the Creator. Yes, what God did for us at the point of justification not only revolutionizes our perception of who we are, but revolutionizes our perception of Who He is as well. When this revolution occurs, everything about our lives is invigorated, not by our own energy, but by His—as we yield to His indwelling presence.

We, as New Testament believers, have the privilege of living life by the life of Another. Stated differently, we have access to what Adam and Eve were originally offered in the Garden of Eden. *"The tree of life"* (Genesis 2:9) was more than a tree named *"life."* The Father's very life resided in the tree. Consequently, had Adam and Eve obeyed, they would have lived by the Father's life—by the life of Another. Instead, they sinned and were barred from the tree (Genesis 3:24) that possessed the only means through which life can be truly enjoyed. Note: A movement exists within Christendom that views God as having caused Adam and Eve to sin so He can have someone (the lost) on which to display His wrath so the elect might appreciate His grace. This view normally perceives God as the cause of all things, even electing the elect to salvation from eternity past. They, as a result, perceive the depraved as incapable of exercising repentance and faith. In fact, they teach that God must first spiritually regenerate the depraved, follow by giving them repentance and faith, before they can repent, believe, and be saved. Our *God's Heart* series addresses this thinking's inconsistencies.

Was the Father caught off guard by Adam and Eve's disobedience that He, for certain, did not cause? Of course not, for Jesus came to demonstrate what Adam and Eve failed to experience due to sin. In other words, He came to demonstrate what life would look like when lived by the life in the tree—the Father's very life:

> *"Do you not believe that I am in the Father, and the Father is in Me? The words that I say to you I do not speak on My own initiative, but the Father abiding in Me does His works.* (John 14:10)

Jesus performed no work due to yielding to the Father (the life in the tree) throughout His First Coming. The Father, through the Son, was responsible for Jesus' miracles. Thus, Jesus stated:

> *"For My yoke is easy, and My load is light."* (Matthew 11:30)

Jesus' *"yoke"* was *"easy"* and His *"load...light"* due to choosing to live by His Father's indwelling presence. As a result, He never sinned, fulfilling the Law completely—so you and I as New Testament believers could live *"under grace"* rather than *"law"* (Romans 6:14). Jesus lived *"under the Law"* (Galatians 4:4) to fulfill the Law so we, once we repented and believed while depraved, could be delivered from the Law to live under grace. Amazing!

Paul's understanding of this truth affected every aspect of the ministry to which he was called. He stated, therefore, that the source of His strength was God's grace:

> *But by the grace of God I am what I am, and His grace toward me did not prove vain; but I labored even more than all of them, yet not I, but the grace of God with me.* (1Corinthians 15:10)

He also wrote:

> *I can do all things through Him who strengthens me.* (Philippians 4:13)

Paul recognized that yielding to Christ's life is always, in every case, the key to victorious living—never applying self-effort to a series of rules or regulations. His words from Romans 6:13 demonstrate that Jesus is *"God"* (Hebrews 1:8):

> *and do not go on presenting the members of your body to sin as instruments of unrighteousness; but present yourselves to God as those alive from the dead, and your members as instruments of righteousness to God.* (Romans 6:13)

Paul understood that all good things performed through his life resulted from yielding to the Son, Who is yielded to the Father. Through this means Paul lived by the life in the tree—the life originally made accessible to Adam and Eve in the Garden. We can live by this same life. Can you imagine anything more exciting? Only through living by Jesus' life can the New Testament believer enter into *"Sabbath rest,"* resulting in obedience motivated by love—never duty:

> *There remains therefore a Sabbath rest for the people of*
> *God. For the one who has entered His rest has himself*
> *also rested from his works, as God did from His.*
> (Hebrews 4:9-10)

This *"Sabbath rest"* is the ultimate reality for the believer, for its possessors know God's heart, and in turn, live by the life in the tree (a subject addressed in greater depth in the Hebrews course distributed by this ministry). Three levels of "rest" are available to the redeemed (Redemption rest, Canaan rest, and Sabbath rest), each of which are portrayed in 1John 2:12-14:

> *I am writing to you, little children, because your sins are*
> *forgiven you for His name's sake. I am writing to you,*
> *fathers, because you know Him who has been from the*
> *beginning. I am writing to you, young men, because you*
> *have overcome the evil one. I have written to you,*
> *children, because you know the Father. I have written to*
> *you, fathers, because you know Him who has been from*
> *the beginning. I have written to you, young men, because*
> *you are strong, and the word of God abides in you, and*
> *you have overcome the evil one.* (1John 2:12-14)

Here we find that *"little children"* (those new in the faith) know their *"sins are forgiven"* (v.12) and *"know the Father"* as their God (v.13). They have entered Redemption rest. The *"young men,"* those more mature in the Lord, *"have overcome the evil one"* (vv.13-14)—through applying the truth they know—and entered Canaan rest (rest from the enemy). The *"fathers"* on the other hand, the seasoned believers, *"know"* the heart of *"Him who has been from the beginning"* (vv.13-

14). They *"know"* the heart of Christ (have intimacy with Christ) and have entered Sabbath rest. Our ultimate goal is not to realize that our *"sins are forgiven"* (Redemption rest), nor to *"overcome the evil one"* through applying God's truth (Canaan rest), but to *"know"* (intimately) the heart of God's Son (Sabbath rest). Intimacy with the Father is attained only through establishing intimacy with His Son (John 14:7 and 9). Those who experience this intimacy walk in Sabbath rest, and in turn, live by the life in the tree—through yielding to Christ, Who is yielded to the Father. What incredible news!

Just as three levels of "rest" are available to the New Testament believer, three types of salvation are available as well: (1) Salvation from the penalty of sin (Acts 16:31)—once we exercise repentance and faith while depraved (2) Salvation from the power of sin (Romans 5:10)—on a daily basis once we repent and believe (3) Salvation from the presence of sin (Romans 13:11)—when we eject out of our earthly bodies and enter heaven. As indicated above, the salvation that Paul addresses in Romans 5:10 *("saved by His life")* is the second type—salvation from the power of sin in our daily experience. Paul mentions this same salvation in 1Corinthians 1:18:

> *For the word of the cross is to those who are perishing*
> *foolishness, but to us who are being saved it is the power*
> *of God. (1Corinthians 1:18)*

The use of the present tense *("being saved")* points to a daily deliverance from sin's power as we yield to Christ's indwelling presence. The voice is passive in the Greek because the subject is being acted upon by an outside Source once the subject chooses to yield—the Source being Jesus.

As has already been verified, no believer will be judged at the *"great white throne"* (Revelation 20:11-15), a judgment of wrath. A New Testament believer faces *"the judgment seat of Christ,"* a judgment that results in rewards. Each of our works will be tested *"with fire"* (1Corinthians 3:10-15), and we will be rewarded for the deeds done in faith. We will be rewarded for each time we have trusted Christ to perform a particular deed through us, regardless of the outcome. The deeds performed in our own strength will burn, even should good result from our efforts. This judgment serves as additional motivation to enter into *"sabbath rest"* (Hebrews 4:9-10), for those who have ceased working for God (and have learned to live by Christ's life) are rewarded most.

You may say, "I know (in my head) that I have been saved from the penalty of sin, and that daily temptation is overcome through yielding to Jesus' indwelling presence, but how does this reality work in a practical sense?" Great question, for we can talk about being saved (on a daily basis from the power of sin) by Christ's life without knowing much about the subject matter. Considerable time will be invested in Romans 6, 7, and 8 discussing this vital truth. For starters, however, allow me to describe how this powerful reality has <u>begun</u> to work in my own experience. Note my emphasis on "begun."

First, temptation is never overcome by concentrating on the temptation. Should I have a problem with stealing (for instance), I will never gain victory in that area by saying, "I cannot steal." With that mind-set, the responsibility of overcoming my problem depends upon me. However, if I see myself as holy and perfect, as God sees me (due to His having made me holy and perfect subsequent to my exercising repentance and faith while depraved), I will realize the unnaturalness of yielding to the temptation. Consequently, while being tempted, I must remember that Jesus lives in me, yield to His life, and walk away in His strength. Through this means I am *"saved by His life"* (Romans 5:10). Sounds simple, doesn't it? But you know as well as I do that intense spiritual warfare can make living from this vantage point extremely challenging. Therefore, we will invest significant time in Romans 6:1-8:17 learning how this reality can become more than a hit or miss exercise of futility. In fact, it must become a consistent lifestyle if we desire to live victoriously.

I once asked a friend, who has been used of God to encourage countless believers, the following question: "What is the supreme truth you have gleaned from God's Word?" He responded by saying that the truth of Romans 5:10 affected him most, where Paul speaks of being saved on a daily basis by Christ's *"life."* He went on to say that the greatest need within the church today is that she learn to live by the life of Another, the life of Christ, and to practice this reality on an ever-increasing basis. I agree! Yet, I have discovered that most believers lack the passion to pursue the deeper things of God until facing difficulties of epic proportions. A great man (source unknown) once said: "Everything is learned through pain. Everything else is just information." Thus, were it not for extreme pain, this ministry would not exist. Neither would this commentary exist! Thank God, therefore, for the pain (2Corinthians 4:17-18).

In Romans 5:11, Paul states that *"...we...exult in God through our Lord Jesus Christ":*

> *And not only this, but we also exult in God through our*
> *Lord Jesus Christ, through whom we have now received*
> *the reconciliation.* (Romans 5:11)

From Romans 5:2, we know that *"exult"* means to "rejoice." Rejoice we can, because through Christ we have been reconciled and granted a place of favor with the Godhead! Thus, Paul described the *"gospel"* as *"...the glorious gospel of the blessed God..."* (1Timothy 1:11). It truly is *"glorious"!* We will continue to observe the *"glorious"* nature of the *"gospel"* as we walk through the remainder of this study. Isn't this exciting! Romans 5:12-21 is some of the most thought-provoking input in the entire course, so remain alert.

Romans 5:12-21

Adam's Mistake - Jesus' Remedy

This portion of Romans portrays the stark contrast between the awfulness of Adam's disobedience and the greatness of Christ's obedience. Adam's fall brought condemnation to all men. Christ's sacrifice offers reconciliation to all men. This section also provides a deeper revelation of the word *"sin."* Note: All that is included in association with Romans 5:12-21 in *The Foundational Truths of Romans 1-8* (the introductory course associated with this series) is presented here along with additional input. The review, coupled with the new information, should enhance our understanding of this vital portion of God's letter to man.

Before going further turn to the Reference Section located in the back. Nine circle diagrams are provided. If you find it more convenient, make copies for easy reference. The written material may become easier to comprehend when used along side the diagrams.

The content of the next few paragraphs may be initially confusing but becomes extremely palatable as we progress.

In Romans 5:12, we find:

> *Therefore, just as through one man sin entered into the world, and death through sin, and so death spread to all men, because all sinned —* (Romans 5:12)

To properly interpret the phrase, *"...through one man sin entered into the world...,"* we must take into account that Satan, the personification of sin, was present in *"the world"* prior to Adam's sin. Consequently, the phrase *"...through one man sin entered into the world..."* must mean, *"...through one man sin entered into man."* Adam was the *"man,"* for God instructed him to abstain from partaking of *"the tree of the knowledge of good and evil"* in Genesis 2:17. Should he partake of the tree, he would *"die"* instantly in the spiritual sense (Genesis 2:17) and later in the physical sense—it was as simple as that. He ate of the tree in Genesis 3:6 and experienced immediate spiritual death, a death that points to separation rather than extinction. Why separation rather than extinction? *"God is Spirit"* (John 4:24), and Adam's sin separated him from God in the spiritual sense. His physical death came much later, for a son was born to Adam in Genesis 4 after his sinning in Genesis 3, meaning that he remained very much alive physically after his disobedience. Thus, *"sin entered into the world,"* that is, *"entered into"* man, resulting in spiritual separation from God.   Note: Genesis 3:7 verifies that this spiritual death did not prevent Adam from recognizing his spiritual nakedness, confirming that the depraved <u>can</u> comprehend their need for a Savior, exercise personal repentance and faith, and experience God's salvation.

Adam and Eve's one act of disobedience caused them to lose their dominion over the earth, which was granted by God in Genesis 1:24-31:

> *Then God said, "Let the earth bring forth living creatures after their kind: cattle and creeping things and beasts of the earth after their kind"; and it was so. And God made the beasts of the earth after their kind, and the cattle after their kind, and everything that creeps on the ground after its kind; and God saw that it was good. Then God said, "Let Us make man in Our image, according to Our likeness; and let them rule over the fish of the sea and over the birds of the sky and over the cattle and over all the earth, and over every creeping thing that creeps on the earth." And God created man in His own image, in the image of God He created him; male and female He created them. And God blessed them; and God said to them, "Be fruitful and multiply, and fill the earth, and subdue it; and <u>rule over</u> the fish of the sea and over the birds of the sky, and over every living thing that moves on the earth." Then God said, "Behold, I have given you every plant yielding seed that is on the surface of all the earth, and every tree which has fruit yielding seed; it shall be food for you; and to every beast of the earth and to every bird of the sky and to every thing that moves on the earth which has life, I have given every green plant for food"; and it was so. And God saw all that He had made, and behold, it was very good. And there was evening and there was morning, the sixth day. (Genesis 1:24-31)*

Satan ruled over the earth once Adam and Eve disobeyed. Thus, Paul refers to Satan as the small "g" *"god of this world"* (2Corinthians 4:4):

> *in whose case the god of this world has blinded the minds*
> *of the unbelieving, that they might not see the light of the*
> *gospel of the glory of Christ, who is the image of God.*
> (2Corinthians 4:4)

Don't misunderstand. Satan is a defeated foe to the New Testament believer due to Jesus' death, burial, resurrection, and ascension. However, he remains our enemy and *"accuser"* based on Revelation 12:10:

> *"Now the salvation, and the power, and the kingdom of*
> *our God and the authority of His Christ have come, for*
> *the accuser of our brethren has been thrown down, who*
> *accuses them before our God day and night.* (Revelation
> 12:10)

Because Satan despises all believers (all mankind, in fact), he seeks *"someone to devour"*:

> *Be of sober spirit, be on the alert. Your adversary, the*
> *devil, prowls about like a roaring lion, seeking someone*
> *to devour.* (1Peter 5:8)

We as believers are to *"resist him, firm in"* our *"faith"*:

> *But resist him, firm in your faith, knowing that the same*
> *experiences of suffering are being accomplished by your*
> *brethren who are in the world.* (1Peter 5:9)

In Romans 5:12-8:39, Paul vividly describes how Satan can be resisted. Expect our *"adversary"* (Satan—1Peter 5:8) to unleash his arsenal of weaponry against us as God's Word exposes him and his schemes. Remember: Our enemy is nothing more than *"a roaring lion"* (1Peter 5:8) that has lost his bite; for the cross, resurrection, and ascension DE-toothed him.

With the above input in mind, let's take a moment to discuss the ramifications of being born into a world controlled by Satan's system—the world system. Terms are introduced here that will be discussed in greater detail later; so don't become discouraged should understanding be lacking. Understanding will surface as we progress.

When Adam sinned, his spiritual death (separation from God) brought about a change of nature. In fact, his nature became such that sin became natural. Stated differently, Adam's sin and change of nature made him love sin. Prior to his sin, disobedience was unnatural. After his sin, sin (for Adam) was as natural as breathing.

You and I (all mankind) are born in the condition that existed within Adam after Adam sinned. We were born with a bent to sin. We loved sin due to our sinful nature inherited from Adam. Having lacked wisdom (Proverbs 9:10), we listened to Satan's lies and obeyed Satan's promptings—naturally. As a result, we were programmed for failure, programming which occurred in our brains. Yes, like a computer, we were programmed by our enemy—an enemy who desires to destroy us. The fact that this programming was not erased when we met Jesus makes the remainder of this study extremely captivating. Hold on as we allow God's Word to expose our enemy and set us free from his ever-present schemes. Romans 5:12 will be our beginning point.

The word *"sin"* in Romans 5:12, being a noun, can point to something other than man's <u>acts</u> of sin. In fact, it refers to a <u>power</u> called *"sin"*:

> *Therefore, just as through one man sin entered into the world, and death through sin, and so death spread to all men, because all sinned—* (Romans 5:12)

To make certain that Romans 5:12 is covered thoroughly, the passage is divided into phrases and discussed in as much detail as possible.

Observe Circle Diagram 1 *(Man is a Three Part Being)* on the next page.

Diagram 1

Man is a Three Part Being

1Thessalonians 5:23

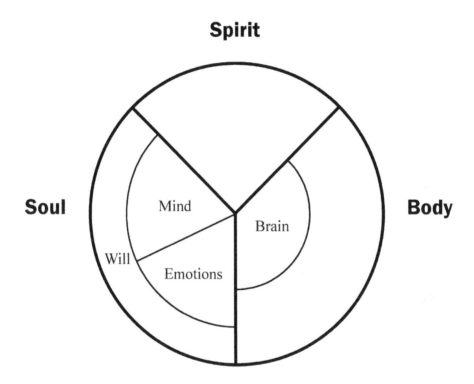

Now may the God of peace Himself sanctify you entirely; and may your spirit and soul and body be preserved complete without blame at the coming of our Lord Jesus Christ, (1Thessalonians 5:23)

Body: What houses the soul and spirit (2Corinthians 5:1-4). Notice that the brain is part of the body.

Soul: Mind, Emotions and Will. Man thinks with his mind, feels with his emotions, and chooses with his will.

Spirit: The part of a New Testament believer that house's God's presence (John 14:16-17, 20, 23). Void of God's presence, this part of man is dead to God (Genesis 2:17; Ephesians 2:1). It is through the avenue of the Spirit that man communicates with God (John 4:24), and God with man (John 14:26).

Therefore, just as through one man sin entered into the world,
(Romans 5:12a)

1.   Before Adam sinned the presence of sin was <u>on</u> earth but not <u>in</u> man. The serpent (evil) was present in the garden <u>before</u> Adam ate of the forbidden fruit.   However, when Adam sinned (Genesis 3:6-7), *"sin entered into"* man through *Adam's* disobedience (Romans 5:12).   Adam truly committed an act of sin.   But the word *"sin"* in some cases, especially in portions of Romans 5-8, refers to a power called *"sin"* which entered into Adam and dwells in man.   This power is called *"the law of sin"* in Romans 7:23, 25 and 8:2, but called *"sin"* in Romans 7:17 and 20.   We will refer to this power in most instances as the power of sin, but in some cases simply as sin.

2.   The contextual view of the word *"sin"* is critical, for it can refer to: (1) An act of sin or (2) The power of sin.   The power of sin will be discussed on numerous occasions as we continue.   Therefore, you will have ample time to comprehend its meaning, even if initially it should seem somewhat confusing.

3.   The power of sin *"entered"* into Adam's spirit, soul, and body when Adam disobeyed.   As a result, Adam's soul was inundated with messages from this power called *"sin."*   Refer to Circle Diagram 2 on the next page titled, *Sin (the Power of Sin) Entered into Man,* and read all the information.   The power of sin is not a demon, but an organized power that has Satan as its master.   The power of sin can be viewed as the opposite of the Holy Spirit.   When God speaks to the soul of man, He speaks through the avenue of the Holy Spirit.   When Satan speaks to the soul of man, he speaks through the avenue of the power of sin.   Thus, the power of sin is Satan's messenger, or agent.

Diagram 2

Sin (the Power of Sin) Entered into Man
Romans 5:12

Just as through one man sin entered into the world, and death through sin, and so death spread to all men because all sinned, (Romans 5:12)

When Adam disobeyed God, the law of sin (the power of sin, sin) moved into Adam's spirit, soul, and body. Adam was then influenced by the messages he received from the law of sin (the power of sin, sin).

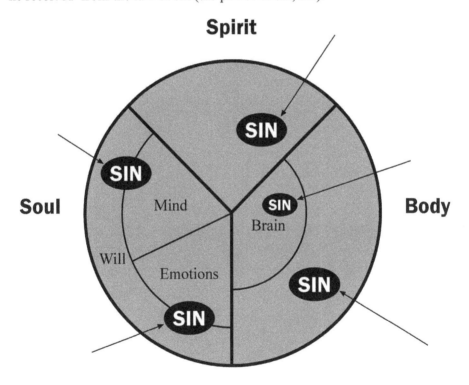

and death through sin,

1.   Adam's act of disobedience brought *"death,"* for the Lord had warned Adam in Genesis 2:17 that he would die should he partake of the forbidden fruit. Remember, the word *"death"* in Scripture can mean "separation" as well as "extinction."

2.   When Adam sinned, his spirit and soul died (they were "separated" from God), at which time the sin nature (Adamic nature, or old man, or old self) was born. Instantly, it was natural for Adam to sin because his very nature was sinful, his nature being both soul and spirit. Refer to Circle Diagram 3 titled *Man without Christ* (on the next page). The terms dead spirit, sin nature, Adamic nature, old man, and old self are synonymous—expressions that consist of different words but possess the same meaning. They refer to the nature that Adam possessed after he sinned—the same nature that you and I possessed until we were made new in Christ. (See Circle Diagram 9 in the reference section.)

Diagram 3

Man without Christ

Romans 5:12

When Adam sinned the Adamic Nature was born, the Adamic Nature being soul and spirit. It was then natural for Adam to be controlled by the Power of Sin that lived in his spirit, soul, and body.

Man is born in the same condition that Adam was in after he sinned. Man is born spiritually separated from God, but not to the degree that he is incapable of exercising personal repentance and faith while depraved. The Power of Sin generates ungodly thoughts that the depraved generally accept as the truth.

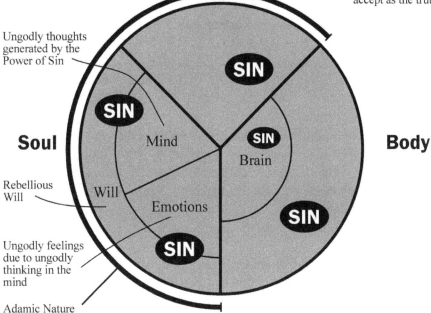

Ungodly thoughts generated by the Power of Sin

Soul

Body

Rebellious Will

Ungodly feelings due to ungodly thinking in the mind

Adamic Nature
(old self, old man, dead spirit, sin nature) - both Spirit and Soul
Also refer to circle Diagram 9.

Just as through one man sin entered into the world, and death through sin, and so death spread to all men because all sinned, (Romans 5:12)

3.   The sin nature (or old man, dead spirit, old self, Adamic nature) enjoys rebelling against God. This fact does not mean that the depraved (the spiritually unregenerated) are incapable of exercising repentance and faith prior to spiritual regeneration, as was verified earlier (this subject is covered extensively in our *God's Heart* series).

4.   Because the nature of man is who man is, Adam was the sin nature (the old man) after he sinned. Refer to Circle Diagrams 1, 2, and 9 in the reference section and read about the spirit and soul of man.

5.   As was mentioned above, *"death"* in Scripture can mean separation. Because *"God is spirit"* (John 4:24), and since the part of Adam that could communicate with God was separated from God subsequent to his disobedience, Adam was dead to God. Thus, when a man's spirit and soul are separated from God, the man is dead, even if he continues to live physically. Hence, the word *"death"* in Scripture does not always point to physical extinction. It can also point to spiritual separation.

6.   When Adam sinned, his spirit and soul died (were separated from God). The power of sin entered Adam's spirit and soul—thereby bringing to life the sin nature (old man, old self, Adamic nature, dead spirit). The power of sin also moved into Adam's body. Adam's soul was then inundated with the power of sin's lies. Refer to Circle Diagrams 2 and 3.

7.   Adam's act of disobedience resulted not only in the immediate death of his spirit and soul, but his physical body eventually died as well. We know that Adam died a physical death several years after he sinned, an event that would not have occurred had he obeyed.

so death spread to all men,

1.   Because we are descendants of Adam, we are born with the nature that Adam possessed after he sinned. We are born with a dead (separated from God) soul and spirit because *"death spread to all men."* The word *"all"* is all-inclusive—pointing to every person who has lived or will live.

2. Physical death also spread to all men, for Adam eventually died physically, as do his descendants.

because all sinned.

1. To understand this phrase, we must tie it in with what is previously stated. *"And so death spread to all men, because all sinned"* simply means that our acts of sin confirm that spiritual death spread to all men. Have you noticed the selfishness of a baby? Cute as they are, babies possess Adam's nature from conception, and as a result, are concerned with only one thing: Getting their needs met. Adults who do not know Christ also exhibit selfish tendencies due to possessing the nature of Adam—a nature out of touch with God so long as rebellion is chosen over submission to Christ. This nature is determined to have its way, thinking of self above all else. Wasn't this Adam's problem in the garden?

2. The lost will not be condemned to hell because of their acts of sin even though *"all sinned"* in Adam. Their nature inherited from Adam will condemn them (Ephesians 2:3—*"...were by nature children of wrath..."*).

> *The lost will not be condemned to hell because of their acts of sin.*

> *for until the Law sin was in the world; but sin is not imputed when there is no law.* (Romans 5:13)

The first part of the verse teaches: *"for until the Law [the Mosaic Law] sin was in the world..."* Man has been committing acts of sin since Adam disobeyed in the Garden. However, these acts of sin are *"not imputed [charged to a person's account] when there is no law."* Man has to break a direct command of God for sin to be counted against him. But no direct command of God was stated from Adam until Moses, since only the moral law written on man's conscience existed during that time span. Why then did men die from the time of Adam until the time of Moses if they were not in violation of any specific law? The answer is simple. The whole race sinned when Adam sinned, for the genes of all of Adam's descendants were in his gene pool when he disobeyed. Therefore, from God's perspective, all mankind broke His command simultaneously with Adam, which explains why God could remain just and, at the same time, allow individuals to die who lived prior to the issuing of the Mosaic Law. Romans 2:12 validates our present discussion. Paul is not insinuating that we existed at the time of Adam's disobedience, rather that our genes were in Adam's gene pool when Adam sinned. In other words, we did not become persons until conception.

The interpretation of Romans 5:14 rests on the above foundation:

> *Nevertheless death reigned from Adam until Moses, even*
> *over those who had not sinned in the likeness of the*
> *offense of Adam, who is a type of Him who was to come.*
> (Romans 5:14)

The first two phrases of this passage offer an insight to why our relationship with Adam caused us to need a Savior.

Romans 5:14 also tells that Adam *"...is a type of Him who was to come"*—*"a type"* of Christ. Neither Adam nor Christ has an earthly father. (The impossibility of Jesus being Joseph's son was addressed earlier.) Just as Adam was created void of a sin nature, Christ was also born void of a sin nature—the heavenly Father being Jesus' Father. (The sin nature would not have been passed down through Mary to Christ because the sin nature is inherited from the earthly father through Adam.) Adam's wife was taken from his side (Genesis 2:21-25), while Christ's wife (the church) was taken from His pierced side (John 19:34). Paul's point is that Adam *"...is a type of Him who was to come."*

In Romans 5:15-19, Paul verifies that Christ's gift through grace supersedes the negativity resulting from Adam's transgression.

> *But the free gift is not like the transgression. For if by the*
> *transgression of the one the <u>many</u> died, much more did*
> *the grace of God and the gift by the grace of the one Man,*
> *Jesus Christ, abound to the <u>many</u>.* (Romans 5:15)

Paul communicates that salvation is a *"free gift."* Due to *"faith"* not being a work (Romans 3:27-28; 4:4-5), salvation is a *"free gift"* (Romans 5:15) granted to those who exercise repentance and faith while depraved. This *"free gift is not like the transgression."* In fact, the *"free gift"* greatly supersedes the transgression. I once heard the following explanation: "Which would be the greater act, to strike a match and ignite a forest fire, or to extinguish the fire after it was raging out of control?" To extinguish the fire, of course, would be the greater act! Jesus' sacrifice (and subsequent resurrection) provided ample grace for all mankind to be saved (He died for all), yet only those who repent and believe while depraved are recipients of this grace. Thus, *"the free gift is not like the transgression"* (Romans 5:15).

We must be careful with the word *"many"* in the phrase, *"For if by the transgression of the one the many died"* (Romans 5:15). *"Many"* in this case means *"all."* This truth was verified in Romans 5:12, for *"all"* died as a result of their genes being in Adam's gene pool when Adam sinned. We must also properly view the word *"many"* in the phrase, *"much more did the grace of God and the gift by the grace of the one Man, Jesus Christ, abound to the many."* The *"many"* in this case means *"all"* as well, verified by Titus 2:11:

> *For the grace of God has appeared, bringing salvation to*
> *all men,* (Titus 2:11)

Jesus' perfect offering brought *"salvation to all men"* (Titus 2:11) in that it provided all that was needed for *"all"* to be saved. Yet, only those who repent and believe while depraved will receive this salvation offered so graciously through the Son. This truth ties in perfectly with Romans 5:16:

> *And the gift is not like that which came through the one*
> *who sinned; for on the one hand the judgment arose from*
> *one transgression resulting in condemnation, but on the*
> *other hand the free gift arose from many transgressions*
> *resulting in justification.* (Romans 5:16)

Again we see that Adam's *"one transgression"* brought *"condemnation"* upon all men. However, Jesus' *"free gift arose from many transgressions resulting in justification"* for the depraved who repent and believe—Jesus having died for all mankind. In other words, the result of Adam's *"transgression"* was *"condemnation."*   *"Many transgressions,"* on the other hand, brought the *"free gift"* of grace into operation for all mankind—the outcome of which is justification (acquittal) for all who accept Christ as Savior.   Those who reject Christ's provision are condemned. Romans 5:17 continues this same theme:

> *For if by the transgression of the one, death reigned*
> *through the one, much more those who receive the*
> *abundance of grace and of the gift of righteousness will*
> *reign in life through the One, Jesus Christ.* (Romans
> 5:17)

Certainly, *"death reigned through the one"* (Adam), but *"those who receive the abundance of grace and of the gift of righteousness will reign in life through the One, Jesus Christ"* (Romans 5:17). What incredible news! We can actually *"reign in life"* through yielding to Christ's indwelling presence (Galatians 2:20; Colossians 1:27), which means that we can live above anything that comes our way. Thus, once we exercised personal repentance and faith while depraved, God not only made us new, but introduced us to the most amazing adventure imaginable—an adventure lived by the life of Another, the life of Christ!

The believer can "reign in life" through yielding to Christ's indwelling presence.

In Romans 5:18, Paul again contrasts the results of Adam's disobedience with the fruit of Christ's obedience:

> *So then as through one transgression there resulted*
> *condemnation to all men, even so through one act of*
> *righteousness there resulted justification of life to all men.*
> (Romans 5:18—emphasis added)

Since our genes were in Adam's gene pool when he sinned, we were born in a condition that gave God no alternative but to condemn us. We were born with a dead spirit, a spirit separated from God. Our soul was separated from God as well. This separated spirit and soul (commonly called the Adamic nature, old man, old self, dead spirit, or sin nature—reference Circle Diagrams 3 and 9) made us *"children of wrath"* before the Father so long as we rejected His provision through Christ (Ephesians 2:3).

The last phrase of Romans 5:18 can be misleading if viewed only at surface level. This passage does <u>not</u> teach that *"through one act of righteousness"* (referring to the cross of Christ) *"all"* descendants of Adam are saved (1Corinthians 6:9-10 and 2Thessalonians 1:1-10 refute the error known as "universalism," or universal salvation, for all lost mankind will be condemned). Rather, Paul is communicating that through the cross *"justification of life"* (salvation) was made available *"to all men"*—to every descendant of Adam. God requires *"repentance"* (2Timothy 2:25; Acts 11:18) and *"faith"* (Acts 16:31; Acts 26:18; Romans 10:9-10) from the depraved prior to His granting new *"life."* Hence, all are not saved, but *"all"* are offered the opportunity to repent and believe. Thus, only some of the *"all"* who are given opportunity to believe do so. *"All"* must be interpreted in its context or error follows.

The same principle applies in Romans 5:19 with the word *"many"*:

> *For as through the one man's disobedience the <u>many</u>*
> *were made sinners, even so through the obedience of the*
> *One the <u>many</u> will be made righteous.* (Romans 5:19)

"Many" means "all" in the first phrase of the verse, as verified by Romans 5:12—for all persons *"were made sinners"* through Adam's misdeed. Yet *"many"* in the last phrase of the verse means "some," not all—for only some of the entirety of mankind are *"made righteous"* by God (the "some" being those who exercise repentance and faith while depraved). Thus, Paul applies two different meanings to *"many"*—as he does in other sections of Scripture. For instance, he records in 1Corinthians 12:12:

> *For even as the body is one and yet has <u>many</u> members,*
> *and <u>all</u> the members of the body, though they are <u>many</u>,*
> *are one body, so also is Christ.* (1Corinthians 12:12)

In this passage, *"many"* in both cases is equivalent to "all." The same principle applies in 1Corinthians 12:14 and 20, where *"many"* also means "all":

> *For the body is not one member, but many.* (1Corinthians 12:14)

> *But now there are many members, but one body.* (1Corinthians 12:20)

Yet, a few verses earlier, Paul uses *"many"* to mean "some."

> *For this reason many among you are weak and sick, and a number sleep.* (1Corinthians 11:30)

Context, at all times, is absolutely essential!
In Romans 5:20, Paul again states the purpose of the Law:

> *And the Law came in that the transgression might increase; but where sin increased, grace abounded all the more,* (Romans 5:20)

The *"Law"* was given *"that the transgression might increase."* The Law was given to be broken; its purpose is to actually make man sin to a greater degree. It was given so man could recognize his sinful state, repent, and receive Jesus as Savior. However, when the *"transgression"* increased, God's *"grace"* increased as well! Consequently, when man's sin increased, God's grace increased accordingly, giving man ample time to repent and come to Christ should he so desire. As a result, Paul records:

> *that, as sin reigned in death, even so grace might reign through righteousness to eternal life through Jesus Christ our Lord.* (Romans 5:21)

Yes, *"sin reigned in death,"* but *"grace"* would *"reign through righteousness to eternal life through Jesus Christ our Lord"* (Romans 5:21). *"Eternal life"* (v.21) is God's kind of life, having no beginning or end—*"life"* that every New Testament believer receives when placed in Christ.

Romans 6:1-6 (Part 1)

The Eradication of the Old Self

Man consists of three parts: *"spirit…soul, and body"* (1 Thessalonians 5:23). The soul consists of three parts: mind, emotions, and will. We will study the soul in more detail later. Review Circle Diagram 1 located in the Reference Section.

Circle Diagrams 2 and 3 portray visually what occurred in Adam when Adam sinned. Adam's sin resulted in spiritual death (spiritual separation from God) and, thus, a change of nature. This nature is referred to in the Scriptures (depending on the version) and by Christians in several ways: Adamic nature, dead spirit, old self, sin nature, sinful nature, and old man. Subsequent to Adam's sin, his acts of sin were natural. Because we are descendants of Adam, we are born in this same condition— *"dead"* to God (Ephesians 2:1), or separated from God, as well as possessors of a nature that enjoys sin.

Not only did Adam's spirit die (being separated from God, who *"is Spirit"*—John 4:24), but also the power of sin (Satan's messenger, representative, or agent) moved into Adam's spirit, soul, and body (note Circle Diagram 2). Adam's mind, being part of his soul, was then inundated with lies from this power.

However, the news is not all bad. Man can be freed from the Adamic nature and united with the life of God through Christ. Circle Diagram 4 shows that when we exercised repentance and faith while depraved, God *"crucified"*

God did not clean up our "old self"; He "crucified" it — eradicated it — did away with it forever.

(Romans 6:6) *"our old self"* (Romans 6:6), who we used to be, and created the new self (2Corinthians 5:17), who we are now. This transformation resulted from Jesus taking up residence in our spirit (Colossians 1:27 and Colossians 3:4), along with the Holy Spirit (John 3:5-6; Romans 8:16), which allowed us to be made alive to God. All of these changes took place at the point of justification (salvation).

God did not clean up our *"old self"; He "crucified"* it (Romans 6:6), eradicated it, did away with it forever. He then created the new self (the new man), which is a holy and perfect being, totally accepted in His eyes. For a review of information regarding the new self (the new man) refer to the notes on Romans 5:1. Statements regarding justification apply to the spirit and soul of the New Testament believer. Your spirit and soul define who you are. Thus, the new man is both soul and spirit (Circle Diagrams 4 and 9).

Hebrews 10:14 is one of the most profound statements included in the Scriptures:

> *because by one sacrifice he has made perfect forever*
> *those who are being made holy.* (Hebrews 10:14 NIV)

Paul's message in Romans 6 is invaluable. God makes our spirit and soul *"perfect"* at the point of justification, even though our behavior is *"being made holy"* on an ongoing basis.

What we do is not who we are, even though who we are has a tremendous impact on what we do.

What we do is not who we are, even though who we are has a tremendous impact on what we do.

We must grasp the change that took place when our *"old self"* (Adamic nature) was eradicated and our new man (new self) was created. The following example, ridiculous as it may seem, has served as a wonderful tool through which to communicate this life changing truth.

If you took a hog (pig), removed its nature and replaced it with the nature of a cat, the resulting creature would use a litter pan. It would have the physical appearance of a hog, but would possess the nature of a cat. So, what would you call the resulting creature? Would you call it a hog or a cat? You would call it a cat, because the nature of a creature, not the way it looks on the outside, makes it what it is. If the resulting creature, the cat, fell into a mud hole, it would lick itself clean because it would hate mud! Cats hate mud; hogs love mud. The same is

If you took a hog (pig), removed its nature and replaced it with the nature of a cat, the resulting creature would use a litter pan.

true of New Testament believers. God, first of all, removed our old nature *("old self,"* sinful nature, Adamic nature), because our old nature was who we used to be. He then replaced it with our new nature (the new man, or new self), who we are now. We hate sin, but will, on occasion, commit acts of sin. However, when we do so, we *"...grieve the Holy Spirit of God..."* (Ephesians 4:30), which results in a desire to confess and repent. The bottom line is that we are no longer capable of enjoying sin.

Some people view the old self (Adamic nature) as wounded, yet alive, in the New Testament believer. In fact, they view the old self (Adamic nature) as eradicated not when we believe, but when we experience physical death. Within theological circles this mindset is known as Positional Truth, a subject addressed briefly in the lesson associated with Romans 5:1. Positional Truth is contradictory as the following example illustrates.

Should the old self (Adamic nature) dwell in us, we would possess two natures, making us part evil and part righteous—the old self being evil, the new self being righteous. Thus, we would be both cat and hog, a "cahog." Being part evil and part righteous would present an impossible situation for the New Testament believer. Should we sin (fall in a mud hole), the hog would be in bliss while the cat would be overcome with grief. On the other hand, should we walk in righteousness (avoid the mud hole), the cat would be in bliss while the hog would be totally demoralized. If we, as New Testament believers, possessed two natures, we could never experience

If we, as New Testament believers, possessed two natures, we could never experience God's peace. The power of sin is not a demon, but an organized power that has Satan as its master.

God's peace. Either the cat or the hog would be out of sorts no matter what choice was made, leaving our souls in a state of constant disarray! Either the *"old self"* (Romans 6:6) was eradicated when we were born again or we have no hope of living in God's *"rest"* (Hebrews 4:9) and *"peace"* (Galatians 5:22).

The necessity of the *"old self"* (Romans 6:6) being eradicated in the New Testament believer will be validated even more when Romans 7:1-

4 is addressed later in this commentary, but let's take a moment to observe how the Old Testament verifies this same truth.

Subsequent to Israel sinning with the golden calf in Exodus 32, Moses desired that God's presence dwell among the Hebrew people:

> *Then Moses said to the LORD, "See, Thou dost say to me, 'Bring up this people!' But Thou Thyself hast not let me know whom Thou wilt send with me. Moreover, Thou hast said, 'I have known you by name, and you have also found favor in My sight.' "Now therefore, I pray Thee, if I have found favor in Thy sight, let me know Thy ways, that I may know Thee, so that I may find favor in Thy sight. Consider too, that this nation is Thy people." And He said, "My presence shall go with **you**, and I will give you rest." Then he said to Him, "If Thy presence does not go with **us**, do not lead us up from here. For how then can it be known that I have found favor in Thy sight, I and Thy people? Is it not by Thy going with **us**, so that we, I and Thy people, may be distinguished from all the other people who are upon the face of the earth?"*
> *And the LORD said to Moses, "I will also do this thing of which you have spoken; for you have found favor in My sight, and I have known you by name." Then Moses said, "I pray Thee, show me Thy glory!" And He said, "I Myself will make all My goodness pass before you, and will proclaim the name of the LORD before you; and I will be gracious to whom I will be gracious, and will show compassion on whom I will show compassion." But He said, "You cannot see My face, for no man can see Me and live!" Then the LORD said, "Behold, there is a place by Me, and you shall stand there on the rock; and it will come about, while My glory is passing by, that I will put you in the cleft of the rock and cover you with My hand until I have passed by. Then I will take My hand away and you shall see My back, but My face shall not be seen."*
> (Exodus 33:12-23)

Moses' desire was that God dwell among the Jewish people (note

Moses' use of *"us"* in verses 15 and 16). However, God preferred that
His presence dwell with Moses (note Jehovah's use of *"you"* in verse
14, pointing to Moses alone). What prompted God's response is the key
to properly interpreting Romans 9:15 (one of the most debated verses in
the New Testament), where Paul quotes God's response to Moses in
Exodus 33:19:

> *For He says to Moses, "I WILL HAVE MERCY ON WHOM I*
> *HAVE MERCY, AND I WILL HAVE COMPASSION ON WHOM I HAVE*
> *COMPASSION."* (Romans 9:15)

Had God dwelt among the people after their sin with the golden calf in
Exodus 32, He would have consumed them:

> *For the LORD had said to Moses, "Say to the sons of*
> *Israel, 'You are an obstinate people; should I go up in*
> *your midst for one moment, I would destroy you. Now*
> *therefore, put off your ornaments from you, that I may*
> *know what I will do with you.'"* (Exodus 33:5)

Even after seeing God's glory in Exodus 34:1-7, Moses remained
committed to God dwelling in the midst of the nation. He uses *"our"* in
Exodus 34:9.

> *And he said, "If now I have found favor in Thy sight, O*
> *Lord, I pray, let the Lord go along in **our** midst, even*
> *though the people are so obstinate; and do Thou pardon*
> *our iniquity and our sin, and take us as Thine own*
> *possession."* (Exodus 34:9—emphasis added)

God's *"mercy"* (Romans 9:15) caused Him to refuse Moses' request.
Had God lived among His people, as Moses desired, He would have
destroyed the nation (Exodus 33:5). Instead, He permitted His presence
to enter the Israelite camp through His representative Moses:

> *And it came about when Moses was coming down from*
> *Mount Sinai (and the two tablets of the testimony were in*
> *Moses' hand as he was coming down from the mountain),*

that Moses did not know that the skin of his face shone because of his speaking with Him. So when Aaron and all the sons of Israel saw Moses, behold, the skin of his face shone, and they were afraid to come near him. Then Moses called to them, and Aaron and all the rulers in the congregation returned to him; and Moses spoke to them. And afterward all the sons of Israel came near, and he commanded them to do everything that the LORD had spoken to him on Mount Sinai. When Moses had finished speaking with them, he put a veil over his face. But whenever Moses went in before the LORD to speak with Him, he would take off the veil until he came out; and whenever he came out and spoke to the sons of Israel what he had been commanded, the sons of Israel would see the face of Moses, that the skin of Moses' face shone. So Moses would replace the veil over his face until he went in to speak with Him. (Exodus 34:29-35)

Paul speaks of this account in 2Corinthians 3:5-18:

Not that we are adequate in ourselves to consider anything as coming from ourselves, but our adequacy is from God, who also made us adequate as servants of a new covenant, not of the letter, but of the Spirit; for the letter kills, but the Spirit gives life. But if the ministry of death, in letters engraved on stones, came with glory, so that the sons of Israel could not look intently at the face of Moses because of the glory of his face, fading as it was, how shall the ministry of the Spirit fail to be even more with glory? For if the ministry of condemnation has glory, much more does the ministry of righteousness abound in glory. For indeed what had glory, in this case has no glory on account of the glory that surpasses it. For if that which fades away was with glory, much more that which remains is in glory.

Having therefore such a hope, we use great boldness in our speech, and are not as Moses, who used to put a veil over his face that the sons of Israel might not look intently

> *at the end of what was fading away. But their minds were hardened; for until this very day at the reading of the old covenant the same veil remains unlifted, because it is removed in Christ. But to this day whenever Moses is read, a veil lies over their heart; but whenever a man turns to the Lord, the veil is taken away. Now the Lord is the Spirit; and where the Spirit of the Lord is, there is liberty. But we all, with unveiled face beholding as in a mirror the glory of the Lord, are being transformed into the same image from glory to glory, just as from the Lord, the Spirit.* (2 Corinthians 3:5-18)

What a wonderful demonstration of God's *"compassion"* (Romans 9:15), for He spared Israel by refusing Moses' request. In other words, God displayed *"mercy"* and *"compassion"* (Romans 9:15) by exhibiting His glory through *"Moses' face"* (Exodus 34:29-35) rather than personally dwelling in the *"midst"* of the people (Exodus 33:5). By doing so, He confirmed His words of Exodus 33:19, *"I will be gracious to whom I will be gracious, and will show compassion on whom I will show compassion."* Yes, He was very *"gracious"* and compassionate, for had His presence dwelt among the people in the manner that Moses requested, the entire nation would have been consumed (Exodus 33:5)!

Viewing Romans 9:15 in context (by applying it to the events in Exodus 32-34), we find that it has nothing to do with God choosing (electing) Moses, Israel, or anyone else to salvation from eternity past (as some believe), for no one is elected and predestined to salvation prior to physical birth. In fact, no one is elected or predestined to salvation period. Rather, believers are elected and predestined to blessings once they repent and believe while depraved and experience God's salvation (a subject covered extensively in Our *God's Heart* series). Therefore, Romans 9:15 pertains to God showing *"mercy"* and *"compassion"* toward His chosen, sinful people (Israel) by not personally dwelling among them and, in turn, consuming them, after their sin with the golden calf. Hence, God will not take up permanent residence inside an unholy environment.

This truth relates extremely well to the Old Testament tabernacle along with our present study of Romans 5.

Moses was instructed to build a tabernacle according to God's specifications:

> *And let them construct a sanctuary for Me, that I may dwell among them. According to all that I am going to show you, as the pattern of the tabernacle and the pattern of all its furniture, just so you shall construct it.* (Exodus 25:8-9)

The tabernacle consisted of three compartments: (1) Outer Court (2) Holy Place (3) Holy of Holies. God dwelt *"between the two cherubim"* situated *"above the mercy seat"* in *"the holy of holies"*:

> *And you shall make a mercy seat of pure gold, two and a half cubits long and one and a half cubits wide. And you shall make two cherubim of gold, make them of hammered work at the two ends of the mercy seat. And make one cherub at one end and one cherub at the other end; you shall make the cherubim of one piece with the mercy seat at its two ends. And the cherubim shall have their wings spread upward, covering the mercy seat with their wings and facing one another; the faces of the cherubim are to be turned toward the mercy seat. And you shall put the mercy seat on top of the ark, and in the ark you shall put the testimony which I shall give to you. And there I will meet with you; and from above the mercy seat, from between the two cherubim which are upon the ark of the testimony, I will speak to you about all that I will give you in commandment for the sons of Israel.* (Exodus 25:17-22)

> *And you shall put the mercy seat on the ark of the testimony in the holy of holies.* (Exodus 26:34)

Scripture refers to the most central portion of the tabernacle as *"the holy of holies"* due to God's holy presence residing there. God's essence will not inhabit anything that is not perfectly sanctified (holy). Thus, His presence entered the tabernacle in Exodus 40:33-38, for Moses had built the tabernacle according to God's specifications—perfect in every way:

*And he erected the court all around the tabernacle and
the altar, and hung up the veil for the gateway of the
court. Thus Moses finished the work. Then the cloud
covered the tent of meeting, and the glory of the LORD
filled the tabernacle. And Moses was not able to enter the
tent of meeting because the cloud had settled on it, and
the glory of the LORD filled the tabernacle. And
throughout all their journeys whenever the cloud was
taken up from over the tabernacle, the sons of Israel
would set out; but if the cloud was not taken up, then they
did not set out until the day when it was taken up. For
throughout all their journeys, the cloud of the LORD was
on the tabernacle by day, and there was fire in it by night,
in the sight of all the house of Israel.* (Exodus 40:34-38)

Exodus 32-34 substantiates that God's presence will not inhabit an unholy environment.

This truth doesn't contradict the fact that God's Spirit temporarily lived in (and empowered) certain men <u>for ministry</u> during Old Testament times, men who were only declared righteous prior to the cross but made righteous later through the cross (Old Testament believers were saved on credit, not being made righteous until Jesus died). Bezalel, Joshua, and Ezekiel were men whom God's Spirit entered prior to Jesus' crucifixion. He (the Spirit) most definitely did not enter to bring new life (spiritual regeneration):

*And He has filled him [Bezalel] with the Spirit of God, in
wisdom, in understanding and in knowledge and in all
craftsmanship;* (Exodus 35:31)

*So the LORD said to Moses, "Take Joshua the son of Nun,
a man in whom is the Spirit, and lay your hand on him;*
(Numbers 27:18)

*Now Joshua the son of Nun was filled with the spirit of
wisdom, for Moses had laid his hands on him; and the
sons of Israel listened to him and did as the LORD had
commanded Moses.* (Deuteronomy 34:9)

> *And as He spoke to me* [Ezekiel] *the Spirit entered me and set me on my feet; and I heard Him speaking to me.* (Ezekiel 2:2)

> *The Spirit then entered me* [Ezekiel] *and made me stand on my feet, and He spoke with me and said to me, "Go, shut yourself up in your house.* (Ezekiel 3:24)

This <u>temporary</u> indwelling of the Spirit (for ministry) was rare, for in almost every case in Old Testament Scripture God's Spirit was <u>upon</u> rather than within those fortunate enough to experience this special empowering.

> *Then I will come down and speak with you there, and I will take of the Spirit who is upon you, and will put Him <u>upon</u> them; and they shall bear the burden of the people with you, so that you shall not bear it all alone.* (Numbers 11:17)

> *But Moses said to him, "Are you jealous for my sake? Would that all the* LORD'S *people were prophets, that the* LORD *would put His Spirit <u>upon</u> them!"* (Numbers 11:29)

> *So the Spirit of the* LORD *came <u>upon</u> Gideon; and he blew a trumpet, and the Abiezrites were called together to follow him.* (Judges 6:34)

> *Now the Spirit of the* LORD *came <u>upon</u> Jephthah, so that he passed through Gilead and Manasseh; then he passed through Mizpah of Gilead, and from Mizpah of Gilead he went on to the sons of Ammon.* (Judges 11:29)

> *When they came to the hill there, behold, a group of prophets met him; and the Spirit of God came <u>upon</u> him mightily, so that he prophesied among them.* (1Samuel 10:10)

> *Now it came about when they had crossed over, that*
> *Elijah said to Elisha, "Ask what I shall do for you before*
> *I am taken from you." And Elisha said, "Please, let a*
> *double portion of your spirit be <u>upon</u> me."* (2Kings 2:9)

> *Now the Spirit of God came <u>on</u> Azariah the son of Oded,*
> (2Chronicles 15:1)

> *Then the Spirit of the LORD fell <u>upon</u> me, and He said to*
> *me, "Say, 'Thus says the LORD, "So you think, house of*
> *Israel, for I know your thoughts.* (Ezekiel 11:5)

God's Spirit is also mentioned as resting <u>upon</u> individuals in Numbers 11:25-26, Judges 3:10, 14:6, 19, 15:14, 1Samuel 10:6, 11:6, 16:13, 19:20, 1Chronicles 12:18, 2Chronicles 24:20.

Unlike Old Testament times, the Spirit of God does not come <u>upon</u> a New Testament believer, nor does it temporarily live in a New Testament believer. He takes up residence (dwells) in a New Testament believer (Romans 8:9; 1Corinthians 6:19)—along with the Father and Son (John 14:23). This indwelling of God brings new life (John 6:63), a total transformation of our person (our souls and spirits)—an indwelling that remains eternally. This conveyance of the presence of the Triune God into the New Testament believer's spirit is radically different from the temporary filling (entering) of the Spirit in a few Old Testament believers—who were not made righteous until the cross. Therefore, just as God temporarily entered the camp on Moses' face (Exodus 34:29-35; 2Corinthians 3:7-18), much less of an entrance than Moses had originally requested, God's Spirit (on extremely rare occasions) temporarily entered certain Old Testament believers to empower them for service. This arrangement was permissible but entirely different from God's presence permanently indwelling New Testament believers who have been made holy and blameless.

What we have gleaned ties in perfectly with Jesus' suffering on the cross; at Gethsemane Jesus *"offered up both prayers and supplications"* to the Father *"with loud crying and tears"* (Hebrews 5:7; Matthew 26:36-44). (To supplicate is to cry for mercy or favor in the midst of trying circumstances.) He asked the Father *"to save Him from death"* (Hebrews 5:7), but the words *"from death"* actually mean *"out of death."* Jesus was not seeking deliverance from the physical pain of the cross, for the cross was the main purpose of His coming (John 12:27). Evidently, He was asking the Father to raise Him from both the physical and spiritual deaths He would endure on the cross. I believe too that spiritual separation from the Father—spiritual death—was Christ's greatest concern. From eternity past He and His Father had lived in perpetual, unbroken, uninterrupted fellowship. For Jesus to even think of being separated from Him for one moment must have produced agony beyond anything we can imagine. Compared to this suffering, the pain involved in Jesus' physical death must have seemed insignificant.

Jesus died spiritually before He died physically. Matthew 27:45-46 tells that *"darkness fell upon all the land"* from *"the sixth hour"* (noon) *"until the ninth hour"* (3 p.m.), at which time Jesus said, *"My God, My God, why hast Thou forsaken Me?"* This order of events confirms that from noon until 3 p.m., God the Father turned His back on the Son.

The Father had no alternative since His holiness prohibits Him from communing with sin (during this time the sin of all mankind was placed on Christ—2Corinthians 5:21; 1John 2:2). In fact, for the first (and last) time the Father and Son broke fellowship. This experience had to be excruciating for Jesus (and the Father as well), for prior to the cross Jesus spoke of the Father's presence that resided within Him (John 10:38; 14:10-11; and 17:21). Thus, Jesus died spiritually, for *"death"* in Scripture can mean separation as well as extinction—depending on the context. But the good news is that Jesus was resurrected spiritually even before He died physically, as verified by Luke 23:44-46. Immediately after *"the ninth hour"* (3 p.m.), after His *"spirit"* had been resurrected (Luke 23:44-46), Jesus said, *"Father, into Thy hands I commit My spirit"* (v.46). He then died physically: *"And having said this, He breathed His last"* (v.46). Three days later, *"on the first day of the week"* (Luke 24:1-5), Jesus' bodily resurrection occurred.

To comprehend the significance of the bodily resurrection of Christ, read 1Corinthians 15:12-17. His bodily resurrection verified that His spiritual resurrection had previously occurred, and that He is the holy Son of God. The fact that the Father and Spirit resided within Jesus (John 10:38; 14:10-11; and 17:21) during His First Coming validates that He was born void of a sin nature and is, therefore, the Father's Son—not the offspring of Joseph, Mary's husband.

Let's take this truth relating to Jehovah's holiness (that He will never eternally inhabit an unrighteous environment) and apply it to our previous cat and hog illustration. God would never take up eternal residence inside a "cahog" (old man plus new man), for the hog (old man) is unholy. However, because the hog (old man) has been eradicated and replaced with the new man (who is *"holy and blameless"*—Ephesians 1:4), Paul is free to teach the *"mystery"* that so amazingly empowered him as he took the gospel to the Gentiles:

> *to whom God willed to make known what is the riches of*
> *the glory of this mystery among the Gentiles, which is*
> *Christ in you, the hope of glory.* (Colossians 1:27)

Yes, Jesus, Who is *"spirit"* (John 4:24), and *"Holy"* (John 6:69), came to eternally dwell in your spirit—which is now holy due to your having accepted Him as Savior. Should the unholy old man (Adamic nature) remain within you in any shape, form, or fashion, such an arrangement would be impossible. Jesus (John 14:18-20; Galatians 2:20), the Father (John 14:23), and the Holy Spirit (John 14:17) would never move into your spirit should it be only partially righteous. Note: Your soul was also made righteous, the soul being part of the new man— reference Circle Diagram 9. You have received *"the mind of Christ"* (1Corinthians 2:16), the mind being part of the soul. However, God the Father, Son, and Spirit do not inhabit your soul, but your spirit (Romans 8:16).

The power of sin, dwelling in the spirit, soul, and body of unbelievers, bombards their minds with lies on an ongoing basis (Circle Diagrams 2 and 3). However, the power of sin is only able to send messages to the mind of a New Testament believer through the avenue of the body, using the believer's brain, a piece of flesh, as the conduit (Circle Diagram 4). Once you are born again (justified), your body is the only avenue through which the power of sin can send a message to your mind.

Don't misunderstand; the body is not evil. It is, however, the avenue through which the power of sin operates as it attempts to influence your mind. Sin desires to influence your mind because your mind influences your will, which controls your behavior. Thus, if sin can disrupt your thought processes it can disrupt the manner in which you conduct your life.

Two truths need to be emphasized before continuing: (1) Sin (the power of sin) cannot send messages to your mind through the avenue of the spirit, for the power of sin does not inhabit your new spirit since Christ dwells there (Colossians 3:4; 1John 4:4). (2) The power of sin cannot enter your soul for the purpose of placing thoughts in your mind, the mind being part of the soul (refer to the circle diagrams). Therefore, when the power of sin sends a message to your mind, it is the thought, and not sin itself (the power of sin), that enters. In other words, the power of sin cannot infiltrate the mind of a New Testament believer— the New Testament believer (the new man) being both soul and spirit (Reference Circle Diagram 9).

What we are discussing here will serve you well the remainder of your days. If you are having difficulty following, don't be discouraged. We will revisit these subjects later. Become very familiar Circle Diagrams 1-4, as they will be useful in your everyday life, especially when confronted with spiritual warfare. We are equipping ourselves for battle.

I highly recommend Dr. Bill Gillham's work, *Lifetime Guarantee* as an additional resource. It covers several of the truths addressed in Romans 5-8 and has been a source of encouragement to many followers of Christ.

Romans 6:1-6 (Part 2)

Verses 1-6 of Romans 6 are some of the most fascinating verses in this entire epistle because they display a side of the cross that can revolutionize every aspect of our walk with Christ.

Paul's Gospel Challenged

Paul's enemies had accused him of proclaiming a gospel that granted license (Romans 6:1):

> *What shall we say then? Are we to continue in sin that*
> *grace might increase?* (Romans 6:1)

License promotes the falsehood that believers can live in habitual sin, enjoy sin, and continue to receive God's blessings. Paul's enemies probably said, "Paul, if what you teach regarding justification is true, a person can accept Christ, wallow in sin, enjoy every second of it, and rest assured that God is pleased with it all." We know that such thinking is contrary to Paul's teaching, for how can a cat, under

To know Christ and enjoy a lifestyle of habitual sin is impossible.

any circumstance, enjoy mud. In Romans 6:2, Paul makes the strongest statement possible when he says, *"May it never be."* He then goes on to say, *"How shall we who died to sin still live in it?"* In other words, to know Christ and enjoy a lifestyle of habitual sin is impossible. Yes, we will sin at times. But repentance and confession will soon follow. Paul's teaching left no room for half-hearted commitments.

The Awesomeness of Scriptural Baptism

Romans 6:3 is one of the most misunderstood verses in all of Romans.

211

"Or do you not know that all of us who have been baptized into Christ Jesus have been baptized into His death?" (Romans 6:3)

"Baptized," does not always refer to water baptism. In fact, when we see the word *"baptized,"* or baptism, water should not automatically come to mind. For example, *"baptism"* in Luke 12:50 refers to Jesus' crucifixion, not to His water baptism of Luke 3:21-22. Thus, *"baptized"* can have different meanings, depending on the context.

According to 1Corinthians 12:13, water is not the means through which New Testament believers are *"baptized into Christ."*

"by one Spirit we were all baptized into one body." (1Corinthians 12:13)

The *"body"* mentioned here is Christ's *"body,"* which proves that the phrase, *"baptized into Christ Jesus"* (Romans 6:3), refers to *"Spirit"* baptism, a baptism that occurs in association with justification—a baptism which places a repentant (depraved) sinner seeking salvation *"into Christ"* so he can be made new. Water can't accomplish such a feat!

The purpose of water baptism is to say to the world that we have died with Christ, that we have been buried with Christ, and that we have been raised with Christ to new life—all through the avenue of the Spirit. Water baptism is a symbolic act, a picture of what the Spirit has

Water baptism is a symbolic act, a picture of what the Spirit has already done in the realm of the invisible. Thus, water baptism does not save.

already accomplished in the realm of the invisible. Thus, water baptism does not save. God saves through placing us in Christ through the avenue of His Spirit subsequent to our repenting and believing while depraved.

To *"...have been baptized into His death"* (Romans 6:3) means to be identified with His death. This truth is displayed vividly in 1Corinthians 10:2:

> *And all were baptized into Moses in the cloud and in the sea;* (1Corinthians 10:2)

The Israelites, while exiting Egypt, were *"baptized into Moses"*—meaning that they were identified with Moses their leader. The word *"baptized"* in this case means identification rather than the act of water baptism.

The following diagram displays the answer to how we could *"have been baptized into His death"* (Romans 6:3)—identified with *"His death"*?

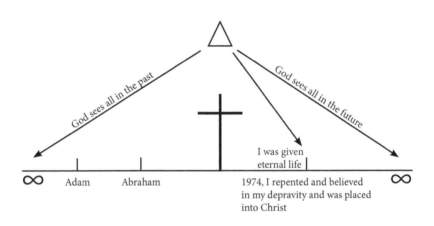

When we were *"baptized"* into Christ through the power of the Holy Spirit (1Corinthians 12:13), we simultaneously received eternal life which has no beginning and no end. When the Holy Spirit *"baptized"* us into Christ and we received eternal life, the Father saw us as having always been in Christ. He will

When the Holy Spirit "baptized" us into Christ and we received eternal life, the Father saw us as having always been in Christ.

213

continue to view us in this manner throughout eternity. Did you comprehend that? When the Holy Spirit *"baptized"* us into Christ and we received eternal life, the Father saw us as having always been in Christ and He will continue to view us in this manner throughout eternity! (As a friend of mine stated recently, God not only gave us a new future, but a new past as well.)

The way God sees us is reality. This new past explains how we could have been in Christ when He was nailed to the cross (Galatians 2:20), when He was buried (Romans 6:4; Colossians 2:12), and when He was resurrected (Ephesians 2:6). This wonderful transformation came about as a result of receiving His kind of life, eternal life, at the point of justification. Remember this truth as we continue.

In Romans 6:4, Paul writes that *"...we have been buried with Him [Christ] through baptism into death...."* The phrase, *"buried with Him through baptism into death,"* simply means that we have been identified with Christ's *"death."* Because we have been placed (baptized) into Christ through the avenue of the Spirit and are perceived by the Father as having always been in Christ, our death, burial, and resurrection with Christ are realities. As a result, we can *"walk in newness of life,"* Christ's resurrected *"life,"* a life lived from God's perspective and by His power:

> *Therefore we have been buried with Him through baptism into death, in order that as Christ was raised from the dead through the glory of the Father, so we too might walk in newness of life.* (Romans 6:4)

This truth ties in perfectly with Romans 5:10 and Romans 5:17:

> *For if while we were enemies, we were reconciled to God through the death of His Son, much more, having been reconciled, we shall be saved by His life.* (Romans 5:10)

> *For if by the transgression of the one, death reigned through the one, much more those who receive the abundance of grace and of the gift of righteousness will reign in life through the One, Jesus Christ.* (Romans 5:17)

To *"be saved by His life"* (Romans 5:10) on a daily basis (from Satan's schemes) means to *"reign in life through the One, Jesus Christ"* (Romans 5:17). Therefore, to *"walk in newness of life"* (Romans 6:4), we must learn to live by the life of Another, Christ's very life, as we face the "circumstances" of our day. Is it not amazing how consistently Paul's teaching ends up at the same place? He realized that imitating Christ through our own self-effort is an act of futility and places the believer under Law. Intimacy with Jesus, on the other hand, results in a desire to yield to His indwelling presence every moment of the day. Truly, *"...the letter kills, but the Spirit gives life"* (2Corinthians 3:6).

Thus, we could have been with Christ when He died (v.3), when He was *"buried"* (v.4), and when He was resurrected (v.4). In fact, Ephesians 2:4-6 states:

> *"God...made us alive together with Christ...and raised us*
> *up with Him, and seated us with Him in the heavenly*
> *places, in Christ Jesus."* (Ephesians 2:4-6)

The tense used in Ephesians 2:4-6 is the past tense. Also, all of these changes occurred as a result of our being placed *"in Christ Jesus."*

Romans 6:5 should now come alive. It states that *"...we have become united with Him [with Christ] in the likeness of His death...."* Paul continues by writing: *"...we shall be also in the likeness of His resurrection."* Yes, at some point in the future we will receive a glorified body. But Paul is also saying that we can live in Christ's resurrected power in the here and now!

The Old Self Crucified

In Romans 6:6, we observe *"that our old self,"* inherited from Adam, *"was crucified with Him* [Christ]":

> *knowing this, that our old self was crucified with Him,*
> *that our body of sin might be done away with, that we*
> *should no longer be slaves to sin;* (Romans 6:6)

215

What a tremendous statement! It means that the person we used to be *"was crucified"*! Also, the verb tenses prove that this act occurred in the past, on the cross, and is thus a completed act. This change could transpire due to the kind of life, eternal life, we received once we were placed in Christ. For this reason, and a host of others, I believe that the *"old self"* was completely eradicated when we received Christ (when we were justified). Refer to Circle Diagram 4.

Some believers perceive the *"old self"* (Romans 6:6) as being <u>declared</u> dead by God yet alive in the New Testament believer. They view God as somehow pretending that the *"old self"* is dead due to their belief that it is alive, yet wounded. They maintain, that the *"old self"* (Romans 6:6) is only <u>positionally</u> dead—that we must deal with it until physical death, at which time it is eradicated. Paul's statement is strong proof that such a situation is impossible. The *"old self"* (Romans 6:6) was eradicated at the point of justification (when we received eternal life), since it died on the cross with Christ.

> *A battle takes place inside every church saint between the new self and the power of sin.*

A battle takes place inside every church saint not between the old self and the new self, but between the new self and the power of sin. Two verses besides Romans 6:6 speak of the death and eradication of the *"old self."* Colossians 3:9 states that *"the old self"* has been *"laid aside"* (eradicated):

> *"Do not lie to one another, since you <u>laid aside the old self</u> with its evil practices."* (Colossians 3:9)

No cause for argument here.

> *"that, in reference to your former manner of life, you <u>lay aside the old self</u>, which is being corrupted in accordance with the lusts of deceit."* (Ephesians 4:22)

The wording of Ephesians 4:22 seems to indicate (on the surface at least) that the old self is still alive in the New Testament believer—that

216

the saint is to *"lay aside the old self"* on a moment-by-moment basis. This error stems from a misunderstanding of the aorist infinitive *"lay aside"* (Greek infinitives are sometimes difficult to translate). However, should Ephesians 4:22 teach that the *"old self"* remains alive (but wounded) after spiritual regeneration/salvation (as is communicated in many Christian circles) it would indeed create a contradiction.

As I sought to reconcile this "apparent" contradiction in Paul's epistle, I discovered that John Murray believed the grammar allowed and the exegesis demanded that the infinitive *"lay aside"* is an infinitive of result. He went on to say that the "past tense" is indicated here. Murray's translation resolves the matter:

> "so that *ye have put off*, according to the former manner of life, the old man."

As a result, Murray interpreted Ephesians 4:21-22 as follows:

> "You were taught in Christ with regard to the fact that your old man <u>was laid aside</u>."[11]

Praise God that our *"old self"* (old man, sinful nature, dead spirit, Adamic nature) was eradicated through the cross and will never be dealt with again! We would face a major dilemma should we be required to continually *"lay aside the old self"* for the *"old self"* to be laid *"aside."* Ephesians 4:23-24 produces an additional quandary:

> *and that you be renewed in the spirit of your mind, and put on the new self, which in the likeness of God has been created in righteousness and holiness of the truth.*
> (Ephesians 4:23-24)

Should New Testament believers be required to *"put on the new self"* on an ongoing basis, we would be lost and without Christ during those times when we failed to lay the *"old self"* aside and put him (the new self) on! During such times, the *"old self"* alone would live in us— making us *"children of wrath"* (Ephesians 2:3). Yet, the Scriptures teach that we became the *"new self"* for all eternity once we were placed in Christ through the power of the Holy Spirit (1Corinthians 12:13; 2Corinthians 5:17; Ephesians 1:13) subsequent to repenting and believing while depraved.   Therefore, we are <u>not</u> required to continually put on the *"new self"* to remain the *"new self."* Should we be required to put off the *"old self,"* yet fail to do so, and at the same time put on the *"new self,"* we would be dual natured (a "cahog"—old self plus new self), a state which Paul classifies as adulterous (Romans 7:1-4—verses studied in much depth shortly).   Scripture validates time and time again that the *"old self"* has been eradicated (crucified and disposed) and that the *"new self,"* being eternal, lives on.

Romans 6:6, Colossians 3:9, and Ephesians 4:22 are in agreement. Paul's words in Galatians 2:20 serve as "the final nail in the coffin," for they place the crucifixion of the old self (old man) in the past, never to be repeated:

> *"I have been crucified with Christ; and it is no longer I*
> *who live, but Christ lives in me; and the life which I now*
> *live in the flesh I live by faith in the Son of God, who*
> *loved me, and delivered Himself up for me.* (Galatians
> 2:20)

The phrase, *"have been crucified,"* is in the perfect tense in the Greek, pointing to past action, completed action, with a resulting state of being. Thus, the old self (sinful nature, old man) was *"crucified with Christ"* and eradicated the moment we repented and believed—never to turn up again.

Some theologians use Galatians 5:24 in an attempt to prove that the old self (sinful nature, old man) is alive, yet wounded in the New Testament believer.   Such a mindset is invalid.   Knowing that Paul contrasts *"the deeds of the flesh"* to *"the fruit of the Spirit"* in Galatians 5:16-23 is necessary to properly interpret Galatians 5:24:

> *Now those who belong to Christ Jesus have crucified the*
> *flesh with its passions and desires.* (Galatians 5:24)

We must understand that Scripture makes a distinction between the *"flesh"* of Galatians 5:24 and the *"old self"* of Romans 6:6. The *"old self"* (Romans 6:6) is who we used to be prior to salvation (justification) and has been *"crucified"* and eradicated (Romans 6:6). The *"flesh"* (Galatians 5:24), on the other hand, is dealt with on an ongoing basis. Romans 8:4 and Romans 8:12-13 teach that the New Testament believer can walk in one of two places— *"according to the flesh"* or *"according to the Spirit"*:

> *in order that the requirement of the Law might be fulfilled in us, who do not walk according to the flesh, but according to the Spirit.* (Romans 8:4)

> *So then, brethren, we are under obligation, not to the flesh, to live according to the flesh — for if you are living according to the flesh, you must die; but if by the Spirit you are putting to death the deeds of the body, you will live.* (Romans 8:12-13)

The *"flesh"* is what we *"walk"* in when we believe the power of sin's lie sent into our minds through the avenue of the habit patterns in the brain—the brain being a piece of *"flesh"* (Circle Diagram 7 addresses this subject and will be studied in depth later.) Thus, to *"walk according to the flesh,"* (Romans 8:4) as a New Testament believer, is to buy the power of sin's lie as the truth. Therefore, the *"flesh"* and the *"old self"* (sinful nature) are not synonymous—something the NIV fails to take into account in Romans 7:17, 8:4-5, 12, and others, where it incorrectly renders *"flesh"* as *"sinful nature."* The NIV commits this mistake because the individuals responsible for translating Romans 7 and 8 erroneously think that believers during the church age possess two natures—the old self (sinful nature) and the new self. This inaccuracy resulted in their perceiving the *"flesh"* and the *"sinful nature"* (the old man, old self) as being equal (the same thing) in the New Testament believer. (This subject is addressed in more depth in the materials associated with Romans 8.)

Take special note of the fact that *"the flesh"* (Galatians 5:24) is crucified by the New Testament believer on an ongoing basis, whereas the crucifixion of the *"old self"* (Romans 6:6) was a single act performed by God through Jesus' death on the cross. Thus, the *"old self"* (Romans 6:6) was eradicated by God and will never be dealt with again. *"The flesh"* (Galatians 5:24), however, is *"crucified"* (Galatians 5:24) daily by New Testament believers as they consider themselves dead to the power of sin's lie and yield to Christ's indwelling presence. Hence, we crucify *"the flesh"* when we consider ourselves dead to the lies the power of sin sends into our minds through the avenue of the habit patterns in the brain (the brain being a piece of *"flesh")* and walk in the truth supplied by God through the Holy Spirit.

Conclusion: Galatians 5:24 teaches that *"the flesh"* (which is not the *"old self"* of Romans 6:6 or sinful nature) is crucified daily (as a lifestyle) by New Testament believers as they consider themselves dead to the power of sin's lies and, in turn, walk in God's truth. Hence, New Testament believers who walk in fellowship with God will find themselves looking back and seeing that they have crucified *"the flesh"* on a decently consistent basis. This crucifixion of *"the flesh"* (Galatians 5:24) continues so long as we live in our earthly bodies. The eradication of the *"old self"* (Romans 6:6), on the other hand, was carried out by the Triune God the moment we met Christ. Hence, the *"old self"* is long gone, never to rear its ugly head again. After all, God *"crucified"* (eradicated) the *"old self"* (through Christ's *"body")* when He saved (justified) us (Romans 6:6; Romans 7:4; Galatians 2:20). This truth can provide incredible encouragement during times of intense warfare. (If our discussion of the *"flesh"* seems confusing at this juncture, know that Romans 8 will help.)
Romans 6:6 states:

> *...that our body of sin might* be *done away with...*
> (Romans 6:6)

Vine's Expository Dictionary of New Testament Words defines *"body of sin"* as:

> "a governing principle or power...an organized power,
> acting through the members of the body."[12]

Coupling this input with the fact that *"done away with"* actually means "made powerless," or "to be rendered idle," we can conclude that the *"body of sin"* (power of sin) has been "made powerless," or "rendered idle," due to the *"old self"* having been eradicated. How liberating!   To yield to the power of sin's influence is, therefore, unnatural. Yes, we will commit acts of sin (when we deem the power of sin's lie to be truth) so long as we live in earthly bodies, but every act of disobedience will be an unnatural event. Thus, the last phrase of Romans 6:6 states, *"...that we should no longer be slaves to sin."* Isn't Romans a tremendous book!

Romans 6:7

Forgiveness Complete

I can hardly wait to cover this passage. If it affects your life the way it has mine, you are in for a treat!

The great news is that we have been released from the power of sin through our death with Christ on the cross:

> *for he who has died is freed from sin.* (Romans 6:7)

The *"old self"* (Adamic nature) has been *"crucified"* (Romans 6:6), and we are free to say "no!" to any thought the power of sin sends into our minds. Paul's message is that no *"crucified"* man can respond to any sort of stimulus. The eradicated *"old self,"* who naturally desired to sin, can no longer respond to the power of sin's lies. The new man, therefore, who naturally desires righteousness, can refuse any thought from the power of sin's arsenal of untruths. The answer to why some New Testament believers continue to sin is provided later, but a short detour is mandatory.

We are no longer enslaved to the <u>power</u> of sin. Our *"old self"* was eradicated on the cross (Romans 6:6-7). But, are we also freed from the <u>penalty</u> of sin? In other words, how many of our acts of sin were forgiven when we were made new in Christ? Were only our past sins forgiven, or were our future sins also forgiven? We need to settle this issue, for a life of victory is unattainable without a thorough knowledge of the depths of God's forgiveness.

The Greek tenses of the verbs and participles contained in Ephesians 4:32, Colossians 2:13, Hebrews 9:26, 10:10, 10:14, and 1John 2:12 (all of which address the subject of forgiveness) are often aorist and perfect. ("Aorist" is a Greek term that in this instance points to past action. "Perfect" points to past action as well.) These tenses tell us that forgiveness had to be dealt with in the past, at one particular point in time—at the cross.

When we accepted Christ we were placed into Christ (1Corinthians 12:13; 2Corinthians 5:17). We received eternal life, and God sees us as having always been in Christ—as having always been holy, perfect, complete, blameless, and forgiven. We are a finished product in the eyes of the Father because of this transformation that occurred at the point of justification.

Forgiveness need not be received on an ongoing basis. Christ would have to be re-crucified each time we sin as New Testament believers if we needed forgiveness more than once. Hebrews 10:10 states:

> *"By this will we have been sanctified through the offering of the body of Jesus Christ once for all."* (Hebrews 10:10)

We are not obligated to seek forgiveness for sins committed <u>after</u> salvation.

Christ's body was offered once, never to be offered again. Thus, all forgiveness is complete when Christ's blood is initially applied to our lives. This total clemency is the meaning of justification; it allows God the Father to make us holy, blameless, <u>and forgiven</u>. We are not obligated to seek forgiveness for sins committed <u>after</u> justification (salvation). In fact, we live in a state of forgiveness.

Some people misunderstand the forgiveness granted to the New Testament believer and incorrectly conclude that New Testament saints no longer sin. They use 1John 3:9 in an attempt to validate their beliefs:

> *Whosoever is born of God doth not commit sin; for his seed remaineth in him: and he cannot sin, because he is born of God.* (1John 3:9 KJV)

The fact that the word *"commit"* is a present, active, indicative verb in the Greek verifies that John is speaking of a lifestyle of habitual sin, unrestrained sin, the frequency of sin experienced by those who are unbelievers. The NASB takes this fact into account and renders the passage as:

> *No one who is born of God practices sin, because His seed abides in him; and he cannot sin, because he is born of God.* (1John 3:9 NASB)

Even the word *"sin"* in the phrase, *"and he cannot sin,"* is a present tense verb, indicating again the habitual sin experienced by the unredeemed.

A great disparity exists between practicing and enjoying sin as a lifestyle (that which occurs with unbelievers) versus being grieved while walking in occasional sin (that which occurs with believers). Again, if you remove the nature of a hog and replace it with the nature of a cat, you have an animal that looks like a hog in appearance but actually hates mud. The animal (the cat), in fact, avoids mud at all costs, although at times makes unwise choices that allow the grimy substance to adhere to its body. These occurrences are loathed by the cat—never enjoyed. Hogs, on the other hand, love, pursue, and bask in them.

Another verse that validates our findings is 1John 1:8:

> *If we say that we have no sin, we are deceiving ourselves,*
> *and the truth is not in us.* (1John 1:8)

Writing to believers, John states that we would deceive ourselves by perceiving New Testament saints as incapable of committing sin. Oh, the value of the full counsel of God's Word!

Another pertinent subject that must be considered is "confession." Even though we are no longer required to ask for forgiveness when we sin, we <u>are</u> required to confess sin once it is committed. Confession means to speak the same thing about sin that God speaks about sin— calling sin what it is before Him. Repentance is a change of attitude that involves both a turning from sin and a turning to God (2Corinthians 7:9-10). Thus, we are required to <u>confess</u> and repent of sins committed after salvation (justification), not to receive forgiveness, but for the restoration of <u>fellowship</u> with the Father. We are eternal beings who have been eternally forgiven. Why would the Lord require us to ask for something we already have? That situation would be totally unreasonable!

The Lord requires us to confess and repent because sin severs our <u>fellowship</u> with God. God created us for the purpose of fellowship. When we sin, the broken fellowship is our problem—not God's. God took care of His side of the problem on the cross. Consequently, He waits (in His mercy and grace) until we repent and confess, at which time fellowship is restored.

Confession can be beneficial in other ways as well. For example, a young couple asked that I hold them accountable prior to marriage. They wanted to remain pure until the wedding day, so they suggested that I ask them (on a weekly basis) if they were abiding by the guidelines they had established for their relationship. I agreed, and the outcome was enormously encouraging. They both said that their relationship grew deeper as a result of their decision, and that their accountability with me was a tremendous motivation to remain pure. That accountability provided incentive because they both realized that compromise would require a face-to-face confession before the man holding them accountable. God knows that the accountability of confession stimulates us to say "no!" to temptation. Thus, God uses confession and repentance for our good—to enhance our desire to walk in holiness.

Conclusion: We are to confess and repent of sins for two reasons: (1) To have fellowship restored with the Father (2) To motivate us to walk away from temptation through yielding to Christ's life within (Romans 5:10).

Some believers maintain that after salvation (justification), we are forgiven for each sin committed when we ask for forgiveness. A verse used to support this position is 1John 1:9, which in actuality reveals nothing regarding <u>when</u> the New Testament believer's sins are forgiven—that is, the sins committed <u>after</u> salvation.

> *If we confess our sins, He is faithful and righteous to forgive us our sins and to cleanse us from all unrighteousness.* (1John 1:9)

The verbs *"forgive"* and *"cleanse"* are in the subjunctive mood, and time is not indicated by this mood. The subjunctive mood indicates <u>kind</u> of action, not <u>time</u> of action; so 1John 1:9 <u>cannot</u> teach that New Testament believers are required to seek <u>forgiveness</u> for sins

If sins had to be forgiven after salvation, church saints who died with unconfessed sin would enter heaven with sins not yet forgiven.

committed subsequent to salvation.   If sins had to be forgiven after salvation, church saints who died with unconfessed sin would enter heaven with sins not yet forgiven. Impossible! The longer I walk with Christ the more I detect hidden areas of immaturity and disobedience—a condition that will remain until physical death.   Thus, the entire forgiveness issue had to be completed at the point of justification. How else could God accept us into His family?

Another verse that <u>seems</u> to indicate that we are to seek forgiveness for sins committed after salvation (justification) is Matthew 6:12. This verse is very familiar because it is included in the Lord's Prayer. Here Jesus said:

> *"And forgive us our debts, as we also have forgiven our debtors."* (Matthew 6:12)

On the surface it seems that the Lord is instructing <u>all believers</u> to ask for forgiveness once sin is committed.   Before jumping to this conclusion, we must consider whether Jesus made this statement before or after the cross. Obviously, He made it prior to His crucifixion— <u>before</u> the forgiveness issue had been settled. In fact, we learned earlier that none of the Old Testament sacrifices took away sin (Hebrews 10:4, 11); they only covered sin by serving as atonement for sin. Scripture must be interpreted in the context in which it is stated, and Matthew 6:12 is no exception. Jesus was addressing individuals who lived prior to the cross, meaning that their forgiveness would occur in the future. Therefore, their seeking forgiveness was proper. Things changed after the cross, for we are privileged to have had all sin removed in the past. Please don't hear me saying that the teachings of Jesus are outdated or irrelevant. I am simply trying to communicate that all Scripture must be interpreted in context, even the teachings of Jesus.

Some theologians perceive Acts 8:9-24 as proving that the New Testament believer is to continue to seek forgiveness for sin.   Their thesis (view) is based on Peter's statement to Simon in Acts 8:22:

> *"Therefore repent of this wickedness of yours, and pray the Lord that if possible, the intention of your heart <u>may be forgiven you</u>.* (Acts 8:22)

Simon *"believed"* and was water *"baptized"* in Acts 8:13—prior to Peter's statement in Acts 8:22. Yet the events of Acts 8:14-24 verify that he was not a born again saint of God (read verses 18-21 and 23-24), but a hypocrite. Thus, Peter's words were stated to an unregenerated soul in need of forgiveness. *"The demons also believe and shudder"* (James 2:19). These verses also verify as well that water baptism does not save, for Simon was water baptized yet remained lost.

To determine <u>when</u> a New Testament believer's sins are forgiven, 1John 2:12 must be considered:

> *I am writing to you, little children, because your sins are forgiven you for His name's sake.* (1John 2:12)

*W*hen Christ's blood was applied to our lives, at the point of justification, forgiveness was thorough and complete.

Here the word *"forgiven"* is in the indicative mood, a mood which <u>can</u> express time. Its perfect tense indicates <u>completed action with a resulting state of being</u>. Ephesians 4:32, Colossians 2:13, Hebrews 9:26, Hebrews 9:28, Hebrews 10:10, Hebrews 10:12, Hebrews 10:14, Jude 24 and other passages also indicate that all sin was dealt with when Jesus died. We can conclude, therefore, that when Christ's blood was applied to our lives, at the point of justification, forgiveness was thorough and complete.

We must remember this magnificent news and renew our minds with this truth on an ongoing basis. The following statements summarize what has been expressed.

1.   When we were lost (depraved), we exercised personal repentance and faith. Then God saved us by eradicating our *"old self"* and, in turn, forgiving our sin.

2.   At the point of salvation (justification), our past, present, and <u>future</u> sins were forgiven. We were also given eternal life and made into eternal beings. As a result, God sees us as having always been in Christ and as having always been forgiven. In fact, we live in a state of

forgiveness!! Justification means to be forgiven and made not guilty for all eternity.

3.   After we are saved (justified), we continue to confess and repent of sin realizing that our sin was forgiven <u>prior</u> to our bringing it before the Father. We must constantly remember that God forgave all past, present, and <u>future</u> sin at the point of justification, subsequent to our exercising personal repentance and faith while depraved.   Confession and repentance after salvation are for the purpose of restoring <u>fellowship</u> with the Father, not for the purpose of receiving forgiveness.

4.   Having become aware of this wonderful truth, we should be less prone to harbor unconfessed sin. In fact, we should be motivated to rush to the Father the instant we disobey, knowing that He will receive us with open arms (Hebrews 4:14-16).   Isn't it

Confession and repentance after salvation are for the purpose of restoring fellowship with the Father, not for the purpose of receiving forgiveness.

freeing to realize that once we are born again we don't confess sin for the purpose of receiving forgiveness, but that confession restores fellowship instead?

Understanding this truth transforms how life is perceived. In fact, our love for Christ becomes the incentive for service (Galatians 5:6)—not duty or law. His heart becomes our treasure, not the temporal which fades away. In fact, our passion to walk in constant fellowship with the Creator will become our motivation for daily living. Only then will the world see Jesus in and through us and, hopefully, desire to know this wonderful, loving, forgiving God Who is our life.

Thank you, Lord, for your indescribable gift!

Romans 6:8-11

Romans 6:8 states that *"...we...died with Christ...":*

> *Now if we have died with Christ, we believe that we shall*
> *also live with Him,* (Romans 6:8)

Paul has made it extremely clear that our old self (Adamic nature, old man, dead spirit, or sin nature) died (was crucified and eradicated) on the cross with Christ—as was explained in our study of Romans 6:1-6. Verse 8 states that *"...we shall also live with Him."* What thoughts run through your mind when you consider living with Jesus? Thinking about our eternal home can assist us immeasurably while facing the trials in the here and now.

Verse 9 is inundated with encouraging news as well:

> *knowing that Christ, having been raised from the dead, is*
> *never to die again; death no longer is master over Him.*
> (Romans 6:9)

Jesus was *"raised from the dead"!* We know that this miraculous event was not a fabrication of the apostle's imagination because Jesus appeared first to a woman. If the Gospel writers were attempting to perpetrate a hoax, they would have avoided such an arrangement because the oral law restricted what women could say in a court of law. Therefore, the fact that Jesus first appeared to a woman (Mark 16:9) makes the resurrection even more believable in that, from the Jewish perspective, the testimony of a woman concerning such matters would have been rejected. Anyone desiring to fabricate a hoax would have had the fake Jesus appearing to a man—never a woman! As it was, Mary's testimony concerning Christ's resurrection was disbelieved by even the disciples (Mark 16:10-11; John 20:18).

Christ's second appearance was to women as well (Matthew 28:9). Thus, Jesus' resurrection was not make-believe.

Paul's words from 1Corinthians 15:3-8 verify the reality of Christ's resurrection:

> *For I delivered to you as of first importance what I also*
> *received, that Christ died for our sins according to the*
> *Scriptures, and that He was buried, and that He was*
> *raised on the third day according to the Scriptures, and*
> *that He appeared to Cephas, then to the twelve. After that*
> *He appeared to more than five hundred brethren at one*
> *time, most of whom remain until now, but some have*
> *fallen asleep; then He appeared to James, then to all the*
> *apostles; and last of all, as it were to one untimely born,*
> *He appeared to me also.* (1Corinthians 15:3-8)

Jesus appeared to the eleven apostles on an appointed mountain in Galilee (Matthew 28:16; 1Corinthians 15:5). (Note that the eleven apostles are referenced as *"the twelve"* in 1Corinthians 15:5.) Upon seeing Him the apostles worshipped, but some of them were doubtful (Matthew 28:17). He also *"appeared to more than five hundred brethren at one time"* (1Corinthians 15:6). Many people who saw Jesus at this time (in 30 AD) and believed in His bodily resurrection were still alive when Paul wrote First Corinthians, probably about 55 AD—further verifying the validity of the resurrection account. Had a hoax been involved, the twenty-five years between Jesus resurrection and the writing of First Corinthians (30 AD to 55 AD) would have been ample time for some to recant—but their stories remained steadfast. This fact substantiates the reality and validity of Jesus' resurrection. However, the most important proof is His indwelling presence in our hearts. Truly, what a Friend we have in Jesus!

How important is Christ's resurrection to our faith? Paul recorded the answer in 1Corinthians 15:12-19:

> *Now if Christ is preached, that He has been raised from*
> *the dead, how do some among you say that there is no*
> *resurrection of the dead? But if there is no resurrection*
> *of the dead, not even Christ has been raised; and if Christ*
> *has not been raised, then our preaching is vain, your faith*
> *also is vain. Moreover we are even found to be false*
> *witnesses of God, because we witnessed against God that*
> *He raised Christ, whom He did not raise, if in fact the*
> *dead are not raised. For if the dead are not raised, not*

even Christ has been raised; and if Christ has not been
raised, your faith is worthless; you are still in your sins.
Then those also who have fallen asleep in Christ have
perished. If we have hoped in Christ in this life only, we
are of all men most to be pitied. (1Corinthians 15:12-19)

Paul emphasized Christ's resurrection in Acts 17:8, 23:6, 26:8, and Romans 1:4. Is it any wonder that God's enemies so desperately attempt to discredit this miraculous event? In fact, prove that Jesus remained in the grave and Christianity becomes extinct.

Romans 6:9 also states that Christ will *"never...die again."* This truth confirms forgiveness is complete when Christ's blood is initially applied to a New Testament believer; all past, present, and future sins are forgiven at the point of justification/salvation.

Due to the resurrection, *"death no longer is master over Him* [Jesus]" (Romans 6:9). Because Jesus lives in us, and we have received His type of life (Colossians 3:4), *"death"* no longer is *"master over"* us (Romans 6:9). Thus, Paul recorded in 2Corinthians 5:8:

we are of good courage, I say, and prefer rather to be
absent from the body and to be at home with the Lord.
(2Corinthians 5:8)

The moment the body dies we are ushered into God's presence in heaven. Therefore, the writer of Hebrews penned:

Since then the children share in flesh and blood, He
Himself likewise also partook of the same, that through
death He might render powerless him who had the power
of death, that is, the devil; and might deliver those who
through fear of death were subject to slavery all their
lives. (Hebrews 2:14-15)

The New Testament believer can walk in freedom from the fear of death due to only one reason: Jesus exited the grave and ascended to the right hand of the Father. What a magnificent gospel!

In Romans 6:10 we find that Jesus *"died to sin":*

> *For the death that He died, He died to sin, once for all;*
> *but the life that He lives, He lives to God.* (Romans 6:10)

Jesus died <u>for</u> the sin of all mankind. His blood was the means through which our sins were forgiven once we repented and exercised faith while depraved. (We will confirm later that His <u>body</u> was the means through which our sinful nature was eradicated. When Jesus submitted to the cross, He also died *"to"* the power of sin (Satan's agent) that attacked Him in the process. In fact, throughout His First Coming He considered Himself dead *"to"* the power of *"sin."* Had this not been the case, He would have sinned and in the process aborted His mission as Savior. Thus, He, as our *"high priest,"* can understand our weaknesses (Hebrews 2:17-18; 4:15)—having been tempted by the same power that entices us daily.

Jesus was born void of a sin nature. He was the Father's Son—not Joseph's son (as addressed in Romans 1). He also possessed a brain free of sinful habit patterns—for He never sinned. Yet, had he sinned, He would have walked according to the flesh.

The New Testament believer walks according to the flesh when he believes the power of sin's lie sent into the mind by means of a sinful habit pattern in the brain—the brain being a piece of flesh (reference Circle Diagram 7). However, new sinful habit patterns have developed in our brains (the brain being a piece of flesh) since becoming part of God's family. They were established by listening to the power of sin's lies in new areas of temptation. Hence, we are capable of walking according to the flesh in areas where sinful habit patterns have not yet been developed. Thus, Jesus would have walked according to the flesh had He sinned, even though He possessed no sinful habit patterns in His brain. He can understand our weaknesses, having been bombarded with the power of sin's lies beyond anything we could imagine.

Romans 6:10 also states that Jesus *"lives to God."* As was the case during His First Coming, Jesus *"lives"* by the Father's life, allowing the Father to do the work through Him rather than expending excessive amounts of energy performing the work Himself (John 14:10). Paul understood this principle well, verified by the combination of Romans 12:1 and 1Corinthians 15:10.

The practical side of how we function as believers can be examined by building on the foundation of Circle Diagrams 1 through 4 with Circle

Diagram 5, *How We Operate,* which depicts that man consists of three parts: body, soul, and spirit. The soul includes the mind, emotions, and will—you think with your mind, feel with your emotions, and make choices with your will. The brain is part of the body, and the brain houses our habit patterns. Lines drawn through the brain represent these habit patterns. Some habit patterns are larger (stronger) than others, which explains the differences in their widths.

Diagram 5

How We Operate

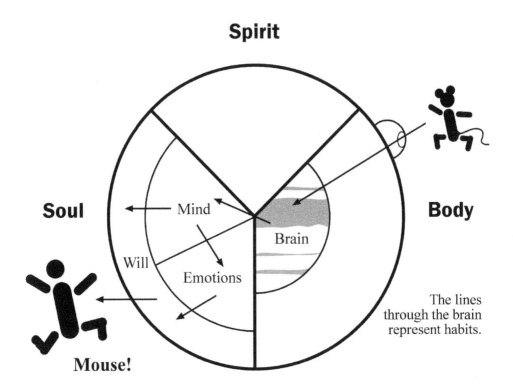

Using Circle Diagram 5 as a visual aid, suppose you are fearful of mice. If these ferocious little monsters should petrify you, a habit pattern that can cause you to respond irrationally in their presence will be formed in your brain, which is a piece of flesh (meat). In fact, when your eye spots one of these fierce creatures, the information will travel up the optic nerve to the brain. The brain will then process this data and signal the mind. Because a large, negative habit pattern regarding mice is stored in the brain, the outgoing information enters the mind as a catalyst for action in the soul. In fact, when the mind receives this information from the brain, the emotions are automatically aroused. Both the mind and emotions give input to the will. At that point the will chooses to operate the body in high gear and move it as fast as possible from the impending danger. Finally, it is safe!

Believe it or not, individuals are alive and well who have no fear of mice. They simply do not possess a large habit pattern that causes them to respond negatively to these "cute" little creatures. In fact, such persons can grasp a mouse by its tail and place it in a safe environment— totally out of harm's way from those who view these "furry friends" as life threatening.

We can be greatly controlled by what we see, touch, taste, hear, and smell. Therefore, we should guard our senses from ungodly influence.

Circle Diagram 6 titled *How the Power of Sin is Defeated,* illustrates how the power of sin (Satan's messenger, or agent) is defeated when you walk in God's Spirit. Paul says to *"consider"* yourself *"dead to sin, but alive to God in Christ Jesus":*

> *Even so consider yourselves to be dead to sin, but alive to*
> *God in Christ Jesus.* (Romans 6:11)

You are forgiven of your acts of sin and released from the penalty of those sins if you are born again. Now that you live *"in Christ,"* the power of *"sin"* can be overcome as well. In fact, because Jesus overcame sin's power and you now live in Him (2Corinthians 5:17) and He in you (Galatians 2:20), you can also *"consider"* yourself *"to be dead to sin* [dead to the power of sin], *but alive to God in Christ Jesus"* (Romans 6:11) and walk victoriously.

This situation can be experienced in a practical sense if, for instance, you struggle with depression, especially on cloudy days? In such cases, a habit pattern will have been formed in your brain (probably prior to your believing in Christ) relating to this behavioral issue. This habit pattern was formed through repeatedly believing the power of sin's lie. Therefore, *"sin"* will use the stimulus (clouds) in an attempt to ruin your day (Circle Diagram 6) by sending messages to your mind such as, "I always feel depressed on cloudy days. I think I will just lie in bed until this feeling subsides," or, "I don't think I can make it through this day." The pronoun "I" is prominent in these statements because sin's goal is to deceive you into believing that the thought, which is a lie, is the truth. In fact, by sending the message into your mind through the ungodly habit pattern etched in your brain, sin's lie enters your mind sounding like you generated it. Consequently, the voice you hear is identical to your voice, including accent and dialect. At this point Romans 6:11 comes into play. Sin's lie can immediately be replaced with the truth by considering yourself *"dead"* to what you have just heard. You can do so only because the being who consistently believed sin's lie to be truth, the *"old self,"* has been eradicated (Romans 6:6). Yes, because the old self has been replaced with the new self, you, the new self, have been *"freed from"* [the power of] *sin"* (Romans 6:7). (Reference Circle Diagram 6 for assistance in understanding this life changing truth.) The power of sin cannot enter your mind now that you are a believer; it is sin's thoughts that enter your mind. It sends messages to your mind through the avenue of the ungodly habit patterns lodged in your brain.

The power of sin's mission is to trick you into responding to its lies. These thoughts (lies) can be overcome only through the truth of God's Word. Matthew 4:3-11 validates this fact, for Jesus processed evil thoughts without committing sin. After all, to respond to Satan as He did, He was required to process Satan's lies—proving that a thought does not become an act of sin until we believe it to be truth and act accordingly.

We can respond to the power of sin in a similar fashion. When evil thoughts bombard our minds, we must immediately appropriate truth. The first thing required is to remember *"...our old self was crucified..."* (Romans 6:6), for it serves as a reminder that sin is no longer a natural act. Although we will commit acts of sin so long as we dwell in earthly bodies, sin is an unnatural response because of our new nature— remember the cat illustration. Second, we must *"consider"* ourselves *"dead"* to sin's thoughts *"...but alive to God in Christ Jesus"* (Romans

6:11). To respond in this manner we simply say, "I am dead to this lie floating around in my mind, and I take authority over it in the name of Christ." At that point we should yield to the truth sent into our minds by means of the Spirit, truth that relates to our particular situation. This truth, empowered by the Holy Spirit, overrides the evil thought and we are immediately delivered through Jesus' indwelling presence (a subject addressed in more detail in Romans 6:13).

As you probably realize, this godly response is much easier to talk about than to experience in daily living. We will have ample opportunity to use what we are learning, for God doesn't teach so truth might lie dormant. He is preparing us for spiritual warfare, so remain alert.

Reference Circle Diagram 6 titled *How the Power of Sin is Defeated*. When the power of sin attempts to stimulate depression (by sending negative thoughts into our minds through the ungodly habit patterns in our brains), the emotions respond immediately. We will begin to feel depressed, especially on cloudy days, as indicated by the diagram. The key at such times is to *"consider"* ourselves *"dead"* to these thoughts (Romans 6:11) and *"alive"* to the truth, truth such as Psalm 118:24:

> *"This is the day the Lord has made; let us rejoice and be glad in it."* (Psalm 118:24)

Through faith, which is an element of the mind, we can choose to set our minds on the absolutes of God's Word. The mind can also force the will to accept its input and reject the input from the emotions, even when the emotions are totally out of sync with reality—meaning that as we walk in the Spirit we will many times act in one way while feeling another. In other words, if we refuse to allow our emotions to control our behavior, we will frequently find ourselves responding in an obedient manner while feeling depressed. The great news is that the emotions will eventually settle, and the habit patterns that once derailed us will become manageable. In fact, the Lord greatly reduces the strength of these negative habit patterns as we mature in the faith. Life is bliss when the emotions line up with reality, but these seasons are typically short in duration and cannot be expected to remain.

Emotions can't always be trusted, especially during times of intense spiritual warfare. If we choose to walk opposite of how we feel, the power of sin will attempt to convince us that we are nothing more than hypocrites playing an imaginary game. To stand, we must realize that many times we will respond positively to truth while <u>feeling</u> like doing just the opposite. This emotional battle is what Jesus faced in Luke 22:44. At Gethsemane, His emotions were out of control, even to the point that *"...His sweat became like drops of blood...."* But, He set His mind on truth, told His will to disregard His emotions, and walked to the cross in the Father's strength. Was He a hypocrite by responding in this manner? Of course not, but we can rest assured that the power of sin was telling Him otherwise.

If we can grasp what we are studying here, through the assistance of the Holy Spirit, we will be amazed at the difference it will make in our ability to persevere in God's strength. We will study more about this topic shortly, so don't be discouraged if understanding is lacking. This subject matter will come together very soon.

Romans 6:12-23

Freed from the Power of Sin

The New Testament believer is no longer enslaved to the power of sin. Reference Circle Diagrams 7 and 8, *Sin in Control* and *Spirit in Control,* as we continue.

> *Therefore do not let sin reign in your mortal body that*
> *you should obey its lusts,* (Romans 6:12)

The word *"sin"* in Romans 6:12 refers to the power of sin. If we are not careful, we will allow this power to *"reign"* in our bodies. When this predicament occurs, we have believed the power of sin's lie and responded accordingly. The behavior which follows resembles that of the unredeemed, for Satan, the power of sin's boss, knows no truth. Thus, when we sin, we respond to the variables of life much like the lost respond to these same variables. Yes, sin can *"reign"* if we refuse to remain alert (1Peter 5:8). When we allow this situation to transpire, we should immediately

The New Testament believer is no longer enslaved to the power of sin.

confess our sin, set our mind on truth, and walk in the truth that the Spirit supplies. It takes *"good"* to *"overcome evil"* (Romans 12:21), and nothing can *"overcome"* the power of sin but the *"good"* truth of the Word of God empowered by the Holy Spirit.

Romans 6:13 holds the key to victorious living:

> *and do not go on presenting the members of your body to*
> *sin as instruments of unrighteousness; but present*
> *yourselves to God as those alive from the dead, and your*
> *members as instruments of righteousness to God.*
> (Romans 6:13)

While under attack, we are to *"present…*[ourselves] *to God as those alive from the dead"* (Romans 6:13) by first recognizing that we are powerless against the enemy's schemes. After acknowledging this fact, we then yield to the only Source of deliverance, the *"God"* Who lives in us (Romans 6:13). Because we are *"...seated...in the heavenly places, in Christ Jesus"* (Ephesians 2:6) with the *"old self"* (Adamic nature) eradicated (Romans 6:6), the power of sin has lost its grip on our lives. Consequently, the physical *"members"* of our *"body"* (hands, feet, eyes, etc.) are free to respond *"as instruments of righteousness"* as we *"present"* ourselves *"to God"* (Romans 6:13), the Omnipotent Creator. This sequence of events describes what it means to be *"saved by"* Christ's *"life"* (Romans 5:10), Jesus being *"God"* (Hebrews 1:8). Truly, what a wonderful adventure awaits those who choose the road less traveled.

When we commit sin we have presented *"the members of"* our *"body to sin as instruments of unrighteousness"* (Romans 6:13). In other words, we have submitted our hands, arms, legs, feet, eyes (our entire bodies) to sin's authority—to the power that longs to destroy us.

Satan desires to control our minds, for faith dwells in the mind. We must, therefore, guard our thoughts; the power of sin does not slumber when left unattended. We are holy and blameless saints. But even so, *"...when lust has conceived, it gives birth to sin..."* (James 1:15), *"sin"* that must be confessed for fellowship to be restored.

In Romans 6:14, Paul verifies why *"sin"* (the power of sin) is no longer *"master"* over the New Testament believer:

> *For sin shall not be master over you, for you are not*
> *under law, but under grace.* (Romans 6:14)

"Sin" holds no mastery because we are *"not under law, but under grace."* The power of sin responds to *"law,"* by gaining strength! In other words, its power intensifies. Thus, before we were saved, the harder we strove to keep the Law the more the power of sin increased in strength. Finally, when the Law had accomplished its purpose, we saw (while depraved) our need for a Savior, surrendered to Christ, and were justified (saved) by the God of *"grace."* We then began living under *"grace,"* and sin's power was broken. The power of *"sin"* can still *"reign in"* our *"body"* (Romans 6:12), but only when the new man is caught off guard. In fact, we commit acts of sin because we choose to

sin, not because sin is a natural act. This topic will be discussed in more depth when we study Romans 7.

Paul next presents a question that his enemies frequently posed:

> *What then? Shall we sin because we are not under law*
> *but under grace?* May it never be! (Romans 6:15)

Paul's critics not only rejected his theology but also accused him of granting believers a license to sin (much the same as in Romans 6:1). Paul again uses the strong Greek expression, *"May it never be"* (Romans 6:15), proving that these accusations were totally unjustified. He wrote in Colossians 3:25 that we suffer consequences in this life from the sins committed as believers:

> *For he who does wrong will receive the consequences of*
> *the wrong which he has done, and that without partiality.*
> (Colossians 3:25)

Paul makes a statement in Romans 6:16 that entirely settles this issue. As we study this passage, we must keep in mind that New Testament believers are made totally righteous in their person at the point of justification/salvation but become increasingly righteous in their behavior as they mature in the faith.

> *Do you not know that when you present yourselves to*
> *someone as slaves for obedience, you are slaves of the*
> *one whom you obey, either of sin resulting in death, or of*
> *obedience resulting in righteousness?* (Romans 6:16)

New Testament believers are the *"slaves of the one"* they *"obey,"* whether it is *"sin,"* which leads to *"death,"* or *"obedience,"* which results *"in righteousness"* (v.16). Therefore, if *"sin"* brings *"death,"* why would Paul preach a gospel that promotes disobedience? He couldn't, and that is his point! Note: The word *"death,"* as it relates to New Testament believers, can point to physical death as in 1 Corinthians 11:30 and other similar passages. It can also describe the emptiness experienced by believers while walking in unconfessed sin. Sin can cause believers to live as though they are dead (spiritually dead) for short seasons of time, but as was the case with David, once repentance and confession are exercised, a zest for life is restored.

The truths of Romans 6:16 can also apply to the lost (depraved). So long as they continue in rebellion, they remain sin's slave and are spiritually dead (separated from God). However, those who choose to repent and believe (obey) are made totally righteous.

Paul continues by teaching that while we were without Christ, we *"...were slaves of sin..."* (Romans 6:17):

> *But thanks be to God that though you were slaves of sin,*
> *you became obedient from the heart to that form of*
> *teaching to which you were committed,* (Romans 6:17)

In our lost state, we loved sin, basked in sin, submerged ourselves in sin, sinned in many ways and on a variety of occasions. We did so because we were the old self, and sin came as natural as breathing. This sinful state doesn't mean that we were incapable of repenting and believing while depraved, but rather that we were sin's slave so long as we refused to repent and exercise faith. We will discover shortly that we as believers are slaves of righteousness, yet sometimes sin. Therefore, we are capable of acting against (contrary to) our strongest inclination, a subject examined in more depth in Romans 7.

Paul, in Romans 6:17, continues by writing: *"...you became obedient from the heart...."* Some individuals who have not become *"obedient from the heart"* claim to know Christ and are, therefore, lost. All who are born of God's Spirit receive a new *"heart,"* a new nature, and desire to obey their Master. As a result, they possess a transformed attitude regarding sin. A person who has *"become obedient from the heart"* experiences a radical change of lifestyle.

When we became *"obedient from the heart"* (Romans 6:17), we were *"freed from"* both the power and penalty of *"sin"* (Romans 6:18). We also *"became slaves of righteousness"* (Romans 6:18):

> *and having been freed from sin, you became slaves of*
> *righteousness.* (Romans 6:18)

Be sure to understand Paul's point here. The power of sin can control us only if we are caught off guard, for we have become *"slaves of righteousness"* due to our new nature. Consequently, the *"members"* of our body should behave more righteously—not as they behaved prior to our being made new (Romans 6:19):

> *I am speaking in human terms because of the weakness of*
> *your flesh. For just as you presented your members as*
> *slaves to impurity and to lawlessness, resulting in further*
> *lawlessness, so now present your members as slaves to*
> *righteousness, resulting in sanctification.* (Romans 6:19)

Paul states that if we *"present"* the *"members"* of our bodies *"as slaves to righteousness"* (on an ongoing basis), then *"sanctification"* results. However, Romans 5 tells that our spirits and souls were sanctified (made holy and perfect) the moment we were justified/saved. Is Romans 6:19 a contradiction? Of course not! In verse 19, Paul is saying that we will progressively live out in our experiences what has already taken place in our spirits and souls. In other words, we will start to behave in a more sanctified (holy) manner due to having already been sanctified in our spirits and souls at the point of justification/salvation. Hebrews 10:14 addresses this subject as well as any verse in the Scriptures:

> *For by one offering He has perfected for all time those*
> *who are sanctified* [being sanctified]. (Hebrews 10:14
> NASB—emphasis added)

> *Because by one sacrifice he has made perfect forever*
> *those who are being made holy* (Hebrews 10:14 NIV—
> emphasis added)

The word *"sanctified"* in the NASB actually means "being sanctified." The NIV's rendering is, *"being made holy,"* since the terms *"holy"* and *"sanctified"* are synonymous. Yes, our souls and spirits are made perfect forever at the point of justification, but our behavior is *"being made holy"* (being sanctified) on an ongoing basis. Thus, you can be perfect and holy (sanctified) in your person before your behavior lines up with who you are. Isn't it wonderful to know that we are not on a performance-based acceptance with God, and that what we sometimes do (when we commit acts of sin) is not who we are? In other words, if you tell a lie, you are <u>not</u> a liar. You are a saint who has told a lie, for you have acted in an unnatural manner. Believe me, a tremendous difference exists between these two mind-sets. In fact, what we do is not who we are, even though who we are has a tremendous impact on what we do.

What we do is not who we are, even though who we are has a tremendous impact on what we do.

Paul's words of Romans 6:20-21 are extremely convicting:

> *For when you were slaves of sin, you were free in regard to righteousness. Therefore what benefit were you then deriving from the things of which you are now ashamed? For the outcome of those things is death.* (Romans 6:20-21)

We were without *"righteousness"* while in our lost state (Romans 6:20), *"deriving"* no *"benefit...from the things of which we are now ashamed"*—grossly ashamed (Romans 6:21). (Would it not be wonderful to apologize to <u>the many</u> before whom we played the fool while lost and void of wisdom?) *"But now having been freed from sin and enslaved to God"* [being enslaved to God means that you desire to serve Him with all your heart], we *"derive"* the *"benefit"* of *"sanctification"* and *"eternal life"* (Romans 6:22).

> *But now having been freed from sin and enslaved to God, you derive your benefit, resulting in sanctification, and the outcome, eternal life.* (Romans 6:22)

Great news isn't it!

To be *"enslaved to God"* does not mean that we cease sinning now that we are believers. We will commit sin to the grave, although we were *"freed from"* the power of *"sin"* the moment we repented and believed (Romans 6:22). Consequently, just as being *"enslaved to God"* does not mean that we (as believers) totally cease responding to the power of sin's influence, being enslaved to sin in our lost state did not mean that we were incapable of exercising repentance and faith while depraved.

We can now shout at the top of our voices Paul's words of Romans 6:23:

> *"For the wages of sin is death, but the free gift of God is eternal life in Christ Jesus our Lord."* (Romans 6:23)

*B*eing enslaved to sin in our lost state did not mean that we were incapable of exercising repentance and faith while depraved.

Clearly, *"the wages of sin is death,"* but did you notice that God's *"free gift...is eternal life,"* and that this *"life"* is found *"in...Jesus"*? We should be motivated to communicate these wonderful truths to anyone and everyone who will listen. However, God must instruct you in how to say what is addressed here before you begin instructing others. Many people have jumped the gun and suffered horrendous consequences. Once you are ready, God will give you ample opportunity to spread this magnificent news to a hurting and dying world.

Romans 7

I had heard for years that Romans 7 describes the defeated Christian. One day, I realized it does the opposite. In fact, I found that it reveals the source of the conflict within every New Testament believer and, at the same time, maps out the path to victory.

When I read Romans 7 as a new believer, I became more aware of my own struggles. I wasn't mature enough to understand the source of those struggles. I thought if I could feed the old self (Adamic nature, old man, dead spirit, sinful nature) enough truth and whip him into line, the battle would subside. I did not yet comprehend that my old self had been crucified and made extinct. I soon learned, nonetheless, that the intensity of the battle did not decrease as my Biblical knowledge increased. In fact, I found that the battle intensified as I matured in my walk with Christ. It was then that I discovered a life-changing truth. I learned that my struggle is with the power of sin and <u>not</u> with my old self (Adamic nature). This insight brought new hope and, with it, a greater desire to live life by Christ's life within me. In other words, I was free to explore what it means to live life by the life of Another, the life of my Savior.

*M*y struggle is with the power of sin and <u>not</u> with my eradicated old self (Adamic nature).

Our understanding of spiritual warfare will be enhanced through our study of Romans 7. Don't be surprised if the intensity of the battle increases as we examine this chapter. Satan will do everything within his power to prevent us from seeing this truth, so pray for wisdom before continuing.

Released from Law through Death

Paul first addresses the means by which we are released from the Law, and he uses the marriage relationship to prove his point (Romans 7:1-4):

> *Or do you not know, brethren (for I am speaking to those who know the law), that the law has jurisdiction over a person as long as he lives? For the married woman is*

> *bound by law to her husband while he is living; but if her*
> *husband dies, she is released from the law concerning the*
> *husband. So then if, while her husband is living, she is*
> *joined to another man, she shall be called an adulteress;*
> *but if her husband dies, she is free from the law, so that*
> *she is not an adulteress, though she is joined to another*
> *man. Therefore, my brethren, you also were made to die*
> *to the Law through the body of Christ, that you might be*
> *joined to another, to Him who was raised from the dead,*
> *that we might bear fruit for God.* (Romans 7:1-4)

In marriage, death of one of the partners automatically frees the surviving partner to remarry. Paul's point is that in our lost state we were joined (in a sense, married) to the Law. Because the Law will live forever (1Peter 1:25), our release could be achieved only through the avenue of our own death. Our death (the death and eradication of the old self) occurred on the cross (Romans 7:4; Galatians 2:20; Romans 6:6) through our being placed in Christ subsequent to our repenting and believing while depraved (review what was addressed in Romans 6:1-6 if necessary). Thus, we are free to be *"joined to"* Christ, for the old self is dead and gone. Otherwise, our betrothal to Christ would be an impossibility! Should the old self remain alive, living alongside the new self, the old self would be married to the Law at the same time that the new self is betrothed to Christ. Spiritual adultery would result, creating an irreconcilable situation. Yet many New Testament believers view themselves as dual natured, possessing both the old and new self.

As a result of being *"joined to another,"* we can *"bear fruit for God"* through living by the life of *"another,"* the *"another"* being Jesus Himself (Romans 7:4), Who is *"God"* (Hebrews 1:8). Can you imagine any better news!

Paul continues in Romans 7:5 by stating:

> *For while we were in the flesh, the sinful passions, which*
> *were aroused by the Law, were at work in the members of*
> *our body to bear fruit for death.* (Romans 7:5)

This passage tells that *"...while we were in the flesh* [in our lost condition], *the sinful passions* [affections]*...were aroused by the*

Law...." These *"passions...were aroused"* because the power of sin increases in intensity when exposed to *"the Law."* Consequently, the more we worked at keeping the Law, the more we broke it. We were constantly bearing *"fruit for death,"* that is, producing the fruit of an unbeliever. Don't misunderstand. Paul is <u>not</u> teaching that the depraved are incapable of recognizing their sin and exercising personal repentance and faith, for Adam realized he was *"naked"* after eating of the forbidden fruit and dying a spiritual death (Genesis 2:16-17; Genesis 3:7).

More good news is on the horizon in Romans 7:6:

> *But now we have been released from the Law, having died*
> *to that by which we were bound, so that we serve in*
> *newness of the Spirit and not in oldness of the letter.*
> (Romans 7:6)

This verse confirms that *"...we have been released from the Law..."* through our death with Christ. (Remember: The Law is for the lost, not the saved, according to 1Timothy 1:9-10). This teaching is in total agreement with Romans 6:6, which verifies *"...that our old self was crucified with Him...."* The death and eradication of the *"old self"* frees us to *"...serve in newness of the Spirit and not in oldness of the letter"* of *"the Law"* (Romans 7:6). Yes, we are free to allow the *"Spirit"* of God to provide victory over anything that comes our way. What freedom!

We should take courage from Romans 7:7, for as Paul was accused of teaching error we will be accused of the same:

> *What shall we say then? Is the Law sin? May it never be!*
> *On the contrary, I would not have come to know sin*
> *except through the Law; for I would not have known*
> *about coveting if the Law had not said, "YOU SHALL NOT*
> *COVET."* (Romans 7:7)

Paul's enemies struggled with his theology, making statements such as, "If what you are teaching is true, the Law must be sin." Paul disagreed by responding with, *"May it never be!"* He then said had it not been for *"the Law"* he *"would not have known about coveting."*

"Coveting" is a sin that can be hidden from the unbeliever, but not from the Law. Thus, Paul writes:

> *But sin, taking opportunity through the commandment,*
> *produced in me coveting of every kind; for apart from the*
> *Law sin is dead.* (Romans 7:8)

Had the Law not been present to expose Paul's sin, he would have continued in his self-righteousness, never seeing his need for a Savior. The power of *"sin"* increases in intensity when exposed to the Law.

Romans 7:9 must be studied based on the full counsel of God's Word or misunderstanding will result:

> *And I was once alive apart from the Law; but when the*
> *commandment came, sin became alive, and I died;*
> (Romans 7:9)

This passage is one of many in God's Word where the context of a portion of the verse is obtained from the input from subsequent verses—not from preceding truth. This same principle also applies elsewhere in Romans 7.

The first phrase of verse 9, *"And I was once alive apart from the Law,"* does not communicate that a time existed when Paul was not exposed to the Law. Paul, a Jew, was taught the Law from the womb! The apostle is communicating that a portion of his life was spent viewing the Law incorrectly—as will be verified by the remainder of the verse shortly. In fact, prior to submitting to Christ, he perceived himself as keeping the Law perfectly:

> *...If anyone else has a mind to put confidence in the flesh,*
> *I far more: circumcised the eighth day, of the nation of*
> *Israel, of the tribe of Benjamin, a Hebrew of Hebrews; as*
> *to the Law, a Pharisee; as to zeal, a persecutor of the*
> *church; as to the righteousness which is in the Law, found*
> *blameless.* (Philippians 3:4-6, emphasis added)

According to the last half of Romans 7:9, a day came when Paul perceived the Law from a proper vantage point—as the vehicle used of

God to expose man's sin.   Thus, Paul wrote, *"but when the commandment came, sin became alive, and I died."*   When *"the commandment came"* (Romans 7:9), Paul finally viewed the Law appropriately—as a *"tutor to lead"* him *"to Christ, that"* he might *"be justified by faith"* (Galatians 3:24):

> *Therefore the Law has become our tutor to lead us to*
> *Christ, that we may be justified by faith.* (Galatians 3:24)

Paul follows in Romans 7:10-11 by writing:

> *and this commandment, which was to result in life, proved*
> *to result in death for me; for sin, taking opportunity*
> *through the commandment, deceived me, and through it*
> *killed me.* (Romans 7:10-11)

The *"commandment"* (Law), which Paul originally perceived as imparting *"life"* through obeying its requirements, resulted in *"death"* by convicting him of sin.   In fact, the power of *"sin"* *"killed"* him through intensifying its strength by means of the Law.   Paul states this same truth in different terminology in Galatians 2:19:

> *"For through the Law I died to the Law, that I might live*
> *to God.* (Galatians 2:19)

As a result of the work of the Law, which gave rise to an increase in the power of sin's intensity, Paul saw himself as a sinner, repented of his sin, and accepted Christ as Savior.   Hence, God gave the Law so man might recognize his sinful and depraved state through his increased involvement with sin.   What a wise God we serve!

"The Law is holy" (Romans 7:12); it serves the purpose for which it was given:

> *So then, the Law is holy, and the commandment is holy*
> *and righteous and good.* (Romans 7:12)

The Law makes *"sin...utterly sinful"* (Romans 7:13), doing its job and doing it well:

> *Therefore did that which is good become a cause of death*
> *for me? May it never be! Rather it was sin, in order that it*
> *might be shown to be sin by effecting my death through*
> *that which is good, that through the commandment sin*
> *might become utterly sinful.* (Romans 7:13)

The Battle Between the New Testament Believer and the Power of Sin

Romans 7:14-16 speaks of the battle that occurs inside every New Testament believer. This battle also raged within Paul, so he describes his frustration during the early years of his walk with Christ. Note his use of the word *"Law"*:

> *For we know that the Law is spiritual; but I am of flesh,*
> *sold into bondage to sin. For that which I am doing, I do*
> *not understand; for I am not practicing what I would like*
> *to do, but I am doing the very thing I hate. But if I do the*
> *very thing I do not wish to do, I agree with the Law,*
> *confessing that it is good.* (Romans 7:14-16)

Paul was inundated (saturated) with Law from birth. In fact, prior to salvation he viewed himself as a keeper of the Law:

> *...as to the righteousness which is in the Law, found*
> *blameless.* (Philippians 3:6)

Having studied under Gamaliel, an influential teacher of the Law in Jerusalem (Acts 5:34-40; 22:3), Paul would have been very familiar with the Law (Acts 26:4-5). Thus, prior to salvation, Paul perceived himself as *"blameless"* (Philippians 3:6) in regard to the Law—as fulfilling the righteousness required by the Law in every way. Can you imagine the difficulty he faced while attempting to abandon Law and live under grace subsequent to believing? The width of the habit patterns in his brain relating to the Law must have been enormous! As you and I can attest, habits of thought of this magnitude aren't shed overnight. Coupling this truth with the events of his early years as a believer, could it be that Paul struggled (for a season at least) with the fact that the Law can't assist a believer in righteous living? I think he did, and Scripture seems to agree.

After Paul's conversion, several years transpired before he embarked on his first missionary journey. He had much to learn concerning grace. In fact, after his dialogue with Jesus in Acts 9, he traveled to Damascus (Acts 9:8), journeyed to Arabia (Galatians 1:17), and returned to Damascus (Galatians 1:17). At least *"three years"* passed during this series of events (Galatians 1:18). He then spent *"fifteen days"* with Peter (Cephas) in Jerusalem (Galatians 1:18) and finally moved to *"the regions of Syria and Cilicia"* (Galatians 1:21)—Tarsus, his hometown, was located in this region. Not until Acts 11:25-26 did Barnabas bring him from Tarsus to Antioch. After a short trip to Jerusalem (Acts 11:27-30; 12:25), they embarked on Paul's first missionary journey (Acts 13:1-3).

Several years passed <u>after</u> Paul's conversion before he was properly equipped for service. I am convinced verses 14-17 of Romans 7 describe what he learned during those years of sitting alone with the Lord. In fact, I conclude that he viewed himself as possessing two natures during the early stages of his walk with Christ.   I also conclude (bases on Romans 7:14-16) that he erroneously attempted to whip the old man (sinful nature) into line (a nature which he later discovered had been eradicated) by hooking it to the Law. One day, however, he came to the realization that the old self (sinful nature) had been jettisoned when he repented and believed. Thus, he discovered that the evil thoughts that penetrated his mind as a church saint were not generated by the old self (sinful nature). Rather, they could be traced to the power of sin living in his body. What a profound discovery!

Certainly, the power of sin comes against all church saints. We want to do good but at times find ourselves doing evil. Once we identify the avenue through which the power of sin launches its attack, we are well on our way to victory.

Paul, in verse 17, describes a major turning point in his earlier walk with Christ.

> *"So now, no longer am I the one doing it, but sin which indwells me."* (Romans 7:17).

For correct interpretation, we must properly define the term *"it"* in Romans 7:17. *"It"* points to the evil thoughts generated by the power of sin living in the New Testament believer's body—a truth verified by the context of the remaining verses of Romans 7, especially verses 21 and 23 (addressed shortly). Thus, Paul taught that the sinful thoughts entering his mind were not generated by the old self (Adamic nature) but were the work of the power of sin living in his physical body. Until this time, Paul struggled with the idea that the old self (sinful nature)

The battle raging inside us is between the power of sin and the new self, not between the old self and the new self.

was alive, producing the evil thoughts that bombarded his thinking. He discovered that the old self is dead and gone in a New Testament believer, never to be reckoned with again. This eradication means that the battle raging inside us is between the power of sin and the new self, not between the old self and the new self. How can a battle exist between the old self and the new self when the old self no longer exists?

So long as we allow the power of sin to trick us into believing that the old self is still alive, it can convince us that we are generating the evil thoughts that bombard our minds. Only through understanding that the old self has been eradicated and that the sinful thoughts are generated by the power of sin living in our body can we take authority over the power of sin (through the power of the Holy Spirit) and live abundantly. Understanding this truth radically changed Paul's experience as a New Testament believer. My prayer is that it will do the same for us. A quick review of the circle diagrams might be helpful at this time.

An initial reading of Romans 7:17 suggests that Paul is teaching that he (the new self) did not commit sin, which cannot be true, for 1John 1:8 states:

> *"If we say we have no sin, we are deceiving ourselves, and the truth is not in us."* (1John 1:8)

Paul is <u>not</u> advocating that he no longer sinned, but that the power of sin is the initiator and source of the evil thoughts that penetrate the New Testament believer's mind. Hence, Paul was not teaching sinless perfection. Therefore, the *"it"* of Romans 7:17 points to the evil thoughts generated by the power of sin (living in our body) as it attempts to convince us that the sin nature is still alive (read verses 21 and 23 for verification). These conclusions agree with the truth addressed in Romans 7:18-19.

Verses 18-19 are similar to verses 14-15, for Paul focuses on the battle generated by the power of sin that lived in his *"flesh"*:

> *For I know that nothing good dwells in me, that is, in my flesh; for the wishing is present in me, but the doing of the good is not. For the good that I wish, I do not do; but I practice the very evil that I do not wish.* (Romans 7:18-19)

As has already been determined, Paul realized that the initiator of the *"evil"* is *"sin,"* the power of *"sin,"* as verified by verse 20 of the same chapter:

> *"But if I am doing the very thing I do not wish, I am no longer the one doing it, but sin which dwells in me."* (Romans 7:20)

Again, the word *"it"* (v.20) points to the evil thoughts generated by the power of sin living in the New Testament believer's body. Applying what we have discussed, verse 20 may be more clearly stated:

> *"But if I am doing the very thing I do not wish, I am no longer the one* producing the evil thoughts that wage war against my mind, for they are produced by the power of *sin which dwells in* my body."

Paul is not advocating that the body is evil, but rather that the body houses the power of sin. After all, the New Testament believer's body is the temple of the Holy Spirit (1Corinthians 6:19).

This amazing truth means that through the power of the Holy Spirit we can catch the power of sin at its game and refuse whatever it sends our way. Because the new self is incapable of producing sinful thoughts (even though the new self is capable of committing sin), and since the *"old self"* has been eradicated (Romans 6:6), we can *"consider"* ourselves *"dead"* to these thoughts (Romans 6:11), living abundantly through God's life within (Romans 6:13).

*W*hen we sin as a believer, we are acting contrary to our strongest inclination.

The phrase, *"But if I am doing the very thing I do not wish..."* (Romans 7:20), confirms that Paul, as a New Testament believer, sometimes acted against (contrary to) his strongest inclination. We do the same when we walk in sin, for our strongest inclination is to walk in righteousness. In fact, should you place the new man in a temptation-free environment, he would never sin. Thus, when we eject out of our earthly bodies and are taken to heaven, we will experience sinless perfection (behave perfectly) for the first time in our existence. Our strongest inclination as holy and blameless saints is to obey. Therefore, when we sin we are acting against (contrary to) our strongest inclination. Those people who view the depraved as incapable of exercising personal repentance and faith teach that man <u>cannot</u> respond against (opposite) his strongest inclination. Paul proves such thinking invalid.

Paul made a great discovery—that *"evil"* was *"present"* in him, even though he wished *"to do good"* (Romans 7:21):

> *I find then the principle that evil is present in me, the one who wishes to do good.* (Romans 7:21)

The *"evil"* is the power of sin which lived in Paul's body, the same power Paul mentioned indirectly in verse 18. (The power of sin is an organized power controlled by Satan and must never be viewed as a demon.)

Verses 17 and 20 of Romans 7 (both of which make use of the word *"it"*) are followed by verses that address the power of sin living in the New Testament believer's body. Thus, the contextual view of *"it"* (in verses 17 and 20) points to the evil thoughts generated by the power of sin. In fact, verse 23 records specific information regarding the *"it"* of verses 17 and 20.

Paul *"joyfully"* concurred *"with the law of God in the inner man"* (Romans 7:22), *"law"* in this case meaning "principle":

> *For I joyfully concur with the law of God in the inner man,* (Romans 7:22)

Paul (as a believer) desired to walk with God to the greatest degree possible. However, he had a problem: A *"law"* (or principle—the power of sin) lived *"in the members of"* his *"body,"* which waged *"war against"* his *"mind,"* and made him *"a prisoner of the law of sin"* (power of sin) which was in the *"members"* of his body (Romans 7:23):

> *but I see a different law in the members of my body, waging war against the law of my mind, and making me a prisoner of the law of sin which is in my members.* (Romans 7:23)

Romans 7:23 records truth that set Paul free! I believe he came to realize that the evil thoughts entering his mind were not generated by the old self—which he had incorrectly viewed as alive and well in a New Testament believer. Hence, he was suddenly awakened to the fact that every sinful (evil) thought entering his mind could be traced to the power of sin living in his body. Thus, he records in Romans 7:24-25:

> *Wretched man that I am! Who will set me free from the body of this death? Thanks be to God through Jesus Christ our Lord! So then, on the one hand I myself with my mind am serving the law of God, but on the other, with my flesh the law of sin.* (Romans 7:24-25)

*E*very believer has the option of walking according to God's truth and strength or according to the enemy's (sin's) lies.

"Jesus Christ" had set Paul *"free from the body of this death,"* from having to be controlled by the power of sin as it worked through his physical *"body."* He was *"free,"* therefore, to reject

sin's lie *"through"* the authority and power of *"Jesus Christ our Lord."* When he responded correctly, he served *"the law* [principle] *of God."* When he listened to sin's lie, he served *"the law* [principle] *of sin."* The choice was his, for every New Testament believer has the option of walking according to God's truth or according to the enemy's (sin's) deceptions.

Deliverance through Christ Alone

Some people have wrestled with Paul's words in Romans 7:24. They question why he would refer to himself as *"wretched"* when he taught that his *"old self"* was *"crucified"* (Romans 6:6), that he was *"a new creation"* (2Corinthians 5:17), in fact, a *"holy and blameless"* (Ephesians 1:4) *"saint"* (1Corinthians 1:2). This concern is easily diffused. The word *"wretched"* actually means "distressed" or "miserable." Paul was not saying that he was a *"wretched"* person in the sense of being worthless. He knew well that he was a saint who sometimes sinned, not a worthless, wretched sinner saved by grace. Basically he was communicating his frustration over the battle that raged in his mind due to the power of sin working through his *"body,"* *"the body of this death"* (v.24). However, he found victory through Jesus' life within (v.25).

Romans 7 – The Victorious Christian's Chapter

Romans 7 does not describe the defeated Christian. Rather, it explains how a New Testament believer can (through Christ's indwelling presence) experience victory over the power of sin! Paul realized that the evil thoughts bombarding his mind were not self-generated, but were produced by the power of sin disguising itself as the old self. If the power of sin can convince us that the old self is still alive, we will view ourselves as part evil and part good and, in turn, lowly sinners saved by grace. As a result, we will be unable to appropriate our true identity (the fact that we are saints who through Christ have authority over the power of sin) and will live in defeat. Yes, deception is one of our enemy's most powerful weapons.

Make use of Diagram 9 in the Reference Section as we continue.

Some followers of Christ perceive only the spirit (instead of the spirit and soul) of a New Testament believer as having been perfected at the point of salvation (justification). In such an arrangement, the perfected spirit is viewed as progressively affecting the soul until the soul is eventually made holy and righteous through the spirit's influence. According to this view, the soul of the New Testament believer increases in holiness and righteousness as his behavior increases in holiness and righteousness. This arrangement is impossible, for the cross alone is responsible for perfecting both the spirit and soul of those who believe. Otherwise, the soul would be perfected through good works—an idea totally foreign to the Scriptures. In fact, should our spirit alone have been perfected through Jesus' death, our soul would be on a performance-based acceptance with God. Stated differently, our soul would increase in holiness and righteousness as our behavior increased in holiness and righteousness. Scripture teaches, however, that both the spirit and soul are made perfect through Jesus' work on the cross once the depraved exercise personal repentance and faith.

The soul cannot be made perfect through good works. Nor can it be made perfect through the physical death of the believer. The cross alone is sufficient to accomplish this special work! Hence, both the spirit and soul of a New Testament believer are perfected at the point of salvation (justification).

This truth can withstand the fact that the New Testament believer sometimes disobeys subsequent to salvation/justification (1John 1:8), for a perfect and blameless saint can commit sin and remain a saint in the process. Paul, while addressing the church at Corinth, refers to each of them as saints—even though a man within the church was committing adultery with his own stepmother (1Corinthians 5:1) and several within the fellowship were abusing the Lord's Supper (1Corinthians 11:20-21, 27-34). Again we see that what we do is not who we are, even though who we are has a tremendous impact on what we do. Our person (spirit and soul) was perfected at the point of salvation (justification)—long before our behavior began to line up with who God made us into (in spirit and soul) when we repented and believed. We will not reach the place of sinless perfection (in our behavior) this side of heaven, but we can be certain that our spirit and soul were perfected (never to be improved upon) when God made us new.

Romans 8:1-11

No Condemnation

Has there been a time when a condemning thought ran through your mind, a thought that condemned your person? (If you are human, your answer should be "yes!") Did you believe the thought? Did it cause you to <u>feel</u> discouraged and inadequate? If so, great news is on the horizon! Christ's death, burial, and resurrection occurred that we might, along with many other things, realize that:

> *"There is therefore now no condemnation for those who are in Christ Jesus"* (Romans 8:1).

Thus, any thought that condemns your person is invalid and can be totally disregarded.

That Satan condemns the <u>believer</u>, the believer's person, while the Holy Spirit condemns only the <u>behavior</u> of the believer when necessary, is crucial to comprehend. For instance, suppose I should tell a lie. On the heels of that lie, the power of sin will probably generate the thought, "I am nothing but a worthless liar" (note

There is therefore now no condemnation for those who are in Christ Jesus" (Romans 8:1).

the first person pronoun "I"). And, moreover, it will do so in a voice, including accent and dialect, that sounds just like mine. It will condemn <u>me</u>, my person. The Holy Spirit, however, will say, "I hate lying, but you remain the apple of my eye." A great difference exists between these two concepts. Romans 8:1 is wonderful ammunition against the power of sin's schemes.

Unlike the King James and the New King James, we find that the New American Standard, the New International, the Phillips Translation, the Ryrie Study Bible, along with other versions, do not include the phrase "who walk not after the flesh, but after the Spirit."

> *There is therefore now no condemnation to them which*
> *are in Christ Jesus, <u>who walk not after the flesh, but after</u>*
> *<u>the Spirit.</u>* (Romans 8:1 KJV)

> *There is therefore now no condemnation for those who*
> *are in Christ Jesus.* (Romans 8:1 NASB)

Neither is this phrase found in the most ancient manuscripts accessible today. As a result, the more recent versions omit it, which is perfectly proper. Hence, the idea that condemnation awaits the New Testament believer who walks after the flesh (and sins) is ill founded. No believer is ever condemned by God, even in the midst of his worst state of disobedience. Yes, the <u>behavior</u> of the disobedient child of God is condemned by the Holy Spirit, but <u>the believer is never condemned</u>. Otherwise, the believer would be condemned by God each time sin is committed!

Because *"There is…now no condemnation for those who are in Christ Jesus"* (Romans 8:1), we have the freedom to deal with our acts of sin at the point of disobedience. No more putting them off. No more excuses. The Father is waiting for us to repent and confess so fellowship can be restored, not so He might forgive us—for we are already forgiven. Many church saints put off confessing their sin because they wrongly believe that condemnation awaits them.

No condemnation awaits New Testament believers because they *"are in Christ Jesus."* In fact, they are *"sealed in"* Christ (*"in Him"*) by means of *"the Holy Spirit"* (Ephesians 1:13). They are also in the Father (John 14:20):

> *"In that day you shall know that I am in My Father, and*
> *you in Me, and I in you.* (John 14:20)

How could anyone who has been *"sealed in"* God's holy Son receive the Father's condemnation? Impossible! Thus, *"in Christ"* and *"in Him"* are some of the most important words in all of Scripture. When you have "spare" time on your hands, encourage yourself by recording every instance in the New Testament where *"in Christ"* and *"in Him"* are employed. Also record what we have received through having been placed *"in Him."* (For instance, 2Corinthians 5:17 states that we were made *"a new creature"* the instant we were sealed *"in Christ"*—after repenting and exercising faith while depraved.) For starters, read Romans 3:24, 6:23, 8:39, 1Corinthians 1:2, 4, 5, 2Corinthians 5:21, Ephesians 1:3 and 2:6.

Because *"no condemnation"* (Romans 8:1) awaits the New Testament believer, no church saint will be present at the *"great white throne"* judgment of Revelation 20:11-15 (a subject addressed previously but meriting consideration here). In fact, no believer from throughout the ages will face that horrific sentencing. Only those who reject Christ's free offer of salvation will be present, after which they are *"thrown into the lake of fire"* (Revelation 20:14-15). (How can anyone read these passages and believe in universal salvation—that all mankind will be saved?) Neither will any church saint face the sheep and goat judgment of Matthew 25:31-46, for the *"goats"* will be those Gentiles who refuse to support the Jews during the Tribulation—the church having been taken to heaven prior to the Tribulation. Church saints will face the judgment seat of Christ for the purpose of receiving rewards for deeds done in faith (1Corinthians 3:10-15), but no condemnation is associated with that judgment.

Set Free through Christ Jesus

Paul makes an extremely liberating statement in verse 2:

> *"For the law of the Spirit of life in Christ Jesus has set you free from the law of sin and of death"* (Romans 8:2).

The word *"law"* means "principle" rather than Mosaic Law. Consequently, *"the* [principle] *of the Spirit of life in Christ Jesus has set you free from the* [principle, or power] *of sin and of death."* Certainly, those who walk by God's *"Spirit"* are guaranteed deliverance from the principle (or power) of *"sin"* and its accompanying *"death."* After all, they are *"in Christ Jesus"* (Romans 8:2), and Christ is in them (Galatians 2:20), Who is greater than anything *"the world"* can send their way (1John 4:4):

> *You are from God, little children, and have overcome*
> *them; because greater is He who is in you than he who is*
> *in the world.* (1John 4:4)

Romans 8:3 makes an intriguing declaration:

> *"For what the Law could not do, weak as it was through*
> *the flesh, God did; sending His own Son in the likeness of*
> *sinful flesh and as an offering for sin, He condemned sin*
> *in the flesh,"* (Romans 8:3)

Paul clearly teaches that *"the Law"* cannot save a person from God's condemnation—while the cross and Christ's subsequent resurrection can. God sent His Son *"as an offering for sin,"* an event that removed our sin nature and forgave our sins once we exercised repentance and faith while depraved. This offering also released us from our enslavement to the power of sin. Thus, God *"condemned sin in the flesh"*—that is, the power of *"sin"* which dwells in the New Testament believer's body (*"flesh"*—v.3). This truth fits perfectly with our previous observations.

The Power of God's Spirit

"The Law is holy" (Romans 7:12) and cannot be kept through one's own power, discipline, or strength. An amazing transformation occurs when we exercise repentance and faith and the Holy Spirit invades our spirit to make us new. Paul writes:

> *in order that the requirement of the Law might be fulfilled*
> *in us, who do not walk according to the flesh, but*
> *according to the Spirit.* (Romans 8:4)

The Spirit of God, when released to control our lives, will empower us to walk a path consistent with the moral standard of the Law—without once

> *The Spirit of God, when released to control our lives, will empower us to walk a path consistent with the moral standard of the Law.*

requiring us to submit to the Law. (The New Testament believer has been released from the Law and lives under grace—Romans 6:14). God, in turn, receives all the credit and glory; we in the process learn the true meaning of life.

Walking According to the Flesh Versus the Spirit

Two phrases from Romans 8:4 are absolutely necessary to understand. The first phrase is *"walk according to the flesh."* The second is *"walk...according to the Spirit."* Both phrases refer to a particular state of a New Testament believer (these phrases are displayed graphically in Diagrams 7 and 8 in the Reference Section). The latter phrase refers to those times when we (as New Testament believers) allow the Spirit of God to positively energize the mind—which grants us the wisdom to properly operate the will (Diagram 8). To *"walk according to the flesh,"* on the other hand, points to those times when we (as New Testament believers) allow the power of sin to energize an ungodly habit pattern etched in the brain (Diagram 7). Yes, our habits are stored in the brain (and **the brain is a piece of flesh**—thus the phrase, *"walk according to the flesh"*). We must remember that all of our ungodly habits were not removed when we experienced new birth (salvation). We must remember as well that new ungodly habits are formed when we walk in disobedience *("according to the flesh")*. The great news is that our ungodly habit patterns decrease in size and intensity as we walk *"according to the Spirit."* Their complete removal, on the other hand, will not occur until physical death.

Paul continues to discuss these two phrases *("according to the flesh"* and *"according to the Spirit")* in Romans 8:5:

> *For those who are according to the flesh set their minds*
> *on the things of the flesh, but those who are according to*
> *the Spirit, the things of the Spirit.* (Romans 8:5)

Stated differently, a New Testament believer walks *"according to the flesh"* when he sets his mind on sin's lie sent into the mind through an ungodly habit pattern etched in the brain (the brain being a piece of *"flesh"*), then accepts the lie as truth and responds accordingly (refer to Diagram 7 in the Reference Section). When this process occurs, the new man commits an act of sin. Paul also states that we walk *"according to the Spirit"* when we set our minds on *"the things of the Spirit"* (refer to Diagram 8 in the Reference Section). In this case, the believer (the new man) is walking in obedience. Sounds pretty simple, doesn't it? It may sound simple, but as you well know, it can certainly be difficult in practice.

According to Romans 8:6, to set the mind *"on the flesh"* is *"death"* for the New Testament believer:

> *For the mind set on the flesh is death, but the mind set on*
> *the Spirit is life and peace,* (Romans 8:6)

To live in a compromised state is *"death"* (a place of misery and unrest) for the saint of God, but *"the mind set on the Spirit is life and peace"* (Romans 8:6). Paul then puts the icing on the cake in Romans 8:7:

> *"because the mind set on the flesh is hostile toward God;*
> *for it does not subject itself to the law* [principle] *of God,*
> *for it is not even able to do so."* (Romans 8:7)

Yes, a New Testament believer who sets his mind *"on the flesh"* will sometimes behave much like an unbeliever, but in most cases will repent and confess his sin. If not, he will be extremely miserable, as was David in the midst of his disobedience (read Psalm 51). How can a cat enjoy wallowing in a mud hole? Impossible!

Paul next addresses what it means to be *"in the flesh"* versus *"in the Spirit"* (Romans 8:8-9), for a person who is *"in the flesh cannot please God"*:

> *and those who are in the flesh cannot please God.*
> (Romans 8:8)

Thus, to be *"in the flesh"* is to be lost—which is totally different from walking *"according to the flesh"* (Romans 8:4, 5, 12, 13), which occurs when a New Testament believer is deceived by sin's lie and disobeys. However, we are *"in the Spirit"* and saved *if...the Spirit of God dwells in"* us (Romans 8:9):

> *However, you are not in the flesh but in the Spirit, if*
> *indeed the Spirit of God dwells in you. But if anyone does*
> *not have the Spirit of Christ, he does not belong to Him.*
> (Romans 8:9).

"Those who are in the flesh" (v.8) do not *"belong"* to God because they are void of the *"Spirit of Christ"* (v.9). Only those who repent and believe while depraved can receive the *"Spirit"* and begin to *"please God"* (v.8) on an ongoing basis.

How Misinterpreting the Term "Flesh" Tarnishes One's View of the Scriptures

This section addresses two examples of how misinterpreting the term *"flesh"* has brought confusion to Christ's body. (1) The New International Version's definition of *"flesh"* (2) Reformed Theology's view of *"flesh"* (Reformed Theology being extreme and hyper-Calvinism—observe Diagrams 13-15 in the Reference Section). This portion of our study should be tremendously encouraging, for the identity principles ("who we are in Christ") taught in this *Advancing in Romans* commentary exposes the error in both of these scenarios.

> *There is therefore now no condemnation for those who*
> *are in Christ Jesus. For the law of the Spirit of life in*
> *Christ Jesus has set you free from the law of sin and of*
> *death. For what the Law could not do, weak as it was*
> *through the flesh, God did: sending His own Son in the*
> *likeness of sinful flesh and as an offering for sin, He*
> *condemned sin in the flesh, in order that the requirement*
> *of the Law might be fulfilled in us, who do not walk*
> *according to the flesh, but according to the Spirit. For*
> *those who are according to the flesh set their minds on*
> *the things of the flesh, but those who are according to the*
> *Spirit, the things of the Spirit. For the mind set on the*
> *flesh is death, but the mind set on the Spirit is life and*
> *peace, because the mind set on the flesh is hostile toward*
> *God; for it does not subject itself to the law of God, for it*

269

is not even able to do so; and those who are in the flesh
cannot please God. However, you are not in the flesh but
in the Spirit, if indeed the Spirit of God dwells in you. But
if anyone does not have the Spirit of Christ, he does not
belong to Him. (Romans 8:1-9 NASB)

Reformed Theologians (extreme and hyper-Calvinists) use these passages, especially Romans 8:5-9, in an attempt to uphold their definition of the "T" of the TULIP, Total Depravity—that the depraved (lost) are spiritual corpses incapable of exercising repentance and faith. They do so by viewing the phrases, *"those who are according to the flesh"* (Romans 8:5), *"the mind set on the flesh"* (Romans 8:6), and *"the mind set on the flesh"* (Romans 8:7), as describing the depraved (lost)—never the saved. They draw this conclusion based on their definition of the term *"flesh"*—an extremely important term included in each of those passages. Reviewing what we have gleaned from the Scriptures will allow us to determine whether their assumption is in agreement with the full counsel of God's Word.

God's Word teaches that we were born a child *"of wrath"* (Ephesians 2:3) due to the sinful nature (the *"old self"*—Romans 6:6) inherited from Adam. The compelling news is that the sinful nature (Adamic nature, old self, old man, or dead spirit—all synonymous terms) is eradicated when a person during the church age accepts Christ as Savior (Romans 6:6; 7:1-4; and Galatians 2:20). Hence, when we were justified (saved), the sinful nature *("the old self"*—Colossians 3:9) was replaced by the *"new"* creation (2Corinthians 5:17), the *"new self"* (Colossians 3:9-10), who is *"holy"* (Ephesians 1:4), *"sanctified"* (Hebrews 10:10), *"perfected"* (Hebrews 10:14), *"glorified"* (Romans 8:30), *"justified"* (Romans 5:1), *"forgiven"* (Ephesians 4:32; Colossians 2:13; 1John 2:12), *"complete"* (Colossians 2:10), and much more. This truth verifies that the New Testament believer is not dual natured, *"old self"* and *"new self"* (bad dog and good dog) as some teach, but the *"new self"* only.

Some believers would question the validity of this teaching, for it surely "feels" as if the old self (sinful nature) is alive at times. However, Romans 6:6, 7:1-4, and Galatians 2:20 teach otherwise—that the old self (sinful nature) is totally eradicated in the New Testament saint. Hence, the old self (who we were before we met Christ) does not war against the new self (who we are now). Rather, the *"flesh"* wars against the new self (new man). Thus, Paul wrote to the <u>believers</u> at Galatia:

> *But I say, walk by the Spirit, and you will not carry out*
> *the desire of the flesh. For the flesh sets its desire against*
> *the Spirit, and the Spirit against the flesh; for these are in*
> *opposition to one another, so that you may not do the*
> *things that you please.* (Galatians 5:16-17)

The New Testament believer's struggle is with the *"flesh"*—not the sinful nature. This truth is extremely liberating, for the sinful nature is who we used to be—the Adamic nature, old self, old man, dead spirit—all synonymous terms. The *"flesh"* is certainly not the sinful nature (old self, old man, dead spirit, Adamic nature).

While living in our lost state, with the sinful nature alive and well, we performed deeds that the Bible classifies as sinful. Sitting on the throne of our lives, we lived for "me, my, and I" only. In fact, the most natural thing we did as unbelievers was sin. We sinned not only because it was natural, but because *"sin,"* Satan's agent, placed lies in our minds that we bought as the truth. This reality is verified by Romans 7:7-13, where Paul describes how sin worked through the Law while in his depraved state—Paul eventually realizing his need for a Savior (while depraved) through failing to measure up to the righteous standard required by the Law:

> *What shall we say then? Is the Law sin? May it never be!*
> *On the contrary, I would not have come to know sin*
> *except through the Law; for I would not have known*
> *about coveting if the Law had not said, "You shall not*
> *covet." But sin, taking opportunity through the*
> *commandment, produced in me coveting of every kind; for*
> *apart from the Law sin is dead. And I was once alive*
> *apart from the Law; but when the commandment came,*
> *sin became alive, and I died; and this commandment,*
> *which was to result in life, proved to result in death for*
> *me; for sin, taking opportunity through the*
> *commandment, deceived me, and through it killed me. So*
> *then, the Law is holy, and the commandment is holy and*

righteous and good. Therefore did that which is good
become a cause of death for me? May it never be! Rather
it was sin, in order that it might be shown to be sin by
effecting my death through that which is good, that
through the commandment sin might become utterly
sinful. (Romans 7:7-13)

The remainder of Romans 7 (verses 14-25) describes Paul's battle with *"sin"* <u>after</u> he became a believer.

Continuing our review, *Vine's Expository Dictionary of New Testament Words* defines the noun *"sin"* as "an organized power."[13] *"Sin"* (the power of *"sin")* is not a demon, but a power controlled by Satan himself. (Satan is not omnipresent, so he uses the power of *"sin"* as his agent for the purpose of deceiving man.) As a result of accepting the power of sin's lies as truth while depraved (lost), patterns (habits) were formed in the brain (the brain being a piece of meat, or *"flesh"*) that programmed us to think, feel, and act in particular ways when exposed to sin's stimulus. As you are well aware, all of these sinful patterns (habits) were not erased when we were made new in Christ. Consequently, when the New Testament believer allows *"sin"* (which lives in the New Testament believer's body only—Romans 7:23) to activate one of these ungodly patterns in the brain (the brain being a piece of <u>flesh</u>), he is walking *"according to the flesh"* (Romans 8:4-5). Simple as that! Yet, in some theological circles, *"flesh"* is equated with the sinful nature. Both the New International Version of the Bible (the NIV) and Reformed Theology commit this fatal error, so let's examine the ramifications of their improper thinking.

Man is born with a sinful nature, but the term *"flesh"* (used in Romans 8:4-5 for instance) is definitely not equivalent to the sinful nature inherited from Adam. Yet, the New International Version (the NIV) took the liberty to translate *"flesh"* (NASB) as *"sinful nature"* (NIV) in verses 3, 4, 5, 8, 9, 12 and 13 of Romans 8. (The King James, New King James, Revised Standard, Modern, Amplified, New American Standard—even the Greek Interlinear—use *"flesh"* instead of "sinful nature.") The NIV also translated *"sinful flesh"* (NASB) in verse 3 as *"sinful man"* (NIV), and *"the things of the flesh"* (NASB) in verse 5 as *"what that nature desires"* (NIV*).* Also, in verse 6, the phrase, *"the mind set on the flesh"* (NASB), is translated *"the mind of sinful man"*

(NIV).   This incorrect rendering in the NIV does not affect the overall meaning of <u>some</u> of these verses, but in other instances (such as in Romans 8:5-7) the meaning is altered altogether.   The severity of this problem will become evident as we read Romans 8:1-14 in the NIV, which is recorded below. [Note: I have inserted the NASB rendering in brackets (the proper rendering from the Greek) to reveal how the NIV misrepresents these extremely critical passages.   Evidently, those responsible for generating the NIV viewed the New Testament believer as possessing two natures (sinful nature and new self) and therefore took the liberty to replace *"flesh"* with *"sinful nature"* due to assuming that the *"sinful nature"* and *"flesh"* are one and the same.   They could not have been more mistaken.   Remember, the original Greek (not any particular version or paraphrase of the Bible) has the final say in every case.   Presented below is the rendering of Romans 8:1-14 in the New International Version with the corrections in brackets for clarification.]

> *Therefore, there is now no condemnation for those who are in Christ Jesus, because through Christ Jesus the law of the Spirit of life set me free from the law of sin and death.   For what the law was powerless to do in that it was weakened by the sinful nature* [flesh], *God did by sending his own Son in the likeness of sinful man* [sinful flesh] *to be a sin offering. And so he condemned sin in sinful man* [the flesh], *in order that the righteous requirements of the law might be fully met in us, who do not live according to the sinful nature* [the flesh] *but according to the Spirit.*
> *Those who live according to the sinful nature* [the flesh] *have their minds set on what that nature desires* [on the things of the flesh]; *but those who live in accordance with the Spirit have their minds set on what the Spirit desires.   The mind of sinful man* [the mind set on the flesh] *is death, but the mind controlled by the Spirit is life and peace; the sinful mind* [the mind set on the flesh] *is hostile to God. It does not submit to God's law, nor can it do so.   Those controlled by the sinful nature* [those who are in the flesh] *cannot please God.   You, however, are controlled not by the sinful nature* [are not in the flesh]

273

but by [in] *the Spirit, if the Spirit of God lives in you. And
if anyone does not have the Spirit of Christ, he does not
belong to Christ. But if Christ is in you, your body is
dead because of sin, yet your spirit is alive because of
righteousness. And if the Spirit of him who raised Jesus
from the dead is living in you, he who raised Christ from
the dead will also give life to your mortal bodies through
his Spirit, who lives in you.*

    *Therefore, brothers, we have an obligation-but it is not
to the sinful nature* [the flesh], *to live according to it* [the
flesh]. *For if you live according to the sinful nature* [the
flesh], *you will die; but if by the Spirit you put to death
the misdeeds of the body, you will live, because those who
are led by the Spirit of God are sons of God.* (Romans
8:1-14 NIV)

Interestingly, the NIV sometimes places a number beside *"sinful
nature,"* indicating that the reader is to reference the margin for the more
correct rendering. In such cases, the word *"flesh"* is found in the
margin. Many people who read the Bible disregard the margins. Thus,
speak with individuals who use the NIV and they will normally tell you
that the sin nature is alive and well in the New Testament believer. What
a shame!

Reformed Theology's view of Romans 8 is also affected by
misinterpreting the term *"flesh."* In fact, several extremely visible
Reformed theologians fail to comprehend the difference between the
"sinful nature" and the *"flesh."* Hence, they view the phrase, *"the mind
set on the flesh,"* in Romans 8:7 as pointing to that which is experienced
by the lost (the depraved). Yet, when studied in the context of Romans
8:4-6, Paul is describing the disobedient New Testament believer. The
fact that the believer can be controlled by the *"flesh"* is verified by
Romans 7:25 as well (remember that Romans 7:14-25 describes Paul's
struggle with *"sin"* as a believer):

*Thanks be to God through Jesus Christ our Lord! So then,
on the one hand I myself with my mind am serving the law
of God, but on the other, with my flesh the law of sin.*
(Romans 7:25)

Some people would argue that Romans 7:24 negates this conclusion—that Paul had to be recounting his days prior to believing:

> *Wretched man that I am! Who will set me free from the*
> *body of this death?* (Romans 7:24)

The word *"wretched"* in this case actually means "distressed" or "miserable." Thus, Paul was not saying that he was a wretched person in the sense of being lost, for he knew he was a saint who sometimes sinned, and not a lowly sinner in need of salvation. He was basically communicating that he was "distressed" (as a believer) over the battle that raged in his mind as a result of the power of sin working through the avenue of his body *("the body of this death")*. He eventually matured as a believer and found victory through Christ's life dwelling within him:

> *Thanks be to God through Jesus Christ our Lord! So then,*
> *on the one hand I myself with my mind am serving the law*
> *of God, but on the other, with my flesh the law of sin.*
> (Romans 7:25)

From all indications, Reformed theologians generally agree with the New International Version's definition of *"flesh"* in Romans 8:1-14 (equating it with the sinful nature)—a view which violates the Greek text altogether. Hence, both the NIV and Reformed Theology misinterpret the term *"flesh"* in Romans 8:5-7—the NIV viewing it as confirming that the New Testament believer possesses two natures (sinful nature plus new man), Reformed Theology generally viewing *"flesh"* as confirming that to walk *"according to the flesh" ("according to the sinful nature"*—NIV) is making reference to the lost (depraved).

Romans 8:5-7 (when studied in context) describes New Testament believers—not once mentioning what transpires with the depraved. We again witness the unbiblical conclusions drawn by Reformed Theology while attempting to protect its unjustifiable view of the "T" of the TULIP, Total Depravity. We also observe the fallout when one's preconceived notions are allowed to affect one's view of the Scriptures. Those responsible for generating (producing) the NIV's version of Romans 6-8 evidently viewed the New Testament believer as possessing two natures—resulting in their redefining *"flesh"* as sinful nature. This mistake has generated a theological nightmare beyond comprehension!

Thus, when the *"flesh"* is improperly viewed as synonymous with the sinful nature, we discover that the following errors can occur: (1) The NIV teaches that the New Testament believer is dual natured—old self and new self (2) Reformed Theology normally perceives verses 5 through 7 of Romans 8 as describing behavior exemplified by the depraved.

Paul follows in Romans 8:8-9 by relating what it means to be *"in the flesh"* versus *"in the Spirit"*:

> *and those who are in the flesh cannot please God.*
> *However, you are not in the flesh but in the Spirit, if*
> *indeed the Spirit of God dwells in you. But if anyone does*
> *not have the Spirit of Christ, he does not belong to Him.*
> (Romans 8:8-9 — emphasis added)

The apostle first states that a person who is *"in the flesh"* cannot please God (Romans 8:8). This fact verifies that to be *"in the flesh"* is to be lost—a vast difference from the New Testament believer walking *"according to the flesh"* (Romans 8:4-5). Romans 7:5-6 confirms this same truth:

> *For while we were in the flesh, the sinful passions, which*
> *were aroused by the Law, were at work in the members of*
> *our body to bear fruit for death. But now we have been*
> *released from the Law, having died to that by which we*
> *were bound, so that we serve in newness of the Spirit and*
> *not in oldness of the letter.* (Romans 7:5-6 — emphasis added)

Reformed theologians suggest that Romans 8:8 disproves "free willism" and endorses their view of total depravity—that the depraved cannot repent and believe and are, therefore, spiritual corpses. Does it? Quite the contrary! This verse is not teaching that a person cannot repent and believe while depraved, but rather that the depraved cannot live in a manner that is pleasing to God on an ongoing basis—described as walking *"according to the Spirit"* in Romans 8:4-5, a lifestyle characterized by the Spirit's leading. By missing the context of Romans 8:8 (through misinterpreting the biblical and, thus, contextual meaning of the term *"flesh"),* Reformed Theology improperly interprets Romans 8:5-7. Thus, they present an argument that is a-contextual and false.

Romans 8:5-7 describes New Testament believers—which totally negates the standard Reformed view of these passages (Reformed Theology is addressed in much depth in our *God's Heart* series).

The first phrase, *"in the flesh"* (Romans 8:8 and 9), refers to a person who does not know Christ. The second, walking *"according to the flesh"* (Romans 8:4-5), refers to those times when a New Testament believer gives in to an ungodly habit pattern due to believing the power of sin's lie. As has already been established, the power of sin dwells in the New Testament believer's body and sends messages

The power of sin dwells in the New Testament believer's body and sends messages into the mind by means of the ungodly habit patterns stored in the brain.

into the mind by means of the ungodly habit patterns stored in the brain, which is a piece of *"flesh."*

Is the Body Already Dead?

In Romans 8:10, Paul stresses that in relation to a New Testament believer, *"...the body is dead because of sin..."* Paul is not teaching that our bodies cease functioning after accepting Jesus as Savior. He proves, rather, that we can consider powerless any lie that the power of *"sin"* sends into our minds through the avenue of *"the body."* This teaching ties in perfectly with our discussion regarding Romans 6:11, so you might want to review those notes. (Remember that the power of sin's thought enters the New Testament believer's mind—not the power of sin itself.)

Paul also stresses that *"...the spirit is alive because of righteousness"* (Romans 8:10). In other words, because we know Christ and have been made *"righteous,"* our *"spirit is alive."* After all, we are *"one spirit with...the Lord"* (1Corinthians 6:17), making us *"alive"* indeed (Romans 8:10).

> *But the one who joins himself to the Lord is one spirit with Him.* (1Corinthians 6:17)

Thus, only through the indwelling presence of Jesus can a New Testament believer receive true *"life."*

> *Jesus said to him, "I am the way, and the truth, and the life; no one comes to the Father, but through Me.* (John 14:6)

Paul is not finished, for he confirms that God's *"Spirit"* living inside us gives *"life to"* our *"mortal bodies"* (Romans 8:11).

> *But if the Spirit of Him who raised Jesus from the dead dwells in you, He who raised Christ Jesus from the dead will also give life to your mortal bodies through His Spirit who indwells you.* (Romans 8:11)

The apostle refers to more than receiving our glorified bodies at the Rapture of the church. He also speaks of the privilege we now have of living above our temptations through the power of the Holy Spirit. God did more than deliver us from condemnation through justification—subsequent to our repenting and believing while depraved. He also empowers our lives in the here and now as we yield to His life within us. Christ's blood is the avenue through which our sins were removed; His body is the avenue through which our old self was eradicated. Consequently, we were freed from the penalty of sin through Jesus' blood, but we have been freed from the dominion of the power of sin through our death with Jesus on the cross (Romans 6:6-7; Galatians 2:20). What terrific news! Isn't Romans a phenomenal book?

Romans 8:12-25

Not Obligated to Sin

Isn't it wonderful to know that, *"There is therefore now no condemnation for those who are in Christ Jesus"* (Romans 8:1)? Have you ever heard better news? This truth should encourage us to know the Lord as intimately as possible: To pant after Him *"As the deer pants for the water brooks..."* (Psalm 42:1). The more we know Him, the more we will love Him. The more we love Him, the more we will desire to glorify Him through every thought and deed. Thus, Paul writes:

> *"So then, brethren, we are under obligation, not to the flesh, to live according to the flesh—"* (Romans 8:12)

Paul's use of the pronoun *"we,"* writing to *"brethren"* (believers), confirms that the New Testament believer can *"live according to the flesh."* However, we are not obligated to do so due to our new holy and perfect nature that hates sin. Don't miss the fact that, although we are not obligated to *"live according to the flesh,"* we are capable of doing so when caught off guard—proving that the phrase *"live according to the flesh"* (Romans 8:12) points to behavior that can be exemplified by the redeemed. As we discovered previously,

When I sin, it is the new self who has sinned, since I am the new self.

to *"walk according to the flesh"* (Romans 8:4) means that we have allowed the power of sin, through its use of the ungodly habit patterns stored in the brain, the brain being a piece of *"flesh,"* to influence our behavior. We do so when we believe the power of sin's lies sent into our minds by means of these ungodly patterns. Thus the phrases, *"live according to the flesh"* (Romans 8:12) and *"walk according to the flesh"* (Romans 8:4), are equivalent. Many of these ungodly habits were formed before we met Christ, but some are fashioned <u>after</u> we become believers. Yes, new sinful patterns are produced when I, the new self (the new man), believe the power of sin's lie in a new area and respond

279

accordingly. Therefore, when I sin, the new self has sinned, since I am the new self.

To live *"according to the flesh"* means that we *"must die"* (Romans 8:13):

> *for if you are living according to the flesh, you must die;...* (Romans 8:13)

The margin in my NASB indicates that the phrase, *"you must die,"* can actually be rendered, *"you are about to die."* Indeed, if we (as New Testament believers) live *"according to the flesh"* long enough and don't experience physical death, we find ourselves living as though we are dead. In fact, to live in a prolonged state of disobedience, after having known the peace and joy of fellowship with Christ, results in nothing but defeat and despair. Joy and peace are restored through repentance and confession, but *"consequence"* is reaped from our disobedience the remainder of our stay on earth (Colossians 3:25). Yet, not once does God condemn the believer who exemplifies such unwise behavior (Romans 8:1)!

Paul continues by writing:

> *"...but if by the Spirit you are putting to death the deeds of the body, you will live"* (Romans 8:13).

Truth is amazing in that it exposes and incapacitates deception. As we yield to the *"Spirit"* of God (the *"Spirit"* of Truth), the power of sin which dwells in our physical body is defeated as it attempts to deceive us into being influenced by our ungodly habit patterns (reference Circle Diagram 8). Hence, only through responding to the Spirit's promptings do we really *"live"!* With this fact in mind, consider the following truth regarding our Savior.

Jesus was born void of a sin nature (old self) because he was the Father's Son, not the son of Joseph. On occasion, however, His mind was flooded with thoughts (lies) from Satan, as verified by Matthew 4:1-11. He chose to reject these thoughts (lies) the moment they entered and remained pure and holy. Therefore, Jesus proves that a sinful thought does not result in sin until we allow it to negatively impact our thinking and, in turn, our behavior. Consequently, we must refuse any thought that violates the principles taught in the full counsel of God's Word.

Was Jesus capable of committing sin? After all, His brain was void of sinful habit patterns. The answer comes from a question: Have you sinned in a new area of temptation since becoming a believer? Of course you have! Thus, a person can sin in an area where no habit pattern exists. However, a new habit pattern begins to be formed the moment we commit sin in untried areas of disobedience. Certainly, Jesus was capable of sinning. How else could He relate to our struggle with sin!

Are you developing a greater appreciation for truth? Doesn't this magnificent news encourage you to devour God's Word, to make it *"the joy"* of your *"heart"* (Psalm 119:111)? The truth found in Jesus alone will set us free from anything the enemy sends our way.

Sons, Not Slaves

Paul teaches:

> *"For all who are being led by the Spirit of God, these are sons of God"* (Romans 8:14).

The phrase, *"are being led,"* is a present, passive, indicative verb in the Greek, which indicates present tense action—linear action that is ongoing. Thus, if a man is being *"led by the Spirit"* on a fairly consistent basis, he shows himself to be a son *"of God."* No one, not even the greatest of saints, is *"led by the Spirit"* every moment of the day. Thus, if we are open to the Spirit's leading, it confirms we are believers.

Some people would argue that since believers are *"led by the Spirit of God"* (Romans 8:14), and that the "passive" voice is in play (meaning that the subject is being acted upon *"by the Spirit"),* that the New Testament believer is void of a free will. Such a scenario cannot be the case due to the many passages that encourage believers to choose the Spirit over the flesh (such as Galatians 5:16 and 25)—proving that a choice (on our part) is first required before we can be *"led by"* God's Spirit.

We become *"sons of God,"* and receive the Holy *"Spirit,"* at the point of justification (salvation). But we must learn to be *"led by the Spirit."* We are being *"led by the Spirit"* when we allow the thoughts directed into our minds by means of the *"Spirit"* to control our lives, thoughts that are always in agreement with the Word of God. *"The Spirit"* grants wisdom to make proper choices, which in turn frees us to live as Jesus lived. He taught that *"the Spirit"* is *"the Spirit of truth"* and that He would *"guide"* us *"into all the truth"* (John 16:13). As a result, we grow *"from faith to faith"* (Romans 1:17) and experience the amazing adventure accessible to the redeemed alone.

We are given even more encouraging news in Romans 8:15:

> *For you have not received a spirit of slavery leading to*
> *fear again, but you have received a spirit of adoption as*
> *sons by which we cry out, "Abba! Father!"* (Romans
> 8:15)

Paul states that we *"...have not received a spirit of slavery leading to fear again,"* but *"a spirit of adoption as sons by which we cry out, 'Abba! Father!'"* Hence, the *"spirit of* adoption" we have *"received"* frees us to perceive God as a loving *"Father"* Who has our best interests in mind. Simply put, if we are justified (saved), we are sons of God whether we <u>feel</u> like it or not (John 1:12):

> *But as many as received Him, to them He gave the right*
> *to become children of God, even to those who believe in*
> *His name,* (John 1:12)

This truth is comforting news, especially to those individuals void of an earthly father's love. After all, God is *"A father of the fatherless":*

> *A father of the fatherless and a judge for the widows, is*
> *God in His holy habitation.* (Psalm 68:5)

Hence, the Lord *"supports the fatherless":*

> The LORD *protects the strangers; He supports the*
> *fatherless and the widow; but He thwarts the way of the*
> *wicked.* (Psalm 146:9)

Therefore, no believer should view himself as lacking support. We must communicate these wonderful truths to all who will listen, for an improper view of the Father keeps many people from accepting Christ as Savior.

The *"Spirit"* reveals to us *"that we are children of God,"* through bearing *"witness with our spirit"* (Romans 8:16):

> *The Spirit Himself bears witness with our spirit that we*
> *are children of God,* (Romans 8:16)

No need to be afraid of God, for He is our Father—and He reminds us of this glorious truth on a consistent, never-ending basis. We are also *"...heirs of God and fellow heirs with Christ..."* (Romans 8:17):

> *and if children, heirs also, heirs of God and fellow heirs*
> *with Christ, if indeed we suffer with Him in order that we*
> *may also be glorified with Him.* (Romans 8:17)

When *"all things"* are summed up *"in Christ"* (Ephesians 1:10), we will be *"fellow heirs with"* Him (Romans 8:17)—possessing all that He possesses. We are also *"heirs of God"* (v.17), confirming that we are His offspring and *"heirs"* of everything He has to bestow. What could possibly keep us from becoming legitimate bond-servants of this God Who loves us so?

*H*e *builds character in the fiber of our being through using the difficulties of life for our good—the only thing that will prepare us to reign.*

As a result of being *"heirs of God and fellow heirs with Christ,"* we will *"also be glorified with Him"?* (Remember that the spirit and soul of a New Testament believer are glorified at the point of justification, but no New Testament believer receives his glorified body until the

283

Rapture of the church.)   According to Revelation 3:21 and Revelation 20:4, we will rule with Christ as well.   Consequently, God must train us for such a responsible position by building character in the fiber of our being through using the difficulties of life for our good—the very catalyst, when coupled with truth, that prepares us to reign.

Hope in the Midst of Suffering

> *For I consider that the sufferings of this present time are not worthy to be compared with the glory that is to be revealed to us.* (Romans 8:18)

As we transition into Romans 8:18-25, note how frequently the pronouns *"us," "we,"* and *"our"* are implemented.   These pronouns are major players when pursuing proper definitions of terms such as *"foreknew," "predestined," "called," "justified,"* and *"glorified"* found in Romans 8:27-30.

Paul's maturity allowed him to perceive his *"sufferings"* as unworthy *"to be compared with the glory that is to be revealed to us"* (Romans 8:18).   Abundant *"glory"* will *"be revealed to"* the New Testament believer as a result of being part of Christ's body and the Father's family. When God's presence is manifested, glory is exhibited.   In fact, glory can be defined as "the physical manifestation of God's presence."   This truth is exemplified vividly in Exodus 3 (God's glory was in the *"burning...bush")* and Exodus 20 (God's glory descended on Mount Sinai in the form of *"thunder," "lightning," "the sound of a trumpet," "smoke,"* and a *"thick cloud.")* In each case, man was awestruck by His presence due to His impeccable nature and character!   To state it differently, God is so perfect that glory manifests itself when He appears (as in the tabernacle in Exodus 40:34-38 and later in the temple in 1Kings 8:11 and 2Chronicles 5:14).   Jesus is the *"glory"* of *"the Father"* (John 1:14) and lives *"in"* us (Colossians 1:27), meaning that His *"glory"* is *"revealed to us"* (Romans 8:18) as we pursue His heart! How exciting!

The King James' rendering of this passage differs from the NASB, for it communicates that much "glory" will *"be revealed in us"* (the NASB uses *"to us").*

> *For I reckon that the sufferings of this present time are*
> *not worthy to be compared with the glory which shall be*
> *revealed <u>in us</u>.* (Romans 8:18 KJV)

No problem, for this interpretation also agrees with the full counsel of God's Word. In fact, when we return as Christ's Bride (and body) at His Second Coming (Revelation 19:11-14), having previously received our glorified bodies (mentioned in 1Corinthians 15:50-55) at the Rapture of the church, we will bring much *"glory"* to the Father. Can we even begin to imagine the glory manifested when Jesus returns as the glorified Son with His glorified body, the church? Also, the Second Coming of Christ will occur when the earth is experiencing devastating darkness unique to that day alone:

> *"But immediately after the tribulation of those days the*
> *sun will be darkened, and the moon will not give its light,*
> *and the stars will fall from the sky, and the powers of the*
> *heavens will be shaken, and then the sign of the Son of*
> *Man will appear in the sky, and then all the tribes of the*
> *earth will mourn, and they will see the Son of Man*
> *coming on the clouds of the sky with power and great*
> *glory.* (Matthew 24:29-30)

We can only imagine the thrill of returning with Him in this magnificent state of glory—to be witnessed by every individual inhabiting the earth, believers and unbelievers alike!

Whether Paul is addressing the *"glory that is to be revealed to us"* (Romans 8:18 NASB) or *"the glory which shall be revealed in us* (Romans 8:18 KJV), his statement is extraordinary considering the extreme persecution he encountered while preaching the gospel. Hence, 2Corinthians 11 and 12 are required reading when our difficulties seem overwhelming. 2Corinthians 4:12 is required reading as well, for Paul states:

> *So death works in us, but life in you.* (2Corinthias 4:12)

Paul taught that the suffering he bore worked *"life"* in his readers. They were significantly encouraged, mesmerized in fact, by the grace

Jesus supplied in the midst of Paul's pain. What hope he possessed (Romans 8:18)! In fact, his life was explained in terms of Jesus alone. Paul was severely persecuted, but he considered his *"sufferings"* as nothing compared to *"the glory"* that would follow (Romans 8:18), as evidenced by 2Corinthians 4:17-18:

> *For momentary, light affliction is producing for us an*
> *eternal weight of glory far beyond all comparison, while*
> *we look not at the things which are seen, but at the things*
> *which are not seen; for the things which are seen are*
> *temporal, but the things which are not seen are eternal.*
> (2Corinthians 4:17-18)

And yes, this *"glory"* that Paul and all church saints possess will be fully manifested at Jesus' Second Coming! Truly, what a magnificent day that will be!

Paul had a superb example to follow, having witnessed Stephen's death (read Acts 7:54-60). God's grace exemplified through Stephen's bold (yet loving) stance for the gospel greatly impacted *"Saul"* (Acts 7:58), who would later be known as Paul. Stephen, in fact, was a visible expression of Hebrews 12:3:

> *For consider Him who has endured such hostility by*
> *sinners against Himself, so that you may not grow weary*
> *and lose heart.* (Hebrews 12:3)

Stephen, as a result of considering Jesus in the midst of his brutal treatment, *"endured"* (like Moses), *"as seeing Him who is unseen":*

> *By faith he left Egypt, not fearing the wrath of the king;*
> *for he endured, as seeing Him who is unseen.* (Hebrews
> 11:27)

Paul had to be forever changed through Stephen's powerful witness.

The Creation Waits

For the anxious longing of the creation waits eagerly for
the revealing of the sons of God. (Romans 8:19)

"Creation" is waiting *"eagerly for the revealing of the sons of God."*
Therefore, *"creation"* knows about Jesus' Second Coming! How it
possesses this capability is difficult to fathom. We do know, however,
that the *"invisible attributes"* of God, *"His eternal power and divine*
nature, have been clearly seen, being understood through what has been
made" (Romans 1:20). So somehow, through some means, *"creation"*
knows that Jesus will return. From the day that Adam sinned,
"creation" has lived in agonizing pain. Hence, the *"creation"* longs for
the Second Coming, when Christ returns with His body (the church). It
longs due to the curse it received through Adam's disobedience.

The Creation Possesses Hope

For the creation was subjected to futility, not of its own
will, but because of Him who subjected it, in hope
(Romans 8:20)

God's curse upon creation was not administered void of *"hope."*
The reason for this *"hope"* is given in Romans 8:21:

that the creation itself also will be set free from its slavery
to corruption into the freedom of the glory of the children
of God. (Romans 8:21)

"Creation" lives in hope because a day is coming when it will be
released from its present *"slavery to corruption"* (Romans 8:21). Yes,
"corruption" (stemming from sin) brings about *"slavery"* (bondage). In
fact, Isaiah 30:23-26, Isaiah 35:1-2, and Ezekiel 36:28-38 (only a few of
the many verses that could have been cited) describe the degree to which
creation will be blessed (and *"set free")* when Christ returns with His
bride, the church, at His Second Coming.

The phrase, *"the freedom of the glory of the children of God"* (Romans 8:21), brings amazing comfort. God, who possesses *"glory,"* is totally free. He is unrestricted by sin and its resulting corruption due to His holiness. Thus, when He appears, *"glory"* is manifested. Therefore Jesus, who is God (Hebrews 1:8), and the *"glory of the...Father"* (John 1:14), is not only *"free,"* but capable of giving all who repent and believe while depraved this same freedom:

> *"If therefore the Son shall make you free, you shall be free indeed.* (John 8:36)

Because the greatest freedom experienced by man is found in Christ, we can walk in that same freedom due to living *"in Christ"* (2Corinthians 5:17), the *"glory as of the only begotten from the Father"* (John 1:14). For this reason Paul states:

> *It was for freedom that Christ set us free; therefore keep standing firm and do not be subject again to a yoke of slavery.* (Galatians 5:1)

We are free indeed! However, if we desire to walk in God's power, this *"freedom"* must never be used as "an opportunity for the flesh":

> *For you were called to freedom, brethren; only do not turn your freedom into an opportunity for the flesh, but through love serve one another.* (Galatians 5:13)

The Creation Groans

> *For we know that the whole creation groans and suffers the pains of childbirth together until now.* (Romans 8:22)

"...the whole creation groans and suffers." In fact, it *"suffers the pains of childbirth"*! Having witnessed this pain firsthand (when Kim birthed our son Benjamin), I can't imagine living in such discomfort (flat-out agony) one hundred percent of the time. Yet, the creation endures this agony every second of the day. Although presently cursed, the creation

remains an incredible invention of God. For instance, the earth is tilted 23 degrees in respect to its orbit. Should it tilt just one degree either side of this mark, we would either (1) die due to frigid temperatures or (2) be consumed by the sun's heat. Truly, God is an amazing architect.

The pronoun *"we"* plays a major role in how verses 26-30 are to be interpreted!

We Groan

> *And not only this, but also we ourselves, having the first fruits of the Spirit, even we ourselves groan within ourselves, waiting eagerly for our adoption as sons, the redemption of our body.* (Romans 8:23)

We, as New Testament believers, *"groan"* along with creation. We who possess *"the first fruits of the Spirit"* (God's divine engagement ring) *"groan"* because we are *"waiting eagerly for our adoption as sons, the redemption of our body."* In other words, we *"groan"* because we live in bodies that will die, bodies housing the power of sin. We learned earlier that the new self (the new man—the real us—our soul and spirit) is already redeemed, perfect, holy, blameless, and more. Our bodies are not yet redeemed, for they are mortal and will one day return to dust! Think about this truth for a moment. At the point of physical death, our brains will die, and our ungodly habit patterns will become extinct. Only then will the power of sin cease sending thoughts into our minds, thoughts that sometimes deceive us into believing that error is truth. Thus, only after our physical bodies cease operating will we be perfected in our behavior.

At the point of physical death, our brains will die, and our ungodly habit patterns will become extinct.

Paul taught that the phrase, *"our adoption as sons"* (Romans 8:23), points to *"the redemption of our body."*

> *"...waiting eagerly for our adoption as sons, the redemption of our body."* (Romans 8:23)

This truth proves that the day we receive our glorified, immortal bodies will be the day we are adopted in the fullest sense. We will then be holy, perfect, and blameless, in spirit, soul, and body—not just in spirit and soul as in the present. All church saints, the church having begun in Acts 2, will receive their glorified bodies (and the *"adoption as sons"*) at the Rapture of the church (1Thessalonians 4:13-17). Also, the phrase, *"adoption as sons"* (Romans 8:23), is a major player in properly defining *"predestined"* in Romans 8:29-30!

Some theologians argue that *"our adoption as sons"* occurred when we were justified/saved. The verse cited for support is Galatians 4:5:

> *in order that He might redeem those who were under the*
> *Law, that we might receive the adoption as sons.*
> (Galatians 4:5)

This argument seems valid at surface level. Yet, when studied in depth, we find that *"receive"* is in the subjunctive mood in the Greek—making it impossible to pinpoint the timing of *"the adoption as sons"* using this passage alone. However, Romans 8:23 reveals the timing as being when we receive our glorified bodies—totally negating the idea that *"the adoption as sons"* occurs at justification/salvation.

Don't misunderstand. We became *"sons"* of God at the point of justification/salvation:

> *And because you are sons, God has sent forth the Spirit of*
> *His Son into our hearts, crying, "Abba! Father!"*
> *Therefore you are no longer a slave, but a son; and if a*
> *son, then an heir through God.* (Galatians 4:6-7)

The Galatian believers became *"sons"* when they were justified/saved. Becoming a son, however, is quite different from experiencing the *"adoption as sons"* of Romans 8:23. Hence, becoming *"a son"* of God through justification/salvation (Galatians 4:6-7) is not equal to the *"adoption as sons"* of Romans 8:23—when we will receive our resurrected bodies.

Still, some "theologians" would argue that the *"adoption as sons"* (Romans 8:23; Galatians 4:5) occurs at the point of justification (salvation) due to Paul's words regarding *"a spirit of adoption as sons"* in Romans 8:15:

> *For you have not received a spirit of slavery leading to*
> *fear again, but you have received a spirit of adoption as*
> *sons by which we cry out, "Abba! Father!"* (Romans
> 8:15)

The phrase, *"have received"* (Romans 8:15), is an aorist, active, indicative verb—pointing to past action as well as reality of action. All New Testament believers *"have received a spirit of adoption as sons"*— which occurred when we were *"born again"* (John 3:3-8) of God's Spirit (justified/saved). This "event" is quite different from the *"adoption as sons"* addressed in Romans 8:23 and Galatians 4:5—where we receive our resurrected bodies. We do not yet inhabit resurrected bodies, proving that receiving *"a spirit of adoption as sons"* (Romans 8:15) at the point of justification/salvation is unequal to receiving the *"adoption as sons"* (Romans 8:23) at the Rapture of the church.

One final passage regarding *"adoption":*

> *who are Israelites, to whom belongs the adoption as sons*
> *and the glory and the covenants and the giving of the Law*
> *and the temple service and the promises,* (Romans 9:4)

Paul, while referring to the nation of Israel, mentions that she has been adopted: *"...to whom belongs the adoption as sons..."* This passage does not teach that all Jews are saved, for in the same chapter (verses 1-3) Paul speaks of his grief associated with Israel's overall spiritual ineptitude. Many Jews have died void of spiritual regeneration, suffering the consequence of eternal punishment. The phrase, *"the adoption as sons"* in Romans 9:4 points to God's choice (election) of Israel to prepare the way for the Messiah—a very special office (or position) within His overall strategy for man, a calling she has grossly disregarded. This allows us to understand the context of Deuteronomy 7:6;

> *"For you are a holy people to the LORD your God; the*
> *LORD your God has chosen you to be a people for His*

*own possession out of all the peoples who are on the face
of the earth.* (Deuteronomy 7:6)

The fact that Israel was *"chosen"* as *"a holy people to the Lord"* has nothing to do with where the individual Jews who make up the nation will spend eternity. Many Jews have rejected the office (function) to which the nation was called—due to rejecting God's holy Son, Jesus the Messiah. Yet, God's call was so great upon the nation that He put his name upon the sons of Israel:

*And they shall put my name upon the children of Israel;
and I will bless them.* (Numbers 6:27 KJV)

Individuals can be called (named) to a special office (position, or function) within God's strategy for man and choose to reject that calling—a fact established to a greater degree when we arrive at Romans 8:28.

We can then conclude that the phrase, *"adoption as sons, the redemption of our body"* (Romans 8:23), points to that day when New Testament believers receive their resurrected bodies at the Rapture of the church. Paul's use of the pronouns *"we"* and *"our"* in Romans 8:23 add amazing insight to verses 27-30 of Romans 8. Much fun awaits us when we arrive at those passages.

As we transition into the remainder of Romans 8, remember that our brains, which store our ungodly habit patterns, will vanish along with our physical bodies—since the brain is part of the body. In fact, we will possess new, immortal brains void of ungodly habit patterns once we receive the *"adoption as sons"* of Romans 8:23, *"the redemption of the body."* The behavior exemplified through our bodies will then match who we have been in spirit and soul (holy and blameless saints) since the point of justification/salvation! What an amazing, omnipotent, omniscient, wise, and loving God we serve!!!

Thinking through our Findings

God makes our souls and spirits holy and perfect at the point of justification, even though our behavior will not be perfected until after the death of our physical bodies. Our behavior is not who we are, but that who we are consists of what God makes our souls and spirits into at the point of justification (salvation). We will

We must think long and hard on what we are addressing here, for it is the absolute key to victory.

continue to commit acts of sin so long as we are in our earthly bodies. Sinless perfection is impossible this side of heaven, yet many areas of weakness can be overcome through God's indwelling power. Thus, the ungodly habit patterns, stored in the brain, actually decrease in intensity as we mature in the faith. We must think long and hard on what we are addressing here, for it is the absolute key to victory.

Let's take what we gleaned from Romans 6:6 and attach it to our latest findings. Suppose that the old self (sin nature) remains alive in a New Testament believer—that it was wounded but not eradicated when we were justified (saved). This false assumption would create a theological nightmare, for our souls and spirits would be part evil and part holy under such an arrangement—the old self being evil and the new self being holy. Consequently, we would not be able to enter into God's presence at the point of physical death.

Hence, the eradication of the old self through God's act of justification is a necessity. Physical death <u>cannot</u> remove the old self, for the old self is <u>not</u> part of the body. The old self is soul and spirit (who we were before we were saved), for we received a new soul and spirit at the point of justification. Only the cross is capable of eradicating who we used to be, thus *"our old self <u>was</u> crucified with"* Christ (Romans 6:6). The *"old self,"* therefore, was eradicated at the point of justification, rather than at physical death.

Saved by Hope

For in hope we have been saved, but hope that is seen is not hope; for why does one also hope for what he sees? But if we hope for what we do not see, with perseverance we wait eagerly for it. (Romans 8:24-25)

293

Thus, *"...in hope we have been saved..."* (Romans 8:24-25). This truth ties in perfectly with 1Timothy 1:1:

> *Paul, an apostle of Christ Jesus according to the*
> *commandment of God our Savior, and of Christ Jesus,*
> *who is our hope;* (1Timothy 1:1)

Paul verifies that Jesus (Who we cannot presently see—Romans 8:24) *"is our hope"* (1Timothy 1:1). Thus, *"in hope we have been saved"* (Romans 8:24), Jesus being our *"hope"* (1Timothy 1:1). The *"hope"* supplied through Christ provides incentive to *"wait"* for what God has promised, in fact, to *"wait"* for the unseen.

"Hope" is enhanced through realizing that our present suffering will one day be exchanged for glory beyond our current ability to comprehend. *"The first fruits of the Spirit"* (Romans 8:23), which we now possess as believers, assist us as we *"groan"* (Romans 8:23)— while living in bodies that house the power of sin. Consequently, the remedy to current suffering is a proper view of the *"unseen"* (2Corinthians 4:17-18; Hebrews 11:27). Paul wrote, *"Set your mind on the things above, and not on the things that are on the earth"* (Colossians 3:2), for *"...our citizenship is in heaven"* (Philippians 3:20). From this vantage point we are to view *"the things"* that touch our lives.

We are growing, so be encouraged!

Romans 8:26-39

The Intercession of the Spirit

*And in the same way the Spirit also helps our weakness;
for we do not know how to pray as we should, but the
Spirit Himself intercedes for us with groanings too deep
for words;* (Romans 8:26)

Has there been a time when you needed to pray, but couldn't? You tried to say the words, but they just wouldn't come. Or have you prayed and "felt" like your words were meaningless and empty? If so, astounding news is on the horizon! Paul says that during these seasons, in fact at all times when we pray, *"...the Spirit Himself intercedes for us with groanings too deep for words."*

Amazingly, Paul, the man used mightily of God, the man who wrote (and understood) more regarding the *"mystery"* (Ephesians 3:3; Colossians 1:26-27) of the gospel than any of the apostles, viewed himself as incapable of praying as he should (notice his use of *"we"* in verse 26). Yet, he exhorted the church at Thessalonica to *"pray without ceasing"* (1Thessalonians 5:17), confirming his unwavering commitment to the matter. Knowing Paul's thoughts encourages me greatly, for I doubt if any of us are totally satisfied with the depth of our communication with God.

The Spirit *"helps"* and *"intercedes for"* (as Paul describes) only one group of believers—those who remain on the earth. That conclusion can be drawn from Paul's use of the pronouns *"us," "our,"* and *"we"* in Romans 8:26. Thus, the words *"helps"* and *"intercedes"* are in the present tense in the Greek, pointing to ongoing, linear action that occurred in Paul's day. No need exists for the Spirit to intercede (as prescribed in Romans 8:26) for believers already in heaven, for they are *"face to face"* (1Corinthians 13:12) with the Triune God—Father, Son, and Spirit. Neither would the Spirit intercede in this manner for persons who are lost and living on the earth—even the lost who later choose to repent and believe. Why would the Spirit intercede (in the sense that Paul addresses in Romans 8:26) for individuals who have never desired to pray? The Holy Spirit <u>convicts</u> the depraved according to John 16:8. Only after the depraved choose to pray (and ask Christ into their hearts—

and God makes them new) does the Spirit intercede as Paul describes. Hence, although the specific context of Romans 8:26 applies to believers of Paul's day, we know that what Paul teaches here applies to present-day believers as well. In fact, it applies to any and all church saints so long as they live in their earthly bodies—as is verified in Romans 8:27. The Holy Spirit convicts unbelievers and believers alike of sin, but He *"intercedes"* in the manner described in Romans 8:26 for believers only—so long as they live on the earth.

Jesus, our high priest, also intercedes for the redeemed:

> *Hence, also, He is able to save forever those who draw*
> *near to God through Him, since He always lives to make*
> *intercession for them.* (Hebrews 7:25)

How encouraging!

Conclusion: The Spirit of God *"intercedes for"* (and *"helps"*) New Testament believers from the time they are justified/saved until they are released from their earthly bodies and enter heaven. However, the particular context of Romans 8:26 points to the Spirit interceding for believers in Paul's day alone.

Paul continues discussing the *"Spirit"* in Romans 8:27:

> *and He who searches the hearts knows what the mind of*
> *the Spirit is, because He intercedes for the saints*
> *according to the will of God.* (Romans 8:27)

"The Spirit" possesses a *"mind,"* verifying once again that *"the Spirit"* is a Person. The fact that the Father *"searches the hearts"* should not cause concern. As the Father *"searches"* a New Testament believer's heart, He finds it desiring to do *"good"* alone (substantiated by Paul's words in Romans 7:15-16 and 19-20)—although the New Testament believer sins at times. He takes pleasure in the holy, perfect, blameless saint He has made us into—not once condemning us when we sin (Romans 8:1).

Paul states: *"...the Spirit...intercedes for the saints according to the will of God."* The *"Spirit"* delights in interceding for holy saints! Based on our present findings, why wouldn't He!

"Intercedes" is a significant term, especially since it carries the present tense. Thus, *"the Spirit"* was interceding for believers *("saints")* in Paul's day. Factoring in our discussion surrounding the pronouns *"us," "we,"* and *"our"* of Romans 8:26, the context of the term *"saints"* implemented in Romans 8:27 must point to the *"saints"* (believers) on the earth when this epistle was penned. This information plays a major role in how Romans 8:28-30 is to be interpreted. This truth, by no means, discounts the fact that the Holy Spirit intercedes for us today.

Yes, when we pray, *"the Spirit...intercedes for"* us according to the Father's perfect plan. Wonderful! Paul supplies more valuable input regarding *"the Spirit"* in 1Corinthians 2:11-12:

> *For who among men knows the thoughts of a man except*
> *the spirit of the man, which is in him? Even so the*
> *thoughts of God no one knows except the Spirit of God.*
> *Now we have received, not the spirit of the world, but the*
> *Spirit who is from God, that we might know the things*
> *freely given to us by God,* (1Corinthians 2:11-12)

Paul states that *"the Spirit...knows...the thoughts of God."* He also communicates that *"the Spirit"* was given *"that we might know the things freely given to us by God."* Yes, the Holy *"Spirit"* not only leads us into a deeper understanding of God's heart but reveals what He (God) has *"freely given"* to all New Testament believers subsequent to their exercising repentance and faith while depraved. 1Corinthians 2:10 ties in well here:

> *For to us God revealed them through the Spirit; for the*
> *Spirit searches all things, even the depths of God.*
> (1Corinthians 2:10)

The fact that *"the Spirit searches all things, even the depths of God,"* does not mean that the Spirit reveals everything about God's being and essence to the redeemed during their stay on earth. *"Secret things belong to the Lord our God"* (Deuteronomy 29:29) that we will not understand this side of heaven, maybe even throughout eternity:

297

> *"The secret things belong to the* LORD *our God, but the*
> *things revealed belong to us and to our sons forever, that*
> *we may observe all the words of this law.* (Deuteronomy
> 29:29)

Conclusion: God's Spirit *"intercedes for"* all New Testament *"saints"* (in the manner prescribed in Romans 8:27) from justification/salvation until the day of physical death. However, as was the case with Romans 8:26, the particular context of Romans 8:27 points to the Spirit interceding for believers in Paul's day alone.

All for Good

> *And we know that God causes all things to work together*
> *for good to those who love God, to those who are called*
> *according to His purpose.* (Romans 8:28)

As we begin our study of this powerful passage, we should observe that Paul does not say that God is the cause of all things. He states, rather, *"that God causes all things to work together for good to those who love God, to those who are called according to His purpose."* A great disparity exists between God causing all things (an idea found nowhere in Scripture) and God causing *"all things to work together for good"* for the New Testament believer. Yet, several individuals are accepting as truth the falsehood that God must cause all things to foreknow all things—foreknow meaning "to know beforehand." We will address this error in more depth when we arrive at Romans 8:29-30.

What if we believed (were fully convinced) that God is capable of using everything that crosses our path, in fact, everything that occurs in space and time, *"for [our] good"*? Paul teaches this wonderful truth in Romans 8:28, truth relating to *"...those who are called according to His purpose."* Would worry or anxiety hold a place in our lives should we adopt such a mindset? No way! We would perceive God as totally sovereign, freeing us to live and relax in a state of *"rest"* (Hebrews 4:9). Can you imagine the world's perception of believers should the body of

Christ fully embrace this truth? It would be amazingly different from its view of today!

Interestingly, the Revised Standard Version (the RSV) renders the verse:

> *We know that in everything God works for good with those who love him, who are called according to his purpose.* (Romans 8:28 RSV)

This rendering communicates that God energizes *"those who love him,"* which lines up perfectly with passages such as 1Corinthians 3:9, 1Corinthians 15:10, and 2Corinthians 5:20. Either translation, therefore, is tremendous news for the passionate believer.

Note: As we continue, realize that Reformed theologians (extreme and hyper-Calvinists) conclude that Romans 8:28 validates their theological position—that God's calling brings His elect to salvation (refer to the portion of the Reference Section that describes Reformed Theology, Diagrams 11, 13-15). According to this view, God not only determines (chooses/elects) from eternity past who will be justified/saved but calls them to Himself when He deems it time for them to be justified/saved—never calling the non-elect. The error of this theology will become obvious as we continue.

The word *"called"* in Romans 8:28 is the same Greek word (2822 in Strong's Greek Dictionary) used in Matthew 22:14:

> *"For many are called* [2822], *but few are chosen."* (Matthew 22:14)

Jesus' words, when interpreted in the context of Matthew 22:1-13, confirm that more people are *"called"* (invited) than are *"chosen"* (elected)—verifying that some are *"called"* (invited) who are not *"chosen"* (elected). Thus, should *"called"* point to God's calling of the elect (and only the elect) to salvation (the Reformed view), Matthew 22:14 would teach that some of the elect of Reformed Theology whom God calls are never saved. Such an arrangement would dismantle their view of sovereignty, and in the process, negate their entire system of thought. Yet, this arrangement is demonstrated (and substantiated) in Matthew 22:14—verifying the inaccuracy of the Reformed view.

God calls (invites) individuals to be saved. In fact, He draws all people to Himself (John 12:32), not willing that any perish (1Timothy 2:4; 2Peter 3:9). They must, however, choose to accept Christ in the midst of their depravity before God bestows salvation. Let's consider some Scriptures that seem to address this type of calling. We will label this "Calling #1":

> *God is faithful, through whom you were called* [2564 in Strong's Greek Dictionary] *into fellowship with His Son, Jesus Christ our Lord.* (1Corinthians 1:9)

> *And it was for this He called* [2564] *you through our gospel, that you may gain the glory of our Lord Jesus Christ.* (2Thessalonians 2:14)

> *Fight the good fight of faith; take hold of the eternal life to which you were called* [2564], *and you made the good confession in the presence of many witnesses.* (1Timothy 6:12)

> *But the God of all grace, who hath called* [2564] *us unto his eternal glory by Christ Jesus, after that ye have suffered a while, make you perfect, stablish, strengthen, settle you.* (1Peter 5:10 KJV)

> *But you are A CHOSEN RACE, A royal PRIESTHOOD, A HOLY NATION, A PEOPLE FOR God's OWN POSSESSION, that you may proclaim the excellencies of Him who has called* [2564] *you out of darkness into His marvelous light;* (1Peter 2:9)

We, as New Testament believers, were *"called"* [invited] to be saved (1Corinthians 1:9; 2Thessalonians 2:14; 1Timothy 6:12; 1Peter 5:10; 1Peter 2:9)—pointing to "Calling #1." However, these passages do not teach, especially when coupled with Matthew 22:1-14, that only the elect are called (invited). A person can be *"called into fellowship with"* Christ (1Corinthians 1:9), reject that offer, and never be chosen (elected). It takes repentance and faith on the part of the depraved, all of whom are called, before election results. Thus, the depraved who reject Christ are called (invited) to be saved but not elected (chosen).

Be aware that the word *"called"* in Scripture can mean: (1) "Invited" (invited to be saved), as has been confirmed, or (2) "Named" (named to an office or position that can be appreciated or ignored). "Calling #2" seems to be the prevalent usage in the Scriptures. John 1:42 is such an example:

> *He brought him to Jesus. Jesus looked at him, and said,*
> *"You are Simon the son of John; you shall be called*
> *[2564] Cephas" (which is translated Peter).* (John 1:42)

Jesus changed Peter's name from *"Simon"* to *"Cephas,"* an Aramaic surname whose Greek equivalent is *Petros*, or Peter, meaning "a rock" or "stone." This name speaks volumes regarding Peter's office (position) to which he was *"called"* by the Messiah. The bestowal of this special office had nothing to do with Peter's destiny. He could either function in the office or live as though he had never been called to this privileged position.

Election transpires when the Holy Spirit places New Testament believers in Christ once they repent and exercise faith while depraved (1Corinthians 12:13; Ephesians 1:4)—Christ being God's *"chosen* [elect] *one"* (Isaiah 42:1), Who was chosen (elected) to the office of Messiah—not chosen (or elected) to salvation. The depraved who exercise repentance and faith during the church age are *"crucified"* (Romans 6:6; Galatians 2:20) and made *"new"* (2Corinthians 5:17) in conjunction with being placed *"in Christ."* They are also endowed with a special office, or position, or gifting (1Peter 4:10) due to being part of Christ's body—Christ having been chosen to office rather than destiny. The Scriptures teach that all individuals are called to be saved (many of whom reject God's offer of salvation and remain lost). God's Word teaches as well that New Testament believers are *"called"* to an office, or purpose, or position, once they are placed in Christ subsequent to exercising personal repentance and faith while depraved—just as Jesus serves in the special office of Messiah. Let's take what we have gleaned (regarding "Calling #2") and apply it to specific men addressed in New Testament Scripture:

Paul was *"called as an apostle,"* an office (position) he could welcome or disregard:

> *Paul, a bond-servant of Christ Jesus, called* [2822] *as an apostle, set apart for the gospel of God,* (Romans 1:1)

> *Paul, called* [2822] *as an apostle of Jesus Christ by the will of God, and Sosthenes our brother,* (1Corinthians 1:1)

Paul was *"set...apart"* as an apostle from his *"mother's womb"* to receive this calling:

> *But when He who had set me apart, even from my mother's womb, and called* [2564] *me through His grace,...* (Galatians 1:15—2564)

Keep in mind that Paul was *"set apart"* and *"called"* as an apostle, an office he could welcome or disregard. Hence, his calling had nothing to do with his eternal destiny. His destiny was determined when he exercised repentance and faith while depraved and was placed *"in Christ"* (2Corinthians 5:17) through the power of the Holy Spirit (1Corinthians 12:13).

> *among whom you also are the called* [2822] *of Jesus Christ;* (Romans 1:6)

If you are a believer, you were *"called"* to a unique office (position) as a result of being placed in Jesus, who received the greatest office of all—that of Messiah.

Luke 6:13 reveals the close connection between *"called"* and *"named."* Judas, being one of the *"twelve,"* was *"called"* and *"named"* yet died void of salvation—confirming that the apostles were *"called"* (also *"named")* to office rather than to destiny. They each had the option of either pursuing their calling or throwing it away:

> *And when day came, He called [4377] His disciples to*
> *Him; and chose twelve of them, whom He also named*
> *[3687] as apostles:* (Luke 6:13)

Thus, Paul was *"called* [named] *an apostle":*

> *For I am the least of the apostles, who am not fit to be*
> *called [2564] an apostle, because I persecuted the church*
> *of God.* (1Corinthians 15:9)

1Corinthians 7:17 relates to this subject matter:

> *Only, as the Lord has assigned to each one, as God has*
> *called [2564] each, in this manner let him walk. And thus*
> *I direct in all the churches.* (1Corinthians 7:17)

This calling (in 1Corinthians 7:17) is the call to office (position), as verified by verses 20 and 24 as well:

> *Let each man remain in that condition in which he was*
> *called [2564].* (1Corinthians 7:20)

> *Brethren, let each man remain with God in that condition*
> *in which he was called [2564].* (1Corinthians 7:24)

Ephesians 4:1 provides insight and validation to our findings:

> *I, therefore, the prisoner of the Lord, entreat you to walk*
> *in a manner worthy of the calling [2821] with which you*
> *have been called [2564],* (Ephesians 4:1)

The King James' rendering of this verse greatly illuminates the legitimacy of our conclusions:

> *I therefore, the prisoner of the Lord, beseech you that ye*
> *walk worthy of the <u>vocation</u> [2821] wherewith ye are*
> *called [2564],* (Ephesians 4:1 KJV—emphasis added)

The word *"calling"* in the NASB is rendered *"vocation"* in the KJV, again confirming that *"calling"* and *"vocation"* in this case are synonymous.

Colossians 3:15 defines "when" we were *"called"* to our special office, which lines up perfectly with our previous analysis:

> *And let the peace of Christ rule in your hearts, to which*
> *indeed you were called* [2564] *in one body; and be*
> *thankful.* (Colossians 3:15)

We, as New Testament believers, *"were called in one body"*—meaning that we were not *"called"* to our particular office (position) until we were placed into Christ's *"body"* subsequent to exercising repentance and faith while depraved. This truth does not invalidate God's call on our lives prior to salvation, for He calls all mankind to be saved, not desiring that any perish (1Timothy 2:4; 2Peter 3:9)—even though most reject His offer. Paul uses the pronoun *"you"* in Colossians 3:15 instead of "we" because the believers at Colosse were *"called"* to office once placed in Christ (after repenting and believing while depraved). Paul, on the other hand, was *"called"* to office from his *"mother's womb"* according to Galatians 1:15—prior to being born. The exactness of the Scriptures is amazing!

Paul was *"set...apart"* to his office (of apostle) from his *"mother's womb"* (Galatians 1:15)—prior to being saved. We, on the other hand, were *"called"* to our office once we were placed in Christ subsequent to repenting and believing while depraved. Paul's experience, being quite unusual, does not violate the Scriptures, for Jeremiah was also uniquely called:

> *"Before I formed you in the womb I knew you, and before*
> *you were born I consecrated you; I have appointed you a*
> *prophet to the nations."* (Jeremiah 1:5)

Jeremiah was *"consecrated"* as *"a prophet"* from his mother's *"womb"*—an office (appointment) he could fulfill or disregard. Hence, his calling had nothing to do with where he would spend eternity. His destiny (like Paul's) was determined by his own choice subsequent to physical birth and while depraved—not a choice God made from eternity past.   (Our study, *God's Heart as it Relates to Foreknowledge - Predestination*, addresses Jeremiah 1:5 in much greater depth—proving that Jeremiah's call to office while in his mother's womb in no way confirms Calvinism's view of election to salvation from eternity past.)

That *"called"* can point to being *"called"* to an office is also verified by Hebrews 5:4:

> *And no one takes the honor to himself, but receives it*
> *when he is called* [2564] *by God, even as Aaron was.*
> (Hebrews 5:4)

The calling addressed here is Aaron's call to the office of high priest—which, by no means, dictated where he would spend eternity. Hebrews 5:1 proves this fact by providing proper context:

> *For every high priest taken from among men is appointed*
> *on behalf of men in things pertaining to God, in order to*
> *offer both gifts and sacrifices for sins;* (Hebrews 5:1)

Aaron was *"called"* (Hebrews 5:4), *"appointed"* (Hebrews 5:1), to the office of *"high priest"*—an office he could have welcomed or disregarded. This same truth applies to Abraham's call:

> *By faith Abraham, when he was called* [2564], *obeyed by*
> *going out to a place which he was to receive for an*
> *inheritance; and he went out, not knowing where he was*
> *going.* (Hebrews 11:8)

These events regarding Abraham occurred in Genesis 11-12. He was *"called"* to obey God by leaving his homeland, a calling he was free to ignore.

Additional passages could be cited, but ample Scriptural evidence has proven that the term *"called"* can mean "invited" as well as "named." Interestingly, "named" ("named" to office) seems to be the more predominant usage in Scripture.

Yes, all people are *"called"* (invited) by God to become part of His family, but His invitation is rejected by the majority. However, once we repented and believed while depraved, the Holy Spirit placed us in

Christ; and we were *"called"* (named) to a special office (position) within Christ's body—an office we can welcome or disregard. An incredible journey awaits us as we function in the unique office He has bestowed!

Having observed the close relationship between the words *"named"* and *"called,"* let's address in more detail the relationship between *"called"* and *"chosen."* We have confirmed that New Testament believers are *"called"* to an office (position) once they are placed in Christ (after repenting and believing while depraved). Jesus was even called to the office of Messiah. New Testament believers are also *"chosen"* as a result of being placed in the Father's *"chosen one"* (Isaiah 42:1), Jesus Christ (after repenting and believing while depraved), Who was *"chosen"* to office—the office of Messiah. 2Peter 1:10 makes use of the terms *"calling"* and *"choosing"* as follows:

> *Therefore, brethren, be all the more diligent to make*
> *certain about His calling* [2821] *and choosing you; for as*
> *long as you practice these things, you will never stumble;*
> (2Peter 1:10)

You received a *"calling"* (2Peter 1:10) in conjunction with God *"choosing you"* (2Peter 1:10) once you were placed in the *"chosen one"* (Isaiah 42:1), Jesus Christ—after repenting and believing while depraved.

The last phrase of Romans 8:28 *("who are called according to His purpose")* provides input that will assist us greatly when we study *"predestined"* in Romans 8:29-30. It contains the words, *"according to,"* which are used 790 times in the New American Standard Bible, 725 in the King James, and on occasion are found more than once in some verses. Interestingly, whatever follows the words *"according to"* must precede (in time) what is addressed prior to the words, *"according to."* Consequently:

If **A** is according to **B**

Then **B** precedes **A**

This principle applies in every instance where *"according to"* is used in the Scriptures. If you consult each reference, you will be amazed at the consistency of God's Word. Some examples are listed below. For the purpose of emphasis, the words *"according to"* are underlined in each of the subsequent passages, with commentary following each verse.

> *Thus Noah did; according to all that God had commanded him, so he did.* (Genesis 6:22)

What *"God...commanded"* preceded Noah's obedience.

> *To each one he interpreted according to his own dream.* (Genesis 41:12)

The *"dream"* existed before the interpretation.

> *And the LORD did according to the word of Moses,* (Exodus 8:13)

Moses' words were spoken before the Lord responded *("did")*.

> *Then you shall erect the tabernacle according to its plan...*(Exodus 26:30)

The *"plan"* for the tabernacle existed before *"the tabernacle"* was erected.

> *...to those who are called according to His purpose.* (Romans 8:28)

God's *"purpose,"* which is *"eternal"* (Ephesians 3:11), precedes the New Testament believer's calling. As has been verified, *"called"* (Romans 8:28) points to the special position or office church saints receive once they are placed in Christ—after having exercised repentance and faith while depraved.

The remarkable nature of *"according to"* is addressed in greater depth in our book, *God's Heart as it Relates to Foreknowledge -*

Predestination. Shortly, we will take these powerful words *("according to")* and apply them to *"foreknew"* and *"predestined"* in Romans 8:29. The results will provide a clear (and proper) definition of these highly debated terms. Before focusing on Romans 8:29, however, we must allow Greek grammar to put the finishing touches on Romans 8:28:

> *And we know that God causes all things to work together for good to those who love God, to those who are called according to His purpose.* (Romans 8:28)

"We know" is a perfect, active, indicative verb—pointing to past action, completed action, action that is never repeated. Thus, Paul confirms that his readers knew something they would never forget— *"that God causes all things to work together for good to those who love God, to those who are called according to His purpose."* Intriguingly, *"work together," "who love,"* and *"who are called"* carry the present tense—which adds incredible flavor to this Scripture.

Due to the implementation of the present tense in *"who are called,"* we can know that Paul is addressing the believers of his day only. After all, a New Testament believer's call <u>to office</u> only lasts so long as he remains on the earth. This truth is verified when Romans 12:6-8, Ephesians 4:11-13, and 1Corinthians 12:28 are coupled with 1Corinthians 13:1-13.

> *And since we have gifts that differ according to the grace given to us, let each exercise them accordingly: if prophecy, according to the proportion of his faith; if service, in his serving; or he who teaches, in his teaching; or he who exhorts, in his exhortation; he who gives, with liberality; he who leads, with diligence; he who shows mercy, with cheerfulness.* (Romans 12:6-8)
>
> *And He gave some as apostles, and some as prophets, and some as evangelists, and some as pastors and teachers, for the equipping of the saints for the work of service, to the building up of the body of Christ; until we all attain to the unity of the faith, and of the knowledge of the Son of*

> *God, to a mature man, to the measure of the stature which*
> *belongs to the fulness of Christ.* (Ephesians 4:11-13)

> *And God has appointed in the church, first apostles,*
> *second prophets, third teachers, then miracles, then gifts*
> *of healings, helps, administrations, various kinds of*
> *tongues.* (1Corinthians 12:28)

God has gifted New Testament believers with specific spiritual gifts. Some of these gifted individuals, such as *"prophets," "evangelists," "pastors and teachers,"* are used of God to equip and *"mature"* the *"body of Christ"*—*"until"* believers *"attain...to the measure of the stature which belongs to the fullness of Christ."* However, once New Testament believers enter heaven, no need exists for such gifts to be exercised because once church saints eject out of their earthly bodies, they suddenly see Jesus *"face to face"* and are taught by Jesus Himself:

> *Love never fails; but if there are gifts of prophecy, they*
> *will be done away; if there are tongues, they will cease; if*
> *there is knowledge, it will be done away. For we know in*
> *part, and we prophesy in part; but when the perfect*
> *comes, the partial will be done away. When I was a child,*
> *I used to speak as a child, think as a child, reason as a*
> *child; when I became a man, I did away with childish*
> *things. For now we see in a mirror dimly, but then face to*
> *face; now I know in part, but then I shall know fully just*
> *as I also have been fully known.* (1Corinthians 13:8-12)

The spiritual gifts granted to New Testament saints are *"done away"* (1Corinthians 13:8), or removed, once they enter heaven. Why would a believer with the gift of *"prophecy"* need to prophesy while in the Lord's presence—the Source of all prophecy? The same principle applies to *"evangelists"* (Ephesians 4:11), for evangelism will become obsolete due to all the inhabitants of heaven being believers. Hence, we function in our special calling (office, position) only so long as we live in earthy bodies. Thus the phrase, *"who are called"* (Romans 8:28), being in the present tense, applies in the specific sense to the New Testament believers (on earth) in Paul's day. This truth plays a major role in determining the context of Romans 8:29-30 (which will be studied shortly), so keep it readily accessible. It also supplies insight into Revelation 17:14:

> *"These will wage war against the Lamb, and the Lamb*
> *will overcome them, because He is Lord of lords and King*
> *of kings, and those who are with Him are the called*
> [2822] *and chosen and faithful."* (Revelation 17:14)

The *"called and chosen and faithful"* in this passage are New Testament believers who return with Christ at His Second Coming. They are described as *"called"* due to having received a special calling (position) when placed in Christ (subsequent to repenting and believing while depraved)—a position they relinquished at the point of physical death. Thus, *"called"* is an adjective—describing those previously *"called"* to office at the point of justification—an office they will no longer hold. The present tense would be implemented in Revelation 17:14 should they remain *"called."* Yet, it is nowhere to be found. They are described as *"chosen"* due to having been placed in the *"chosen"* one, Jesus Himself, after repenting and believing while depraved.

Let's observe how these wonderful realities regarding the phrase, *"who are called"* (Romans 8:28), fit the whole of Romans 8:28:

> *And we know that God causes all things to work together*
> *for good to those who love God, to those who are called*
> *according to His purpose.* (Romans 8:28)

Paul is communicating *"that God causes"* (present tense action on God's part—the context of which is action that occurred in Paul's day) *"all things to work together for good to those who love God"* (*"who love God"* is also in the present tense—pointing to the inhabitants of earth who loved God when this epistle was written). This context is proper due to the phrase, *"to those who are called,"* being in the present tense—pointing to those living on earth in Paul's day who were *"called"* to office. Thus, they were *"called according to His purpose"* in conjunction with being placed in Christ after repenting and believing while depraved. None of the believers of Paul's day serve in their previous areas of calling due to presently seeing Jesus *"face to face"* (1Corinthians 13:12). Also, believers in heaven need not be encouraged to view *"all things"* as working *"together for good"* (Romans 8:28)! Why should they when adversity is a thing of the past? This truth confirms that the general context of Romans 8:28 relates to all New Testament believers so long as they live on the earth, the specific context being believers living on the earth in Paul's day?

Conclusion: The specific context of Paul's words in Romans 8:28 applies to believers on the earth when this epistle was penned—who loved God and were *"called"* to a special position (office) within the body of Christ once they were placed in Christ—after repenting and believing while depraved. Upon physical death their calling ended, being no longer necessary in an environment filled with mature followers of Jesus Christ and void of the unsaved. No need for their calling (to office) remains, for Jesus is present to meet their every need. When coupled with the full counsel of God's Word, Romans 8:28 also confirms that we, presently functioning in the area of our calling, will do so only so long as we live in our physical bodies.

Some scholars might argue that Romans 11:29 disproves our findings:

> *for the gifts and the calling of God are irrevocable.*
> (Romans 11:29)

The term, *"irrevocable,"* must be properly understood or confusion results. Paul is not teaching that the *"calling"* (to office) we received at the point of justification remains forever. In fact, the context of Romans 11:29 points to the nation of Israel's *"calling"* to office—a *"calling"* to take the gospel to the Gentiles—a *"calling"* she has yet to fulfill. However, she remains called and will continue to be called until she fulfills her *"calling"* prior to Jesus' Second Coming—by taking the gospel to the world (Matthew 24:14) through the 144,000 Jewish evangelists of Revelation 7. She will not function in this *"calling"* forever, for no unsaved Gentiles will inhabit the eternal order of Revelation 21-22—ushered in after the one thousand year reign of Christ on the earth. Hence, *"irrevocable"* (Romans 11:29) is interpreted *"without repentance"* in the King James:

> *For the gifts and calling of God are without repentance.*
> (Romans 11:29 KJV)

The ASV renders the verse:

> *For the gifts and the calling of God are not repented of.*
> (Romans 11:29 ASV)

This rendering verifies that God will never repent of (change His mind regarding) His *"calling"* on the nation of Israel to take the gospel to the Gentiles—although Israel will eventually cease functioning in this *"calling"* during the eternal order (an environment void of any unsaved Gentiles). Neither will He renege (default) on His promises (or covenants) given to the physical Jewish nation. Numbers 23:19 validates this truth:

> *"God is not a man, that He should lie, nor a son of man,*
> *that He should repent; has He said, and will He not do it?*
> *Or has He spoken, and will He not make it good?*
> (Numbers 23:19)

What God says, God will do. He can be trusted.

This truth regarding the New Testament believer's *"calling"* to office will add tremendous flavor to Romans 8:30. In fact, it allows Romans 8:29-30 to be interpreted free of contradiction. It also validates the free-will of man.

God's Foreknowledge

> *For whom He foreknew, He also predestined to become*
> *conformed to the image of His Son, that He might be the*
> *first-born among many brethren;* (Romans 8:29)

God knows, and has always known, everything that will transpire from eternity past through eternity future. God has given man a free will to choose as he pleases, but God knows beforehand what those choices will be (Psalm 139:1-4). Thus, God possesses foreknowledge.

We must exercise caution here, for some individuals perceive Romans 8:29 as teaching that God determines who will or will not be saved—that God sealed our destiny <u>before</u> we were born. They believe that a person must be *"predestined"* (and elected) to salvation from eternity past if he is to be saved at some point after physical birth. Is this mindset proper, or is Paul communicating something totally different?

*G*od has given man a free will to choose as he pleases, but God knows beforehand what choices man will make. Thus, God possesses foreknowledge.

God possesses foreknowledge. He knows, and has always known, everything that has occurred, is occurring, or will occur from eternity past through eternity future. In fact, all that transpires from eternity past through eternity future is constantly before Him. Consequently, God is not required to cause all things to know all things, as some theologians have incorrectly assumed. Such inappropriate assumptions force one to redefine *"foreknew"* (Romans 8:29) as "foreordained" or "predestined," which is totally unfair to the text.

Those who view God as predetermining man's destiny before man is born (by means of an eternal decree—with the depraved incapable of repenting and exercising faith), must view foreknowledge as equal to foreordination and predestination. This modification is an attempt to extinguish the proper meaning of foreknowledge. So long as "foreknowledge" remains "foreknowledge" (to know beforehand in the sense of foreseeing), man can possess a free will and choose to repent and believe while depraved. Reformed Theology (extreme and hyper-Calvinism) cannot withstand such an arrangement, for according to their view the depraved are spiritual corpses incapable of choosing Christ. Hence, God (according to their view) must cause all things, even determine man's destiny, if He is to remain sovereign. Should such thinking be true, God would be the cause of Adam's sin (the Author of sin), the reason Hitler attempted to exterminate the Jews, the instigator of terrorism, the cause of your next sin—and Satan, instead of being God's enemy, would be His faithful ally, preforming His will. Scripture repudiates not only the Reformed view, but moderate Calvinism and Arminianism as well. (Consult the Reference Section, Diagrams 13-15, for more information regarding Arminianism and the different branches of Calvinism, including Reformed Theology.)

The Scriptural View of Foreknowledge

The following should be read more than once (maybe several times) for proper understanding. Don't become discouraged your first time through. Also, the same truth is stated in a variety of ways. Repetition can be a wonderful tool when properly implemented.

Our search will begin by determining what the Scriptures teach regarding God's purposes (plans), decrees, and works. These subjects, defined correctly, are vital because they reveal the proper definition of foreknowledge.

We will start by confirming that God is *"eternal"* (note that words are underlined for emphasis):

> *"The eternal God is a dwelling place, and underneath are the everlasting arms; and He drove out the enemy from before you, and said, 'Destroy!'* (Deuteronomy 33:27)

> *For a child will be born to us, a son will be given to us; and the government will rest on His shoulders; and His name will be called Wonderful Counselor, Mighty God, Eternal Father, Prince of Peace.* (Isaiah 9:6)

> *but now is manifested, and by the Scriptures of the prophets, according to the commandment of the eternal God, has been made known to all the nations, leading to obedience of faith;* (Romans 16:26)

> *Now to the King eternal, immortal, invisible, the only God, be honor and glory forever and ever. Amen.* (1Timothy 1:17)

> *how much more will the blood of Christ, who through the eternal Spirit offered Himself without blemish to God,*

*cleanse your conscience from dead works to serve the
living God?* (Hebrews 9:14)

Based on Acts 15:18, God has always (eternally) known His *"works."*

*Known unto God are all his <u>works</u> from the beginning of the
world.* (Acts 15:18 KJV).

Known to God <u>from eternity</u> are all His <u>works</u>. (Acts 15:18
NKJV).

God's *"works"* are the natural byproduct of His purposes (plans). If
no purpose (plan) exists, no work can occur. Because God's purposes
(plans) are *"eternal"* (Ephesians 3:11; 2Timothy 1:9), He has always
known them; they have always existed within His heart.

*This was in accordance with the <u>eternal purpose</u> which
He carried out in Christ Jesus our Lord,* (Ephesians 3:11
NASB)

*who has saved us, and called us with a holy calling, not
according to our works, but according to His own
<u>purpose</u> and grace which was granted us in Christ Jesus
<u>from all eternity</u>,* (2 Timothy 1:9 NASB)

Scripture confirms that an eternally known work requires an eternally
known *"purpose"* or plan. Because the same Greek word used for
"eternal" in Ephesians 3:11 is used to describe the eternal King of the
universe in 1Timothy 1:17, we can know that God's purposes are eternal
as well.

*Now unto the King <u>eternal</u>, immortal, invisible, the only
wise God, be honour and glory for ever and ever. Amen.*
(1Timothy 1:17 KJV)

This truth explains Paul's use of the words, *"eternal purpose,"* in
Ephesians 3:11.

According to Job 22:28 and Daniel 11:36b, the function of a *"decree"*
is to establish the certainty of the fulfillment of a purpose or plan.

315

> *"You will also <u>decree</u> a thing, and it will be established for you; ...* (Job 22:28 NASB)

> *"Then the king will do as he pleases, and he will exalt and magnify himself above every god, and will speak monstrous things against the God of gods; and he will prosper until the indignation is finished, for that which is <u>decreed</u> will be done.* (Daniel 11:36 NASB)

If no *"decree"* exists, the fulfillment of a purpose or plan is unattainable.

God's purposes are *"eternal"* (Ephesians 3:11; 2Timothy 1:9) because they have always existed within His heart. In addition, His decrees, which guarantee the certainty of the fulfillment of His purposes, are also *"eternal,"* as confirmed by Jeremiah 5:22.

> *'Do you not fear Me?' declares the LORD. Do you not tremble in My presence? For I have placed the sand as a boundary for the sea, an <u>eternal decree</u>, so it cannot cross over it. Though the waves toss, yet they cannot prevail; though they roar, yet they cannot cross over it.* (Jeremiah 5:22 NASB)

Isaiah 63:16 is in agreement:

> *Doubtless thou art our father, though Abraham be ignorant of us, and Israel acknowledge us not: thou, O LORD, art our father, our redeemer; thy name is <u>from everlasting</u>.* (Isaiah 63:16 KJV)

Because God is both eternal and unchanging (and much, much more), His *"name"* remains the same from eternity past through eternity future. Thus, His *"name"* is eternal. Hence, the words *"from everlasting"* (Isaiah 63:16) confirm that His name has no beginning. His decrees are also eternal, for the identical Hebrew word from which we get *"from everlasting"* (Isaiah 63:16) is rendered *"eternal"* Jeremiah 5:22.

Applying this input to Romans 8:29 greatly impacts how this passage is to be perceived.

According to Romans 8:29, God's foreknowledge must <u>precede</u> that moment when a person is predestined:

> *For whom He foreknew, He also predestined to become conformed to the image of His Son, that He might be the first-born among many brethren*; (Romans 8:29)

Based on 1Peter 1:1-2, foreknowledge is also required to <u>precede</u> the election of a New Testament believer—note that *"Elect"* (KJV) is equivalent to *"chosen"* (NASB), proving that to be elected is equivalent to being chosen:

> *Peter, an apostle of Jesus Christ, to the strangers scattered throughout Pontus, Galatia, Cappadocia, Asia, and Bithynia, <u>elect</u> according to the <u>foreknowledge</u> of God the Father, through sanctification of the Spirit, unto obedience and sprinkling of the blood of Jesus Christ: grace unto you, and peace, be multiplied.* (1Peter 1:1-2 KJV—emphasis added)

> *Peter, an apostle of Jesus Christ, to those who reside as aliens, scattered throughout Pontus, Galatia, Cappadocia, Asia, and Bithynia, who are <u>chosen</u> according to the <u>foreknowledge</u> of God the Father, by the sanctifying work of the Spirit, that you may obey Jesus Christ and be sprinkled with His blood: may grace and peace be yours in fullest measure.* (1Peter 1:1-2 NASB—emphasis added)

Should New Testament believers have been predestined to salvation by means of an eternal decree (as Arminianism and all forms of Calvinism advocate), foreknowledge could not precede such an arrangement—refuting Arminianism and all forms of Calvinism altogether. For further input, study Diagram 10 in the Reference Section titled, *"Why God's Foreknowledge Cannot Precede His Eternal Decrees."*

Conclusion: God's eternally known works are accomplished through His eternal decrees, which make certain the fulfillment of His eternal purposes or plans. Thus, if God's decrees have always existed, they have never been future to Him. To state it differently, God can't foreknow what has always existed. Hence, to foreknow that which has no beginning is impossible. In fact, God has never said, "I knew before I decreed this decree that I would decree it," because His decrees have always existed within His heart. Because God's foreknowledge must precede His decrees, New Testament believers could not have been predestined to salvation by means of an eternal decree. Thus, Reformed Theology must redefine *"foreknew"* (Romans 8:29) in an attempt to justify its view of election and predestination. (Our *God's Heart* series describes in much detail how Reformed Theology attempts to redefine this powerful term.)

Words can't be manipulated, changed, or redefined to validate an unscriptural experience or contradictory ideology. In fact, we are never to allow an experience or system of thought to dictate what we accept or reject regarding God's infallible Word. Rather, we are to always allow God's Word to dictate what we accept or reject

S cripture is never at the mercy of a particular way of thinking. Instead, all ways of thinking are at the mercy of the Scriptures.

regarding all experiences or systems of thought! Scripture is never at the mercy of a particular way of thinking. Instead, all ways of thinking are at the mercy of the Scriptures. Changing the definition or meaning of the terms used in God's holy Word is an indictment against the God Who composed it. This manipulation must never be allowed—no matter who perceives it as proper.

Now that *"foreknew"* has been addressed and properly defined, we will transition into that hugely debated subject known as "predestination." Honestly, its definition is easily obtained when Scripture alone directs one's conclusions.

Predestination

According to Ephesians 1:5, God predestines New Testament believers *"to adoption as sons"*:

> He *predestined us to adoption as sons* through Jesus Christ to Himself, according to the kind intention of His will, (Ephesians 1:5)

Noting Paul's use of *"us"* in this passage, and considering that Paul was a believer while writing to the church at Ephesus, one can easily understand that the full counsel of God's Word teaches that believers aren't predestined until they become believers. Nowhere in the Scriptures do we find that potential believers are predestined from eternity past, as some have incorrectly assumed. Therefore, New Testament believers are not predestined until God makes them new— subsequent to their exercising repentance and faith while depraved. How can we be certain of this? The phrase, *"adoption as sons,"* according to Romans 8:23, points to that day when all church saints receive their resurrected bodies:

> And not only this, but also we ourselves, having the first fruits of the Spirit, even we ourselves groan within ourselves, waiting eagerly for *our adoption as sons, the redemption of our body.* (Romans 8:23)

Linking the phrase, *"our adoption as sons, the redemption of our body"* (Romans 8:23), to the phrase, *"predestined us to adoption as sons"* (Ephesians 1:5), we can conclude the following:

> A New Testament believer is *"predestined"* to receive a glorified *"body"* once he is placed in Christ and made new—after exercising repentance and faith while depraved.

Yes, we were *"predestined"* to one day receive resurrected bodies. We were granted this glorious future destiny once we were placed in Christ through the Person of the *"Spirit"* (1Corinthians 12:13) and made *"new"* (2Corinthians 5:17)—subsequent to our exercising repentance and faith while depraved. The predestination of New Testament believers occurs in time, not from eternity past. We were *"predestined"* in time to blessings associated with salvation, not *"predestined"* from eternity past to one day be saved from the penalty of sin. (Consult Diagram 12 titled *"Scriptural Election/Chosenness and Predestination"* in the Reference Section.)

Teachings about predestination which are contrary to this Scriptural view are responsible for the confusion. Everyone has a free will and can, while depraved, accept or reject Christ (John 1:12, Acts 16:31, Acts 26:18, Romans 10:9-10—along with a hoard of additional passages). Once we exercised repentance and faith while depraved and were placed in Christ through the power of the Holy Spirit (1Corinthians 12:13), we were *"predestined"* (Romans 8:29). To what were we *"predestined"* once we were placed in Jesus? We were *"...predestined to become conformed to the image of His* [God's] *Son..."* (Romans 8:29), a conformity that includes receiving a resurrected body at the Rapture of the church. This truth will be confirmed by interpreting Scripture in context, so we will begin by revisiting Romans 8:29 and build from there.

The proper interpretation of the phrase, *"that He might be the first-born among many brethren"* (Romans 8:29), can be found by noting its relationship to the previous phrases in the passage:

> *For whom He foreknew, He also predestined to become*
> *conformed to the image of His Son, that He might be the*
> *first-born among many brethren;* (Romans 8:29)

Jesus is *"the first-born"* of the Father in the sense that He was the first to receive a resurrected body. Colossians 1:18 validates this fact:

> *...and He is the beginning, the first-born from the*
> *dead...*(Colossians 1:18)

If Jesus is described as *"the first-born"* of the Father due to His bodily resurrection (Colossians 1:18), then Romans 8:29 must point not only to Jesus' bodily resurrection, but also to the future bodily resurrection of all New Testament believers:

...that He might be the first-born among many brethren; (Romans 8:29)

The fact that we are part of the *"many brethren"* confirms that God *"predestined"* us (after we exercised repentance and faith while depraved) to receive a glorified body at the Rapture of the church. Many blessings accompany this wonderful event. Consequently, church saints will live throughout the Millennium and the Eternal Order in a glorified body, responding properly to the variables surrounding them. Each church saint will live in a body, not only void of the old brain, which houses sinful habit patterns (and godly habit patterns as well), but a body void of the power of sin—a power which lives in the body of New Testament believers (and the spirit, soul, and body of unbelievers) while dwelling on earth (Romans 7:23). The New Testament believer has been given a glorious future destiny—that of receiving a glorified body at the Rapture of the church.

> *G*od *"predestined" us (after we exercised repentance and faith while depraved) to receive a glorified body at the Rapture of the church.*

This truth ties in perfectly with 1Corinthians 15:51-55:

> *...we shall not all sleep, but we shall all be changed, in a moment, in the twinkling of an eye, at the last trumpet; for the trumpet will sound, and the dead will be raised imperishable, and we shall be changed. For this perishable must put on the imperishable, and this mortal must put on immortality. But when this perishable will have put on the imperishable, and this mortal will have put on immortality, then will come about the saying that is written, "DEATH IS SWALLOWED UP in victory. O DEATH, WHERE IS YOUR VICTORY? O DEATH, WHERE IS YOUR STING?"* (1Corinthians 15:51-55)

The resurrection addressed in 1Corinthians 15:51-55 is different from Lazarus' experience in John 11. Lazarus was raised back to natural life, back to mortal life, meaning that his body would die a second time. The same principle applies to all individuals who are raised back to natural life, such as Tabitha in Acts 9:36-43. Jesus' body, on the other hand, was resurrected to immortal life, never to die again. Thus, in conjunction with our (old) souls and spirits being placed in Christ and made new (subsequent to our repenting and believing while depraved), we were predestined to receive glorified bodies so we, at the Rapture of the church, can be recipients of this same immortal life in regard to the body.

When a New Testament believer dies, his soul and spirit eject out of the earthly body and instantaneously enter heaven (2Corinthians 5:8), while the physical body returns to dust. At the Rapture, the church saint's soul and spirit will be joined to his resurrected (immortal) body for all eternity (1Thessalonians 4:13-18).

With the above in mind, let's review how easily *"predestined"* is defined by first reading Romans 8:23:

> *And not only this, but also we ourselves, having the first*
> *fruits of the Spirit, even we ourselves groan within*
> *ourselves, waiting eagerly for <u>our adoption as sons, the*
> *redemption of our body</u>.* (Romans 8:23)

The phrase, *"our adoption as sons,"* points to *"the redemption of our body"* (Romans 8:23)—that moment in the future when we receive our resurrected, glorified, immortal bodies. According to Ephesians 1:5, we have been *"predestined"* to this—*"to adoption as sons":*

> *He <u>predestined us to adoption as sons</u> through Jesus*
> *Christ to Himself, according to the kind intention of His*
> *will,* (Ephesians 1:5)

This verse confirms that New Testament believers are *"predestined"* to receive glorified bodies—not predestined (from eternity past) to be saved. When, then, are they *"predestined"*? They are *"predestined"* in conjunction with being placed in Christ subsequent to exercising repentance and faith while depraved. Consequently, if you are a believer, you were *"predestined"* the moment you were justified/saved—meaning that your future destiny is to one day receive a glorified body and experience all the benefits associated with that wonderful transformation.

The word *"predestined"* (Romans 8:29) can be summed up in the following statement:

> We were <u>not</u> predestined to be saved from eternity past by
> means of an eternal decree of God. Rather, in conjunction
> with being saved (justified) through being placed in Christ
> subsequent to exercising personal repentance and faith
> while depraved, we received a glorious future destiny—
> that of one day living in a glorified body.

Predestination has to do with believers only, for we were *"predestined"* when God made us new. Therefore, predestination has nothing to do with who will or will not be saved, but has everything to do with the New Testament believer receiving a glorified body at the Rapture of the church. Because the Father possesses foreknowledge, He knows who will choose (while depraved) to accept Christ and receive this glorious future destiny—foreknowledge meaning "to know beforehand." He also knows who will reject Christ's free offer of salvation and the resulting blessings. Consequently, foreknowledge means "foreknowledge." It cannot be redefined as foreordain or predestine, as some have erroneously assumed.

Predestination has nothing to do with who will or will not be saved, but has everything to do with the New Testament believer receiving a glorified body at the Rapture of the church.

Predestination is simple when studied in context. New Testament believers are predestined (once they are placed in Christ subsequent to repenting and believing while depraved) to receive glorified bodies at the Rapture of the church. Nothing is complicated about that! The contradictory systems of thought have brought the confusion. To pursue the topic further, you can obtain a copy of *God's Heart as it Relates to Foreknowledge - Predestination*.

Before concluding our analysis of Romans 8:29, we must determine the context of the word *"whom."* Although only four letters in length, its impact on how one views Romans 8:29-30 is amazingly significant. In fact, its context refutes both Arminianism and Calvinism:

> *For <u>whom</u> He foreknew, He also predestined to become*
> *conformed to the image of His Son, that He might be the*
> *<u>first-born</u> among many brethren;* (Romans 8:29—
> emphasis added)

A proper view of *"whom"* is unattainable without the assistance of the verses that both precede and follow Romans 8:29, so let's review for a moment what we concluded regarding Romans 8:26-28.

The specific context of verses 26-28 of Romans 8 confirms that Paul was making reference to believers living on the earth when this epistle was penned—although the principles taught in these passages apply to New Testament believers in general. (In other words, should Paul live on the earth today and write us an epistle regarding this same subject matter, he could record the identical statements recorded in Romans 8:28-30; and they would apply, in their specific context, to our day alone.) Therefore, the *"whom"* of Romans 8:29 points to believers of Paul's day. The validity of this conclusion is upheld by the following verse, Romans 8:30, where we find *"whom"* used on three different occasions. We will, therefore, transition into Romans 8:30 at this time:

> *and <u>whom</u> He predestined, these He also called; and*
> *<u>whom</u> He called, these He also justified; and <u>whom</u> He*
> *justified, these He also glorified.* (Romans 8:30)

The *"whom"* of Romans 8:29 is the same group of individuals to whom the *"whom," "whom,"* and *"whom"* of Romans 8:30 refer. Hence, linking Romans 8:29 with Romans 8:30, we will discover that the specific context of *"whom"* in every case points to believers living on the earth when this epistle was written—believers that God not only *"foreknew,"* but had also *"predestined," "called," "justified,"* and *"glorified."* (Remember: Should Paul live on the earth today and write us an epistle regarding this same subject matter, he could record the identical statements written in Romans 8:28-30 and they would apply, in their specific context, to our day alone.) These facts supply proper context for Romans 8:29-30. Are you ready? "Hard thinking" is required, so prepare yourself! I am certain you are up for the challenge, realizing that making the profound simple is always worth the price of admission.

The fact that *"foreknew"* (Romans 8:29), *"predestined"* (Romans 8:29 and 30), *"called"* (Romans 8:30), *"justified"* (Romans 8:30), and *"glorified"* (Romans 8:30) are in the aorist tense in the Greek plays a major role in how these verses are to be interpreted, especially since the aorist in each case points to past action—action that had already occurred. Therefore, Paul was addressing individuals whom God *"foreknew"* and had *"predestined,"* *"called,"* *"justified,"* and *"glorified."* They were *"holy"* (Ephesians 1:4) saints who had been made *"the righteousness of God"* (2Corinthians 5:21) the moment they repented and believed while depraved. They had also been *"sanctified"* (Hebrews 10:10), *"perfected"* (Hebrews 10:14), and *"made complete"* (Colossians 2:10) in their souls and spirits—and much, much more (review materials addressing Romans 5:1 earlier in this study). Hence, God *"foreknew"* these believers in the sense that He had known from eternity past the decisions they would make prior to their making them. He had also *"predestined,"* *"called,"* *"justified,"* and *"glorified"* them after their arrival on the earth (when they repented and believed while depraved)—all of which had occurred prior to Paul writing this epistle. After all, the epistle to the Romans was sent to believers, individuals who were already saved. We will take these thoughts through four distinct groups of believers to validate our findings:

> Church saints who experienced physical death prior to Paul writing this epistle

> Church saints living on the earth when this epistle was written

> Unbelievers who were alive physically when this epistle was written, but later accepted Christ

> Individuals who exist after this epistle was written and accept Christ during the church age

The term *"called,"* located in Romans 8:28 and 30 will be examined first. Remember that *"called"* in Romans 8:28 is in the present tense

while *"called"* in Romans 8:30 is in the aorist tense, or past tense—
"called" in both cases meaning to be *"called"* to office once placed in
Christ after repenting and believing while depraved:

> *And we know that God causes all things to work together*
> *for good to those who love God, to those who are <u>called</u>*
> *according to His purpose. For whom He foreknew, He also*
> *predestined to become conformed to the image of His Son,*
> *that He might be the first-born among many brethren; and*
> *whom He predestined, these He also <u>called</u>; and whom He*
> *called, these He also justified; and whom He justified, these*
> *He also glorified.* (Romans 8:28, 30)

God's employment of *"called"* in the Scriptures (the full counsel of
all the verses) is displayed in graphic form below:

The Context of Called

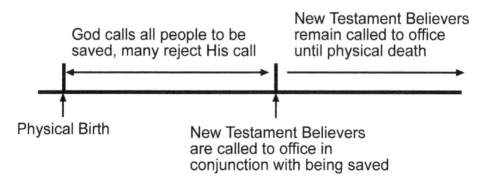

New Testament believers are *"called"* to office in conjunction with
God making them new—subsequent to their repenting and believing
while depraved. We will now take the four previously mentioned groups
of New Testament believers through Romans 8:28 and 30, focusing on

the word *"called."* These four groups are displayed in graphic form below:

**Four Possible Groups to Whom Paul
Was Referring in Romans 8:29-30**

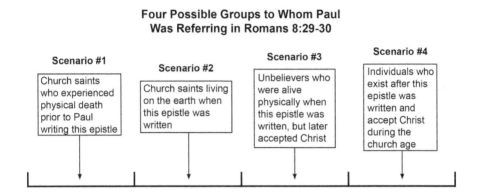

*And we know that God causes all things to work together
for good to those who love God, to those who are <u>called</u>
according to His purpose. For whom He foreknew, He also
predestined to become conformed to the image of His Son,
that He might be the first-born among many brethren; and
whom He predestined, these He also <u>called</u>; and whom He
called, these He also justified; and whom He justified, these
He also glorified.* (Romans 8:28, 30)

*Scenario #1   Church saints who experienced physical death prior to
Paul writing this epistle*

This arrangement will <u>not</u> work (in relation to the word *"called"*) due to deceased New Testament believers no longer functioning in their calling. Thus, the past tense *"called"* in Romans 8:30 applies, but the present tense *"called"* in Romans 8:28 eliminates Scenario #1.

*Scenario #2   Church saints living on the earth when this epistle was
written*

This arrangement will work (in relation to the word *"called"*) because New Testament believers living on earth when this epistle was written served in their area of calling (office)—fulfilling the present tense *"called"* found in Romans 8:28. They had also been *"called"* to office (after having repented and believed while depraved) prior to receiving this epistle, placing their calling to office in the past—fulfilling the past tense *"called"* in Romans 8:30.

Scenario #3   Unbelievers who were alive physically when this epistle was written but later accepted Christ

Scenario #4   Individuals who exist after this epistle was written and accept Christ during the church age

Neither scenario will work (in relation to the word *"called"*) because prospective New Testament believers are not *"called"* to office until they are placed in Christ subsequent to repenting and believing while depraved. Thus, neither the present tense *"called"* of Romans 8:28, or the past tense *"called"* of Romans 8:30, can apply.

The next terms to consider are *"foreknew"* (Romans 8:29.), *"predestined* (Romans 8:29-30),"* *"justified"* (Romans 8:30), and *"glorified"* (Romans 8:30). A series of diagrams will be used to display the error associated with Arminianism and all forms of Calvinism.

Because foreknowledge must precede the election and predestination of a New Testament believer, these readers (those who received this epistle) could not have been predestined and elected to salvation by means of an eternal decree. God's foreknowledge cannot precede what has no beginning (review Diagram 10, *"Why God's Foreknowledge Cannot Precede His Eternal Decrees"* in the Reference Section). Also, *"glorified"* in Romans 8:30 is in the past tense, meaning that these believers had been *"glorified"* in soul and spirit in the past—in fact, they were *"glorified"* (in soul and spirit) the moment they were placed in Christ subsequent to repenting and believing while depraved.

Arminians view the elect as being *"glorified"* at physical death, yet Romans 8:30 verifies that these believers had been *"glorified"* (in soul and spirit) when they were *"justified"* (saved). If Arminianism's view of *"predestined"* were correct (that God predestined all of the elect to salvation from eternity past by means of an eternal decree), the Scriptures would also teach that the elect born after the book of Romans was written (who do not exist until conception) were also *"justified," "called,"* and *"glorified"* in eternity past *("predestined," "called," "justified,"* and *"glorified"* in Romans 8:30 being in the past tense).

Romans 8:29-30
The Arminian View

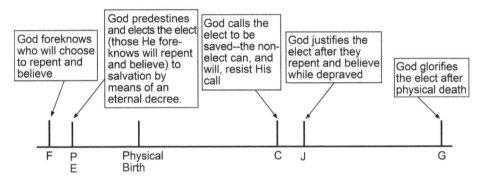

Such an arrangement is impossible for several reasons, two of which are: (1) The elect do not exist until conception. Therefore, how could they have been predestined, called, justified, and glorified prior to existing? (2) The elect would be born *"predestined," "called," "justified,"* and *"glorified"* had they been predestined in eternity past. Yet, Ephesians 2:1-3 validates that all people are born *"children of wrath."* This truth will be addressed in more detail shortly.

> *Among them we too all formerly lived in the lusts of our*
> *flesh, indulging the desires of the flesh and of the mind,*
> *and were by nature children of wrath, even as the rest.*
> (Ephesians 2:3)

Because foreknowledge must precede the election and predestination of a New Testament believer, these readers (those who received this epistle) could not have been predestined and elected to salvation by means of an eternal decree. God's foreknowledge cannot precede what has no beginning (see Diagram 10, *"Why God's Foreknowledge Cannot Precede His Eternal Decrees"* in the Reference Section). Also, "*glorified*" in Romans 8:30 is in the past tense, meaning that these believers had been "*glorified*" in soul and spirit in the past—in fact, they were "*glorified*" (in soul and spirit) the moment they were placed in Christ subsequent to repenting and believing while depraved.

Romans 8:29-30
The Reformed View
(Extreme & Hyper-Calvinism)

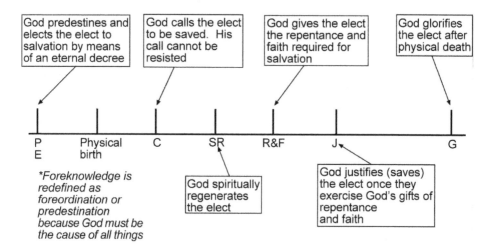

Reformed Theology (Extreme and hyper-Calvinism) views the elect as being "glorified" at physical death, yet Romans 8:30 verifies that these believers had been "*glorified*" (in soul and spirit) when they were "*justified*" (saved). Should Reformed Theology's view of "*predestined*" be correct (that God predestined all of the elect to salvation from eternity past by means of an eternal decree), the Scriptures would also teach that the elect born after the book of Romans was written (who do not exist until conception) were also "*justified*," "*called*," and "*glorified*" in eternity past ("*predestined*," "*called*," "*justified*," and "*glorified*" in Romans 8:30 being in the past tense). Such an arrangement is impossible for several reasons, two of which are (1) The elect do not exist until conception. Therefore, how could they have been predestined, called, justified, and glorified prior to existing? (2) The elect would be born "*predestined*," "*called*," "*justified*," and "*glorified*" had they been predestined in eternity past. Yet, Ephesians

330

2:1-3 validates that all people are born *"children of wrath."* This truth will be addressed in more detail shortly.

Because foreknowledge must precede the election and predestination of a New Testament believer, these readers (those who received this epistle) could not have been predestined and elected to salvation by means of an eternal decree. God's foreknowledge cannot precede what has no beginning (see Diagram 10, *"Why God's Foreknowledge Cannot Precede His Eternal Decrees"* in the Reference Section). Also, *"glorified"* in Romans 8:30 is in the past tense, meaning that these believers had been *"glorified"* in soul and spirit in the past—in fact, they were *"glorified"* (in soul and spirit) the moment they were placed in Christ subsequent to repenting and believing while depraved.

Romans 8:29-30
Moderate Calvinism

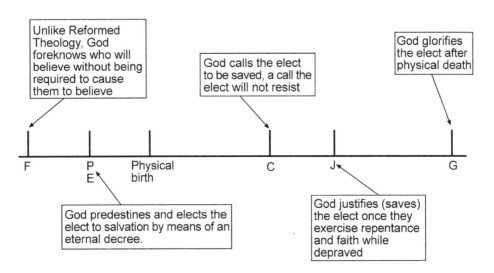

Moderate Calvinism views the elect as being *"glorified"* at physical death, yet Romans 8:30 verifies that these believers had been *"glorified"* (in soul and spirit) when they were *"justified"* (saved). Should Moderate Calvinism's view of *"predestined"* be correct (that God predestined all of the elect to salvation from eternity past by means of an eternal decree), the Scriptures would also teach that the elect born after the book of Romans was written (who do not exist until conception) were also

331

"justified," "called," and *"glorified"* in eternity past *("predestined," "called," "justified,"* and *"glorified"* in Romans 8:30 being in the past tense). Such an arrangement is impossible for several reasons, two of which are: (1) The elect do not exist until conception. Therefore, how could they have been predestined, called, justified, and glorified prior to existing? (2) The elect would be born *"predestined," "called," "justified,"* and *"glorified"* had they been predestined in eternity past. Yet, Ephesians 2:1-3 validates that all people are born *"children of wrath."* This truth will be addressed in more detail shortly.

The Contextual View

Let's reconsider our findings in regard to *"called"* (Romans 8:28) and *"whom," "whom," "whom,"* and *"whom"* (Romans 8:29-30).

> *And we know that God causes all things to work together for good to those who love God, to those who are <u>called</u> according to His purpose. For <u>whom </u>He foreknew, He also predestined to become conformed to the image of His Son, that He might be the first-born among many brethren; and <u>whom </u>He predestined, these He also <u>called</u>; and <u>whom </u>He called, these He also justified; and <u>whom </u>He justified, these He also glorified.* (Romans 8:28-30)

The specific context of these passages relates to believers living on the earth when this epistle was written (Scenario #2 in the diagram presented previously titled *"Four Scenarios that Provide Context to Romans 8:28-30"*). The significance of this discovery is impossible to overemphasize, for it holds the key to a proper view of this highly debated segment of God's infallible Word. New Testament believers are *"called"* (Romans 8:28) to office only so long as they live on the earth—*"called"* (Romans 8:28) being in the present tense, placing the specific context squarely upon believers inhabiting the earth when this God-inspired letter was generated. Thus, the *"whom," "whom," "whom,"* and *"whom"* of Romans 8:29-30 must point to this same group of believers—saints living at that particular time who <u>had been</u> *"predestined," "called," "justified,"* and *"glorified"* the moment they repented and believed while depraved. This view, therefore, allows the past tense (aorist tense) associated with *"predestined," "called," "justified,"* and *"glorified"* to apply void of inconsistency—for the recipients of this epistle were already believers when this epistle was written.

Considering all of this wonderful truth, the specific context of *"foreknew"* of Romans 8:29 relates to this same group of saints. Don't misunderstand. God's foreknowledge is eternal and all-inclusive, for He foreknows all things without being required to cause all things. Yet Paul, in these passages, is emphasizing His foreknowledge of a particular group of believers—the New Testament believers on the earth when this epistle was written (remember that the *"whom"* of *"for whom He foreknew"* of Romans 8:29 also references this particular group of believers). These facts add incredible insight to our study, for they prove that only one of the four previously addressed scenarios applies. All four scenarios are again listed for convenience:

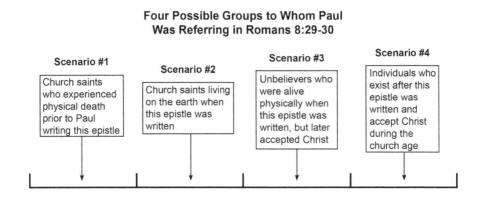

Four Possible Groups to Whom Paul Was Referring in Romans 8:29-30

Scenario #1	Scenario #2	Scenario #3	Scenario #4
Church saints who experienced physical death prior to Paul writing this epistle	Church saints living on the earth when this epistle was written	Unbelievers who were alive physically when this epistle was written, but later accepted Christ	Individuals who exist after this epistle was written and accept Christ during the church age

Paul was led to implement the particular tenses utilized in these passages because he was addressing Scenario #2—"Church saints living on the earth when this epistle was written." The present tense *"called"* (Romans 8:28) proves that Scenario #1 does not apply, for these New Testament saints no longer serve in the office to which they were previously *"called."* They were (and are) basking in the presence of God in heaven (2Corinthians 5:8). Neither does Scenario #3 fit the specific context, for these unbelievers would have been *"predestined,"* *"called,"* *"justified,"* and *"glorified"* prior to repenting and believing had Paul been referencing them. Should Scenario #4 fit the specific context, these individuals would be *"predestined,"* *"called,"* *"justified,"* and *"glorified"* when they arrive on the earth—a total impossibility. Thus, Paul narrows the specific context of *"foreknew"* (Romans 8:29) to believers dwelling on the earth when this epistle was written.

Based on these amazing facts, the P *("predestined"),* C *("called"),* J *("justified"),* and G *("glorified")* of Romans 8:30 can be associated with a particular point on the timeline. New Testament believers are *"predestined,"* *"called,"* and *"glorified"* the instant they are *"justified."* This truth is displayed in graphic form below:

Romans 8:29-30
The Contextual View

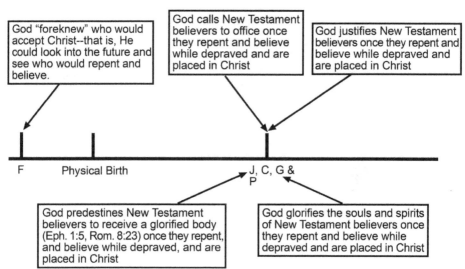

This "Contextual View" of Romans 8:29-30 allows God's foreknowledge to have preceded that moment when the recipients of this epistle (and all other believers on the earth at that time) repented and believed while depraved. Once they repented and believed, they were *"predestined"* (to receive a glorified body), *"called"* (to office), *"justified"* (made not guilty, righteous), and *"glorified"* (in soul and spirit) through the Spirit placing them in Christ—allowing the past tense in each case to apply due to their having been made into all of these wonderful things prior to receiving this epistle. The exactness of the Scriptures is astounding!

The next portion of the study will verify how a correct view of the identity of the New Testament believer (what God makes New Testament believers into the moment they repent and believe while depraved) supplies additional insight into these highly debated and often misinterpreted passages. In this breathtaking journey we will allow God's Word to make the profound simple.

Arminianism and all forms of Calvinism perceive Romans 8:29-30 as teaching that believers are predestined and elected to salvation before they are born (from eternity past by means of an eternal decree). Such an arrangement, however, would allow Romans 8:29-30 to teach that the *"predestined"* of Arminianism and Calvinism who are not yet in existence are presently *"called," "justified,"* and *"glorified"*—since *"predestined," "called," "justified,"* and *"glorified"* are all in the past tense. Stated differently, had future believers been *"predestined"* to salvation from eternity past, they would presently be *"called," "justified,"* and *"glorified."* This arrangement, however, would cause them to be *"justified"* and *"glorified"* prior to existing as well as *"justified"* and *"glorified"* at physical birth. Therefore, Ephesians 2:3 discredits both Arminianism and all forms of Calvinism (including Reformed Theology), since all persons arrive on the earth *"children of wrath."*

In an attempt to circumvent the inconsistencies surrounding their view of foreknowledge and predestination, Reformed Theology (extreme and hyper-Calvinism) teaches that Paul (by inserting the past action *"glorified"* in Romans 8:29-30) is actually stressing the certainty of a future event. In fact, they perceive Romans 8:29-30 as providing the chronological order of events experienced by the elect in regard to salvation (the "golden chain" that cannot be broken according to their interpretation). Yet, the truths associated with the identity of the New Testament believer discredit their reasoning. This fact is confirmed below by first listing the Reformed view and presenting a rebuttal.

The Reformed View of Romans 8:29-30

God can't foreknow what He has not caused. Therefore, *"foreknew"* (Romans 8:29) can be redefined as "foreordained" or "predestined."

God predestines the elect to salvation from eternity past by means of an eternal decree. Thus, all of the elect were *"predestined"* (Romans 8:29-30) to be saved.

When the time arrives for the elect to be saved, they are *"called"* (Romans 8:30) by God through irresistible grace. God then spiritually regenerates them and gives them the gifts of repentance and faith. This repentance and faith become the possession of the elect.

The elect exercise the repentance and faith supplied by God and they are *"justified"* (Romans 8:30).

Once the elect are released from their earthly bodies (at physical death), they are *"glorified"* (Romans 8:30). Although this "event" transpires in the future for the elect living on the earth, the certainty of the action allows the Scriptures to perceive it as having already occurred.

Are any of these five conclusions valid? Let's allow God's Word to answer this question by examining the five—one at a time.

The Scriptural Rebuttal to the Reformed View of Romans 8:29-30

The Reformed view: God can't foreknow what He has not caused. Therefore, *"foreknew"* (Romans 8:29) can be redefined as "foreordained" or "predestined."

Rebuttal: Reformed Theology's unhealthy view of God's sovereignty (where His sovereignty is elevated above all His wonderful attributes, including His love) can't allow God to foreknow what He does not cause. Hence, Reformed theologians perceive God as causing all things, including man's destiny. Thus, they redefine *"foreknew"* (Romans 8:29) as "foreordained" or "predestined."

Words can't be redefined in an attempt to uphold a contradictory presupposition. In fact, should this redefinition of terms be valid, Romans 8:29 would read: *"For whom he predestined he also predestined."* This arrangement of terms would not only be redundant but totally nonsensical. Paul would never yield to redundancy and senseless verbiage while addressing such vital matters.

The specific context of *"foreknew"* in Romans 8:29 was proven earlier to point to God's foreknowledge (pre-knowledge) of the believers inhabiting the earth when this epistle was written. Therefore, the aorist tense (past tense) *"foreknew"* applies void of contradiction, for the recipients of this epistle were not only believers, but were "foreknown" by God prior to receiving Paul's words—thus *"foreknew"* is in the aorist tense (past tense). For God to foreknow these believers in the sense of knowing their thoughts, deeds, and more, prior to their being saved (the full counsel, contextual view) is a far cry from the Reformed view—which has God predetermining every deed they would perform. (Remember that Reformed Theology takes the liberty to redefine *"foreknew"* as foreordained or predestinated.) The *"foreknew"* of Romans 8:29 does not communicate that God *"foreknew"* believers in the sense of predestining them to salvation from eternity past by means of an eternal decree.

> *The Reformed view*: God predestines the elect to salvation from eternity past by means of an eternal decree. Thus, all of the elect were *"predestined"* (Romans 8:29-30) to be saved.

Rebuttal: Should the elect have been predestined to salvation from eternity past by means of an eternal decree (as Reformed Theology supposes), God's foreknowledge could not precede such an arrangement due to foreknowledge meaning "to know beforehand." God cannot foreknow what has always existed. Eternal decrees have always existed. Hence, Reformed Theology is forced to redefine *"foreknew"* of Romans 8:29 as "foreordained" or "predestined," which was earlier proven inconsistent.

Subsequent to exercising personal repentance and faith while depraved, New Testament believers are *"predestined"* (Romans 8:29-30; Ephesians 1:5) to receive a glorified body (Romans 8:23) at the Rapture of the church—as was validated earlier in our study. This order allows the aorist tense (past tense) *"predestined"* to apply void of contradiction. The believers addressed in the book of Romans had been *"predestined"* to receive a glorified body the instant they had been placed in Christ (subsequent to repenting and believing while depraved.) Thus, they were *"predestined"* prior to receiving this epistle, allowing the "past tense" context to remain uncompromised.

> *The Reformed view*: When the time arrives for the elect to be saved, they are *"called"* (Romans 8:30) by God through irresistible grace. God then spiritually regenerates them and gives them the gifts of repentance and faith. This repentance and faith become the possession of the elect.

Rebuttal: God calls everyone to be saved (Matthew 22:14), not desiring that any *"perish"* (1Timothy 2:4; 2Peter 3:9)—although the majority reject His free offer. We have determined that the word *"called"* of Romans 8:30 points to a New Testament believer's "calling" to a position or office within the body of Christ in conjunction with being made new—subsequent to exercising repentance and faith while depraved. In fact, this usage of the term *"called"* seems to be the most prevalent in Scripture. The believers in Paul's day were *"called"* to office the moment they placed faith in Christ and were made new. Thus, the aorist (past tense) fits perfectly, for they were saved (and *"called"*) prior to receiving this epistle but subsequent to exercising repentance and faith while depraved.

Of course, deceased New Testament believers who had been *"called"* to office (after repenting and believing while depraved) had been *"called"* in the aorist tense (past tense) as well. However, the context of *"called"* in Romans 8:28 (being in the present tense) points to New Testament believers who remained in their physical bodies when this epistle was penned. We can conclude that *"called"* in Romans 8:30 points to this same group of individuals—the *"whom"* addressed on four different occasions in Romans 8:29-30.

338

> *The Reformed View*:   The elect exercise the repentance
> and faith supplied by God and they are *"justified"*
> (Romans 8:30).

Rebuttal: Due to the term *"justified"* being in the aorist tense (past tense), we can conclude that Paul is describing believers who graced the earth in his day—who had been *"justified"* before receiving this epistle but after exercising repentance and faith while depraved.   Should the Reformed view be correct (a view which has the elect predestined to salvation from eternity past by means of an eternal decree), all of the elect of Reformed Theology (including those not yet born) would have been *"justified"* as early as Paul's day—*"justified"* being in the aorist tense (past action) in the Greek.   Impossible!   The Scriptures teach that the New Testament believer is predestined to receive a glorified body (Ephesians 1:5; Romans 8:23) in conjunction with being justified—after repenting and believing while depraved.   This arrangement allows the aorist tense (past tense) *"justified"* in Romans 8:30 to apply void of contradiction since Paul's readers had been *"justified"* prior to receiving this epistle.

> *The Reformed View*:   Once the elect are released from
> their earthly bodies (at physical death), they are
> *"glorified"* (Romans 8:30).   Although this "event"
> transpires in the future for the elect living on the earth, the
> certainty of the action allows the Scriptures to perceive it
> as having already occurred.

Rebuttal: The term *"glorified,"* being in the aorist tense (the past tense), must point to what had previously occurred in the souls and spirits of the readers receiving this epistle—who were already justified/saved yet remained on the earth.   The fact that a New Testament believer is made into a finished product (in spirit and soul) at the point of justification/salvation allows the aorist tense (past tense) *"glorified"* to apply in Romans 8:30 void of contradiction.   Therefore, the recipients of this epistle had been *"glorified"* in their spirits and souls prior to receiving this epistle, allowing the past tense to fit the context perfectly—refuting the Reformed view, which has believers glorified in the future (after experiencing physical death).   Of course, New

339

Testament believers' glorified bodies will not be obtained until the Rapture of the church, but that event is not the subject of Romans 8:30. Reformed Theology's idea that the term *"glorified"* is stressing the certainty of a future event is proven invalid.

The "golden chain" of Reformed Theology is broken by the weightiness of its contradictory ideology. Their "golden chain" can't pull the Reformed view out of the ditch in which it is mired. Thus, "mystery" is the artificial remedy to its plethora of inconsistencies. God, on the other hand, classifies contradiction as error—never mystery.

Before completing this portion of our study, let's take time to bask in the profoundness of Romans 8:30 and its ability to insulate the believer from error. We will do so by again addressing the four scenarios previously mentioned:

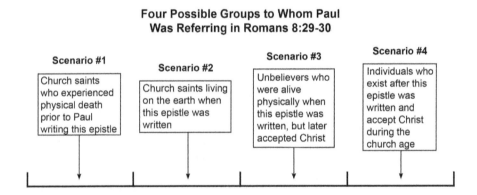

**Four Possible Groups to Whom Paul
Was Referring in Romans 8:29-30**

Scenario #1	Scenario #2	Scenario #3	Scenario #4
Church saints who experienced physical death prior to Paul writing this epistle	Church saints living on the earth when this epistle was written	Unbelievers who were alive physically when this epistle was written, but later accepted Christ	Individuals who exist after this epistle was written and accept Christ during the church age

Church saints who experienced physical death prior to Paul writing this epistle:

> *Predestined*—The past tense *"predestined"* of Romans 8:30 would tie in with Arminianism and all forms of Calvinism were it not for the fact that God's foreknowledge must precede the predestination of a New Testament believer (Romans 8:28)— negating their view due to the impossibility of foreknowledge preceding God's eternal decrees, which have always existed.

Remember, all forms of Arminianism and Calvinism incorrectly view the elect as having been predestined to salvation from eternity past by means of an <u>eternal</u> decree. Not even God can foreknow that which has always existed (God's decrees in this case)—foreknowledge meaning "to know beforehand." The past tense *"predestined"* of Romans 8:30 fits the Contextual View void of contradiction because these believers (*Church saints who experienced physical death prior to Paul writing this epistle*) would have been predestined when they were made new (saved), allowing foreknowledge to precede that moment when they were saved and predestined—prior to Paul writing this epistle.

Called—The past tense *"called"* of Romans 8:30 would fit Arminianism and Calvinism, that is, should they define *"called"* as a call to office. However, the Calvinists I have read view *"called"* of Romans 8:30 as a call to salvation rather than a call to office—a view that is scripturally unsound. The past tense *"called"* of Romans 8:30 fits the Contextual View void of contradiction because these believers (*Church saints who experienced physical death prior to Paul writing this epistle*) would have been *"called"* to office when they were made new (saved), allowing their calling to office to precede the writing of this epistle—thus placing their calling to office in the past tense.

Justified—The past tense *"justified"* of Romans 8:30 would fit Arminianism and all forms of Calvinism, for these believers (*Church saints who experienced physical death prior to Paul writing this epistle*) would have been *"justified"* when they repented and believed—thus, in the past tense. The past tense *"justified"* of Romans 8:30 fits the Contextual View void of contradiction because these believers would have been *"justified"* when they were made new (saved), allowing their justification to precede the writing of this epistle—thus placing their justification in the past tense.

Glorified—The past tense *"glorified"* of Romans 8:30 would fit Arminianism and all forms of Calvinism (that is, in relation to *Church saints who experienced physical death prior to Paul*

341

writing this epistle) due their viewing believers as being glorified at physical death. The past tense *"glorified"* of Romans 8:30 would fit the Contextual View void of contradiction because these believers (*Church saints who experienced physical death prior to Paul writing this epistle*) would have been *"glorified"* in soul and spirit when they were made new (saved)—thus placing their glorification (in soul and spirit) in the past tense.

Church saints living on the earth when this epistle was written:

Predestined—The past tense *"predestined"* of Romans 8:30 would tie in with Arminianism and all forms of Calvinism were it not for the fact that God's foreknowledge must precede the predestination of a New Testament believer (Romans 8:28)— negating their view due to the impossibility of foreknowledge preceding God's eternal decrees, which have always existed. Remember, all forms of Arminianism and Calvinism incorrectly view the elect as having been predestined to salvation from eternity past by means of an <u>eternal</u> decree. Not even God can foreknow that which has always existed (God's decrees in this case)—foreknowledge meaning "to know beforehand." The past tense "predestined" of Romans 8:29-30 fits the Contextual View void of contradiction because these believers (*Church saints living on the earth when this epistle was written*) would have been predestined when they were made new (saved), allowing foreknowledge to precede that moment when they were made new (saved) and predestined—prior to Paul writing this epistle.

Called— The past tense *"called"* of Romans 8:30 would fit Arminianism and Calvinism, that is, should they define *"called"* as a call to office.   However, the Calvinists I have read view *"called"* of Romans 8:30 as a call to salvation rather than a call to office—a view that is scripturally unsound. The past tense *"called"* of Romans 8:30 fits the Contextual View void of contradiction because these believers (*Church saints living on the earth when this epistle was written*) would have been *"called"* to office when they were made new (saved), allowing their calling to office to precede the writing of this epistle—thus placing the action in the past tense.

Justified— The past tense *"justified"* of Romans 8:30 would fit Arminianism and all forms of Calvinism, for these believers (*Church saints living on the earth when this epistle was written*) would have been *"justified"* when they repented and believed— thus, in the past tense. The past tense *"justified"* of Romans 8:30 fits the Contextual View void of contradiction because these believers (*Church saints living on the earth when this epistle was written*) would have been *"justified"* when they were made new (saved), allowing their justification to precede the writing of this epistle—thus placing their justification in the past tense.

Glorified— The past tense *"glorified"* of Romans 8:30 would not fit Arminianism and all forms of Calvinism due their viewing believers as being glorified at physical death. Hence, these believers (*Church saints living on the earth when this epistle was written*) would not have been glorified at this time according to their interpretation—violating the past tense. The past tense *"glorified"* of Romans 8:30 would fit the Contextual View void of contradiction because these believers (*Church saints living on the earth when this epistle was written*) would have been *"glorified"* in soul and spirit when they were made new (saved), prior to receiving this epistle—thus placing their glorification (in soul and spirit) in the past tense.

Unbelievers who were alive physically when this epistle was written, but later accepted Christ:

Predestined— The past tense *"predestined"* of Romans 8:29-30 would tie in with Arminianism and all forms of Calvinism were it not for the fact that God's foreknowledge must precede the predestination of a New Testament believer (Romans 8:28)— negating their view due to the impossibility of foreknowledge preceding God's eternal decrees, which have always existed. Remember, all forms of Arminianism and Calvinism incorrectly

343

view the elect as having been predestined to salvation from eternity past by means of an <u>eternal</u> decree. Not even God can foreknow that which has always existed (God's decrees in this case)—foreknowledge meaning "to know beforehand." The Contextual View of *"predestined,"* on the other hand, is free of contradiction when applied to *Unbelievers who were alive physically when this epistle was written, but later accepted Christ.* The Contextual View depicts the New Testament believers as *"predestined"* to receive a glorified body (in conjunction with being made new, or saved)—never predestined to salvation (from eternity past) and before they repent and believe. Thus, the Contextual View of *"predestined"* is free of contradiction in association with *"Unbelievers who were alive physically when this epistle was written, but later accepted Christ"*—for it never claims to apply so long as they remained unbelievers. (Ponder this thought before continuing.)

Called—"Called" in Romans 8:30 applies to a New Testament believer's call to office in conjunction with being placed in Christ and made new. Most Arminians I have read agree with this interpretation. However, when this view is adopted by the Arminian, *Unbelievers who were alive physically when this epistle was written, but later accepted Christ* would be called to office prior to being made new (or saved)—in fact from eternity past, proving to be contradictory.

The past tense *"called"* (Romans 8:30) also refutes all forms of Calvinism in regard to *Unbelievers who were alive physically when this epistle was written, but later accepted Christ,* for the "called" within Calvinism are called to a salvation that cannot be rejected—a salvation that is instantaneously applied. In other words, when you are called to be saved within Calvinism you are saved the instant you are called. Calvinism also teaches that the elect were predestined to salvation in eternity past, making it a past tense action. This scenario worsens their problem, for all who have been *"predestined"* have also been *"called"*—for both *"predestined"* and *"called"* are in the past tense in Romans 8:30. Should Calvinism be true, therefore, the elect of Calvinism who were unbelievers when this epistle was written were not only predestined by the time this epistle was written but also called! Holding Calvinism accountable to its definition of "called" would have them viewing unbelievers who were part of the elect (when this epistle was written) as having already been made new (saved). Thus, they would have been made new (saved) before they were made new (saved). Wow! How could an unbeliever be called and made new (saved) and remain an unbeliever? Hence, the past tense *"called"* of Romans 8:30 totally refutes Calvinism, especially when applied to the elect of Calvinism who are yet unbelievers. Therefore, Calvinism is totally defused when applied to *Unbelievers who were alive physically when this epistle was written, but later accepted Christ.*

In the Contextual View New Testament believers are *"called"* to office once they are made new (saved)—at the very same time they are *"predestined,"* *"justified,"* and *"glorified."* Thus, the *Unbelievers who were alive physically when this epistle was written, but later accepted Christ,* had not been predestined at the time of the writing of this epistle. Good thing, for had they been predestined to salvation from eternity past (as Arminianism and Calvinism suggest), they would have also been "called" to office while in their unredeemed state—*"called"* and *"predestined"* being in the past tense in the Greek. Hence, the Contextual View is free of contradiction in association with *Unbelievers who were alive physically when this epistle was written, but later accepted Christ.*

The error within Arminianism and all forms of Calvinism is exposed, especially when applied to the *"elect"* (of Arminianism and Calvinism) not yet made new (saved). In fact, by viewing the elect as having been predestined to salvation from eternity past, Arminianism and Calvinism inadvertently teach that the elect not yet made new (or saved) are presently *"called,"* *"justified,"* and *"glorified."* Therefore, should the elect not yet made new (or saved) have been predestined to salvation from eternity past (Arminianism and Calvinism), they would also be, at the present time, *"called,"* *"justified,"* and *"glorified."* In this scenario (in Arminianism and Calvinism), *"predestined"* is equivalent to a locomotive pulling *"called," "justified,"* and *"glorified"* into eternity past! This fact will be confirmed to even a greater degree as we proceed.

Justified—The past tense *"justified"* refutes Arminianism and all forms of Calvinism, for *Unbelievers who were alive physically when this epistle was written, but later accepted Christ* would have been justified prior to repenting and believing should Arminianism and Calvinism be correct. Arminianism and Calvinism teach that the elect were predestined to salvation from eternity past. Yet, Romans 8:30 places *"predestined," "called, "justified,"* and *"glorified"* in the past tense. Hence, should *Unbelievers who were alive physically when this epistle was written, but later accepted Christ* have been predestined to salvation in eternity past (Calvinism's view), they would have also been *"justified"* in eternity past—a total impossibility.

The Contextual View has New Testament believers *"justified"* once they are made new (saved)—at the very same time they are *"predestined," "called,"* and *"glorified."* Thus, the *Unbelievers who were alive physically when this epistle was written, but later accepted Christ,* had not been predestined (according to the Contextual View) at the time of the writing of this epistle. Good thing, for had they been predestined to salvation from eternity past (as Arminianism and Calvinism suggest), they would have also been *"justified"* while in their unredeemed state. Hence, the Contextual View remains free of contradiction in association with *Unbelievers who were alive physically when this epistle was written, but later accepted Christ.*

Glorified— The past tense *"glorified"* refutes Arminianism and all forms of Calvinism, for *Unbelievers who were alive physically when this epistle was written, but later accepted Christ* would have been glorified prior to repenting and believing should Arminianism and Calvinism be correct. Arminianism and Calvinism teach that the elect were predestined to salvation from eternity past. However, Romans 8:30 places *"predestined," "called, "justified," and "glorified"* in the past tense. Hence, should *Unbelievers who were alive physically when this epistle was written, but later accepted Christ* have been predestined to salvation in eternity past (Arminianism and Calvinism's view), they would have also been *"glorified"* in eternity past—a total impossibility.

The Contextual View has New Testament believers *"glorified"* once they are made new (saved)—at the very same time they are *"predestined," "called,"* and *"justified."* Thus, the *Unbelievers who were alive physically when this epistle was written, but later accepted Christ* had not been predestined (according to the Contextual View) at the time of the writing of this epistle. Good thing, for had they been predestined to salvation from eternity past (as Arminianism and Calvinism suggest), they would have also been *"glorified"* while in their unredeemed state. Hence, the Contextual View is free of contradiction in association with *Unbelievers who were alive physically when this epistle was written, but later accepted Christ.*

Individuals who exist after this epistle was written and accept Christ during the church age:

Predestined— The past tense *"predestined"* of Romans 8:29-30 would tie in with Arminianism and all forms of Calvinism were it not for the fact that God's foreknowledge must precede the predestination of a New Testament believer (Romans 8:28)— negating their view due to the impossibility of foreknowledge preceding God's eternal decrees, which have always existed. Remember, all forms of Arminianism and Calvinism incorrectly view the elect as having been predestined to salvation from eternity past by means of an <u>eternal</u> decree. Not even God can foreknow that which has always existed (God's decrees in this case)—foreknowledge meaning "to know beforehand."

The Contextual View of *"predestined"* is free of contradiction in association with *Individuals who exist after this epistle was written and accept Christ during the church age,* for it perceives New Testament believers as *"predestined"* (once they repent and believe while depraved) to receive a glorified body at the Rapture of the church—never predestined to salvation from eternity past (as followers of Arminianism and Calvinism suggest). Thus, the Contextual View allows foreknowledge to precede the New Testament believer's predestination—as required by Scripture. Hence, the Contextual View of *"predestined"* is free of contradiction in association with *Individuals who exist after this epistle was written and accept Christ during the church age,* for it never claims to apply until they are born and choose (while depraved) to repent and believe.

Called—The past tense *"called"* (Romans 8:30) doesn't support Arminianism in regard to *Individuals who exist after this epistle was written and accept Christ during the church age*; even should Arminianism perceive it as pointing to God's call to salvation. God most definitely calls all unbelievers to be saved, not desiring any to perish; He never calls individuals to be saved prior to their becoming human beings. (Ponder this thought before continuing.) Interestingly, most Arminians I have read view the past tense *"called"* (Romans 8:30) as pointing to God's call of the elect to office in conjunction with their being made new (or saved). Even so, Arminianism is grossly contradictory (especially considering the past tense associated with *"predestined," "called," "justified,"* and *"glorified"),* leaving the unbelievers (who later receive Christ) "called" to office prior to their being made new (or saved).

The past tense *"called"* (Romans 8:30) also refutes all forms of Calvinism, for the "called" within Calvinism are called to a salvation that cannot be rejected—a salvation instantaneously applied (once the elect are spiritually regenerated and given repentance and faith, then repent and believe). In other words, when you are called to be saved within Calvinism you are saved the instant you are called. However, Calvinism teaches that the elect were predestined to salvation in eternity past, making it a past tense action. The problem here is that all who have been *"predestined"* have also been *"called"*—for both *"predestined"* and *"called"* are in the past tense in Romans 8:30. Should Calvinism be true, the elect of Calvinism who are yet unbelievers (or not yet born) were not only predestined in the past, but also called in the past! Holding Calvinism accountable to its definition of *"called"* would result in the unbelieving elect being presently made new (saved). Thus, they would presently be made new (saved) <u>before</u> they are made new (saved) at a later date. Wow! How could an unbeliever be called and made new (saved) and remain an unbeliever? Hence, the past tense *"called"* of Romans 8:30 totally refutes Calvinism, especially when applied to the elect of Calvinism who are yet unbelievers— or not yet born. Therefore, Calvinism is totally defused when applied to *Individuals who exist after this epistle was written and accept Christ during the church age.*

The Contextual View of *"called"* is free of contradiction in association with *Individuals who exist after this epistle was written and accept Christ during the church age,* for it perceives New Testament believers as *"called"* to office once they repent and believe while depraved—at the very same time they are *"predestined"* (to receive a glorified body), *"justified,"* and *"glorified"* (in spirit and soul).

Justified— The past tense *"justified"* refutes Arminianism and all forms of Calvinism, for *Individuals who exist after this epistle was written and accept Christ during the church age* would be justified prior to repenting and believing should Arminianism and Calvinism be correct. Arminianism and Calvinism teach that the elect were predestined to salvation in eternity past. Romans 8:30 places *"predestined,"* *"called,"* *"justified,"* and *"glorified"* in the past tense. Hence, should *Individuals who exist after this epistle was written and accept Christ during the church age* have been predestined to salvation from eternity past (Arminianism and Calvinism's view), they would have also been *"justified"* in eternity past—a total impossibility. Remember that should the elect have been predestined to salvation from eternity past, *"predestined"* would be equivalent to a locomotive pulling *"called," "justified,"* and *"glorified"* into eternity past in relation to *Individuals who exist after this epistle was written and accept Christ during the church age*!

The Contextual View of *"justified"* is free of contradiction in association with *Individuals who exist after this epistle was written and accept Christ during the church age,* for it perceives New Testament believers as *"justified"* once they repent and believe while depraved—at the very same time they are *"predestined"* (to receive a glorified body), *"called"* (to office) and *"glorified"* (in spirit and soul). Hence, according to the Contextual View, none of the *Individuals who exist after this epistle was written and accept Christ during the church age* experience justification prior to birth—nor prior to exercising repentance and faith while depraved. The Contextual View, therefore, is void of inconsistency!

Glorified— The past tense *"glorified"* refutes Arminianism and all forms of Calvinism, for *Individuals who exist after this epistle was written and accept Christ during the church age* would have been glorified prior to repenting and believing should Arminianism and Calvinism be correct. Arminianism and Calvinism teach that the elect were predestined to salvation from eternity past. Yet, Romans 8:30 places *"predestined," "called," "justified,"* and *"glorified"* in the past tense. Hence, should *Individuals who exist after this epistle was written and accept Christ during the church age* have been predestined to salvation from eternity past (Arminianism and Calvinism's view), they would have also been *"glorified"* in eternity past—a total impossibility.

The Contextual View of *"glorified"* is free of contradiction in association with *Individuals who exist after this epistle was written and accept Christ during the church age,* for it perceives New Testament believers as *"glorified"* (in soul and spirit) the moment they repent and believe while depraved—at the very same time they are *"predestined"* (to receive a glorified body), *"called"* (to office) and *"justified."*

The proponents of "bad dog" "good dog" theology (that the New Testament believer possesses two natures instead of one) perceive passages such as Romans 8:30 as supporting their view. Thus, they conclude that New Testament believers are *"glorified"* "positionally" (whatever that means) while on earth but in actuality at physical death. Such can't be the case due to the use of the aorist tense (past tense) *"glorified"* in Romans 8:30. The recipients of this epistle were already *"glorified"* in their souls and spirits due to having become the new man at the point of justification—before receiving this epistle and after exercising repentance and faith while depraved. We recognize once again the gross inconsistencies associated with "Positional Truth"— which advocates that the New Testament believer is a dual natured, no good, worthless, sinner saved by grace until entering heaven. Should this theological position be accurate, all New Testament believers would live in spiritual adultery until physical death—with the sinful nature (old self) married to the Law and the new man (new self) betrothed to Christ (Romans 7:4).

The past tense *"glorified"* (Romans 8:30) verifies that God has made our spirits and souls, who we are, into finished products. You may ask, "Doesn't Philippians 3:21 teach that Jesus '...*will transform the body of our humble state into conformity with the body of His glory...*,' and doesn't this transpire at some point after we are released from our earthly bodies?" Most definitely, if you are a follower of Jesus Christ, you will receive your glorified body at some point in the future. But the term *"glorified"* in Romans 8:30 is not referencing that amazing event. *"Glorified"* in this context points to what was done in our spirits and souls in conjunction with our being placed in Christ and made new. Consequently, when we were placed in Christ, subsequent to our exercising repentance and faith while depraved, our spirits and souls were *"glorified"* to the greatest degree possible—in an instant of time! Yes, we will commit occasional acts of sin so long as we live in our physical bodies. But even in the midst of these sinful acts, we are *"glorified"* saints making temporary mistakes—not lowly, second-class citizens of the kingdom.

God's Awesome Provision and Protection

Considering all that Paul has taught in this wonderful epistle, when I read the words, *"What then shall we say to these things?..."* (Romans 8:31), all I can *"say"* is "Wow"! What a fascinating work the Lord assembled through His apostle to the Gentiles. I have found no section of Scripture that presents the gospel more concisely than does the epistle to the Romans.

Paul's answer to the question, *"What then shall we say to these things?..."* (Romans 8:31), is:

> *...If God is for us, who is against us?* (Romans 8:31)

Should enemies attempt to disrupt what God is doing in and through us, He alone is (and always will be) the answer to our dilemma. Try as hard as we may, we could never imagine anything greater in intelligence, power, and authority than our God. Hence, the indwelling Creator sees us through by means of a limitless energizing flow from His Person alone. Adding to this thrilling news, Paul writes:

> *He who did not spare His own Son, but delivered Him up for us all, how will He not also with Him freely give us all things?* (Romans 8:32)

God will *"...freely give us all things"* (v.32)—meaning that He will abundantly supply all future needs. We must be careful with the phrase, *"delivered Him up for us all."* Paul is not teaching the "L" of the TULIP, Limited Atonement (that Jesus died for the elect of Calvinism alone), for if such were the case it could also be concluded that Jesus died solely for Paul and the believers at Rome. Remember as well Paul's words from Romans 5:6, which prove that only the elect of Calvinism would be born *"ungodly"* should Limited Atonement be true:

> *For while we were still helpless, at the right time Christ died for the ungodly.* (Romans 5:6)

> *Who will bring a charge against God's elect? God is the one who justifies; who is the one who condemns? Christ*

> *Jesus is He who died, yes, rather who was raised, who is*
> *at the right hand of God, who also intercedes for us.*
> (Romans 8:33-34)

Paul follows in verses 33 and 34 by declaring that no one can *"...bring a charge against God's elect...."*—the *"elect"* being those New Testament believers who have been placed in God's *"elect"* one (Isaiah 42:1 KJV), Jesus Christ, and made new, after repenting and believing while depraved. Why can no one *"bring a charge against God's elect"?* *"...God is the one who justifies"* (Romans 8:33; Romans 5:1). Because Jesus died, rose, and *"intercedes for us"* in heaven (Romans 8:34), we cannot be condemned (Romans 8:1). Yes, God is in our corner, covering us on every front. Truly, He is our Friend!

Do you at times question God's love? Should you face pain and hardship, does it mean that God has ceased caring for you? Paul was equipped to answer questions of this sort, as verified by Romans 8:35-36:

> *Who shall separate us from the love of Christ? Shall*
> *tribulation, or distress, or persecution, or famine, or*
> *nakedness, or peril, or sword? Just as it is written, "FOR*
> *THY SAKE WE ARE BEING PUT TO DEATH ALL DAY LONG; WE*
> *WERE CONSIDERED AS SHEEP TO BE SLAUGHTERED."*
> (Romans 8:35-36)

After intense trial and persecution, Paul still writes:

> *But in all these things we overwhelmingly conquer*
> *through Him who loved us.* (Romans 8:37)

Paul teaches that Christ's indwelling presence could conquer any hardship (confirmed by 2Corinthians 11-12), for Christ was his *"life"* (Colossians 3:4). However, to understand the significance of Christ's presence in our lives, suffering is normally required. In fact, pain allows us to say with Paul:

> *For I am convinced that neither death, nor life, nor*
> *angels, nor principalities, nor things present, nor things*

353

> *to come, nor powers, nor height, nor depth, nor any other created thing, shall be able to separate us from the love of God, which is in Christ Jesus our Lord.* (Romans 8:38-39)

Are you yet *"convinced"* (v.38)? If not, you can rest assured that God knows what is required for this change to transpire. Due to His unfathomable love, He is absolutely determined that we learn to live from His perspective—the only perspective that provides hope in the midst of societal chaos, turmoil, and despair.

My prayer is that God might use what we have studied to transform not only your life, but also the lives within the sphere of your influence. We should take every opportunity to know our Lord as intimately as possible. We will then stand amazed as He, through our unique personalities, enriches and deepens the lives of those seeking the excellent way.

Please think on the things you have heard. Several people who have studied with us have returned months (even years) later and said, "I am finally understanding how to apply what I learned in Romans 1-8. It took some challenging circumstances to bring it about, but they were used of God to catapult me to where I am today. I am so very appreciative of His incredible grace."

Thankfully, the Lord is responsible for maturing us as we face the variables of our day. Therefore, we must take hold of His huge, powerful hand and allow Him to lead us through the sunshine and the rain, realizing every step of the way that He is working it all for our good! Shalom.

Diagram 1

Man is a Three Part Being
1Thessalonians 5:23

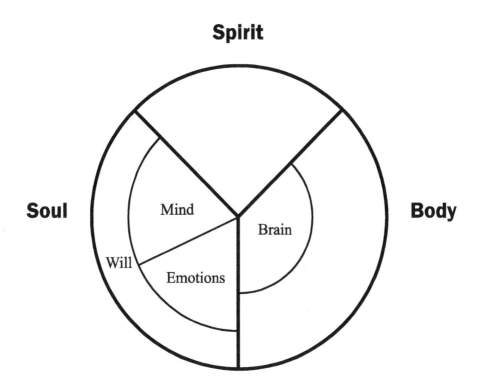

Now may the God of peace Himself sanctify you entirely; and may your spirit and soul and body be preserved complete without blame at the coming of our Lord Jesus Christ, (1Thessalonians 5:23)

Body: What houses the soul and spirit (2Corinthians 5:1-4). Notice that the brain is part of the body.

Soul: Mind, Emotions and Will. Man thinks with his mind, feels with his emotions, and chooses with his will.

Spirit: The part of a New Testament believer that house's God's presence (John 14:16-17, 20, 23). Void of God's presence, this part of man is dead to God (Genesis 2:17; Ephesians 2:1). It is through the avenue of the Spirit that man communicates with God (John 4:24), and God with man (John 14:26).

Diagram 2

Sin (the Power of Sin) Entered into Man
Romans 5:12

Just as through one man sin entered into the world, and death through sin, and so death spread to all men because all sinned, (Romans 5:12)

When Adam disobeyed God, the law of sin (the power of sin, sin) moved into Adam's spirit, soul, and body. Adam was then influenced by the messages he received from the law of sin (the power of sin, sin).

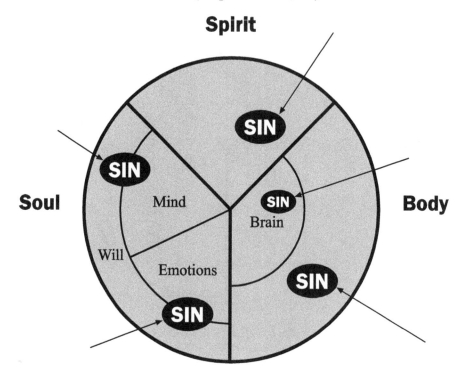

Diagram 3

Man without Christ
Romans 5:12

When Adam sinned the Adamic Nature was born, the Adamic Nature being soul and spirit. It was then natural for Adam to be controlled by the Power of Sin that lived in his spirit, soul, and body.

Man is born in the same condition that Adam was in after he sinned. Man is born spiritually separated from God, but not to the degree that he is incapable of exercising personal repentance and faith while depraved. The Power of Sin generates ungodly thoughts that the depraved generally accept as the truth.

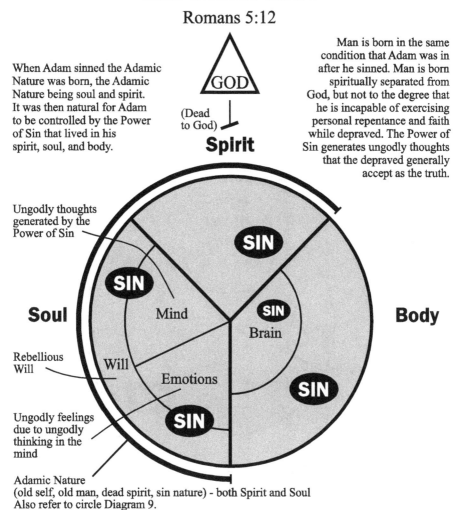

Ungodly thoughts generated by the Power of Sin

Soul

Rebellious Will

Ungodly feelings due to ungodly thinking in the mind

Adamic Nature
(old self, old man, dead spirit, sin nature) - both Spirit and Soul
Also refer to circle Diagram 9.

Just as through one man sin entered into the world, and death through sin, and so death spread to all men because all sinned, (Romans 5:12)

The terms old self, old man, dead spirit, sin nature, and Adamic Nature (listed above as the spirit and soul of lost mankind) are all synonymous. When you see one of these terms, either in the course or in Scripture, know that it refers to the nature that Adam possessed after he sinned. Since we are descendants of Adam, we are born with this same nature. This nature is rebellious toward God, but not so much so that it can't repent and exercise faith.

Make sure that you don't confuse the sinful nature with the power of sin (sin). They are different in that the sinful nature has to do with the nature of lost mankind, while the power of sin (sin) is Satan's messenger (Satan's agent).

Diagram 4

Man with Christ
2Corinthians 5:17

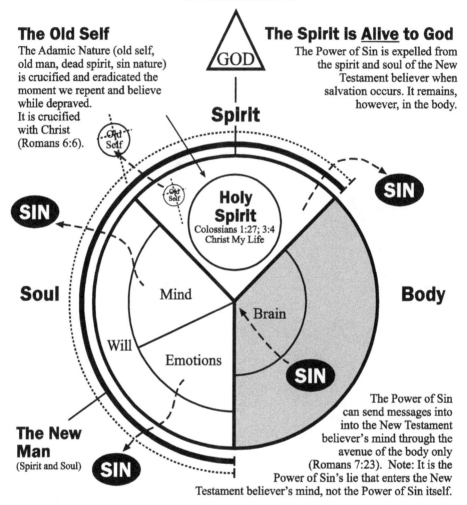

The Old Self

The Adamic Nature (old self, old man, dead spirit, sin nature) is crucified and eradicated the moment we repent and believe while depraved. It is crucified with Christ (Romans 6:6).

The Spirit is <u>Alive</u> to God

The Power of Sin is expelled from the spirit and soul of the New Testament believer when salvation occurs. It remains, however, in the body.

Spirit

Holy Spirit
Colossians 1:27; 3:4
Christ My Life

Soul

Mind

Will

Emotions

Brain

Body

The New Man
(Spirit and Soul)

The Power of Sin can send messages into into the New Testament believer's mind through the avenue of the body only (Romans 7:23). Note: It is the Power of Sin's lie that enters the New Testament believer's mind, not the Power of Sin itself.

... Christ in you, the hope of glory. (Colossians 1:27)

When Christ, who is our life,... (Colossians 3:4)

Therefore if any man is in Christ, he is a new creature; the old things passed away; behold new things have come. (2Corinthians 5:17)

Knowing this, that our old self was crucified with Him,... (Romans 6:6)

...greater is He who is in you than he who is in the world. (1 John 4:4)

But I see a different law in the members of my body, waging war against the law of my mind, and making me a prisoner of the law of sin which is in my members. (Romans 7:23)

Diagram 5

How We Operate

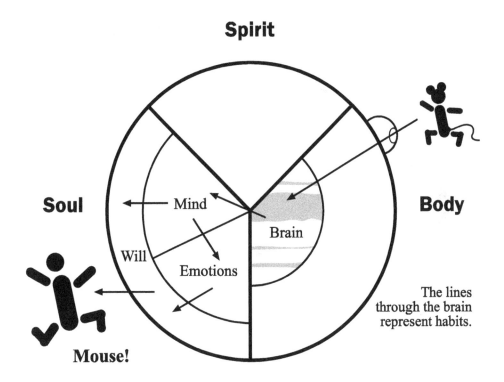

The lines through the brain represent habits.

Diagram 6

How the Power of Sin is Defeated

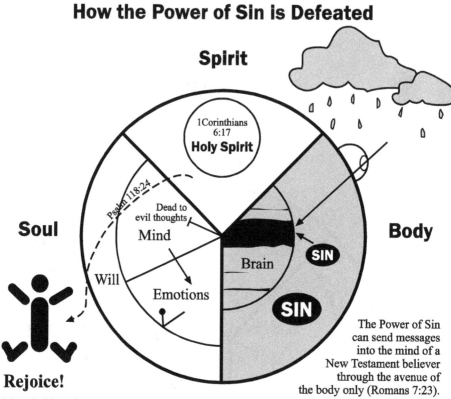

Rejoice!

My mind is no longer enslaved to evil thoughts. My new spirit and the Holy Spirit are one. Therefore, I can consistently respond to the truth ushered into my mind through the power of the Holy Spirit and walk in victory.

> *But the one who joins himself to the Lord is one spirit with Him.* (1Corinthians 6:17)

> *This is the day which the Lord has made; Let us rejoice and be glad in it.* (Psalm 118:24)

All our habits (good and bad) are stored in the brain, and our brain is part of our physical body. While living in our lost condition, we developed many ungodly habits. We also develop ungodly habits after we become believers. We do so by repeatedly yielding to the Power of Sin's lie in a particular area of our lives. Satan's messenger (the Power of Sin) sends sinful thoughts into our minds through the avenue of these ungodly habit patterns (Romans 7:17, 20, and 23). It does so for two reasons: (1) To make us think that we generate the sinful thoughts entering our minds (2) To attempt to trick us into believing that the old man is still alive.

Note: These ungodly habit patterns are reduced in size (intensity) as we mature in the Lord and learn to walk by His Spirit.

Diagram 7

Sin in Control
Romans 6:12

Walking (or Living) According to the Flesh
Romans 8:4-5

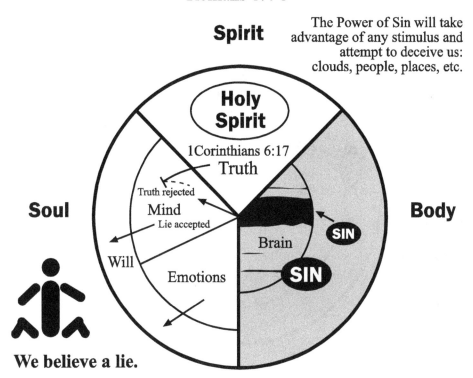

We believe a lie.

When we walk according to the flesh, we have failed to consider ourselves dead to the lie that the Power of Sin has sent into our minds (Romans 6:11). We have also failed to respond to the truth that the Spirit of God has sent in our minds. Thus, when this occurs, the new man sins.

> *Therefore do not let sin reign in your mortal body that you should obey its lusts,* (Romans 6:12)

> *in order that the requirement of the Law might be fulfilled in us, who do not walk according to the flesh, but according to the Spirit. For those who are according to the flesh set their minds on the things of the flesh, but those who are according to the Spirit, the things of the Spirit.* (Romans 8:4-5)

When we walk according to the flesh, we have believed the Power of Sin's lie and walked according to one of our ungodly habit patterns stored in our brain (the brain being a piece of flesh).

361

Spirit in Control

Romans 6:13

Walking (or Living) According to the Spirit

Romans 8:4-5

Spirit

The Power of Sin will take advantage of any stimulus and attempt to deceive us: clouds, people, places, etc.

Holy Spirit

Psalm 118:24

TRUTH ACCEPTED

Lie rejected

Mind

Soul

Will

Emotions

Brain

SIN

SIN

Body

We do not believe a lie!

My mind is no longer enslaved to the evil thoughts generated by the Power of Sin.
My new spirit and the Holy Spirit are one (1Corinthians 6:17).

When we walk according to the Spirit, we have considered ourselves dead to the lie that the Power of Sin has sent into our minds (Romans 6:11). We have also responded to the truth that the Spirit of God has sent into our minds and, thus, have not allowed the Power of Sin to reign (Romans 6:12).

> *And do not go on presenting the members of your body to sin as instruments of unrighteousness; but present yourselves to God as those alive from the dead, and your members as instruments of righteousness to God.* (Romans 6:13)

> *in order that the requirement of the Law might be fulfilled in us, who do not walk according the flesh, but according to the Spirit. For those who are according to the flesh set their minds on the things of the flesh, but those who are according to the Spirit, the things of the Spirit.* (Romans 8:4-5)

362

Diagram 9

The Old Self was Soul and Spirit

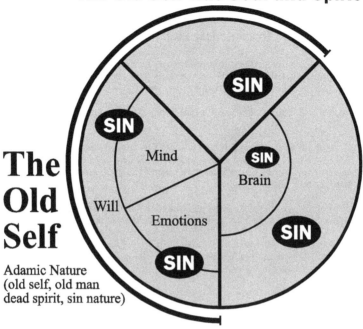

The New Self is Soul and Spirit

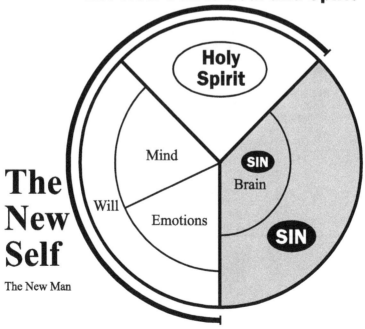

Diagram 10

Why God's Foreknowledge Cannot
Precede His Eternal Decrees

Calvinism and Arminianism adhere to the idea that the elect were elected (chosen) and predestined to salvation from eternity past by means of an eternal decree. This arrangement is impossible, and the following explains why.

Scripture teaches that God's decrees are eternal (Jeremiah 5:22), having always existed in His heart.

> *'Do you not fear Me?' declares the LORD. 'Do you not tremble in My presence? For I have placed the sand as a boundary for the sea, an eternal decree, so it cannot cross over it. Though the waves toss, yet they cannot prevail; though they roar, yet they cannot cross over it.* (Jeremiah 5:22)

Scripture also requires God's foreknowledge (which means to know beforehand) to precede the predestination and election (choosing) of a New Testament believer.

> *For those whom He foreknew, He also predestined to become conformed to the image of His Son, so that he would be the firstborn among many brethren;* (Romans 8:29)

> *Peter, an apostle of Jesus Christ, to those who reside as aliens, scattered through-out Pontus, Galatia, Cappadocia, Asia, and Bithynia, who are chosen according to the foreknowledge of God the Father, by the sanctifying work of the Spirit, to obey Jesus Christ and be sprinkled with His blood: may grace and peace be yours in the fullest measure.* (1Peter 1:1-2)

Should God's foreknowledge, meaning "to know beforehand," precede His eternal decrees, eternity would have a beginning (a starting point)--a total impossibility.

Because God's decrees are eternal (Jeremiah 5:22), and foreknowledge is required to precede the predestination and election (choosing) of the New Testament believer (Romans 8:29; 1Peter 1:1-2). for God to have predestined or elected (chosen) New Testament believers to salvation from eternity past by means of an eternal decree is impossible.

The Scriptures teach that New Testament believers are elected and predestined to blessings (rather than to salvation), a predestination and election that occur when they are placed in Christ subsequent to their exercising personal repentance and faith while depraved. This truth allows God's foreknowledge to precede the predestination and election of a New Testament believer, as displayed below.

	Predestination of New Testament believers when they are spiritually regenerated (saved). Election/Chosenness of New Testament believers when they are spiritually regenerated (saved).
Foreknowledge	
∞	∞

Diagram 11

Calvin's Beliefs

Election
Predestination
(God's Foreknowledge=Foreordination or Predestination

Calvin believed that God, from eternity past and by means of an eternal decreee, elected (chose) and predestined the elect to salvation. This view contradicts Romans 8:29 and 1Peter 1:1-2, both of which require God's foreknowledge to precede the election (chosenness) and predestination of a New Testament believer. Calvin's theology fails to provide room for foreknowledge to precede the election (chosenness) and predestination of a New Testament believer. Consequently, Calvin deemed foreknowledge as synonymous with foreordination or predestination. In other words Calvin redefined foreknowledge as foreordination or pre-destination, which required the writing of volumes of materials in an effort to remedy such contradiction. Calvin arrived at this error due to equating the blessings associated with salvation with salvation itself.

Diagram 12

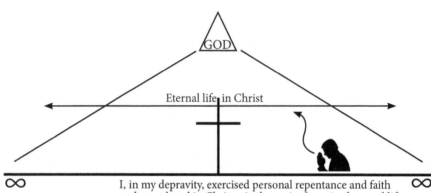

Scriptural Election/Chosenness
and Predestination

I, in my depravity, exercised personal repentance and faith
and was placed in Christ. At that point I received eternal life.

The Holy Spirit places those seeking salvation during the church age into Christ when they repent and exercise faith while depraved (1Corinthians 12:13). Once this occurs, God makes them new (2Corinthians 5:17). He also predestines them (at that time) to receive glorified bodies at the Rapture of the church (Ephesians 1:5, Romans 8:23, 1Corinthians 15:35-58, IThessalonians 4:13-18). They are also elected/chosen (at that time) to office due to having been placed into Christ, the Father's elect/chosen One (Luke 9:35, Isaiah 42:1), Who was elected/chosen to the office of Messiah. The office to which New Testament believers are elected/chosen is the special office or position (gift) they receive (1Peter 4:10) in conjuction with being placed in Christ and made new. Therefore, New Testament believers were not predestined and elected/chosen to salvation from eternity past by means of an eternal decree. They are predestined the moment they are made new in Christ subsequent to repenting and believing while depraved; predestined to receive a new body (Ephesians 1:5, Romans 8:23) at the Rapture of the church. They are also elected/chosen to office when placed in Christ, subsequent to repenting and believing while depraved, Christ having been elected/chosen to office, the office of Messiah. Ephesians 1:4 states:

> *just as He chose us in Him before the foundation of the world, that we should*
> *be holy and blameless before Him.* (Ephesians 1:4)

Once New Testament believers are placed in Christ, they receive His kind of life, eternal life (Romans 6:23), Colossians 3:4), life with no beginning and no end. As a result, the Father sees them as having always been in Christ, even *"before the foundation of the world"* (Ephesians 1:4). Consequently, their point of entry into Christ is when they repent and believe while depraved; but once they are placed in Him through the power of the Holy Spirit (1Corinthians 12:13), the Father sees them as having always been in His holy Son. He will continue to view New Testament believers in this manner throughout eternity.

Diagram 13

Reformed Theology
(Extreme and Hyper-Calvinism)

	Stage 2 God spiritually regenerates the elect and they are born again	**Stage 3** God immediately gives faith and repentance to the spiritually regenerated elect	**Stage 4** The spiritually regenerated elect choose to repent and believe and are saved
Stage 1 Man is born totally depraved			

This view is contradictory because Scripture equates spiritual regeneration and being born again with salvation. With Reformed Theology's configuration, believers would be saved twice--a total impossibility.

The Scriptural View

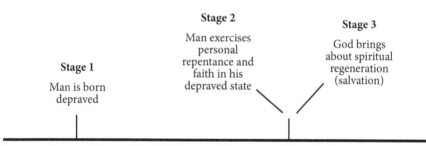

Stage 2

Man exercises
personal
repentance and
faith in his
depraved state

Stage 3

God brings
about spiritual
regeneration
(salvation)

Stage 1

Man is born
depraved

Be aware that man is brought out of his state of depravity and into the kingdom in an instant. Therefore, the brevity of time between man's choice to repent and believe while depraved and God's act of spiritual regeneration (salvation) is impossible to imagine.

Diagram 14

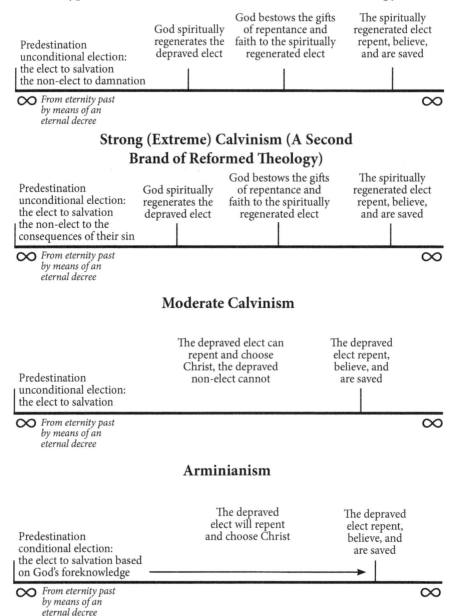

Hyper-Calvinism (One Brand of Reformed Theology)

Predestination
unconditional election:
the elect to salvation
the non-elect to damnation

God spiritually
regenerates the
depraved elect

God bestows the gifts
of repentance and
faith to the spiritually
regenerated elect

The spiritually
regenerated elect
repent, believe,
and are saved

∞ *From eternity past
by means of an
eternal decree*   ∞

Strong (Extreme) Calvinism (A Second Brand of Reformed Theology)

Predestination
unconditional election:
the elect to salvation
the non-elect to the
consequences of their sin

God spiritually
regenerates the
depraved elect

God bestows the gifts
of repentance and
faith to the spiritually
regenerated elect

The spiritually
regenerated elect
repent, believe,
and are saved

∞ *From eternity past
by means of an
eternal decree*   ∞

Moderate Calvinism

Predestination
unconditional election:
the elect to salvation

The depraved elect can
repent and choose
Christ, the depraved
non-elect cannot

The depraved
elect repent,
believe, and
are saved

∞ *From eternity past
by means of an
eternal decree*   ∞

Arminianism

Predestination
conditional election:
the elect to salvation based
on God's foreknowledge

The depraved
elect will repent
and choose Christ

The depraved
elect repent,
believe, and
are saved

∞ *From eternity past
by means of an
eternal decree*   ∞

368

Diagram 15

How the Various Forms of Calvinism View Salvation

Calvinism is generally divided into three branches—hyper, extreme, and moderate (for lack of better terms). Many Calvinists would take issue with these "labels," but they exist as a means to classify the varying opinions that inundate Calvinism's overall system of thought. The following definitions are not exhaustive, but contain pertinent information regarding the present subject matter.

Hyper-Calvinism

God predestined the elect to salvation and the non-elect to damnation from eternity past by means of an eternal decree. Man, in his depraved state, cannot choose Christ. Consequently, God must spiritually regenerate the elect, as well as give them the gifts of repentance and faith, before they can repent, believe, and be saved. This branch of Calvinism adheres to limited atonement.

Comment: Even though I adamantly disagree with this system of thought, I view the hyper-Calvinists as more straightforward regarding their views than the other branches of Calvinism.

Extreme Calvinism

God predestined the elect to salvation from eternity past (by means of an eternal decree) but left the non-elect to the consequence of their sin. Man, in his depraved state, cannot choose Christ. As a result, God must spiritually regenerate the elect, as well as give them the gifts of repentance and faith, before they can repent, believe, and be saved. This branch of Calvinism adheres to limited atonement.

Comment: Bottom line, extreme and hyper-Calvinists believe the same thing. What difference exists between God leaving the non-elect to the consequence of their sin, with no opportunity to believe (extreme Calvinism), versus predestining the non-elect to damnation in eternity past (hyper-Calvinism), if only the elect in both cases will be saved? No difference exists, for in extreme Calvinism the non-elect are predestined to damnation by default (that is, if extreme Calvinism is held accountable to its bottom line).

Moderate Calvinism

The depraved <u>can</u> repent and exercise faith in Christ due to possessing a free will. However, only the elect, chosen to salvation by God from eternity past by means of an eternal decree, can, and will, choose to believe. This branch of Calvinism normally adheres to unlimited atonement.

<u>Comment</u>: What difference would it make for the depraved to possess a free will to choose Christ should only the elect be capable of repenting and believing? Under such an arrangement, God, not man, would determine where man spends eternity. Therefore, bottom line, moderate Calvinism eliminates free will altogether in regard to salvation and inadvertently places itself in the same category as extreme and hyper-Calvinism. Note: Diagram 14 in the Reference Section portrays the three branches of Calvinism in graphic form.

Note: Diagrams 1-9 originally appeared in *Romans, The Foundational Truths of Romans 1-8,* ©1991 The Hill Publishing, LLC. Diagrams 10-14 originally appeared in *God's Heart as it Relates to Foreknowledge – Predestination,* ©2012 The Hill Publishing, LLC. Diagram 15 is from *Jacob Have I Loved, A Study of Romans 9,* ©2014 The Hill Publishing, LLC

Scripture Index

[1] Jamieson, Robert, Fausset, A. R., & Brown, David. (Reference on Jude 1:7, "Strange

[2] Merriam Webster, <http://www.merriam-webster.com/dictionary/natural>.

[3] Simmons, Rabbi Shraga. Ask.com Religion and Spirituality>Judaism>Reincarnation. <http://judaism.about.com/library/3_askrabbi_o/bl_simmons_reincarnation.htm>.

[4] Ross, Hugh (1993, 1995, 2001), *The Creator and the Cosmos; how the greatest discoveries of the century reveal God*, Published by Reason To Believe, Navpress, pages 73-74, Used by permission.

[5] Hunt, Dave. *What Love Is This?* Bend, OR: The Berea Call. 2006

[6] Ibid

[7] Mickelsen, A. Berkeley, *et al*. Edited by Pfeiffer, Charles E. & Harrison, Everett F. *Wickliffe Bible Commentary*. Chicago: Moody Publishers. 1990

[8] Gerrish, Jim. *Does God Play Favorites? God's Unique Relationship With Israel*, Originally published by Cornerstone Publishing, 2007. <http://www.churchisraelforum.com/favorites-11/>.

[9] Lightfoot, John. *A Commentary on the New Testament from the Talmud and Hebraica*. Peabody, MA: Hendrickson Publishers. 1989. Used by permission. All rights reserved.

[10] Ibid

[11] Murray, John. *Principles Of Conduct, Aspects Of Biblical Ethics.* Grand Rapids, MI: Wm. B. Eerdmans Publishing Co. www.eerdmans.com. 1957. Used by permission.

[12] Vine, W.E., Unger, Merrill F., & White, William Jr. *Vine's Expository Dictionary of New Testament Words,* Nashville: Thomas Nelson. 1996. Used by permission. All rights reserved.

[13] Ibid